Measure Learning Rather than Satisfaction in Higher Education

Measure Learning Rather than Satisfaction in Higher Education

Edited by Ronald E. Flinn and D. Larry Crumbley

Published by the
Teaching, Learning and Curriculum Section
of the American Accounting Association

American Accounting Association
5717 Bessie Drive
Sarasota, Florida 34233-2399

Library of Congress Control Number: 2009929009
ISBN 0-86539-093-2

Printed in the United States of America

The editors, Teaching, Learning and Curriculum Section, and American Accounting Association appreciate the financial support of Tim Tribe and EPPS CPA Consulting PLLC to help publish this monograph. The editors appreciate the word processing and editorial assistance provided by Zariat Afrin, Marsha Huber, and Yingqin Zhang.

Table of Contents

About the Editors ix

Measuring Accounting Learning Monograph Committee xi

Preface xiii
Ronald E. Flinn and D. Larry Crumbley

Chapter 1
A Balanced Look at the Use of Contingent Faculty in Accounting Education 1
Marsha M. Huber, Shirine L. Mafi, and Ronald E. Flinn

Chapter 2
Why We Should Measure Student Learning: A Glossary of Collegiate Corruption 17
Patrick Moore

Chapter 3
Academic Freedom, Tenure, Promotion, and Student Evaluation of Faculty (SEF): Retrospective and Abstracted Summaries 29
Robert E. Haskell

Chapter 4
The Games Professors Play in the Dysfunctional Performance Evaluation System Used in Higher Education: Brainstorming Some Recommendations 41
D. Larry Crumbley and G. Stevenson Smith

Chapter 5
Bias, the Brain, and Student Evaluations of Teaching 59
Deborah J. Merritt

Chapter 6
The Limitations of Measuring Student Learning 91
Patrick Moore and Ronald E. Flinn

Chapter 7
Inputs to the Measurement of Teaching Quality: Moving Beyond Student Evaluations of Teaching 111
Ronald J. Huefner

Chapter 8
Assessing Critical Thinking 119
Rebekah Heath

Chapter 9
Multiple Teaching Performance Measurements Needed: SET Management Similar to Earnings Management 133
Ronald E. Flinn and D. Larry Crumbley

Chapter 10
Improving Teaching and Learning through SMART Classroom Assessment Techniques... 157
Marsha M. Huber

Chapter 11
Grades, Performance, and Reputation: Adjusting Ratings Using Expected Grades......... 175
Karen Leppel and Hamid Zangeneh

Chapter 12
Assessment Testing in the First Intermediate Accounting Course: A Three-Year Study in Comparison to Bloom's Taxonomy.. 181
Michael J. Krause

Chapter 13
Distance Learning in Accounting Education: Current State and Future Directions......... 191
Vasant Raval

References.. 199

ABOUT THE EDITORS

Dr. Ronald E. Flinn, Associate Professor, has taught accounting and tax courses at Creighton University since 1986. He has published a two-day AICPA course on Executive Compensation. Professor Flinn has published articles in accounting and tax practitioner journals including the *CPA Journal*, *Journal of Accountancy, Taxes—The Tax Magazine, The Adviser, Tax Strategies,* and the *Oil, Gas & Energy Quarterly*. He has written the "Environmental Corner" column for the *Oil, Gas & Energy Quarterly* for more than ten years. His hobbies include reading and golf.

Dr. D. Larry Crumbley is KPMG Endowed Professor at Louisiana State University. He was the Chair of the then Teaching and Curriculum Section of the American Accounting Association for 2007–2008, when he conceived of the idea to publish a monograph to develop alternatives to the student evaluation of teacher performance measurement. He is the author of more than 350 articles and 55 books, including 12 educational novels that teach specific subject matters. Professor Crumbley has been editor of the *Oil, Gas & Energy Quarterly* for more than 30 years and the *Journal of Forensic Accounting* since 1991. He won the Society of Louisiana CPA Lifetime Achievement in Accounting Education Award in 2007.

Measuring Accounting Learning Monograph Committee (2007–2009)

PREFACE

A previous Teaching and Curriculum committee (Calderon et al. 1996, 4) produced a learned framework for encouraging effective teaching, indicating that student evaluation of teaching (SET) are "useful but limited in scope." Since little has changed in over a decade except more grade inflation and possibly coursework deflation, we decided to take a more aggressive and critical approach to this dysfunctional evaluation system. Most professors are no longer in the teaching business, but rather are in the satisfaction business.

The Spellings Commission in 2006 stated that there are indications that many who earn university and college degrees have not mastered the reading, writing, and thinking skills that are expected of graduates. The Commission's suggestions were to urge educators to "embrace new pedagogies, curricula, and technologies to *improve student learning* to correct shortcomings" (U.S. Department of Education 2006, 4; emphasis added).

PricewaterhouseCoopers (PWC) issued a position paper on accounting education in 2003, stating that "accounting programs must be successful in attracting the right students, *provide a vigorous and challenging curriculum*, and maintain adequate resources to ensure the viability of the education process" (PricewaterhouseCoopers 2003, 3; emphasis added). One of PwC's ten specific recommendations involved "fostering students' ability to solve problems in complex business environments where the best answer is difficult to identify" (PricewaterhouseCoopers 2003, 3).

Neither the Spellings Report wake-up call nor the PwC position paper point out that the major problem is the inappropriate teaching performance measurement system in higher education. Student Evaluation of Teachers (SET) has a long history, ostensibly created to provide formative feedback to a teacher about his or her teaching effectiveness. However, administrators now use it almost exclusively as a summative evaluative measure. A major fallacy behind this approach is the belief that if something can be quantified, then it is both reliable and valid. Nowhere, however, is there any linkage between student satisfaction (SET) and demonstrative learning as called for in the Spellings and PwC reports.

Mark Oppenheimer in the *New York Times* summarized this pervasive dysfunctional control system operating in higher education:

> But to many, it's the system itself that is choking higher education. When students in the 1960s demanded more say in academic governance, they could not have predicted that their children would play so outsized a role in deciding which professors were fit to teach them. Once there was a student revolution, which then begat a consumer revolution, and along with more variety in the food court and dorm rooms wired for cable, it brought the curious phenomenon of students grading their graders. Whether students are learning more, it's hard to say. But whatever they believe, they're asked to say it. (Oppenheimer 2008)

This mess in higher education can be explained by the agency theory, the most popular model used by accounting researchers. Legislators for public universities and Boards of Trustees in private universities tell administrators to evaluate the teaching effectiveness of university professors, and they in turn hire the inventory (students) to evaluate (e.g., audit) the professors. While using students in this manner may be an inexpensive and quick way to evaluate professors, this method does not measure learning. In fact, this system has reduced respect for professors and the higher education process. Administrators prefer higher Student Evaluation of Teachers (SET) scores, which lead to higher grades, higher student retention rates, and more tuition and tax revenues. As the chart below illustrates, common sense dictates that professors will focus on pecuniary benefits and inflate grades and decrease their course work to survive because they are caught between a rock and a hard place.

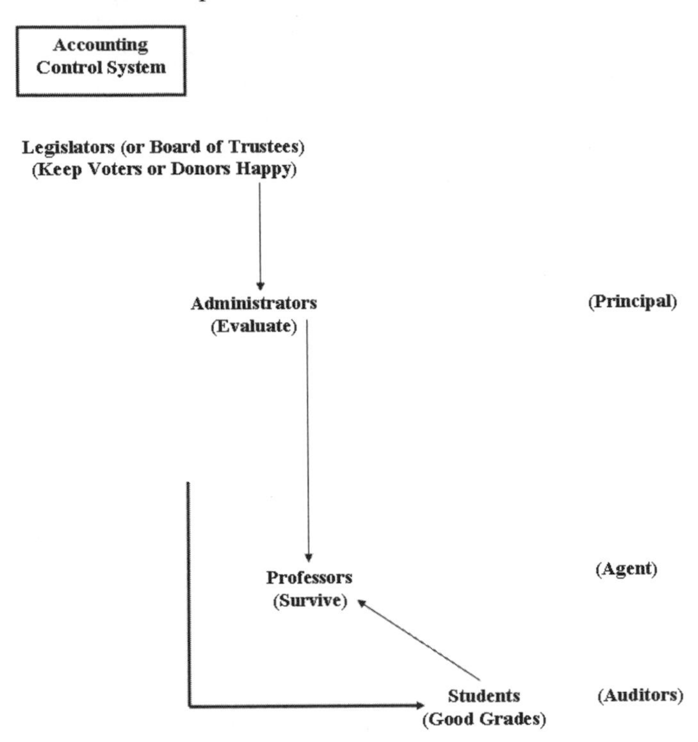

Professors today are hired, rewarded, promoted, tenured, punished, and fired largely based on student opinions at the end of each semester about their professors' teaching. Each semester professors face the classic prisoners' dilemma as outlined below:

	Professor B (hard)	**Professor B (inflates)***
Professor A (hard)	Each get slightly lower evaluations	Professor A: much lower evaluations Professor B: much higher evaluations
Professor A (inflates)*	Professor A: much higher evaluations Professor B: much lower evaluations	Each get slightly higher evaluations

* Grade inflates and coursework deflates.

Professor A can accurately say, no matter what Professor B does, "I personally am better off inflating my grades rather than trying to really educate my students. Therefore, my rational decision is to inflate my grades and deflate my coursework." This inflation and deflation occurs even if easy professors do not get higher evaluations as long as a significant number of professors believe easy grading results in higher evaluations. The resulting ever-increasing grade inflation and course work deflation are a negative sum game as student learning and education are shortchanged. See http://www.gradeinflation.com. Thus, the current SET control system results in a dysfunctional reward system and does not create goal congruence between a professor's behavior and student learning (regardless of whether students lie on the SET questionnaires). The SET process is counterproductive to the Spellings Commission's call for "a culture of continuous innovation and quality improvement in pedagogies, curricula, and technologies to improve learning."

In the words of Charles Murray, "dumbed down courses, flaky majors and grade inflation have conspired to make the letters B.A. close to meaningless. The light workload alone can make college today a joke." He believes the "demanding professor is close to extinct" (Murray 2008). Recent accounting education research strongly suggests that some students will not simply work hard enough to be successful accounting practitioners (Milliron 2008). But these students are allowed to evaluate their professors' teaching effectiveness. Many professors believe they have the right to increase their SET scores, even if learning decreases and the other professors' SET scores decline. The motto "All is fair in love, war, and teaching" is the direct result of the widespread reliance on the inappropriate use of SET scores as summative measures of teaching effectiveness by administrators and students.

Just imagine if, starting in the seventies, sports coaches were hired and fired based upon anonymous questionnaires completed by their players (rather than their win-loss record). Eventually, coaches would play all of their players an equal number of minutes at the position selected by the player. College sports would be entirely different today with such a dysfunctional reward system. Certainly education is as important as college sports.

As Robert Haskell says in his article (herein), we have had enough research in SET, because we will never reach a scientific level of certitude. "If the control mechanism is not constrained, this dysfunctional system will continue to endanger the integrity of tenure, promotion, and academic freedom." If mankind can send a person to the moon, surely we can develop a system to more appropriately measure student learning (and not satisfaction) and correctly reward professors. Our major educational institutions must acknowledge this runaway system and attempt to fix it if higher education is to survive (e.g., American Accounting Association).

The Spellings Commission pushed for higher education to develop readily comparable ways of measuring student learning (U.S. Department of Education 2006). As could be expected, two groups (Association of Colleges and Universities and the Council for Higher Education Accreditation) issued in January 2008 a reply to the Spellings Report by shunning the idea of higher education to develop ways of measuring student learning. They wish individual institutions to decide themselves what to measure and how to measure (New Leadership for Student Learning and Accountability 2008). Obviously, administrators do not wish to give up the dysfunctional SET internal control system that controls professors.

The National Governors Association, however, believes that "governors can help restrain college costs—while extending a quality postsecondary education to a larger segment of the population—by insisting that student learning outcomes become an integral part of state higher education accountability systems." An Issue Brief indicates that governors can:

- Call for the development of minimum general educational learning outcomes for undergraduates educated at a public college or university, and require assessment of these outcomes.

- Require student competencies to be assessed and publicly reported through appropriate metrics, such as a combination of statewide sampling and institutional assessments (Linn 2007).

We encourage governors and others concerned with the integrity of higher education and student learning to scrutinize the current internal control mechanism that allows administrators to increase retention rates at the expense of learning. As administrators multiply, their salaries skyrocket, professors decrease, and adjuncts increase, governors and Board of Trustees must realize that it's the control system, stupid.

If the SET system is not replaced, then some form of exit examination or alternative assessment process is needed before a student is allowed to graduate from colleges and universities. Administrators must begin to visit their faculty classes randomly each semester, and peer reviews of faculty teaching must be inaugurated. A teaching model of productivity must be used in place of the current use of student satisfaction scores. Finally, class rankings and grade point percentiles on transcripts could restore some of the comparative curve at the university level. Corrective action is essential to avoid a Sarbanes-Oxley solution being imposed on higher education.

Ronald E. Flinn
Creighton University

D. Larry Crumbley
Louisiana State University

CHAPTER 1

A Balanced Look at the Use of Contingent Faculty in Accounting Education

Marsha M. Huber, Otterbein College
Shirine L. Mafi, Otterbein College
Ronald E. Flinn, Creighton University*

The American Association of University Professors (AAUP) reports that there has been a dramatic shift in the employment of faculty at many colleges (AAUP 2006a). The most rapid growth in recent years has been in the areas of part-time positions and fixed-term contracts (AAUP 2006a). Furthermore, in all business fields (especially accounting), there is a shortage of academically qualified faculty, which means that, for better or worse, an increasing number of business courses will be taught by faculty members who do not have Ph.D.s in their respective teaching fields (Plumlee et al. 2006; Sharman 2007; Swartz et al. 2007). Because of the shortage of accounting Ph.D.s, colleges and universities are searching for alternative faculty members to teach accounting classes (Douglas et al. 2006).

The implications regarding these shifts should concern all stakeholders of accounting education. What are the repercussions on the curriculum, accounting programs, faculty morale, governance, ability to attract and retain accounting majors, and more importantly, on students and their learning? Economic necessity and market forces have driven many institutions to increase their use of contingent faculty, but at what cost? And to what gain? What are the differences in learning achieved by students taught by full-time faculty and adjuncts? And ultimately, what are the long-term implications for the accounting profession?

The purpose of this article is to present a balanced view and to dispel myths concerning the use of contingent faculty in accounting education. This article examines and discusses the increase in the use of contingent faculty, reasons for these changes, relevant accreditation standards, benefits and consequences to accounting education, and presents recommendations to help maintain and improve the standards of academic excellence in accounting education.

WHO ARE CONTINGENT FACULTY?

Contingent faculty is instructors who are part-time faculty, graduate teaching assistants, or post-doctoral fellows who do not and cannot earn tenure (AAUP 2006a). These faculty members

* Drs. Marsha M. Huber, CPA (mhuber@otterbein.edu) and Shirine L. Mafi are Associate Professors at Otterbein College, and Dr. Ronald E. Flinn, CPA, CMA is Associate Professor at Creighton University.

are sometimes called "adjuncts," or "clinicians" with nearly 72 percent of them having at least one job outside their teaching position (Gappa and Brawer 1997; Leslie and Gappa 2002). They often have a master's degree and professional certification such as a CPA or CMA. Thus, for most "adjuncts" teaching is a peripheral activity, and not their main source of income.

On average, contingent faculty members have less than four years of experience on their campuses (Benjamin 2003a). A small minority, however, are former tenured faculty who are over 70 years old, yet stay on as part-time faculty (Cross and Goldenberg 2003). Graduate assistants, of course, are inherently transitional, and teaching tends to delay their graduation. Even after graduation, some freshly-minted Ph.D.s can not obtain full-time teaching positions, thereby taking temporary part-time positions or multiple fellowship positions. Recent studies of contingent appointments highlight certain problematic characteristics including lower pay, fewer benefits, and consequently, an inferior or "second-class citizen" status on campuses (Benjamin 2003a; Sonner 2000).

The national trends regarding the use of adjuncts could be considered alarming. The AAUP (2006) reported that in 1975, 57% of all faculty were either tenured or tenure track with 30% of classes being taught by contingent faculty (Exhibit 1). In 2003, the tenured numbers declined to 35% with 46% of all classes being taught by contingent faculty (AAUP 2006a). To today's college student that means that more than half of their curriculum is taught by non-tenured faculty members.

Trends concerning accounting faculty coincide with the national trends. Exhibit 2 reveals that only the Research/Doctoral institutions have increased the number of full-time accounting faculty lines (AAA 2008). The other degree granting institutions (including at the master's level) have shifted more than 50% of the accounting teaching responsibility to contingent faculty.

The most disturbing trend is perhaps with the four-year, non-doctoral programs. In 1993, 63% of accounting classes were taught by full-time faculty; whereas in 2004, full-time coverage declined to 47%.

EXHIBIT 1
Trends in Faculty Status, 1975–2003

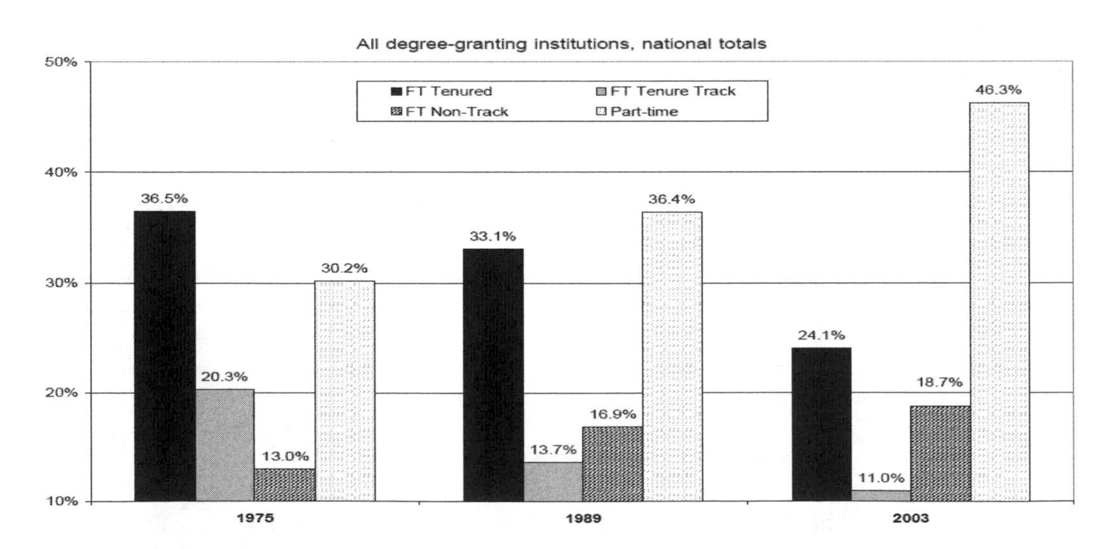

Source: AAUP 2006a

EXHIBIT 2
Number of Full-Time and Part-Time Faculty by Institution 1993–2004

Institution Type	1993 Full-Time	2004 Full-Time	1993 Part-Time	2004 Part-Time
Research/Doctoral	2,853	3,072	2,163	851
4-Year Non-Doctoral	4,572	3,169	2,714	3,555
2-Year	2,274	2,287	4,601	3,911
Total	9,699	8,528	9,478	8,317

Source: AAA 2008

Although the percentage of adjunct over full-time faculty varies by type of institution (public or private, two-year or four-year), state, discipline, and type of program (graduate or undergraduate, certificate, on-line, evening or weekend), it is evident that the ratio of adjunct to full-time accounting faculty is increasing in all institutions except some doctoral institutions. The use of contingent faculty at community colleges is even more prevalent. At two-year colleges, almost 65% of all accounting classes are taught by contingent faculty (Exhibit 2).

DISPELLING MYTHS

Contrary to common beliefs, contingent faculty members are not vagabonds or "freeway flyers." Only a minority would be considered "professional" adjuncts who teach a variety of courses at multiple institutions at the same time. At one Midwestern college, one adjunct reported he taught a total of nine classes in one quarter at three different institutions to maximize his income. The majorities of adjuncts, however, are attracted to teaching because of their interest and love for teaching (Eagan 2007; Cohen and Brawer 2003; Gappa and Brawer 1997) and not necessarily to maximize their income.

The contingents are also increasing in their age and experience in teaching. According to a survey of the National Study of Postsecondary Faculty (U.S. Department of Education 2006a), full-time faculty saw their average employment duration at the same institution increased from 11.3 years to 12.2 years from 1993 to 2004; whereas, the part-timers' average increased from 5.9 years to 7 years in that same period (Eagan 2007). The full-time and part-time average age is about the same. The average age of accounting full-time faculty increased from 48.5 to 51.6 years; whereas, the part-time ages increased from 45.4 to 50.5 from 1993 to 2004 (AAA 2008). A national survey of 2000 community college faculty members found that contingent faculty has similar attitudes and motivation levels toward teaching as full-time faculty members (Leslie and Gappa 2002). This survey provides evidence that further dispels the popular stereotype that contingents are transient and inexperienced faculty.

Students report that the contingent faculty members are often passionate instructors that bring "real world" experience to the classroom (Wallin 2007, Fagan-Wilen, et al. 2006). Some adjuncts have specialized areas of expertise and are up-to-date on professional developments in their disciplines. Many contingent faculty members are committed to teaching, and feel that they add to the students' lives (Wallin 2005). As time passes, adjuncts are growing in their experience, presence, and influence on campuses.

THE AACSB RESPONSE TO THE HIRING CRISIS

The Association to Advance the Collegiate Schools of Business (AACSB) has tried to cope with a shortage of business and accounting Ph.D.s. For over two decades, the top fifty schools granting doctorate degrees in business, have decreased the number of Ph.D.s awarded in business by 18% (Olian et al. 2004), and in the five largest Ph.D. programs, the number has decreased by 27.1% (AACSB 2003b). In fact, the AACSB (2003b) reported that although student applications for admission for doctoral programs increased, actual admissions decreased.

As a result, the number of business doctorates graduating from accredited schools is not keeping pace with the demand for vacant teaching positions. The degrees conferred in business are increasing, both undergraduate and graduate. Business graduates with undergraduate and master's degrees increased nearly 400% from 127,000 in 1970 to 454,000 in 2005; whereas, new Ph.D.s only doubled from 620 in 1970 to 1,500 in 2005 (AACSB 2003b). Accounting degrees conferred from 1999 to 2004, increased 12.33% (American Accounting Association 2008).

In 2012, the projected Ph.D. shortage of business faculty members to fill vacant business and accounting positions will be 2,419 (Exhibit 3) (AACSB 2003b). Specifically in accounting, from 2006–2008, there were 590 accounting faculty needed, but only 330 Ph.D graduates available—a 55.9% shortage (Plumlee et al. 2006). In fact, the American Accounting Association (AAA) projects future demand over the next 5–10 years to be about 500 replacement faculty per year with an available supply of new accounting Ph.D.s at 140 per year with half of those being foreign nationals (AAA 2008).

"Academically Qualified" versus "Professionally Qualified"

Rather than classify faculty as "contingent," the AACSB now uses a different classification using the terms "academically qualified" (AQ) and "professionally qualified" (PQ) to categorize faculty regarding their academic qualifications. In order to deal with the shortage of qualified business and accounting faculty, the AACSB allowed schools to fill faculty positions with lower cost instructors in 2003, which would not have been qualified under the previous standards (Mangan 2003). The AACSB prescribes that a minimum of 50% of the courses be taught by an "AQ" faculty member, 40% by "PQ" faculty, and 10% could be taught by "unqualified" faculty.

EXHIBIT 3
Projected U.S. Doctoral

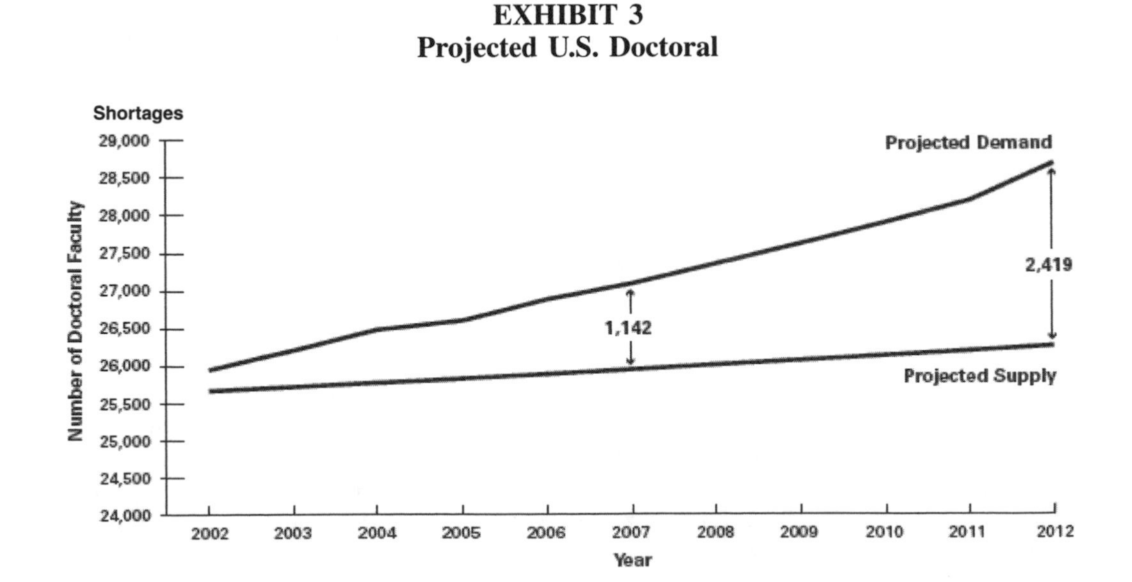

Source: AACSB 2003b

The "AQ" designation normally means the faculty member has a terminal degree in their teaching area. The standards, however, allow for Ph.D.s in other disciplines to teach accounting. In fact, there are four levels of faculty that could be considered to be "AQ" for accounting. A Master's degree in taxation is considered "AQ" for teaching taxation. The remaining faculty categories include those with Ph.D.s in a business-related field; those without Ph.D.s in accounting, but with academic preparation in accounting; and those without Ph.D.s and/or academic coursework in accounting. For non-accounting Ph.D.s, the greater the disparity in the degree from accounting, the more specialized training, coursework, professional development, and scholarship in accounting are needed to show the faculty member is qualified to teach accounting.

"AQ" faculty is expected to maintain their qualifications by publishing in their respective areas. The unspoken rule of thumb is to have a minimum of "two refereed journal articles published every five years." Faculty members are considered to be "AQ" the first five years after earning a Ph.D., but the faculty member will lose "AQ" status if scholarship productivity is not maintained. For some faculty, this scholarship requirement is a difficult standard to fulfill, and they move to or teach at a non-AACSB institution.

"PQ" faculty is those who do not have Ph.D.s in accounting, but rather professional experience. Their highest degree is usually a Masters' degree, and they usually have a professional certification such as a CPA or CMA. In addition, they may have executive level experience such as serving as a Chief Financial Officer (CFO) for a corporation or as a partner at a "Big 4" firm. They are often called "clinical" faculty.

"PQ" faculty usually receives less compensation than "AQ" faculty. They often teach more classes than "AQ" faculty, and are not expected to conduct research or service. "PQ" faculty members, however, are expected to maintain their qualifications by remaining active in the accounting profession. They are expected to sustain their professional currency through professional development and their qualifications through consulting, serving on Board of Directors, and being active in professional organizations.

The AACSB has been criticized for contradicting the basic laws of "supply and demand" by allowing colleges to hire lower costing "PQ" faculty members. Consequently, any action on the part of the AACSB that reduces starting salaries theoretically prevents necessary market corrections (Basil and Basil 2006; White et al. 2005). If market salaries adjusted upward (Francisco et al. 2008), then more new entrants presumably would be attracted to Ph.D. programs (White et al. 2005). Furthermore, the "PQ" status works to diminish potential salary increases that new faculty members could make "to at least recapture the equity premium that exists for new Ph.D.s when compared to new MBA graduates" (Francisco et al. 2008, 28).

Participating versus Supporting

AACSB business schools have not experienced the same prolific growth in the use of contingent faculty due to accreditation standards. The AACSB prescribes that 75% of the accounting faculty be "participating" faculty member and 25% can be "supporting." According to Exhibit 2, doctoral institutions were staffed 94% by full-time accounting faculty (of which many are AACSB-accredited). Those numbers decline, however, for non-doctoral four-year and two-year institutions (most of which are not AACSB-accredited).

A "participating" faculty member is one that participates in duties beyond teaching including advising, research, and service (AACSB 2003a). The school considers "participating" members to be "long-term" regardless of their contract status, (e.g., full or part-time). On the other hand, "supporting" faculty members do not participate in intellectual or operational duties beyond teaching (AACSB 2003a). They are usually hired on an *ad hoc* basis without an expectation of continuation.

A "supporting" faculty would include most of the faculty that the AAUP would describe as "contingent." As mentioned earlier, contingent faculty will teach 34% of business courses in 2008 (AACSB 2008a). Thus, some contingent faculty members become "participating" faculty members for colleges to meet the 75% participating faculty AACSB staffing ratio. To counter the proliferation of contingent faculty used in business education, the AACSB has served as a buffer. Faculty-student interaction is one key to student learning (AACSB 2003a) and, at least, the AACSB standards help to ensure that faculty-student interaction happens. The question still remains, however, on how "AQ-PQ" and "participating-supporting" designations impact student learning.

The AACSB "Bridge" Programs

Because of the severe shortage in "AQ" accounting faculty, the AACSB has begun a controversial "bridge" program to convert non-business and non-accounting Ph.D.s to "AQ" status. These programs began in the summer of 2008, and are untested. The programs' time spans are from seven weeks to two years, depending on the institution. The tuition for the programs ranges from $14,000 to $45,000 with an AACSB endorsement of five programs, which are advertised on the AACSB website.

The "bridge programs," like the "PQ" status, could have negative implications for business and accounting faculty (Francisco et al. 2008). Salaries could be lower for the new bridge "AQ" faculty causing further salary compression. There are also questions to the validity of the concept. Can a bridge program "convert" a non-accounting Ph.D. into an accounting Ph.D. in a matter of weeks? For example, can a statistics Ph.D. become "AQ" in accounting without having the academic and experience requirements to sit for the CPA examination? Will business schools hire the new "bridge" graduates?

Discussions on web boards question the academic preparation of faculty from the bridge program, arguing that professional experience makes for a better faculty member than a summer "bridge" course for non-business Ph.D.s. The proposed solution by the AACSB to produce more eligible business faculty is too new to evaluate its impact on the quality of accounting education.

WHY SO MANY CONTINGENTS?

There are many reasons for the hiring of contingent faculty. One reason is simply supply is not keeping up with the demand for accounting faculty. Surprisingly, much of the blame for the shortage in Ph.D.s in accounting can be placed on Ph.D. granting institutions themselves. As discussed earlier, the top doctoral institutions decreased admissions to their programs. The doctoral granting institutions claim they are not admitting as many students to their programs because the quality of the applicants has decreased (AACSB 2003b). The AACSB gives other reasons for declining admissions into doctoral programs.

First, doctorate programs are not profit centers. Since most doctoral students are not funded, Ph.D. programs do not produce revenue streams for universities. In addition, business school rankings often reward MBA programs at the expense of Ph.D. programs (AACSB 2005b; Haka 2008). Second, there is lack of program responsiveness to students' individual research that could reduce student retention (Haka 2008). Often students are required to conduct research interests in their advisor's areas of interest, which may or may not, coincide with their own. Simply stated, there are few incentives offered to professors to work with Ph.D. students unless they are motivated by intrinsic rewards such as satisfaction and possible collaboration for future research (AACSB 2003b; Haka 2008). Third, it is taking longer to complete a doctorate. It now takes over six years for a business doctoral student to complete a Ph.D. whereas in 1995, the time frame was previously closer to five years (AACSB 2003b). Fourth, there are misperceptions in the marketplace in the salaries for new Ph.D.s. Many prospective students underestimate the earning potential of an accounting Ph.D. compared to their professional careers. Fifth, more and more money is being spent on administrators rather than professors. Lastly, the attractiveness of academic life is declining due to less flexibility and more pressure, regulations, and accountability placed on faculty (AACSB 2003b).

The profession also "appears to be suffering from competition for new talent, whether because pay is insufficiently competitive to attract new Ph.D.s or because the workload for current faculty has increased to a functional limit ..." (AAA 2008, 32). The AAA (2008) reported the following trends for accounting faculty from 1993 to 2004:

- Faculty members spent 7% more time on the job; whereas business counterparts remained unchanged.
- Teaching loads for accounting faculty increased by 9%, but the reverse was true for other business faculty.
- Time spent on research increased 52% over the same time period for accounting faculty.

From the view of potential doctoral students, the work profile of the accounting faculty member, "may diminish the attractiveness of the field" (AAA 2008, 29).

But perhaps, the most disturbing reality is how much less adjuncts cost to employ than full-time faculty. Strictly for budgetary reasons, adjuncts are much less expensive than full-time faculty and doctoral students and generally can be dismissed at any time. For example, the average accounting professor might earn $90,000 plus fringe benefits to teach six courses per academic year. To hire an adjunct to carry the same load might cost the college $3,000 per course (Townsend 2003) for a total of $18,000 with no benefits. Can accounting program budgets absorb the teaching cost of hiring all "AQ" faculty (if they were available) as some would suggest? The current usage of contingent faculty is almost impossible to reverse, thus effectively making the adjunct faculty positions permanent (Cross and Goldenberg 2003).

Lastly, who would bear the cost of hiring all terminally qualified faculty? There is a trade-off between the number of "AQ" faculty and the tuition costs. Either the government by increasing aid, or students by paying higher tuition, would have to bear the additional cost. Neither of these stakeholders would likely agree to incur this added expense. Since the average accounting full professor earned $118,100 and average new hire earned $114,800 in 2005–2006 (AACSB 2006), how can institutions, especially IIA and IIB schools afford these faculty?

Exhibit 4, developed from 2005–06 AACSB (2006) and 2007–08 AAUP (2008b) salary data, shows the disparity between what an average new hire (AVE New Hire) and average accounting faculty member (AVE Acct) costs in relation to the different classes of institutions—I (Doctoral), IIA (Masters) and IIB schools, (Bachelors)—and the average salaries of faculty by rank. The gap between the new hires and average salaries for other institutions could be substantial depending on the type of institution.

IMPLICATIONS FOR ACCOUNTING EDUCATION

Budgetary constraints, decreasing state support for public institutions, lack of accounting faculty, retirement cycles, and changing enrollment patterns all play a role in hiring of adjunct faculty (Green 2007). The fundamental concern regarding the increase in contingent faculty in accounting education is not only the alarming rate of growth, but its implications for the quality of education (Benjamin 2003a). There are ethical implications for institutions, educational implications regarding students, and broader issues that could impede the future of progressive business thought.

EXHIBIT 4
Average Salaries

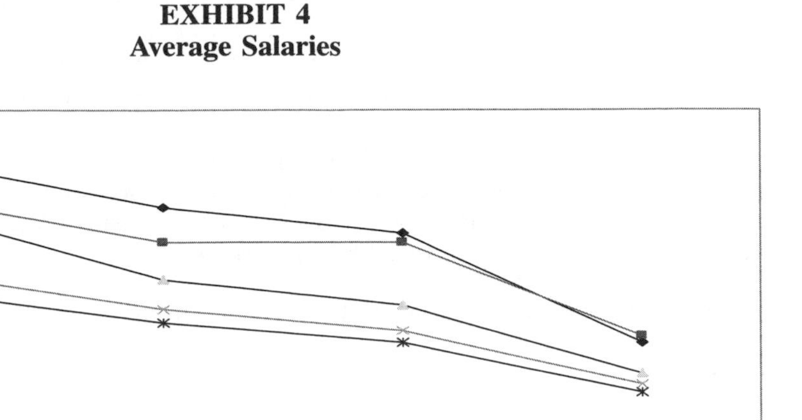

Ethical Issues

The central concern is not only the growing numbers, but also "institutional neglect of this critical mass" (Wyles 1998, 92). Contingent faculty are hired and fired almost at will (Sonner 2000). The problem with contingent faculty members is not necessarily their credentials to teach, but the lack of support structures and rights regarding academic freedom (AAUP 2006a). Those employed on contingent contracts face different and often more difficult working conditions, employment contracts, and lack of rank in the academic environment.

Critics would describe the treatment of adjuncts as exploitive. Overall, the contingent faculty lack job security and have little support in development of their scholarly or professional careers. They often lack resources such as offices, campus telephones, computer technology, and in some cases have no library access. They are not eligible for sabbatical leaves, travel monies, professional development funds, or grants often awarded to full-time faculty. Their classes can be cancelled due to low enrollments, and adjuncts may have no control over content, textbook, or course design. They often "teach in isolation" with little contact with full-time faculty (Quinn 2005; Green 2007).

Worse yet, the evaluation process of contingent faculty is often lacking and unfair, where their only evaluation might be based on SET scores. Adjuncts could be fired for no reason other than low SET scores or student complaints. For most adjuncts there is no real formal evaluation process, faculty development program, due process, or job protection. Given the lack of job security and peer support, they may fear of speaking on controversial issues in class—a loss of academic freedom. They may grade inflate and reduce course content to maintain high student evaluations.

Lack of Due Process

One documented example of alleged mistreatment of a contingent faculty member occurred at the University of New Haven in 2007, where Ms. Marianna Vieira was fired over nine student complaints (formal and informal) stretching over a period of seven years. These complaints ranged from her giving a student an "F" for plagiarism, enforcing department attendance policies, dismissing a student for lighting a cigarette in class, grading disagreements, and a student complaining that her class was too rigorous. Her department recommended both contract renewal and promotion, but the administration dismissed her for a "pattern of student complaints" stating:

> Each of these students approached Ms. Vieira with a relatively mundane concern, and in each instance, as a direct result of Ms. Vieira's hostile conduct, these concerns were transformed into student complaints requiring the attention of the dean's office and other administrative offices (AAUP 2008a).

Because of her termination, the AAUP censured the University of New Haven for doing so without "adequate cause" (AAUP 2008a). Although there were student complaints, the University's own General Grievance Committee found that the administration had "denied Ms. Vieira the basic safeguards of academic due process." The University stated that it has two distinct categories of faculty, and it does not grant those without tenure track the same procedural rights as tenurable or tenured faculty (AAUP 2008a). What happened at New Haven is not an isolated incident when it comes to the treatment of contingent faculty (Wilson 2005).

Second Class Citizens

Even if contingent faculty members receive full-time appointments with job protections, they often carry the burden of teaching more classes than full-time tenured faculty. They are excluded from governance since most department meetings are held during working hours, and they often have no status. They can become "second class" citizens with sometimes several teaching jobs at different institutions, teaching classes no one else wants to teach. Sadly, for most contingent faculty, their part-time jobs rarely translate into full-time teaching jobs (Finkelstein and Schuster 2001).

Even if included into governance, would other campus faculty treat contingent faculty members as peers? Can a business dean make the case that an MBA with "PQ" status is at par with a history professor with a Ph.D. (White et al. 2005)? In addition, the "AQ" faculty without Ph.D.s in their respective teaching areas can pose problems. By allowing non-business Ph.D.s to teach business courses, other programs such as hospitality or sports management may feel that there is no reason for their students to take business classes. They can develop and teach their own accounting, marketing, finance, and management courses since a Ph.D. in accounting or business is apparently not needed to teach in those fields any longer (White et al. 2005).

Unionization

Another important issue is the trend of unionization of contingent faculty. In response to lower pay and the prospect of reduced job security, more adjunct faculty are turning to unions for protection of their economic interests. The Coalition of Contingent Academic Labor (COCAL) is a grass roots effort to solidify adjunct faculty members. At this year's annual conference there will be sessions on organizing coalitions on college campuses (COCAL 2008).

This trend can have a profound impact on the culture and character of higher education institutions (Cross and Goldenberg 2003). Several institutions that have organized coalitions for its contingent faculty are Syracuse University, Cornell University, University of Massachusetts–Boston, City University of New York, and University of Colorado at Denver, to name a few (Schell 2001). Is this movement strong enough to replace the institution of tenure with a system of union contracts? The contingent faculty's growing presence on campuses across the country could ultimately change the systems of faculty governance, collegiality, and terms of employment (Cross and Goldenberg 2003).

Quality of Instruction Issues

The greatest concern in using "contingent" faculty is the consequences to students and their learning. The quality of education is threatened for several reasons. The first problem recognized by the AACSB standards is the lack of faculty-student interaction. Adjuncts or "supporting" faculty often lack a significant presence on campus, fewer or no office hours (Benjamin 2003b), and can be difficult to contact outside of the classroom. Given that many adjuncts have full-time professional careers, they may read their e-mail only periodically. In addition, adjuncts are often given last minute appointments resulting in a lack of preparation time, potentially with several different classes, and lack of consistent course offerings. The students may also be shortchanged due to the lack of proper course planning (Thompson 2003).

Carroll (2003) argues, however, that full-time faculty also do not have time for students, given their commitments to committee work, service, and research. Even if this is the case, two wrongs do not make a right. The pressures placed on adjuncts from excessive teaching and work obligations detract from their involvement in student learning. In addition, part-time faculty is significantly more disengaged from campus life than their full-time counterparts (Green 2007; Umbach 2007).

A second problem is the level of knowledge of the subject matter and teaching pedagogy that contingent faculty possess. Haeger (1998) believes that because part-time faculty have less education (Master's degree), the quality of instruction is threatened. Much of this research related to quality of education is based on comparisons of traditional end-of-semester student evaluations. For instance, Grenzke (1998) reported that adjuncts are evaluated more often than their full-time colleagues. In some cases, students generally do not rate adjuncts as highly as full-time faculty (Jackson 1986), but in other cases, there was no significant difference in SET satisfaction scores (Webb 2008). One study, however, found that full-time faculty members have been rated higher in subject knowledge and presentation of the materials (Jackson 1986).

Clark (1990) compared scores on a standardized test for differences between students who were taught by adjuncts and those who had full-time faculty. The final exam scores were identical for the two groups. Bolge (1995) found similar results where groups of students who were taught mathematics by full-time faculty and adjuncts showed no significant difference. Adjuncts with professional experience and credentials (i.e. CPA or CMA) are considered by many students to be superior instructors (Wallin 2007). A study of non-tenured faculty in four Research I institutions found that adjuncts were quite effective. Evaluations for these individuals were consistently higher than for tenure-track faculty and higher still when compared with graduate teaching assistants (Cross and Goldenberg 2003). Lastly, findings on skill levels showed no significant differences in 19 of the 20 skill areas (Marshall et al. 2006) between faculty with Ph.D.s in accounting and those with Ph.D.s in other areas who taught accounting. The one area that showed a difference was the non-accounting Ph.D.s reported it easier to integrate topics other than accounting into their courses than accounting Ph.D.s (Marshall et al. 2006).

Does an instructor with a master's degree and a CPA or a CMA have the same depth of knowledge and scholarship that someone with a Ph.D. may have (Haeger 1998)? While many adjuncts may be entertaining in the classroom, the quality of instruction suffers (White, et al. 2005). Keim and Biletzky (1999) found that adjuncts often employ traditional and neglect newer teaching strategies. Full-time instructors emphasized classroom discussion and participation, cooperative learning, research projects, journals, and on-line assessment; whereas, part-time instructors focused on objective tests—multiple choice and true-false (Thompson 2003; Lei 2007; Lei 2008). Most adjuncts did not use field trips, guest lecturers, and media in their classes. Assignments did not allow students to participate in small group discussions or activities that promoted higher skills such as critical thinking (Keim and Biletzky 1999).

A third problem is that contingent faculty members were often assigned to teach the first and second year courses (Townsend 2003). If "gatekeeper classes" are taught by contingent faculty, students are significantly less likely to return their sophomore years (Glenn 2008). In addition, students are more likely to drop out of classes taught by adjuncts and are less prepared for more advanced courses (Burgess and Samuels 1999). Burgess and Samuels (1999) found that full-time instructors better prepared students for their second courses than part-time instructors. Furthermore, Cross and Goldenberg (2003) found non-tenure track instruction is expanding, albeit at slower pace, into junior-senior courses. In addition, they found that adjunct faculty occasionally moves into non-instructional roles such as student advising or internship supervising.

A fourth problem and a peripheral consequence of the increase in the use of non-AQ faculty means that there are fewer and fewer tenured faculty to oversee course development and curriculum planning. Institutions are beginning to suffer other adverse effects (Nutting 2003). The ratio of part-time to full-time faculty at community colleges was highly correlated with negative graduation rates. Student motivation and ability also have declined leading to higher dropout rates (Jacoby 2006).

A fifth problem with adjunct faculty is grade inflation (Kezim et al. 2005; Sonner 2000). Sonner (2000) found that adjunct faculty often gave higher grades than their full-time counterparts even when the other potentially biasing factors were accounted for. Since adjuncts are employed on a part-time basis, most of them face the pressure of earning high SET scores as their passport for being retained in the adjunct pool (Sonner 2000). Student satisfaction is often equated with higher grades and less rigorous courses, thus students may reciprocate by giving adjunct faculty higher student evaluations (Fajardo 2004). In fact, adjuncts may feel less responsible for maintaining academic integrity in the classroom (Freeland 1998; Rifkin 1998).

A final problem with the use of non-accounting Ph.D.s is the lowering of the quality of accounting education. Unarguably, the integrity of programs is maintained by full-time faculty members who are committed educators. Tenured faculty members are not as easily moved by trends, SET scores, student complaints, or internal and external pressures to increase enrollments, inflate grades, dumb-down classes, or lower program costs. Few accounting faculty members would say they chose the teaching profession solely for money, but rather for the love of teaching or research or both. One problem with the "bridge" programs is that money is touted as a primary reason to enroll in the programs. The implications of these issues in accounting education are not positive at this time.

Despite the many disadvantages of using adjunct faculty in higher education, there are benefits to students, institutions, and the accounting profession. Adjuncts can offer to the classroom rich work experiences, current practices, and connections with the real world (Green 2007; Lyons 1999; Thompson 2003). In fact, some studies that found no differences between the quality of full-time and adjuncts' teaching (Leslie and Gappa 2002). The positive findings of these studies regarding adjuncts show that the use of contingent faculty can be effective at some institutions and under certain conditions.

RECOMMENDATIONS

The differences in the treatment of full-time "AQ" faculty and contingent faculty are pronounced. Whereas the appointment of tenure-track faculty is closely monitored and regulated by university policies, non-tenure track faculty are often selected by department chairs or program directors (Cross and Goldenberg 2003) with little due process or input by AQ faculty. When hired, new non-tenured faculty are integrated into the institutional culture, policies, practices, and department processes through formal programs that could include mentoring programs, professional learning communities, or other programs promoted by Teaching and Learning Centers (Wyles

1998). Adjunct faculty members are often handed a textbook and syllabus and instructed to just teach. For ethical reasons and for the sake of our students' learning, we need to create sustainable strategies for the contingent faculty to better integrate into college life, to improve their teaching, and to contribute to accounting programs in a positive manner.

Create Contingent Faculty Development Programs

Adopting faculty development programs for contingent faculty could have a dramatic impact on success in the classroom and on student satisfaction (Lyons 1999). Elman (2003) recommended that the use of contingent faculty should be aligned with the mission and the purpose of the college. The institution should develop explicit expectations for contingent faculty, and contingents should be given a voice in academic governance.

Indian River Community College in Fort Pierce, Florida developed a faculty development program that had four elements that could easily be adopted by other institutions. Those elements include:

1. Instructor effectiveness training where adjuncts are taught course planning, syllabus development, how to conduct a first class, effective teaching and learning practices, and methods of student assessment.
2. Structured orientation from the department chair where department policies are shared with the adjunct.
3. Mentoring program with full-timers helping adjuncts through meetings.
4. Resource center with books on teaching issues that could be accessed by adjuncts.

In addition to limiting exploitation, hiring and evaluation cycles need to be more predictable. Bates College in Lewiston, Maine allows part-time faculty to improve in rank (to senior lecturer) and compensation. The results of the Bates program were greater recognition and an improved sense of belonging for part-time faculty members. Bates also adopted long-term contracts for adjuncts on three year cycles, and then after nine years, five year cycles. By giving extended contracts, however, do contingent faculty members have the right to sue for de facto tenure if released after seven years? AAUP policy states that:

> for full-time faculty, the probationary period should not exceed seven years, and those who are reappointed beyond seven years should be recognized as having the protections that would accrue with tenure—termination only for adequate cause and with due process (AAUP 2006b).

The matter of *de facto* tenure is often a matter for the courts to decide, based on the circumstances. Thus, even with extended contracts, contingent faculty members are not guaranteed lifetime employment like tenured faculty members. If fact, some colleges limit all employment of contingents to six years to avoid the problem of de facto tenure (Wilson 2005).

An economical approach is for institutions to join together to develop contingent faculty development programs. One coalition of seven colleges developed an Academy for Part-time Teaching with four training modules to educate part-timers on teaching, planning, assessment, technology, on-line delivery, online discussions using the web, teacher partnering, teaching evaluations, and final capstone reflection papers (Wallin 2007). In addition to improving adjuncts' quality of teaching, such faculty development programs help adjuncts feel less like strangers, but more like integrated members of the community (Roueche et al. 1995).

Develop Quality Control Programs

Do accounting programs need a quality control system beyond AACSB "standards?" Some good news is that the American Institute of CPAs (AICPA) core competency framework can be used as quality control program (Daigle et al. 2007). Ward and Dugger (2002, 5) argue that:

> A key component of the success of any discipline is the demonstrated satisfaction of its customers. ... (Others believe) employer satisfaction with graduates, graduate satisfaction with employment, career mobility, starting salary, and the ability of graduates to function effectively in industry without additional training would be appropriate in improving the method for assessing the effectiveness of each program.

As part of the quality control program, contingent faculty need the same training and support as full-time faculty. Mentoring, supervision, partnership with full-time faculty, and continuing education for adjuncts can help improve their quality of instruction. Furthermore, Fulton (2000) recommends that contingent faculty should only teach in specialty areas related to their disciplines, thereby enhancing program quality. Adjuncts also can participate in supervision of interns and co-ops in the workplace as well as serving as advisor to student professional organization as ways to increase their engagement in the college campus and culture.

Careful data collection and management is a must (Cross and Goldenberg 2003). For instance, there should be a distinction between graduate assistant and adjunct faculty categories for proper tracking. Although most institutions will know how many tenure-track faculty members are employed and how many full-time equivalents (FTEs) they represent, they are less aware of the numbers of adjunct faculty and often are amazed when they understand the extensive utilization of contingent faculty (Cross and Goldenberg 2003). Once tracked, institutions can gauge the percentages of classes taught by adjuncts versus full-time faculty to see if the ratios are in line with the institutional mission.

Fellingham (2007, 161) believes that "nonacademic measures, such as student evaluations and school rankings, are increasingly used to decide who teaches and what they teach." Universities should conduct their own studies regarding quality of instruction, grades, and use course-embedded assessment to ensure quality instruction is occurring in their classes.

Sustain Academic Respectability

Having a Ph.D. and engaging in research does not ensure that one will be a good teacher. But the growing use of "PQ" faculty, non-Ph.D.s in accounting, and adjuncts, no matter how caring, hardworking, or professionally qualified they may be, inevitably raises an old question which accounting has never solved: Does accounting really belong in the academy (Demski 2007; Fellingham 2007)? Accounting is still viewed by some as a vocational topic worthy of high school study and on-the-job training. Demksi (2007) and Fellingham (2007) argue that academic accountants have not done nearly all they should have to combat those lingering largely vocational and nonacademic images of accounting.

Trends presented in Exhibit 2 reflect the perception in the Academy that the role of accounting faculty is largely vocational. Only the doctoral institutions increased their hiring of full-time faculty; whereas, more than half of the accounting classes at other institutions are taught by contingent faculty. Fellingham (2007, 161) laments the fact that "teaching of accounting is being done, increasingly, by instructors (clinical faulty) who do not have academic training and academic values" that full-time "AQ" faculty have. The argument that a doctorate is not necessary to teach undergraduate courses neglects the fact that doctoral education not only requires a dissertation, but also a minimum of two years of additional coursework (Benjamin 2003b).

Recent work by Fogarty and Markarian (2007) and Van Wyhe (2007a and 2007b) paint a rather dismal picture of accounting education today. Compared to the important theoretical tools created by financial economics such as the Modigliani-Miller theorem and the Black-Scholes option pricing formula (Barone 2008), accounting seems to have come up short. Combined with the large decline in interest in traditional accounting Ph.D. programs (Fellingham 2007, 161) in the face of a growing demand for well-trained accountants (Nance-Nash 2007; Thomson et al. 2008), one has to wonder what is going on? Even with the AACSB interfering in the supply side of the demand and supply equation through the "PQ" classification and the "bridge program" initiative, the accounting faculty shortage is projected to grow worse.

The reality is that the accounting profession in the United States is becoming less vocational every day. With the "Big Four" firms outsourcing tax preparation work to India, higher skill sets are required of today's accounting graduate. It is the ratio of PQ and contingent faculty to full-timers that is the difference between "institution offering education and one that offers training" (AAUP 2006a, 17). Education visionaries such as Gardner (2006) state that today's graduate needs higher learning skills leading to a disciplined, synthesizing, creating, respectful, and ethical mind to compete in the future.

The mindset of adjuncts is often on content and the practical, which students like, but the development of critical thinking skills and challenge are often lacking (Keim and Biletzky 1999). Thus, for contingent faculty members, it becomes even more important that they are integrated into academia (Liu 2007). In reality, how can anyone expect adjuncts, given the low pay, to try to gain an understanding of traditional academic values? For accounting education to succeed, we need competent, engaged, and committed faculty, both part and full-time, to meet the challenges that our students will face in the future.

WHERE WILL OUR FUTURE THINKERS COME FROM?

With fewer and fewer Ph.D.s in accounting (and business), where are the future leaders of business and accounting education going to come from, and who will conduct accounting research? Accounting research has led to valuable ideas in areas including tax policy, derivatives, portfolio analysis, auditing, and management accounting. With fewer minds committed to research, there could be a loss of leadership in the accounting profession, education, professional organizations, and a lessened influence on government policies. Furthermore, as "the ranks of tenure-track faculty continue to erode, who will be the arbitrators of quality? Who will have the academic freedom to make decisions? How will administrators know what is being taught and who is really teaching effectively? And what happens when administrators get outsourced along with teaching?" (Thompson 2003, 47).

The long-term impacts of these staffing trends need to be fully examined, but there is adequate evidence to suggest the consequences outweigh the benefits. Hiring adjuncts is one way to make college more affordable for the masses, but often at the expense of student learning and exploitation of contingent faculty. Rhetoric of exploitation, second class citizens, and the outsourcing of higher education reflect an uncomplimentary, but too often realistic view of contingent faculty. But how can institutions afford, especially private institutions, to pay the typical new Ph.D. in accounting a salary with benefits starting in excess of $140,000?

How do we as faculty deal with the changed AACSB standards and increase in the hiring of contingent faculty? How do we ensure that our accounting students receive an education that prepares them for the challenges of the profession in a global market? As mentioned earlier, faculty development and quality control programs can help integrate contingent faculty into the academic environment and provide fairer treatment. The larger issue is ultimately how to increase the supply of business Ph.D.s, especially in accounting.

There are market forces at work regarding wages and the attractiveness of the higher education as a profession. When students observe the exploitation of adjuncts (even those with Ph.D.s), why would students pursue this profession (Thompson 2003)? Professors may not realize the influence they have on Master's students (Schuster 2003). Out of about twelve students in one graduate level tax class at Miami University in 1981, three now have Ph.D.s, another is "PQ" and teaching accounting, and one more, currently a partner at a CPA firm, is planning to get his Ph.D. when he becomes 50 years old. Over time, these students decided that their professors were "living the good life" compared to pursuing a long-term career in public accounting. In addition, Miami University offered instructor positions to promising graduates (3-year contracts) at a competitive pay rate, allowing graduates to "test" drive the academic life.

More can be done to increase the supply of new accounting doctorates. Ph.D. programs could welcome and accept more talented accounting students into their programs. In her presidential keynote speech given to the American Accounting Association in 2008, Susan Haka (2008) spoke to program administrators. She recommended that each doctoral program in the United States accept one more accounting doctoral student. This strategy would add 102 new Ph.D.s to the future employment pipeline. She also encouraged Deans of Business Schools to reward doctoral faculty with incentives to advise Ph.D. students.

Business deans also should examine the workload equity among business and accounting faculty. The teaching and research workloads of accounting faculty have increased continuously from 1993 to 2004 (AAA 2008). This increase was even more prevalent at research and doctoral institutions (AAA 2008). In order to attract new talent to the field, expectations for accounting faculty should be adjusted to a more equitable level.

Businesses could and are "chipping in" to give financial assistance to support doctoral students. Professional organizations could award fellowships to doctoral students. For example, the AICPA awarded 22 doctoral accounting fellowships to minority students entering into Ph.D. programs in 2007. The AICPA is also in the process of raising $15 million from industry and state societies to give $30,000 per year for four years to 120 new Ph.D. candidates beginning in 2009.

The government and foundations need to recognize the shortage and related consequences and should invest in the education of future accounting Ph.D.s. Accounting professors too, need to encourage their best students to think about doctoral education as a career choice (Haka 2008). Without these joint efforts, more than accounting education is at peril.

CONCLUSION

Long-term perspective, collective responsibility and joint effort will be needed to help battle the severe accounting Ph.D. shortage problem. As a community of accounting educators, practitioners, consultants, and public policy advisors, we have a greater responsibility not only to our students, but also to the future of the accounting profession and society's economic well-being. The shortage of qualified accounting educators, scholars, and researchers not only negatively impacts the students' learning, but hinders the growth of scholarship, thus limiting the innovative concepts to improve practice. By taking a short-term focus of cutting costs, we sacrifice the long-term sustainability of the profession. Our challenge is to educate the future generation of accountants by constantly germinating the field with new knowledge to help accounting maintain its respectability and critical role in influencing government policies and business practices.

CHAPTER 2

Why We Should Measure Student Learning: A Glossary of Collegiate Corruption

Patrick Moore, University of Arkansas at Little Rock*

Why is measuring or assessing learning an important priority in U.S. higher education today? The short answer is, collegiate corruption: too many college graduates are incompetent; many cannot write a simple English sentence (Quible and Griffin 2007). The longer answer is that changes in U.S. socio-economic conditions in the past 40 years and the increased use of Student Evaluations of Teaching (SET) to judge teaching effectiveness have created perverse incentives for some students, professors, administrators, legislators, and business executives. Although some in the academy have resisted those incentives, many have not. Those perverse incentives have led to infantilized classes, inflated grades, college graduates who are deficient in basic skills, and many other problems.

This article is not the place for a thorough analysis of all the socio-economic conditions in the past 40 years that have led to the current situation. I summarize just two: (1) The "higher" in many institutions of higher education is largely gone. (2) Higher education in the U.S. became monetarized in the 1970s and 1980s, to the detriment of many and to the detriment of student learning in general (Spellings 2006).

The ideas of philosopher John Rawls have played a significant role in the loss of quality in many colleges. Rawls (1971) made popular the "difference principle" in his influential book, *A Theory of Justice.* The difference principle is "a strongly egalitarian conception in the sense that unless there is a distribution that makes both persons better off (limiting ourselves to the two-person case for simplicity), an equal distribution is to be preferred" (1971, 76). In a later work, Rawls elaborates on how to achieve justice: "Social and economic inequalities are to satisfy two conditions: first, they are to be attached to offices and positions open to all under conditions of fair equality of opportunity; and second, they are to be the greatest benefit of the least-advantaged members of society (the difference principle)" (2001, 42–43). Rawls' ideas have been used to justify the policy of admitting almost everyone in the U.S. into higher education and subsidizing their education. His ideas also have encouraged U.S. culture to value fairness over meritocracy in higher education. As a result, the goal of higher education in the U.S. in many schools is no

* Patrick Moore is Associate Professor of English at the University of Arkansas at Little Rock; epmoore@att.net.

longer to advance learning, but to pursue other goals related to fairness: equity, accessibility, open admissions, and retention.

The resulting educational and financial policies have encouraged dumbed down classes and curricula and inflated grades, have diminished student learning in order to keep many underperforming and incompetent students in college, and have enabled many free riders to exploit higher education (Zimmerman 2002). Rawls' ideas make equity the highest value in higher education, not efficiency, accountability, or even learning itself.

As Edward St. John, one of Rawls' supporters, says: "There is no higher aim in policy research on education and public finance than to frame analyses in order to inform the public interest in ways that are fair and just" (2004, 245). But that raises the question, "fair and just to whom?"

Too many manipulators and free riders are getting away with too much, which is one reason why appropriately measuring student learning is so important now.

The second socio-economic condition is the monetarization of higher education. Beginning in the 1970s and 1980s, students were no longer human beings, but FTEs (Full-Time-Equivalents) or SSCH (Student Semester Credit Hours). FTEs and SSCH are pegged to dollar amounts according to the funding formulas of federal and state governments. In the 1970s and 1980s, the primary goal of many American colleges and universities shifted from educating to collecting money. That money is students. It is more important now in many schools to keep students happy and passing their classes no matter what.

The U.S. Congress helped to create this new arrangement. They passed laws that made it much easier for almost anyone to get money for college—good students or bad. The Congress also guaranteed the government would repay banks and loan companies for defaulted student loans, and Congress guaranteed good profits to banks and loan companies for student loans. (For a summary of this legislation, see Dillon 2007.)

Because of these laws, money became available to almost anyone to attend college. Today, the U.S. spends over $300 billion annually on post-secondary education (Knapp et al. 2007, Table 3). In the 2004–2005 school year, 75% of all first-time undergraduates in the U.S. received some kind of student aid (Knapp et al. 2007, Table 7). That number would be higher were it not for the fact that the U.S. has millions of millionaires, who cannot make a case for needing aid.

The huge sums of money, the complicated eligibility rules surrounding them, and the lack of accountability attracted profiteers from the ranks of business managers, academic administrators, students, and politicians. For example, the chairman of the board and the CEO of Sallie Mae, the big federal student loan corporation, paid themselves $367 million in total compensation from 1999 to 2006 (Kamenetz 2006). That money came from the profits that the government guaranteed to Sallie Mae.

University presidents began to command large salaries. One executive compensation survey in 2006 showed 112 college presidents had salaries and benefits over $500,000 per year (Fain and June 2006). Several presidents of private colleges earned over one million dollars a year (Fain and June 2006). In 2004–2005, the president of the University of Delaware earned $979,571 in total compensation (Fain and June 2006). Presidents make these salaries because of the huge sums of money that flooded colleges, and because of the ways students and instructors are manipulated. See the discussion of *academic freedom, code of silence, confidentiality, deniability, heresthetic, intimidators,* and *remedial education* below.

Predatory students have also profited. The vast majority of the 6,000 plus U.S. post-secondary institutions have open admissions, and obtaining loan money is easy. If new college students cannot read, write (Quible and Griffin 2007), or compute well, they can find the easy graders on the faculty through the grapevine or through Internet sites such as ratemyprofessor.com. Or they can manipulate the hard graders, or cheat with the help of fellow students or with the help of the many Internet sites that sell pre-written essays. Many college instructors are aware of student cheating, but some do not care and will not read student essays that they assign. Some faculty pass student cheaters after they discover their dishonesty. They feel helpless to do much about it due to the lack of support from college administrations or because prosecuting student cheaters through the college bureaucracy takes so much time and effort.

Predatory students have discovered that *change checks* give them a tidy living while they fake attendance in college. *Change checks* are the money returned to students after they present their aid and loan checks to the college cashier for payment of tuition and fees. Some students register for classes, collect their *change checks,* and vanish. Other free riders sign up for easy teachers, collect their *change checks,* cut class, cheat, or do as little work as possible, and still get a grade point average (GPA) high enough to qualify them for more aid and loan checks. They can do this for years.

State legislators also profit from the monetarization of higher education. Because of the flood of state and federal money, state legislators from poor districts can establish a college in their area and pump millions into the local economy and win reelection. Even a small community college with 1,500 students can bring millions of dollars annually into a poor district, money that comes from state taxes, from student aid payments for tuition and fees, and from *change checks.*

Many legislators do not acknowledge that many college degrees are debased. They do not explain that for higher education to be meaningful, it must be *higher:* graduates must know more than high school students, preferably a lot more. The monetarization of higher education creates powerful incentives to infantilize courses and inflate grades: since students are money and throwing away money is wasteful, faculty are pressured to inflate grades and dumb down classes. Reports of grade inflation in all disciplines, especially the humanities, have become widespread (Rosovsky and Hartley 2002; Johnson 2003). One result of grade inflation is that the quality of a college education is declining. For example, the 2003 National Assessment of Adult Literacy has shown that college graduates are becoming less and less proficient in reading (Romano 2005).

The federal and state legislators who create these problems can do little to improve college education. For the existing system to improve, post-secondary institutions would have to raise admission standards, eliminate remedial courses, and create rigorous exit exams. Such changes could eliminate half of the 18 million current U.S. post-secondary students, which in turn would close many public and private schools, lay off half of all U.S. postsecondary instructors, and lay off half of all support staff. Those are a lot of votes.

These two social conditions—the loss of quality and the monetarization of higher education—coupled with such well-known human traits as greed and shirking responsibility, have encouraged more meaningful measurement of student learning in U.S. higher education. But the usual problems—i.e., dumbed down classes and inflated grades—provide an incomplete picture of the range of collegiate corruption in U.S. colleges and universities. Below is a more comprehensive glossary and discussion. Some of the items in this glossary (e.g., *academic freedom* and *confidentiality*) are not in themselves acts of corruption, but like any value, they can be exploited by unscrupulous people to do wrong.

GLOSSARY OF COLLEGIATE CORRUPTION

Academic Freedom: For many college faculty, academic freedom is the right to present the startling facts, innovative conclusions, and occasionally controversial interpretations that arise from legitimate academic inquiry and research. For other college faculty, academic freedom is the right to loot and pillage the public's resources: to dumb-down classes, to inflate grades, to steal time, to engage in *time-laundering,* to propagandize, and to do whatever they want in their classes and on their jobs short of criminal misconduct. Students, parents, taxpayers, legislators, and other stakeholders often do not have any effective property rights to offset the abuses of academic freedom. That is, while many faculty have academic freedom, tenure, and control over the curriculum, students, parents, and legislators do not have the right, for example, to discover if graduating college seniors can actually read, write, and compute at the tenth-grade level of high school.

Access: Accessibility in higher education is not necessarily related to the ramps, elevators, and other special accommodations that justifiably exist for people with disabilities. Accessibility is more commonly associated with *open-admissions colleges and universities.* More than 90 percent of the 2,200 four-year colleges in the U.S. have non-selective admission practices (Maeroff 2005, 14). The emphasis on accessibility results in part from the Rawlsian emphasis on fairness. According to this view, everyone should be admitted to college and have access to money for college because it is fair. Some educators see such access as a corrective to the "elitist" colleges and universities who select only the highly able from their pools of applicants. These educators believe that access is good because it is fair and democratic. But when access is a high priority, then higher education is not focused on learning or knowledge but on other things such as *retention,* dumbed down classes, and inflated grades.

Aid Kiters: Students who exploit faculty goodwill or corruption and the float time between the beginning and end of the term in order to gain undeserved financial support. Aid kiters register for college classes, receive aid money to pay tuition and other expenses (including living expenses), and fulfill few or no course requirements during the term. Then, later in the term, aid kiters go to their professors with excuses to get incompletes, exemptions from course requirements, or *gratuity grades* to keep up their grade point averages and collect more aid for the subsequent term. If the required minimum GPA for renewing aid is low (e.g., a C), aid kiters can skip a class entirely, collect an F, and still get more aid money, because two or three A's or B's from grade inflators or *course infantilizers* will offset one F.

Anti-humanists: Humanities professors who attack the corporate, scientific, engineering, government, and technology sectors and find them lacking in humanity, fairness, and other kinds of cultural or moral capital. Anti-humanists have narrowed broader definitions of humanism to exclude anyone who does not reflect their *utopian* and *moral supremacist* ideals. Broadly defined, humanism is the Renaissance perspective that shifted attention away from divine subjects and onto human concerns, including scientific pursuits, reason, and human interests and pursuits in the physical world. Today, anti-humanists reject that earlier definition. They declare members of the corporate, scientific, engineering, government, and technology sectors to be excessively focused on financial profits, materialism, expediency, domination, hierarchy, imperialism, and exploitation, among other defects. Anti-humanists believe they can solve the world's problems if they can run society in accordance with their *utopian* beliefs.

Bottom Feeders: Students who search for easy graders. The best source of information about faculty grading policies is other students. Valerie Milliron (2008, 405) found that today's students "place a significantly higher value on low workload and less importance on analytical and computational assignments." During pre-registration periods at *open-admission* and less-selective schools, students can be heard asking each other if a professor is an easy or hard grader. A second source of information is websites that provide information about faculty grading policies. Two websites, www.myprofessorsucks.com and www.ratemyprofessors.com, tell prospective students if professors are easy or hard graders.

Change Checks: Change checks are legitimate financial instruments issued by colleges and universities. They represent the difference between the student's aid check and the tuition and fees that the school charges. For example, a student may submit an aid check of $3,000 to pay a $2,000 bill for tuition and fees. The college then writes a change check to the student for $1,000. Change checks commonly range from a few hundred to several thousand dollars. Students who get aid from several sources (e.g., grants, scholarships, loans) may get change checks totaling eight to ten thousand dollars and use the money for books, supplies, and paying their living expenses (Appleby 2002).

Child Extortionists: A student who uses a child to threaten to disrupt a class if the instructor does not allow the student to cut a class, an exam, or another course requirement. Many students in college today have children. Some students use their children as a weapon to extort exemptions or other privileges from their instructors. A child extortionist will call an instructor before a class, claim to have a sick or fussy child, and request an exemption from a class or exam. If the instructor says no because the student has missed many previous classes, the student will threaten to bring the child to class to disrupt it.

Code of Silence: Like the Sicilian mafia, the mortarboard mafia has its code of silence. Any faculty member who violates the code by complaining publicly risks retaliation, unless the professor works for a school with a strong union or with a strong tradition of academic freedom. Administrators and faculty can prevent ethical resistors from teaching summer classes or courses in their specialties, force them to teach every day a week or teach early morning and evening classes, summon the resistor to an administrative office for an intimidation ritual, deny the resistor access to opportunities that are available to other faculty, and, among other things, fire the resistor.

Confidentiality: Evaluating others (e.g., students, applicants for professorships, peer review of teaching, manuscripts for publication, applicants for promotion and tenure) is central to academic life. Professors have a right to secrecy on many occasions, especially when deliberating over personnel matters. Ostensibly a professor's right to secrecy is meant to protect a student's or job applicant's privacy. But in some cases private academic meetings are opportunities for faculty members to bully political opponents, to violate federal and state hiring laws, and to get their stories straight before making their conclusions public. Some faculty use the confidentiality of those meetings to engage in misconduct and then to deny that anything wrong happened. Even when one faculty member violates federal law (e.g., discriminates against a job applicant because of gender, age, etc.), others will not testify against the malefactor out of concern for getting the school sued, for the confidentiality of the evaluation process, and for the *code of silence.* See *deniability* below.

Course Infantilizers: Faculty who dumb down their classes. Open-admissions and less-competitive colleges and universities often admit *unprepared students* who have social passes out of high school. These students typically take remedial classes in college. But once these students get social passes through their remedial classes, they often cannot do college work. In order to retain these students and, more importantly, their aid checks, some faculty infantilize their classes so that anyone can pass the assignments. See *gratuity grades* and *remedial education.*

Deniability: The ability to speak or act in one way in one context and avoid responsibility for those words or acts in another context. This privilege is the foundation of most collegiate corruption. In the United States, many colleges lack a comprehensive exit exam that prevents inept students from graduating. Thus, no one knows if graduating seniors can read, write, and compute at the tenth-grade level. When business people or legislators complain that college graduates do not know much, faculty and administrators can dismiss their concerns by offering anecdotal information about the success of a few *showcase* students, and by offering, as Frank Newman says, a "well-polished argument about the importance of higher education, the danger to the process and to academic freedom of external meddling, and the mystic and immeasurable basis of the liberal education" (Burd 2003, A23). Tenured college faculty have strongly enforced property rights to academic freedom—freedom that includes the right to dumb down classes and inflate grades—but many faculty abuse those rights. Unfortunately, taxpayers, students, and legislators can do little because they have no information to make the injustice visible. See also *confidentiality* and *code of silence.*

Drama Kings/Queens: Students who begin shouting, crying, or playing the victim on little pretense to pressure faculty into letting them avoid course requirements or to gain *gratuity grades.* Some students put on ostentatious shows of victimhood in class to encourage other students to gang up on a professor who is insufficiently corrupt. Some students brag openly about crying to manipulate faculty into giving higher grades. See also *intimidators* and *professional victims.*

Economics of Grade Inflation: To paraphrase Lionel Robbins' famous definition, economists study the use of scarce resources that have alternative uses (1935, 16). Among other resources, colleges and their faculty need money, time, and goodwill. Inflating grades earns all those scarce resources.

(a) *Making money:* If faculty give passing (or higher) grades to all comers, then those students return to college for the subsequent term and pay their tuition and fees. Those students do not spend their money attending trade schools or in other possibly more worthy pursuits. Every returning student—literate, subliterate, or totally illiterate—assures to some degree the jobs, raises, and pensions of college faculty and administrators for the next term. A significant 73.7 percent of accounting administrators admit that an important goal of their institution is to improve retention rates (Crumbley and Fliedner 2002).

(b) *Saving time:* If faculty give passing (or higher) grades to all comers, then they do not have to give students many assignments, give much feedback on student work, hold many office hours, or spend their time with students who appeal low grades to the administration. Grade inflators can hold second or third jobs, research and publish more, spend more time with their families, or convert their job to a sinecure and become semi-retired on full pay.

(c) *Creating goodwill:* If faculty give passing (or higher) grades to all comers, they often earn higher course evaluations, they stay in favor with many administrators at least in the short run, and they avoid the stress—not to mention the injuries and fatalities—of coping with angry and retaliatory students. See *retaliators, self-appointed 'A' students,* and the *law of reciprocal grading.*

Grade Inflation: A rise in the level of students' grade point averages over time without an attendant rise in the quality of student performance is grade inflation. Grade inflation is sometimes hard to prove because many colleges and universities do not make public the records of past student grades. But Valen Johnson's book, *Grade Inflation* (2003), and the report by Rosovsky and Hartley (2002) present strong evidence about the prevalence of grade inflation. Literally dozens of articles, academic and non-academic, have documented or bemoaned the prevalence of grade inflation in American colleges (e.g., Abbott 2008; Addy and Herring 1996; Cluskey et al. 1997; Crumbley 1995; Cushman 2003; Fajardo 2004; Grimes, Millea, and Woodruff 2004; Kurtz 2006; Neath 1996; Pressman 2007; Sax 2003; Sonner 2000; Wilson 1999; Yunker and Yunker 2003; Zimmerman 2002). Grade inflation exists because colleges need to retain students to maintain their cash flow (see *retention*), because instructors want to avoid harassment and retaliation from students and administrators (see *hostage takers, intimidators, professional victims, racial extortionists, retaliators*), because instructors want to manipulate SET (see *student evaluations of teachers*), and because instructors want to appear fair to disadvantaged and unprepared students (see *unprepared students*). Also, many faculty admit—privately, of course—to inflating grades. See the *economics of grade inflation.*

Grading Differentials: The difference between academic specialties in the stringency of their grading. As Johnson states, "Generally speaking, humanities and most social science departments have adopted grading policies that provide comparatively lucrative reward structures for student performance, while natural sciences, mathematics, and economics departments have adopted more miserly distribution schemes" (2003, 225). Grading differentials have several socially destructive consequences. One is that they discourage students from taking classes in science, mathematics, and economics. Another is that they often create lower student evaluations for teachers in science, mathematics, and economics.

Gratuity Grades: Some students earn gratuity grades by playing on the sympathy or self-interest of instructors. Some instructors will give students passing grades for courses even if a student has done little or no work and has attended few classes. Instructors may issue gratuity grades if they are sufficiently weak-willed, if their institutions pressure them to pass non-performing students to keep collecting their tuition and aid checks, or if a student makes a case for sympathy.

Heresthetic: "[S]tructuring the world so you can win" is William Riker's definition (1986, ix) of heresthetic. In *The Art of Political Manipulation,* Riker explains that heresthetic is based on "a simple and rather specialized form of the social choice model" (1986, 143). Riker focuses his analysis on four variables: (1) people and their values and tastes, (2) alternative choices, (3) dimensions, which are the measurable properties of the alternatives and individuals' tastes, and (4) ways of choosing, which for Riker is majority rule, but in other situations might be an individual's power to decide (1986, 143). Heresthetic is important in measuring student learning, because single individuals or groups can structure academic rules, procedures, and environments to ensure grading policies that favor their private agendas. As Johnson explains, at most colleges and universities, faculty groups oversee changes in grading policies: "Unfortunately, many faculty councils are populated by the very individuals who benefit most from inequitable grading policies" (2003, 240). Similarly, heresthetic is important in state government. If enough legislators from poor districts are on a state legislature's educational appropriations committee, they can structure their votes and legislation to create new community colleges in their districts or move funding from one state university or college system to another.

Hostage Takers: Hostage takers come in three types: those who take themselves, the class, or others (e.g., their children or families) hostage.

(a) Students who take themselves hostage claim that faculty must give them good grades to enable students to get more aid money, to keep them from losing a scholarship, to keep them from being dismissed from college, or to avoid hurting students' chances for future success. Sometimes these students claim that strict instructors are mean or are using punitive grading if they give low grades for inept performance. See *professional victims.*

(b) Students who take the class hostage threaten to disrupt the class (e.g., by throwing tantrums or bringing fussy children) if they are not given exemptions from course requirements, extra absences, or other benefits. See *Drama Kings/Queens* and *child extortionists.*

(c) Students who take others hostage typically claim that their children or families will be hurt if the student gets a low grade and loses aid money.

Intimidators: Intimidators can be students, faculty, or administrators. Student intimidators, among other things, throw tantrums, threaten physical violence, threaten to go to an instructor's superior (i.e., department chair or Dean), or threaten to sue the instructor or the school. Student intimidators often have little to lose if they threaten instructors in private. Faculty can also intimidate by throwing tantrums in departmental meetings, by posting insulting emails to listservers, by refusing to call (or attend) a committee meeting if the faculty member is the chair, by privately threatening untenured faculty with retaliation if the untenured person does not vote the right way, and so on. Administrators can intimidate faculty by using the same strategies as faculty members and by threatening to not approve of sabbaticals, promotions, tenure, course reductions, summer school teaching, curriculum changes, leaves, travel subsidies, equipment subsidies, new hires, etc.

Law of Reciprocal Grading: This law states, "If you give me a high grade, I will give you a high course evaluation." The law of reciprocal grading is based on the common experience that if instructors give poor students undeserved high grades, the students will not complain. But if instructors give the same poor students low grades that they do deserve, they will complain, very likely give the faculty low end-of-term evaluations, tie up faculty time in appeals to the administration, defame faculty at every opportunity, and possibly kill the instructor. See *hostage takers* and *retaliators.*

Moral Supremacists: People who pose as superior to others, by virtue of their education, their association with the so-called "humanities" (see *anti-humanists*), their *utopian* beliefs, and their access to free time. In academia, moral supremacists anoint themselves the guardians of society's moral and cultural capital, and exploit *heresthetic* to give themselves leverage and power. Their education often gives them exposure to wide reading in philosophy, art, literature, and political theory (including the ideas of Rawls) from which they draw ideas and examples, and it gives them many rhetorical strategies to present allegations of diminished morality against their political opponents. Their professional associations with universities, publishing and media outlets, social networks, and libraries give them access to the infrastructure of cultural life. Their *utopian* assumptions provide them with an ideology and worldview of unshakable self-righteousness. Their plentiful free time enables them to read widely, write voluminously, and promote their accusations continuously. Moral supremacists typically find workers in the corporate, science, technology, government, and engineering sectors to be inhumane, unfair, anti-humanistic, insensitive, hierarchical, racist, sexist, elitist, profiteering, domineering, discriminatory, imperialistic, or capitalistic, among other defects.

Open-Admissions College or University: Also known as non-competitive, less-selective, or down-market schools, they register any student who can fog glass, borrow money, and has a social pass out of high school. See *unprepared students and access.*

Professional Victims: In the moral economy of the West, victims now have high social status. Some students find it easy and profitable to play the victim when attending college. They overload themselves with responsibilities that interfere with their college classes: e.g., children, one or more jobs, caring for sick relatives, coping with their own health problems, maintaining their car, house, and other possessions. Then these students get aid money to attend college. Because they are overextended, they always have a reason to avoid their course work. Many instructors excuse professional victims, who can get aid for years because *open-admission* and less-competitive colleges want to keep students in school to collect their aid checks. Professional victims typically do not complete their course requirements with excuses involving a personal illness or injury, a sick or injured child, a dead or dying relative, a computer malfunction, or a problem with the job, the car, or the law.

Racial Extortionists: Racial extortionists can be of any race, because instructors can be of any race. Racial extortionists notice that their race is not the same as the instructor's and use that difference to harass the instructor. If racial extortionists earn a low grade on an assignment or are warned against disrupting the class, they accuse the instructor of racial harassment.

Remedial Education: Remedial programs for subliterate or subnumerate college students began to flourish in recent decades, at considerable profit to colleges. For example, students may be charged $500 each in tuition and fees for a 3-hour remedial writing class with 20 students, earning the school a total of $10,000 per class. The part-time instructor for the class might be paid $2,000, making a profit of $8,000 per section for the college. These numbers will vary from school to school according to the greed of the school and local conditions.

Resource Sinks: Historically, resource sinks are individuals, groups, or institutions that consume disproportionately large quantities of resources, including cultural capital, without giving back. *Anti-humanists, child extortionists, drama kings/queens, hostage takers, intimidators, moral supremacists, professional victims, racial extortionists,* and others want disproportionate shares of cultural or moral capital, and they want to prevent others from having such resources.

Retaliators: Faculty and administrators with high or even middling standards risk retaliation from students. Among other things, retaliators slash tires, make bomb threats, write anonymous threatening notes, disrupt classes, physically attack faculty, and defame faculty on websites and in student newspapers. Retaliators also murder faculty, administrators, and fellow students. James Kelly was a graduate student at the University of Arkansas who was dismissed. He killed an English professor, John Locke, on the first day of class in August, 2000 (Wood 2007, 279). Peter Odighizuwa, a failing student at the Appalachian School of Law in Grundy, Virginia, killed the dean of the school, one of his professors, and a fellow student in January, 2002 (Wood 2007, 280). Robert Flores Jr., a failing student at the University of Arizona, killed three of his nursing school instructors in October, 2002 (Wood 2007, 279–80). Such students do more than kill: their acts create a climate of fear in colleges and universities. Instructors, and especially part-timers, adjuncts, and even tenured and non-tenured full-time faculty, will think twice about giving low grades to any student (Sonner 2000).

Retention: Keeping students in college rather than failing them when they will not attend classes, buy books, read books, do assigned work, or perform assigned work acceptably. Retention is absolutely vital to keep money flowing from state and federal aid sources into the public colleges and universities in poorer legislative districts. Some state legislators establish a community college or university in their district to improve the district's income. Education money from outside the district enters through the academic jobs that a community college brings (e.g., the faculty, staff, and administrators) and from the increased service jobs in the surrounding community (e.g., fast food restaurants, gas stations, and copy shops). *Change checks* give hundreds or thousands of district residents thousands of dollars of extra cash every year. In such funding schemes, some legislators emphasize retention, because faculty who fail bad students cut into a poor legislative district's cash flow. Besides *heresthetic,* legislators can use the ideas of Rawls and his disciples to give themselves moral capital as they debase higher education and simultaneously roll money into their districts.

Self-Appointed "A" Students: "I am an A student" or "I am an A writer" is the response of such students when they receive an assignment with any grade less than an A. When such students matriculate at *open-admission* or less-competitive public colleges, they may have many A's on their transcripts from grade-inflating or course-infantilizing faculty, or from faculty who gave in to the pressure and bought the students' silence with an undeserved A.

Showcase Students: To gain a publicity edge on other state schools, some *open-admission* and less-competitive public colleges and universities will lavish money, attention, and services (e.g., trips and tutorials and workshops from senior faculty) on a tiny percentage of their best or most photogenic students in order to help them win awards and graduate fellowships so that the school can feature the student in advertising, publicity releases, and college catalogs and brochures. The vast majority of students at the state school do not have access to those services.

Student Evaluations of Teachers (SET): SET are questionnaires completed by students at or near the end of a school term to measure the teacher's performance on a number of variables usually expressed as statements. Each statement about a teacher's performance (e.g., "the instructor graded fairly," "the instructor explained the material clearly," "the instructor returned the tests and assignments promptly") is followed by a Likert-scale measurement (e.g., where 1 = strongly disagree and 5 = strongly agree). The responses of every student in the class to each statement are reduced to a mean score and summarized in a report to the instructor and the college administration. SET have many problems:

(a) They are easy to manipulate (Martin 1998, Naftulin et al. 1973, Williams and Ceci 1997, McPherson 2006).
(b) They have dubious validity as a measure of student learning (Langbein 2008, Newton 1988, Yunker and Yunker 2003, Grimes, Millea, and Woodruff 2004, Wallace and Wallace 1998).
(c) They can be abused by administrators who evaluate faculty for tenure, promotion, and raises (Crumbley 1995, Addy and Herring 1996, Neath 1996).
(d) They can create perverse incentives. One instructor who was rebuked for his low SET scores dramatically increased his numbers by the next semester by throwing a pizza party for his students, by making his tests easier, and by making the final exam optional (Crumbley 1995, 71). Instructors often can easily buy higher SET scores by inflating student grades (McPherson 2006).
(e) They give unqualified students too much power over faculty. Bale and Dudney (2000) suggest that when teaching finance to undergraduates, faculty should use instruction strategies that assume that students have some characteristics of adults and children. But if undergraduates have some characteristics of children, that does not qualify them to evaluate accurately the teaching and knowledge of faculty on SET.
(f) They create considerable stress for faculty being evaluated (Chonko 2006).

Other articles by Crumbley and Smith and by Moore and Flinn in this monograph discuss the limitations of SET at greater length.

Time Laundering: Corrupt professors typically steal time rather than money. To succeed, however, corrupt professors need some way to legitimate their theft. To do so, they exploit the practices and traditions of academic life, just as the mafia exploits legitimate businesses. The most common time-laundering opportunity is the professor's class. Some professors fill up their class time by showing films, by making students give hours of team projects and reports, by having students draft essays in class, or by having students do group work in class which does not require the instructor's participation. Many faculty use these classroom activities for legitimate reasons, but some do not. Other time-laundering devices include having office hours but not being there, canceling classes on any pretense, frequently coming to class late, or dismissing classes early. Some faculty use sabbaticals to launder time. See the *economics of grade inflation.*

Unprepared Students: Parents, administrators, fellow teachers, school boards, and students themselves often pressure teachers into giving students social passes out of high school. These unprepared students can barely read and write, but they are welcomed at *open-admission* and less-selective colleges because they can easily obtain financial aid. They become income delivery devices for these schools. Once in college, unprepared students typically have to take remedial classes for no credit (see *remedial education*), but faculty in those classes are frequently untenured and are themselves pressured to "process through" such students (see *retention*). Once unprepared students get through their remedial classes, some seek out grade inflators and *course infantilizers,* and they use many strategies (e.g., see *aid kiters, bottom feeders, child extortionists, hostage takers, intimidators, racial extortionists, professional victims*) to collect more aid money and course credits. Other unprepared students decide to study, attend class regularly, do their assigned work competently, and earn an education.

Utopians: "Utopia" literally means "no place." The name is associated with highly idealized social and political visions. Contemporary utopians believe that people are perfectible, that sufficient resources can usually be assembled to solve problems, that most if not all problems have solutions, and that experts can solve those problems. Pragmatists believe that people are not perfectible, that resources are typically scarce, that many problems cannot be solved to everyone's satisfaction, and that solutions to problems, if they exist at all, often evolve slowly through social traditions and market adjustments (see Pinker 2002, chapter 16; Sowell 2002).

Weil's Law of Academic Hiring: In his autobiography, mathematician Paul Halmos (1985) explained a logarithmic law described by one of his famous colleagues, André Weil. Weil believed that first-rate scholars and administrators tend to hire other first-rate scholars, but second-raters tend to hire third-raters, third-raters tend to hire fifth-raters, and so on, until quality diverges towards minus infinity (1985, 123). Weil's law of academic hiring partially explains the collegiate corruption in the U.S.

CONCLUSION

Many of the problems in colleges and universities revolve around property rights. Property rights include, among other things, the right to benefit from one's property and to exclude others from it. Compared to the public and most other employment situations, college faculty have disproportionately strong property rights. Academic freedom and tenure mean that faculty can usually do what they want in their classes, including dumb them down, inflate their grades, waste time (and launder it), and then deny their responsibility for inept student performance. Many students are aware of faculty property rights, because they use the strategies named above to pressure faculty into abusing the privileges associated with their property rights.

The imbalance between the property rights of faculty and the property rights of tax- and tuition-payers should be rectified by legal changes. Parents, taxpayers, and legislators need stronger academic property rights themselves. Those property rights should include the following:

1. The right to know whether high school graduates can read and write at the level of a high school senior. If high school graduates lack basic educational skills, it is unfair and unethical to admit them to college, because if they cannot do college work, they will reduce the level of instruction and achievement for their classmates, or they will promptly flunk out. Given the political and economic realities of contemporary open-admissions and less-competitive colleges, weak students will more likely reduce the level of instruction. Information about the academic ability of entering college freshmen is available. The American College Test company (ACT), for example, distributes its "Class Profile Service Report" to colleges. Schools should make that data public.
2. The right to know what students' grades mean. What does it mean to get an A in a class? Did everyone else in the class get an A or just 10% of the students? What does it mean to be a graduating senior with a 3.5 GPA (out of 4.0)? Is the average GPA in the graduating class a 3.9 or a 2.2? Students should not have to waste their resources pursuing a high grade that is awarded to every subliterate in their graduating class. One solution to this problem is to print the average grade for all the members of a class next to the student's grade on his or her semester grade report and college grade transcript.
3. The right to know if one's fellow graduates can pass competency exams. Parents, taxpayers, and students themselves should not have to pay for four or more years of college only to find out the student has a tenth-grade education upon graduation. Collecting this information would be expensive, but, as we shall see shortly, it could save tens of billions of dollars a year in wasted tuition and aid.

Righting the imbalance between the property rights of college faculty and everyone else does not mean that faculty must lose tenure, confidentiality, or academic freedom. But faculty must lose *deniability.* College faculty and administrators should not profit from dumbed down classes or from giving high or passing grades to subliterates.

Unfortunately, many faculty—and their institutions—do profit from collegiate corruption. Many *open-admission* and less-competitive public colleges are *de facto* income redistribution programs: They admit many unprepared students, collect their tuition and aid checks, process them term after term through infantilized classes with inflated grades, and exploit deniability, *confidentiality, retaliators,* and the *code of silence* to ensure that the collegiate corruption is never exposed. These *open-admission* and less-competitive public colleges are jobs programs for faculty and administrators, entitlements programs for students, and vote-getting programs for legislators.

Because of *deniability,* it is difficult to measure how much money is wasted on higher education in the U.S. each year. But the following data are suggestive. Today, post-secondary institutions spend $300 billion a year (Knapp et al. 2007, Table 3). In their report on post-secondary retention, Berkner et al. (2002) said that the graduation rate (after six years) was 58% for students who were entering freshmen at four-year institutions in the 1995–96 school year (2002, 16). The 2003 National Assessment of Adult Literacy found that between 1992 and 2003, "prose and document literacy declined for adults with some college or with higher levels of education" (Kutner et al. 2007, v).

If a little less than 60% of students are graduating college in six years, and if the literacy of adults with some college or with higher levels of education is declining, then $100 billion (and maybe a lot more) could be wasted each year on faculty who pretend to teach and on students who pretend to learn. Of course, given the present situation, we will never know. Because of the power of academic property rights, that is, the professors' power to deny their misconduct, and because of the professors' use of *heresthetic,* there is no way to determine exactly how much money is wasted in U.S. higher education. More accurate measures of student learning will help reduce this problem.

Many college and university administrators and faculty (especially faculty in the so-called "humanities") exploit their disproportionate share of cultural capital (e.g., their educations, distinctions, and command of rhetoric) and their powerful property rights (e.g., their *academic freedom,* tenure, *deniability, confidentiality,* and control of the curriculum) to steal money and moral authority from the public. Many professors and administrators do not want to be held accountable for their abuses of their cultural capital or of their property rights. They want to be laissez-faire cultural capitalists. The time is ripe to adjust academic property rights so that the public can get back some of the money and moral authority that some professors and administrators are stealing. Those are some reasons why we should measure student learning.

CHAPTER 3

Academic Freedom, Tenure, Promotion, and Student Evaluation of Faculty (SEF): Retrospective and Abstracted Summaries

Robert E. Haskell, University of New England*

RETROSPECTIVE

In 1997, I wrote a series of four articles on student evaluation of faculty (SEF) that were published in the refereed journal, *Education Policy Analysis Archives* (Haskell, 1997a; 1997b; 1997c; 1997d). The collective thrust of these articles was that SEF, as used, infringe not only on the integrity of the tenure and promotion process but, more importantly, that they abrogate academic freedom. At the time few if any articles addressed these particular consequences of SEF. Let me say up front, I am not against SEF, only the way the data are gathered, processed, and used.

The articles began as a simple series of informational papers for colleagues on campus after it became increasingly clear that SEF instruments were seriously flawed and were being misused in deciding faculty promotion and tenure. I should note up front here my bona fides. First, I always received "above average" student evaluations—whatever this means given the flawed instrument and its interpretation. Second, I successfully, and without mentionable problem, traversed the promotion and tenure process, culminating in my being promoted on schedule to the rank of full professor. Accordingly, I had and have no personal axe to grind. Indeed, I have always been concerned with effective instruction (Haskell 2000). Furthermore, serving as department chair for four years where I was required to evaluate colleagues, I am familiar with administrative issues, problems, and practices involving SEF.

Since the publication of these articles, I continue to receive emails about them. In fact, of all of my publications, these SEF articles have received—by far—the most attention, being widely cited and summarized. The emails come from multiple countries around the world. Some of these emails either invited me to speak at conferences, to write follow-up articles, or to testify in court about their (un)scientific basis. Until now my response has consistently been to say, "Sorry, I am no longer in the SEF business."

I maintained this stance because I came to the conclusion in 1997 that despite the increasing volume of research on SEF that not much was going to change any time soon; and it has not.

* Dr. Haskell is Professor of Psychology at University of New England; rhaskell@une.edu.

When Professor Larry Crumbley, whose name I recognized from his involvement in the SEF issue ten years previous, invited me to contribute to this volume, I accepted. I accepted out of a continuing, gnawing commitment to the academy; to make one last contribution that might make a difference.

Obviously, there has been a kind of perverse irony in the use of SEF by institutions of higher education. The irony is this:

> *While a major defining mission of institutions of higher education is the pursuit of valid knowledge through rigorous controlling methodologies, the manner in which knowledge of faculty is gathered by SEF instruments and applied by both faculty tenure and promotion committees and by administrators would receive an unquestionable failing grade in any introductory course on research methods.*

At risk of seeming hyperbole, this situation is really scandalous.

In brief, SEF as used for tenure, promotion and merit salary increases—even if they were valid—create strong financial and political pressures for faculty to (1) assent and adjust their teaching to whatever level of student the (open enrollment) institution elects to admit, (2) conform to student demands in the classroom by lowering standards which include, (3) lower curricular demands on students, (4) make tests less rigorous, (5) inflate grading, (6) require fewer classroom requirements and prerequisites, (7) make courses easier with less course content, (8) to adjust courses to popular culture belief and notions, and (9) to set up a conflict of interest between the instructor and quality of education, all of which result in the opposite of the original intent of SEF which was the improvement of instruction. Under the current system, faculty who do not conform to these student pressures tend to receive lower SEF scores. They are thus more likely to not be awarded tenure or promotion, to say nothing about their academic freedom being abrogated (to assume otherwise doesn't pass the giggle test). Even as used in business and management training, instructor evaluation instruments are, recognized as, and called, "smile sheets" (See Haskell 1998).

With the recent advent of a post-tenure review process, the use of flawed SEF is compounded. We know for example, that along with the demographic variables of gender and ethnicity, that age typically and negatively influences faculty evaluation. Accordingly, post-tenure reviews using SEF, in an inordinate degree, impacts older faculty.

The Cooling-Out Function of SEF

What sustains SEF and their associated problems of negatively impinging on the awarding of tenure, abrogating academic freedom, and lowering academic standards is a complex one, involving both negative and positive reinforcement patterns where all parties seem to gain from their use. First, given the current system, faculty gain by conforming to what students want (e.g., easier grading, etc.) and thereby achieve higher SEF scores; they are then rewarded for these scores by promotion and tenure committees and by administrators doling out merit raises. Faculty who do not conform tend to be weeded out of the system. Second, students gain by faculty reducing their requirements and standards as they do not have to study as hard and can show they are achieving 'superior' grade point averages. Third, academic departments gain by retaining and acquiring students over departments that do not conform to student demands to the same degree, which then increases the department's budget. Fourth, Deans gain because they can show presidents student growth and retention within their administrative units. Fifth, college presidents gain by demonstrating to board of trustees that with the growth and retention of students come increased revenues that then justifies the constructing of new buildings and higher salaries for administrators. Sixth, all administrators gain as SEF functions as a means of faculty control. Seventh, trustees also gain by demonstrating that they oversee an economically upwardly mobile institution. Finally, parents gain when their children, who might not otherwise earn a college degree, do acquire one and indeed graduate with honors on the Deans List, a list that has become so large on some campuses that it is no longer published.

The above describes what is called a closed, mutually reinforcing, escalating process; what systems engineers would recognize as a runaway system. The system is also uncomfortably similar to the classic "con game," where "the mark" does not complain about being sold a fake piece of art either because s/he gains from the transaction or does not report it to law enforcement because s/he is embarrassed by his/her complicit role in the process. Thus, the mark has been "cooled out." As a colleague of mine has reminded me, the situation is similar to what Burton Clark (1960) classically identified as "The Cooling Out Function of Higher Education," where—in this context—students are like the mark in the con game: they think they are earning something (e.g., a college diploma or a 3.5 grade point average) when they are in fact receiving counterfeits.[1] They too have been "cooled out." Unfortunately, in such a system, change may have to come from external sources like accrediting agencies.

To close this section, let me say something that I really dislike hearing myself say: Enough research into SEF. More than a sufficient amount has been and continues to be conducted. This research has become a substitute for not dealing with the situation. As with most research, it could continue endlessly never reaching a scientific level of certitude (see below). Significant action is now required. If the control mechanism of SEF is not constrained, this dysfunctional system will continue to endanger the integrity of tenure, promotion, student learning, and academic freedom. Without tenure and academic freedom, however, one does not have a university; one has something else. To play the higher education game without a valid tenure process or with academic freedom abrogated, is like playing chess without a King.

I would like to make a fundamental point, one that was "buried" in my third article, but which merits repeating up front here:

> *From a scientific perspective, since institutional administrators initiated SEF claiming their validity and their appropriateness for use in deciding tenure and promotion, the burden of proof is not on faculty but on the institutions making the claim to show they are scientifically valid as well as demonstrating that—if valid—their application is likewise valid.*

Response to Responses and Commentaries

In this section, I would like to briefly present a generalized response to critiques of my four articles (see Stake, 1997; Theall, 1997), the most reasoned of which was Cisneros-Cohernour (2005).

See also my replies (Haskell, 1997e; Haskell, 1997f). First, in my initial article I laid out the constraints of the paper. Regarding these constraints I said, "In explicating SEF, many closely related issues must be substantially bracketed ... they can only be addressed here in so far as they directly impact the focus on SEF and academic freedom." The main issue bracketed was not pronouncing on the ultimate validity of SEF research findings. Despite these constraints, many of the responses to my articles ignored the statement of the boundaries and critiques ensued accordingly.

Second—the above constraint notwithstanding—clearly there is always going to be disagreement around a research area. Some of the critiques are disagreements about what the research on SEF shows or does not show. But such disagreements are not just with my view of the research, but the view of many others who read the literature as I have read it.

Third, to further extend my above reluctant comment that more than a sufficient amount of research on SEF has been conducted, that continued research will only—indeed has—become a substitute for not dealing with the situation, it could continue near endlessly never reaching a significant scientific confidence level. Clearly there is sufficient disagreement in the literature to conclude that a scientific consensus has not been reached claiming the validity of SEF and its ensuing application.

Research Findings and the Construction of Policy

I see the role of science in the construction of policy on the use of SEF as an overlooked issue. Understandably, most academic disciplines have a built-in tendency to base any claims about reality on solid and rigorous research. However, in the everyday world, it is not always possible to do so. Given this, on what basis is any given policy to be constructed? There is an answer based on precedent in environmental science, where a "precautionary principle" has been invoked (e.g., Lemons 1996).

In essence, this principle says that when making policy decisions about environmental harm, given (1) a certain level of possible harm, (2) the complexity/uncertainty of data, and (3) the high level of proof (typically a 95 percent confidence level) required for a scientific finding to be accepted by most scientists. Setting policy should not be based on this level of scientific proof. The reason: to wait for such a confidence level may be too risky given the level of harm that may be indicated (by the existence of data with a lesser confidence level). In short, using scientific criteria that have been adopted for doing science may often not be appropriate criteria for making policy decisions.

There are several implications for the Precautionary Principle as applied to SEF. First, given (1) the lack of consensus among researchers on the validity of SEF and the appropriateness of their use, (2) the level of possible harm of accepting SEF for purposes of salary increases, promotion, denial of tenure or non-reappointment, and (3) the effects of SEF used for such purposes likely have on the quality standards of higher education, should not administrators and faculty evaluation committees apply for the same reasons, a similar Precautionary Principle stance? A kind of Precautionary Principle is used by courts in what is called Disparate Impact cases (Haskell 1997c).

This legal principle refers to the use of assessment procedures that are on their surface neutral in their treatment of different groups, but which produce evaluation outcomes that inadvertently fall more harshly on one group than on another. Proof of a discriminatory motive is not necessary to establish a disparate impact claim. To establish a *prima facie* case of such adverse impact, a minority need only show a causal connection between the facially neutral employment practice and the disproportionate negative or adverse effects on him or herself as a member of a protected group. In this regard, it would seem that disparate impact could be invoked for many variables influencing SEF, especially gender and age.

In the interest of the most efficient and comprehensive way to achieve an overview of the integral issues addressed in my four 1997 articles, and because the articles are easily accessed, I will present the Abstracts, Table of Contents, and Summaries of the major headings and points. These will provide a detailed map of what is contained in each of the four articles. Let me finally say that, unfortunately, most critiques have only been based on the first article, as if the other three integral papers did not exist. In fact, the four papers are effectively all of a piece.

ACADEMIC FREEDOM, TENURE, AND STUDENT EVALUATION OF FACULTY: GALLOPING POLLS IN THE 21ST CENTURY PART I

http://olam.ed.asu.edu/epaa/v5n6.html

ABSTRACT: Despite a history of conflicting research on the reliability and validity of student evaluation of faculty, use of SEF for summative evaluation purposes has typically not been viewed as an infringement on academic freedom. When suggesting that SEF may impinge on academic freedom, it is often considered an attack on either student rights, or on the process of evaluating faculty performance in general. Faculty and educational administrator views and surveys are reviewed since SEF data is used in salary, promotion and tenure decisions. The literature shows that SEF infringe on instructional responsibilities of faculty by providing a control mechanism over curricular, course content, grading, and teaching methodology. Further, SEF play a significant role in current attacks on tenure, and that its role in a demographically diverse 21st century educational system has changed from its benign historical origins. Concluding, contrary to current views, SEF is a serious unrecognized infringement on academic freedom. A number of findings are summarized from the abstracted textual material.

Summary

As currently used (and perhaps under more stringent conditions as well) the validity of SEF as used in salary, promotion, and tenure decisions are in question relative to methodology: (1) untrained interpreters using (2) intuitive, and (3) eyeballing methods of analysis to analyze SEF, (4) not controlling for contaminating variables such as (a) level of course, (b) instructor standards (c) grading practices, (d) subject matter or discipline, (e) personality and (f) interest of student, (g) academic level of student, (h) required course vs. elective course, (i) class size, (j) age, and (k) gender of instructor, and (l) a host of other variables. (5) Validity is also in question regarding student ability to validly render judgments regarding instruction and curricular.

Administrative Pressures To Relinquish Faculty Control: SEF (6) are typically required by administrative policy, (7) are therefore involuntary, (8) are used for salary, promotion, and tenure decisions, which allow (8) administrative intrusion into the classroom, (9) create economic incentives for shaping faculty behavior to assure (10) assent to general consumer demands for the type and level of education, (11) assuring classroom changes in accordance with educational fads, (12) political ideology, (13) pressure to teach in a manner that results in student satisfaction, (14) leading to the retention of students, (15) for their tuition dollars, for facilitating in (16) institutional growth.

Control Over Academic Standards: Given the above, pressures are created (17) for faculty to assent and adjust their teaching to whatever level of student the (open enrollment) institution elects to admit, (18) for conforming to student demands in the classroom by lowering standards which include (19) to lower curricular standards, (20) to make tests less rigorous, (21) to inflate grading, (22) for fewer classroom requirements and prerequisites, (23) for easier and less course content, (24) to adjust courses to popular culture belief and notions, (25) to set up a conflict of interest between the instructor and quality of education, all of which result (26) in the opposite of the original intent of SEF which was the improvement of instruction.

General Legal Implications: Depending on their use, SEF (27) is often in conflict with usual personnel practices and procedures, (28) and when published can lead to defamation of faculty reputation, (29) can be discriminatory with regard to age, gender, race, and other variables, (30) is involuntarily imposed, and (31) do not meet what is considered contractual informed consent of faculty for their use.

Academic Freedom and Tenure: SEF can be used to (32) inappropriately dismiss competent faculty, (33) abrogate tenure, and (34) abridge academic freedom.

ACADEMIC FREEDOM, PROMOTION, REAPPOINTMENT, TENURE AND THE ADMINISTRATIVE USE OF STUDENT EVALUATION OF FACULTY (PART II)

Views from the Court

http://olam.ed.asu.edu/epaa/v5n17.html

ABSTRACT: Although a controversial history of research on the reliability and validity of SEF exists, this situation has not been typically viewed as an infringement on academic freedom, promotion, reappointment, and tenure rights. As a consequence, legal aspects of SEF are neither readily apparent, nor available. Unlike academic freedom, tenure, and other issues, which exist as legal categories, SEF as a category is virtually absent in legal compendia on higher education law. The question of its judicial standing is important to any suggestion of abridging faculty rights. In this second of four articles, legal rulings are categorized and abstracted verbatim from cases where SEF is integral to the denial of academic freedom, tenure, promotion and reappointment and are reviewed and provide an initial resource of legal ruling on SEF. My findings are summarized from the abstracted textual material.

Summary

Reliance on SEF v. Peer Evaluation: From these decisions, one can see that court rulings range from holding that (1) relying primarily or solely on student evaluations is acceptable, (2) to placing little exclusive reliance on SEF, (3) in rare cases SEF cannot be permitted to stand in the way of promoting or retaining professors who are excellent in non-teaching areas, (4) tenure decisions can not be based solely on SEF by students who have not been made aware of the ramifications of their evaluations, (5) anonymous documents or those "based on hearsay" should not be included in a faculty member's personnel file, (6) students should be made aware of the purpose and ramifications of their evaluations of faculty, (7) anonymous student evaluations should not be used, and (8) peer evaluations also must be a part of evaluating teaching.

Popularity and Effectiveness: In these disputes, the court rulings range from saying that (9) in cases of exceptional research faculty, popularity should not play a role in termination due to teaching, to (10) in normal cases that a measure of popularity is related to teaching effectiveness.

Transcendent Value of a Professor Over Teaching Quality: Courts have ruled that (11) the courts and educational administrations cannot allow low SEF to stand in the way of promoting or retaining professors who may be world renowned scientists, (12) if deemed nationally or internationally exceptional as a researcher, courts have variously ruled that SEF may be disregarded and not disregarded, and (13) at least in two cases the courts did not find the faculty exceptional.

The Courts' Approach to the General and Psychometric Accuracy/Validity of SEF: With regard to establishing the general and statistical accuracy of SEF in the above disputes, the range of opinions go from (14) statistical analyses may be a part of a plaintiff's effort to establish discriminatory treatment if it reached proportions comparable to those in cases establishing a *prima facie* racial discrimination, (15) cautioning that statistics are not irrefutable, with their usefulness depending upon the surrounding facts and circumstances of a case, (16) the Court maintaining that it need not consider them and is under no obligation to establish the accuracy of administrative interpretations of SEF, (17) that tenure criteria are not drawn with "mathematical nicety," (18) administrator's failure to perform statistical comparisons is not arbitrary and is reasonable, especially (19) if such is not required by a Faculty Association Contract, (20) nearly any use made of SEF is acceptable if it followed the standard practice of the university, (21) and that creativity, rapport with students and colleagues, teaching ability, and other qualities are intangibles which cannot be measured by objective standards.

Numerical Ranking of Faculty: Numerical scores often result in faculty (22) being compared relative to other faculty, (23) being ranked relative to other faculty, (24) and with distinctions often being made on the basis of tenths of a decimal, and (25) with most courts accepting these fine decimal distinctions.

Acceptance of Administrative Subjective Judgments of SEF Data: Courts have tended to accept administrative subjective judgments if (26) they are deemed sincere, (27) grounded on some evidentiary basis, (28) made on the "vigor and variety of student criticisms," (29) "not arbitrary or capricious and were exercised honestly upon due consideration," (30) based upon "much experience in reviewing student evaluations," (31) reasonably draw on that experience, (32) and have ruled that presidents are not bound by factual findings made by a majority members of a faculty.

Use of Qualitative Written Student Comments: The use of student comments ranges from (33) placing importance on a single comment (34) to several comments as significant information, (35) maintaining that statistical analyses of SEF need to be bolstered by individual comments, (36) to maintaining that while some very negative—e.g., racist, sexist—comments may be found, the court may find that they do not render the SEF unreliable, (18) that such instances or "impressions" may be validated after the fact, (37) negative comments often seem to outweigh positive ones, and (38) comments may often outweigh numerical data to the contrary, (39) negative comments need not be verified before acting on them, and (40), that negative comments can not be used to undermine otherwise generally favorable comments received in an annual performance review.

Mixed Student Comments: With regard to non-numerically assessed written student comments, they are often qualitatively characterized as (41) a few were ambivalent, (42) a considerable number, (43) of mixed result, and selectively recognized. (44) It would only be fair to add that there were a number of comments in favor, but (45) there also were some negative comments, (46) sometimes placing the greater weight on past evaluations of teaching over current comments, and (47) sometimes placing greater weight on current comments over past positive evaluation of teaching.

Variables Not Taken Into Account When Assessing SEF: Student bias variables include (48) being a demanding teacher, (49) thus thwarting student expectations, (50) difficult examinations (51) grading, and (52) heavy workload in a course. (53) While most courts ignore these student biases in SEF, (54) occasionally a court will recognize that difficult courses have to be given to the students and that such material is difficult for even the best teacher to teach the material.

Other Variables: The variables noted in these court cases include (55) not controlling for class size (i.e., those obtained in small seminars from those obtained in large lecture classes), (56) those obtained for tenured faculty from those obtained for non-tenured junior faculty, (57) not performing appropriate comparisons of SEF with other faculty, (58) noting SEF in all courses, not just to problem courses, (59) not mistaking student 'response' figures for actual student enrollment figures when using them to determine student attraction to a course, (60) using all courses taught, (61) taking into consideration the faculty teaching a wide range of courses, versus those with lighter teaching loads, (62) number of new courses taught in a year, (63) whether graduate courses were taught at the same time as teaching undergraduate courses, (64) selectively mentioning only negative student comments, or (65) overly weighting negative comments, and (66) different procedures for gathering student opinion.

Impact on Academic Standards: From the above limited cases, the courts have clearly said (67) universities must be allowed to set (68) standards, including (69) course content, (70) homework load, and (71) grading policy.

Methods of Instruction and Academic Freedom: Teaching method (72) because it is an action, not speech, (73) is not a form of free speech, nor (74) covered under academic freedom, (75) except if noted in specific contractual faculty agreements.

Release of SEF To Students and To the Public: (76) Unlike most personnel records, SEF can be released to students and the public, on the grounds, that (77) students are not considered the general public, and (78) that SEF are public records and withholding them from public access does not outweigh the public interest in them.

ACADEMIC FREEDOM, PROMOTION, REAPPOINTMENT, TENURE AND THE ADMINISTRATIVE USE OF SEF (PART III)

Analysis and Implications of Views from the Court in Relation to Accuracy and Psychometric Validity

http://olam.ed.asu.edu/epaa/v5n18.html

ABSTRACT: Two previous papers noted that while a controversial history of research on the reliability and validity of student evaluation of faculty exists, the use of SEF as an evaluation tool has not been typically viewed as an infringement on academic freedom, promotion, reappointment, and tenure rights. As a consequence, legal aspects of SEF are neither readily apparent, nor available. Legal rulings, their implications and assumptions in relation to their accuracy and psychometric validity where SEF are integral to the denial of academic freedom, tenure, promotion, and reappointment are reviewed along with the legal principles of Disparate Treatment and Disparate Impact, and the scientific Precautionary Principle in policy decisions.

Summary

Studies demonstrate the following confounding variables: (1) age, (2) gender, (3) class size, (4) year of student, (5) level of student, (6) instructor style, (7) subject matter, (8) major or elective course, (9) student interest in subject matter, (10) instructor grading difficulty, (11) anonymous vs. signed ratings, (12) whether students are informed of their use, (13) instructor present vs. instructor absent while completing the evaluation (see for example, Divoky and Rothermel, 1988), and (14) length of class period, and a host of other variables.

The Courts' Approach to the General Accuracy and Psychometric Validity of SEF: An issue directly related to the reliance of SEF for administrative purposes is its validity. Presumably the more valid SEF data in a given case, the more justifiable is the reliance on it for administrative purposes. From the legal cases reviewed (in Haskell 1997b), in general the courts tend to accept SEF data as presented to them by institutions.

With regard to requiring the general and statistical accuracy of SEF, legal reasoning and rulings can be summarized (see Haskell 1997b) as ranging from: (1) accepting statistical analyses as a part of a plaintiff's effort to establish discriminatory treatment if it reaches proportions comparable to those in cases establishing a *prima facie* racial discrimination, (2) cautioning that statistics are not irrefutable, with their usefulness depending on surrounding facts and circumstances of a case, (3) maintaining that the court need not consider validity and is under no obligation to establish the accuracy of administrative interpretations of SEF, (4) that tenure criteria are not drawn with "mathematical nicety," (5) administrator's failure to perform statistical comparisons is not arbitrary and is reasonable, (6) especially if such is not required by a Faculty Association Contract, (7) nearly any use made of SEF, regardless of its validity, is acceptable if it followed the standard practice of the university, (8) that creativity, rapport with students and colleagues, teaching ability, and other qualities are intangibles which cannot be measured by objective standards.

Acceptance of Administrative Subjective and Untrained Evaluator Judgments of SEF Data: With regard to accepting the subjective judgments of administrators' evaluation of SEF, the legal reasoning and rulings can be summarized as ranging from: (1) accepting administrative subjective judgments if (2) they are deemed sincere (3) grounded on some evidentiary basis, (4) if made on the "vigor and variety of student criticisms," (5) "not arbitrary or capricious and were exercised honestly upon due consideration," (6) based upon "much experience in reviewing student evaluations, (7) reasonably draw on that experience, and (8) have ruled that presidents are not bound by factual findings made by majority members of a faculty.

Not only have the courts not traditionally examined faculty evaluations rigorously, they have tended not to require that evaluators be trained in the use, analysis, and interpretation of evaluation instruments. In general, state courts reviewing teacher evaluation practices will not analyze directly the substantive criteria used to evaluate teachers, nor the qualifications of the raters (Rebell, 1990). There are exceptions, however.

Instructional Variables: The variables noted in the legal cases reviewed include (1) not controlling for class size (i.e., those obtained in small seminars from those obtained in large lecture classes), (2) those obtained for tenured faculty from those obtained for non-tenured junior faculty, (3) not performing appropriate comparisons of SEF with other faculty, (4) noting SEF in all courses, not just to problem courses, (5) not mistaking student 'response' figures for actual student enrollment figures when using them to determine student attraction to a course, (6) using all courses taught, (7) taking into consideration faculty teaching a wide range of courses, versus those with lighter teaching loads, (8) number of new courses taught in a year, (9) whether graduate courses were taught at the same time as teaching undergraduate courses, (10) selectively mentioning only negative student comments, or (11) overly weighting negative comments, and (12) different procedures for gathering student opinion. Courts sometimes weigh these variables heavily; in most cases, however, the courts either ignore them or do not weigh them heavily in the total context of a particular case.

Student Biases Variables: Student bias variables include reactions to (13) academically demanding faculty, that (14) thus thwart student expectations, (15) difficult examinations, (16) and tough grading policy, (17) heavy workload in a course. (18) While most courts ignore these student biases in SEF, (19) occasionally a court will recognize that difficult courses have to be given to the students and that such material is difficult for even the best teacher to get across.

Popularity Variables and Effectiveness: Court rulings range from holding that (20) in situations of exceptional research faculty that popularity should not play a role in termination due to teaching, to (21) in normal cases that a measure of popularity is related to teaching effectiveness. While not noted frequently, popularity appears to be generally assumed to be involved in teaching effectiveness. But again, the courts are mixed on this issue as well. In terms of the research literature, there is little or no support for popularity being a measure of teaching effectiveness in higher education.

Reliance on SEF v. Peer Evaluation: From the cases analyzed, it can be seen that court rulings range from saying that (1) relying primarily or solely on student evaluations is acceptable, to (2) placing little exclusive reliance on SEF, (3) in rare cases SEF can not be permitted to stand in the way of promoting or retaining professors who are excellent in non-teaching areas, (4) tenure decisions can not be based solely on SEF by students who have not been made aware of the ramifications of their evaluations, (5) anonymous documents or those "based on hearsay" should not be included in a faculty member's file, (6) students should be made aware of the purpose and ramifications of their evaluations of faculty, (7) anonymous student evaluations should not be used, and (8) peer evaluations must also be a part of evaluating teaching.

Again, courts range widely on the exclusiveness or non-exclusiveness of SEF, even though books on how to conduct faculty evaluation by authors who basically accept the validity of SEF (e.g., Seldin 1993a; Theall and Franklin 1990) for some time now have consistently emphasized that SEF should not be used as the only and/or primary method for assessing teaching effectiveness.

Numerical Ranking of Faculty: From the cases reviewed, numerical scores from SEF often result in faculty (9) being compared relative to other faculty, (10) being ranked relative to other faculty, (11) with distinctions often being made on the basis of a tenth of a decimal, and (12) with most courts accepting these fine decimal distinctions.

Use of Qualitative Written Student Comments: For the use of student comments, court views range from (13) placing importance on a single comment (14) to several comments as significant information, (15) maintaining that statistical analyses of SEF need to be bolstered by individual comments, (16) maintaining that while some very negative—e.g., racist, sexist—comments may be found, the court may find that they do not render SEF unreliable, (17) that such instances or "impressions" may be validated after the fact, (18) negative comments often seem to outweigh positive ones, and (19) may often outweigh numerical data to the contrary, (20) negative comments need not be verified before acting on them, to (21) that negative comments can not be used to undermine otherwise generally favorable comments received in an annual performance review. Clearly, the views from the court suggest the legitimacy of not only using what is in fact anecdotal data, but often to raise it above more systematic (averaged) data.

Mixed Student Comments: With regard to non-numerically assessed written student comments, they are often qualitatively characterized as (22) a few were ambivalent, (23) a considerable number, (24) of mixed result, and selectively recognized, (25) it would only be fair to add that there were a number of comments in favor, (26) there were also some negative comments, (27) sometimes placing the greater weight on past evaluations of teaching over current comments, (28) sometimes placing greater weight on current comments over past positive evaluation of teaching.

Transcendent Value of a Professor Over Teaching Quality: (19) The courts and educational administrations can not allow low SEF to stand in the way of promoting or retaining professors who may be world renowned scientists, (20) deemed nationally or internationally exceptional as a researcher, courts may nevertheless disregard SEF, (21) at least in these two cases the courts did not find the faculty exceptional. One wonders if what the court seems to accept in principle exists in fact. These collective categories abstracted from court cases are illustrated by a denial of tenure case, by a (non-litigated) case that contains an interesting difference from most of the cases reviewed here.

ACADEMIC FREEDOM, PROMOTION, REAPPOINTMENT, TENURE AND THE ADMINISTRATIVE USE OF SEF (PART IV)

Analysis and Implications of Views from the Court in Relation to Academic Freedom, Standards, and Quality Instruction

http://olam.ed.asu.edu/epaa/v5n21.html

ABSTRACT: Three previous papers noted that while a controversial history of research on the reliability and validity of SEF exists, this history has not been typically viewed as an infringement on academic freedom. As a consequence, legal aspects of SEF are neither readily apparent, nor available. Moreover, SEF has not been generally seen as an infringement on, and detriment to, academic standards and quality instruction. The article is a review of SEF legal rulings analyzed in terms of their implications for academic freedom and quality of instruction in higher education.

Summary

This final article continues to examine legal rulings on SEF cases involving the denial of tenure, promotion, and reappointment decisions in relation to its implications and assumptions regarding academic freedom and quality of instruction. The issue of what sustains SEF and its associated problems of academic standards and of maintaining student tuition is a complex one, including positive reinforcement patterns by all parties involved. Assuming that the situation calls for at least some modicum of change, it cannot be accomplished on an individual level; it has to be accessed on a systems level.

On a macro level, this means changing cultural values about education, the university's economic orientation, administrative practices, student orientation to learning, and faculty collective action. We must change the reward structures so that each party does not gain from the situation. Currently, parents gain when their children who might not otherwise earn a college degree do acquire one; college presidents gain by demonstrating to boards of trustees that they are constructing new buildings; trustees gain by demonstrating an economically viable institution, other administrators gain because they can show the president growth within their own administrative units; other units within the university like academic departments gain because department budgets tend to be based on student enrollment numbers; students gain because they do not have to study hard to attain an A or B grade-point average; and finally, faculty gain because they are rewarded both by student evaluations and administrators. The current system is called a closed, mutually rewarding, escalating system with little to no restraining feedback. Systems engineers would recognize this as a runaway system. Unfortunately, change may have to come from external sources like accrediting agencies.

CHAPTER 4

The Games Professors Play in the Dysfunctional Performance Evaluation System Used in Higher Education: Brainstorming Some Recommendations*

D. Larry Crumbley, Louisiana State University
*G. Stevenson Smith,** Southeastern Oklahoma State University*

Student ratings were first used in the 1920's at the University of Washington. SET became popular in the early 1960s, and administrators began using them in the early 1970s. During the 1960s and early 1970s "college faculties around the country lowered expectations, abolished examinations, and either discarded grades altogether or nullified them through rampant inflation" (S. M. Cahn 1986, 30–31). At Westminster College in Utah the average grade is A−, and administrators debate how to reduce the number of students who receive graduation honors (Saje 2005).

Higher education is experiencing the simultaneous phenomena of widespread use of student evaluation of teachers (SETs), grade inflation (T. R. Bar et al. 2007; Yunker and Yunker 2003; Cluskey et al. 1997; Addy and Herring 1996; Oldenguist 1983), student moral decline resulting in widespread cheating and plagiarism, and increasingly lower student motivation. SAT scores declined from 1972 until 1997 and started increasing in 1998. They declined again in 2006 and 2007. Rosovsky and Hartley (2002) identified the beginning of grade inflation and the drop in SATs with the introduction of SETs.

STUDENT RETENTION RATES

As pointed out in the Preface, the holy grail in higher education is student satisfaction, and student retention has become a proxy for earnings in a profit-making organization. According to statistics released by the *Chronicle of Higher Education,* salaries for public university presidents in 2007 rose 7.6 per cent. Salaries for public university presidents have risen 35 percent since 2003. Fifteen presidents of public universities received at least $700,000 in 2007–08. Their median

* Portions of this article were published in 1995 in *Accounting Perspectives.* See: Crumbley, L. 1995. The dysfunctional atmosphere of higher education: games professors play, *Accounting Perspectives* 1 (1): 27–33.

** Dr. Crumbley is KPMG Endowed Professor at Louisiana State University, and Dr. Smith is the John Massey Endowed Professor of Accounting at Southeastern Oklahoma State University.

salary is $427,400. The highest-paid public university president at $1,346,000 is Gordon Lee at Ohio State University. The highest-paid community college leader at $610,670 is Michael McCall at Kentucky Community and Technical College System.

The highest-paid private university president at $2.8 million in 2006–07 was David Sargent at Suffolk University in Boston. Donald E. Ross at Lynn University, Boca Raton, Florida in 2003–04 was drawing $5,042,315. When Benjamin Ladner at American University left his job in 2006, he was receiving $4.3 million in pay and benefits. Chatham University has almost 2,200 students with a president with a salary of $734,576. Of course, other administrators have multiplied like rabbits in recent years, and their salaries also outpace professors' salaries.

Publicly traded companies under §162(m) have a $1 million deduction limitation for the top five executives. Recently, Congress reduced this $1 million limit to $500,000 (including performance based compensation) for companies benefiting from the Treasury's Troubled Asset Relief Program. For closely-held companies, IRS agents can disallow unreasonable compensation paid to employees. These restrictions do not apply to universities and colleges, and there are no major public or private gatekeepers (e.g., SEC or PCAOB) to monitor public and private universities and colleges.

ATMOSPHERE IN HIGHER EDUCATION

The atmosphere in higher education today has been illustrated by Peter Sacks (1996) in *Generation X Goes to College: An Eye-Opening Account of Teaching in Postmodern America.* Sacks, a reporter, went underground to teach journalism at the college level. He finds that administrators, faculty, nor students seem to care about learning or academic standards. Administrators want students to be satisfied, and students want good grades with little effort. They blame the faculty if they do not get good grades.

Sack's chairperson suggested he take an acting course to improve his class-satisfying ability. His peers advised him to teach to the evaluations. He engages in a so-called Sandbox Experiment by lowering standards and expectations and learning to entertain. He raised his evaluations and survived.

Sacks outlined these beliefs and attitudes of today's college students:

- They are consumers purchasing education and grades as a commodity.
- Hard work outside the classroom should not be a requirement.
- Teachers should be entertainers.
- They are disrespectful and often contemptuous of their teachers.

A persuasive case can be made that the increased use of SET has caused higher education to become dysfunctional, resulting in a steep, slippery slide in the quality of student learning (Langbein 2008; Winsor 1977; Renner 1981). Fellingham (2007) worries those nonacademic measures, such as *student evaluations* and school rankings, are increasingly being used to decide who teaches and what they teach.

A Harvard University graduate had this to say about his fellow students (Douthat 2005):

> Harvard students are creatively lazy, gifted at working smarter rather than harder. Most of my classmates were studious primarily in our avoidance of academic work, and brilliant largely in our maneuverings to achieve a maximal GPA in return for minimal effort. It was easy to see the classroom as just another résumé-padding opportunity, a place to collect the grade (and recommendation) necessary to get to the next station in life. If a grade could be obtained while reading a tenth of the books on the syllabus, so much the better.

As more and more research questions the validity of summative SET as an indicator of instructor effectiveness, ironically there has been a greater use of SET (Campbell et al. 2005; Adams 1997; Haskell 1997; Newton 1988; Wright et al. 1984; Powell 1977; Ditts 1980; DuCette and Kenney 1982; Howard and Maxwell 1982; Worthington and Wong 1979; Brown 1976; Porcano 1984; Dowell and Neal 1983; Stumpf and Freedman 1979). A typical SET questionnaire has at least one question which is a surrogate for overall teaching effectiveness. In 1984, two-thirds of liberal arts colleges were using SET for personnel decisions, and this percentage grew to 86% in 1993 (Seldin 1984; Seldin 1993a). Most business schools now use SET for decision making, and 95% of the deans at 220 accredited undergraduate schools "always use them as a source of information," but only 67% of the department heads relied upon them.[1] By 1997, 95 percent of accounting departments used SETs to measure teaching effectiveness (Calderon and Green 1997). Yet, only 20.4% of 559 accounting professors in 1988 agreed with the statement that SET are indicative of an instructor's teaching effectiveness and should be used directly in calculating annual salary increases (Bures et al. 1988). Langbein (2008) believes that the inexpensive, socially destructive SET process drives out the more costly better measures, but in the long-run SET use is more costly because of the unwarranted behavior caused by this control mechanism (Baker 1992).

More than 71 percent of accounting administrators agree that students are not qualified to judge many areas of teaching skills, 48 percent believe that summative SET have caused grade inflation, and 38.6 percent believe dysfunctional techniques are used by professors to improve SET scores (Crumbley and Fliedner 2002).

An instructor's grading policy (easier grading = higher evaluations) and course difficulty (easier course = higher evaluations) can be significant factors in determining an instructor's SET scores. Nichols and Soper (1972) found that an increase of 1 point (on a 4.0 scale) in the mean expected grade will result in an increase of 0.53 in the mean rating of a professor. Certainly many instructors believe in this leniency concept (Newton 1988), and they take corresponding actions to improve. Unfortunately, results of research on the web-based Ratemyprofessor.com found significant correlations between "quality and easiness" and "quality and hotness." The authors state that their research "cast considerable doubt on the usefulness of in-class student opinion surveys for purposes of examining quality and effectiveness of teaching" (Felton et al. 2008).

This badgering of professors for higher grades occurs as either demand-pull or cost-push grade inflation. Demand-pull comes from the student pressures. Cost-push occurs when difficult grading causes enrollment drops in a professor's classes and cost per student increases make the professor vulnerable to a critical evaluation. If an entire department should grade strictly, the department or college runs the risk of losing students and having upper-level courses canceled (Pressman 2007). Students move to the easy departments or schools, and their tuition monies and funding support moves with them.

MANAGING SET RESULTS

If an instructor can choose teaching styles, grade difficulty, and course content, he or she will prefer the choices that are expected to result in higher SET scores. According to Medley (1979), if teachers know the criteria on which decisions affecting their careers are based, they will meet the criteria if it is humanly possible to do so. As an instructor inflates grades, they will be much more likely to receive positive evaluations (Worthington and Wong 1979). Many enhancement choices are anti-learning, resulting in grade inflation, coursework deflation, and pander pollution

[1] One Texas dean in 1993 said that "students are the best judge of teaching competence," and a Massachusetts' dean said that "we rely on student ratings more than on any other source of data on teaching" (Crumbley and Fliedner 2002).

(PP) behavior. Pander pollution may be defined as purposeful intervention by an instructor inside and outside the classroom with the intention of increasing SET scores which is counterproductive to the learning process. Widespread use of SET has bred a vast army of pandering professors engaged in pander pollution semester after semester. This pander pollution increases each year as instructors try to enhance their SET scores.[2] Ironically, accounting researchers have published as many as 1,000 articles condemning abusive earnings management; yet there are few, if any, accounting articles condemning abusive SET management. Executives go to prison for cooking the books and managing earnings, but professors are praised and rewarded for abusive SET management and such behavior continues.

At a well-attended meeting of the college faculty at a large southern public university an Associate Dean gave the following glowing praise to the winner of the Best Teaching Award presented to a tenured faculty member. This Dean stated that during Professor X's first semester at the university he/she gave all A's. Thereafter, the Dean counseled the professor that he/she could not give all A's. The following semester Professor X gave all A's except for one B. The Associate Dean said that the Dean decided to reassign this professor from teaching undergraduate students to Ph.D. courses and everything was fine. What was so depressing about this event was that the Associate Dean felt that he was praising the faculty for his actions. Professor X received at least two best teaching awards while at the university.

Consider the teaching awards system on most campuses. The awards committees are made up of previous awards winners who had high SET scores and probably inflated their grades. High SET scores play prominently in any decision with little recognition of learning in the classroom. Student satisfaction is the key driver, and the system is self-perpetuating.

Tagomori (1993) performed a content analysis of 4,028 evaluation items on 200 SET instruments. He found that 54.6 percent of the items were ambiguous, unclear, and/or subjective. Another 24.5 percent of the items did not correlate with classroom teaching performance. A total of 79.1 percent of the items were either flawed or did not identify with teaching performance. His conclusion was that the evaluation instruments used were unreliable.

Smith (2004) concluded from a qualitative review of course evaluations collected from a sample of 267 U.S. accounting programs that the instruments largely measure student satisfaction, and states that, it is expected that without feedback about teaching methods, U.S. accounting students will remain deficient. Saje (2005) says that students actually write on their course evaluation that "I'm not paying this kind of money to get a B."

Martin (1998) explains the invalidity of student evaluations by outlining the 133 variables that influence the SET scores of a professor, many not under the control of a professor. These variables are grouped into four categories:

1. Environmental and course related variables (26).
2. Student characteristics (28).
3. Teacher-related characteristics (34).
4. Controllable teacher practices related to course and students (45).

Because of these numerous variables, faculty use gaming techniques to improve ratings. According to Martin (1998, 1087–1088):

> ... evaluating teaching effectiveness based on student opinions encourages game playing, which becomes more and more competitive and compelling as more

[2] Federal and state laws highly regulate financial statements to reduce income manipulation and opportunistic behavior, yet there is no regulation of SET. Most administrators blindly accept them as truth. Instructors have a high incentive to manage SET, even more so than managers have the incentive to enhance earnings (Holthausen 1990, 83–110).

gaming techniques are used, many to the detriment of quality education. Using student opinions to evaluate faculty promotes a system where students move forward unprepared for the next level. This promotes even more gaming behavior at the higher levels. Unfortunately, this behavior is advertently driven by an indeterminable number of university administrators who pretend to evaluate teaching effectiveness with little or no empirical evidence.

DYSFUNCTIONAL BEHAVIOR TECHNIQUES USED TO SUPPORT SET SCORES

Many of the steps taken by instructors to improve their SET are counterproductive to teaching effectiveness and the learning process (McPherson 2006). These dysfunctional techniques include grade inflation, course work deflation, and keeping grade expectations high. For example, one freshman history professor, in a conversation, calls it "hosing students." "We give easy or no grades during the semester, distribute the SET questionnaires, and then give a tough final examination to weed out the students." Another sociology professor gives a few minor quizzes and short papers during the semester, collects the SET data, and then assigns a difficult term paper project. These forms of faculty deception work best in required freshman and sophomore classes where students are forced to take the difficult instructor because of a limited number of classes.

Suppose airline pilots were rewarded and fired based upon anonymous satisfaction questionnaires given to passengers at the end of a flight. The key criteria for a favorable rating would be a timely arrival, so imagine the chaos in our skies as pilots jockey for on time arrivals. Or suppose Internal Revenue Service (IRS) agents were fired and rewarded based upon anonymous questionnaires from their auditees. Soon IRS agents would issue only no change reports and our tax receipts would be greatly reduced.

Suppose external auditors' performance was based solely on satisfied clients. Soon we would be only consultants, and there would be many more Enrons, WorldComs, and HealthSouths. Suppose prison guards' performance was based upon satisfied prisoners? As Dr. Mike Davis often said, in education we now have the inmates in charge of the system, and they are clearly aware of their power over professors. We have this dysfunctional system in higher education.

Dysfunctional behavior caused by a control system such as SET fits within the following categories (Lawler and Rhode 1976):

Category	**Description**
Rigid Bureaucratic Behavior	Behave in ways which will help an instructor look good on the measures that are used in the SET system (e.g., inflate grades and deflate course work).
Strategic Behavior	Temporary action designed solely to influence the SET system so the instructor will look acceptable (e.g., keep grade expectation high as long as possible, give parties, etc.).
Invalid Data Reporting	Invalid data about what can be done and invalid data about what has been done (e.g., "stuff" the SET system, pander pollution).
Resistance	SET is seen as a threat to the satisfaction of many needs and significantly changes the power relationships in the department (e.g., pits one friend against another, breaks up social groups).

There are recognized methods, known here as the ***Rules of the Trade*** to maximize SET scores. With the exception of Rule 1, these rules can be varied from term to term.

1. First and foremost, inflate your student's grades.[3]
2. Reduce the course material covered and drop the most difficult material first.
3. Give easy examinations (e.g., true-false; broad, open-ended discussion questions; take home exams; open book exams).[4]
4. Join the college party environment by giving classroom parties on SET day. Sponsoring student's officially-approved class skipping days to ball games, etc., is a means to increase student satisfaction. One Oregon professor prepares cupcakes on the day the SET questionnaires are distributed.
5. Give financial rewards such as establishing connections to potential employers.
6. Spoon-feed watered-down material to the students.
7. Give answers to exam questions beforehand. Either pass them out in class or if you want the students to work harder, put them on reserve in the library or on the Internet.
8. Do not risk embarrassing students by calling on them in the classroom.
9. Hand out sample exams, or take your examination questions from the student's online exercises provided by the textbook publisher.
10. Grade on a wide curve.
11. Give SET as early as possible in the term and then give hard exams, projects, etc.
12. Keep telling students how much they are learning and that they are intelligent.
13. Delete grading exams, projects, and other material. If they turn in work, give them credit. The correctness of the work is not an issue.
14. Teach during the bankers' hours (9:00–3:00) favored by the students.
15. Give the same exams each semester allowing the answers to get out and grades to move higher and higher each semester.
16. Avoid the effort of trying to teach students to think (e.g., avoid the Socratic method).
17. Provide more free time (e.g., cancel classes on or near holidays, Mondays, Fridays, etc.)
18. Avoid giving a cumulative final exam.
19. Do not give a final exam and dismiss the class on the last class day. Even if the final is administratively required there are methods to avoid the final exam.
20. Use simple slides so the students do not need to read the book and post the slides to the course website from which test questions will be taken.
21. Where multiple classes are taught by different instructors, always ensure that your classes have the highest GPA.
22. Allow the students to participate in determining material coverage and the number of points assigned to difficult test questions.
23. When possible, teach classes where common exams are used; then help students pass "this bad exam" for which you are not responsible.
24. Allow students to re-take exams until they pass. It helps to put a page reference next to each question so the students can find the answer during an open-book examination.
25. Give significant above-the-curve extra or bonus credit.[5]

---

[3] More than 90 percent of the Harvard University class of 2001 had earned grade-point averages of B-minus or higher. Half of all the grades given the year before at Harvard were A's or A-minuses; only six percent were C-pluses or lower. By way of comparison, in 1940 C-minus was the most common GPA at Harvard, and in 1955 just 15 percent of undergraduates had a GPA of B-plus or higher (Douthat 2005). A Yale student newspaper suggests that Yale's median GPA is between 3.6 to 3.7. The median at Princeton University is between 3.2 and 3.3 (Yang 2006). Certainly at most private universities the saying is correct: "you pay your fees, and you get your B's."

[4] Changing to an all true/false exam can dramatically improve a class average and therefore SET scores (e.g., each student starts off—on an average—with 50 points).

[5] A physics professor at Georgia Tech University states that "a physics major could obtain a degree without ever answering a single written examination question completely" by simply obtaining partial and extra credit (Weisenfeld 1996).

26. Remember to spend the first ten minutes of class schmoozing and joking with the students.
27. In online courses allow the students a two-day window to take the posted online examination.
28. Allow anonymous taking of online examinations by students (i.e., do not use a test center).

Why work to become a better teacher (from the point of view of student learning), when an instructor can more easily inflate grades, deflate coursework, and keep grade expectations high? There is an almost universal assumption among administrators that an increase in SET scores is good and a decrease is bad. This myth is a naive and dangerous assumption for learning. Pandering professors are playing along with the myth as they knowingly inflate their grades and deflate course requirements without concern about the level of student learning.

A high SET score may indicate a poor teacher. For example, in a major west coast private university an administrator took control of a master of taxation program and decided to review the effectiveness of his instructors by visiting their classrooms. One instructor consistently scored 5 out of 5 on his SET scores in prior years, so the administrator waited until the last class period to review this "superior" instructor's estate and trust taxation class. The administrator found that the instructor had yet to introduce the concept of a complex trust (which should have been introduced before the middle of the semester). Upon further investigation, the administrator found that the instructor (a partner in a big-six CPA firm) was taking all of his students to a local bar after every class and feeding them dinner and drinks. This instructor was merely using the classroom to recruit students (not to educate).

There is another universal assumption that students must like an instructor to learn. Not true. Even if they dislike you and you force them to learn by hard work and low grades, you may be a good educator (but not according to SET scores). SET largely measures whether or not students like you, and not necessarily whether you are expanding their knowledge in the field. Instructors should be in the business of educating and teaching students—not SET enhancement. Until administrators learn this simple truth, there is little chance of improving higher education. "Teaching is a professional relationship, not a popularity contest. To invite students to participate in the selection or promotion of their teachers exposes the teachers to intimidation" (Frankel 1968, 30–31).

There are many adverse consequences of abusive SET management for student learning, and universities should attempt to reduce these adverse consequences. Many instructors devote much of their teaching time and effort to massaging SET results for administrator and student consumption. Costs to an instructor for SET enhancement by inflating grades or decreasing course work are insignificant as few instructors are penalized for giving high grades or deflating coverage. Since many of the students in college and university today are of much lower quality, these same students are likely to modify evaluations in response to grade manipulations. So, given objectively equivalent teaching skills, lenient graders will tend to receive more positive evaluation ratings than stringent graders (Worthington and Wong 1979). The concept is simple: summative SET + PPs = US, where PP is pander pollution and US is undereducated students.

Of course, the use of student opinions reduces the work load of administrators since they do not have to spend time in the classroom evaluating professors or helping professors improve their teaching effectiveness. They avoid legal and other potential problems that would likely arise if they had to visit classrooms and formally give professors evaluations of their teaching effectiveness along with suggested improvements.

If administrators continue to use this seemingly low cost performance measurement device until nothing but As are given, what will replace universities? Rosovsky and Hartley (2002) assert that employers will turn to personal contacts, letters of recommendation, internships, and co-ops for recruiting. The authors are uncertain these alternatives are more informative and less costly than developing accurate performance measurement of professors.

An inverse relationship may exist between evaluation ratings and student learning. That is, the result of trying to facilitate high student achievement may be low ratings and vice versa (Sullivan and Skanes 1974). Not surprising, at least two professors (Neath 1996; Trout 1997) have provided tips on how to improve teaching evaluations without improving teaching effectiveness and student learning.

Ian Neath (1996) provides a list of 20 such ways to improve SET scores without improving teaching, including these fourteen.

1. Be organized. "Start class on time, end class on time, bring extra chalk or overhead pens to class, and keep all of your lecture notes in three-ring binder with neatly punched holes."
2. Grade leniently because grading harshly is a sure way to lower evaluations.
3. Do not leave the classroom when you administer your evaluations. Administer them after a particularly entertaining lecture.
4. Administer ratings before tests and not after a test. Inform students of their potential "high" grades before administering the questionnaires.
5. Provide the instructions that the purpose of the evaluations is for administrative purposes rather than actual course improvements. "These evaluations will be used by the administration to determine whether my children, age 4 and 6, will eat for the next six months."
6. Teach smaller classes (e.g., 25 or less students); not large classes.
7. Teach higher level classes rather than lower level courses. Especially avoid introductory classes with non-majors.
8. Required courses are the worst, unless there is a department examination that you can blame on someone else. You are here to help them pass the exam. Give them answers to the questions on the exam.
9. Show lots of films, perform demonstrations, and use the latest technology. In other words, covering less material makes the exams easier.
10. Entertain the students with as little content as possible. Play music. Play games.
11. Teach the course less rigorously than the normal expectations of the students.
12. Be like your students. Be more liberal at Berkeley, but more conservative at Baylor. Teach what they want, and how they want it.
13. Prevent poor students from taking your course.
14. Closely review your evaluations because there can be mistakes that you need to identify.

Paul Trout (1997) also suggests additional ways to improve your evaluations without improving your teaching and student learning. He asserts that "administrators want satisfied student consumers (and happy parents and taxpayers). Thus, administrators use SET to make sure that classroom instruction does not seriously displease student "customers." Some of his suggestions are:

1. Remember the first day impressions are very important.
2. Increase your immediacy effect by smiling, using gestures, being relaxed, moving among students, and looking them in the eyes.
3. Dress casually like the students.
4. Use powerful words with a confident delivery.
5. Demonstrate with stories that you are warm and nurturing.

6. Be personable and charismatic. College teaching has less to do with knowledge and information and more with entertaining the students.
7. Give lots of high grades.[6] Max Hocutt (1987–1988, 57) asserts that,

   A study of several thousand courses at my home university has recently confirmed what most professors have always suspected: students definitely give a higher rating to teachers who grade higher. The coefficient of correlation is a low but significant .38. This correlation might have been higher had the study considered not actual but expected grade.

8. Teach undemanding courses.
9. Individually flatter the political biases of your students. Remember this is a risky technique.
10. Suck up to students (this is more intense than impression management). In the words of Paul Trout (1997):
    (a) Oprah students. Let them know that you are a victim and that you have *suffered* (spouse left you, mother just died, etc). Students, many of whom are soap-opera junkies, will cut you some slack.
    (b) Rosie O'Donnell students. Fawn over them and praise them lavishly! Tell them they are wonderful and God's gift to the college system. Inflate your evaluation numbers by inflating their egos.
    (c) Bribe students. Lay on the goodies. For example, bring cookies to exams, let them out early on a regular basis and cancel a lot of Friday classes. Another way to get better ratings from them is to throw a party for them! For the biggest bang for the buck, throw it at the end of the semester, *before* evaluations are given out. No researcher has yet analyzed the correlation between end-of-the-semester suck-up behavior and evaluation scores, but the rewards must be worth it because some instructors invest a whole lot of money into bringing pizza to class.

And as Peter Sacks reasoned (1996, 86, 310), considering the benefits and punishments professors face thanks to those evaluation forms, "pandering becomes quite rational and justifiable, however unfortunate its collective results." He explains his sandbox theory as follows:

> And so, in my mind, I became a teaching teddy bear. In the metaphorical sandbox I created, students could do no wrong, and I did almost anything possible to keep all of them happy, all of the time, no matter how childish or rude their behavior, no matter how poorly they performed in the course, no matter how little effort they gave. If they wanted their hands held, I would hold them. If they wanted a stapler (or a Kleenex) and I didn't have one, I'd apologize. If they wanted to read the newspaper while I was addressing the class or if they wanted to get up and leave in the middle of a lecture, go for it. Call me spineless. I confess. But in the excessively accommodative culture that I found myself in, "our students" as many of my colleagues called them, had too much power for me to afford irritating them with demands and challenges I had previously thought were part and parcel of the collegiate experience.

[6] The best approach is to give really high grades to really poor students inducing the Santa Claus effect. Snyder and Clair (1976) found that students who received higher grades than they expected tended to give "very positive teacher evaluations" (a happy birthday effect). Worthington and Wong (1979) came to the same conclusion.

THE CUSTOMER MYTH

Complaints are often voiced that students are not qualified to evaluate many areas of instructor effectiveness. A senior in high school is not qualified to evaluate high school teachers, yet four or five months later this *same* freshman in college has developed the maturity and judgment to evaluate higher education.[7] At the same time that our student population is becoming less motivated and more dishonest, we continue to inflate grades and deflate our courses. As the student population becomes more dishonest and less motivated (Fishbein 1993, A52; White, 1993, A44), we in the academy give their opinions more and more credibility. Some administrators explain this dichotomy by stating that students are our customers. Students are not our customers—they are our products. We need to improve students' value by educating them. Society and employers are our customers. Students are workers and apprentices (George 2007).

Steven M. Cahn, Provost and Vice-President at City University of New York, debunks this ludicrous student as customers argument by pointing out that passengers on an airplane do not certify pilots, and patients do not certify physicians. "Those who suffer the consequences of professional malfeasance do not typically possess the requisite knowledge to make informed judgments" (Cahn 1986, 37). Imagine the chaos if we certified dentists, nurses, CPAs, lawyers, engineers, architects, air conditioning repair people, etc. with questionnaires from customers. Saje (2005) equates professors and teaching to waiting tables at an upscale restaurant. "It's like working for a tip, except the payoff isn't cash under the plate; it's having one's contract renewed."

There is a vast difference between customers and products. If the raw materials coming into higher education are deficient, we need to work even harder to maintain an outflow of qualified students. This improvement cannot be done easily as competition for better SET scores causes severe grade inflation and course work deflation. Just as U.S. businesses are attempting to improve the value of their products, we must improve our efforts to help our students think and learn. In the long run, producing increasingly less educated students is self-defeating for universities. Soon society will look elsewhere for quality employees and indications of competence.

REGULATED CLASSES

As severe as grade inflation has been, it would be worse without the introduction of regulated classes in many lower level courses. Highly regulated classes reduce the conflict level between instructors and students. In regulated classes the course content is the same, there are common exams, and the cut-off scores for the grades are set by the department. The instructor is in the classroom helping the students overcome these hurdles imposed by someone else. Administrators try to restrict the free-market educational system in order to reduce both PPs. In general, SET scores may be much higher in regulated classes than in nonregulated classes because of the reduced conflict between the student and instructor.

For example, Temple's basketball coach John Chaney might have a hard time surviving in a physics class. According to Chaney, "I'm always looking for kids whose heads I can turn. A coach should develop good human beings. Tough love and respect make good human beings." Says Chaney: "Try coming late ... and feel my wrath. I punish them by working them to death" (Blauvelt 1933, C-1 and 2). Working students hard in today's modern classrooms is a kiss of death to the instructor. Of course, Chaney is evaluated by how many games his team wins—not

[7] The Program for International Student Assessment (PISA) compares the scores of U.S. 15-year old students in science and mathematics literacy to the scores of their peers internationally. In 2006, the PISA results show the average combined science and mathematics literacy score of U.S. students to be lower than the OECD average of fifty-seven jurisdictions participating in PISA. In science, the U.S. had a lower score than countries such as Czech Republic, Austria, Hungary, and Iceland. Similarly, the U.S. scored lower in math literacy scale than Czech Republic, Hungary, Poland, and Slovak Republic. The high school students from this group, who within a few years enter college, are judged qualified to evaluate their learning. See especially Milliron, 2008.

by how his players evaluate him on a questionnaire. Student athletic programs may be the last arena in higher education where student motivation is important.

STRATEGIC CONSEQUENCES

The consequences of using traditional SET as customer satisfaction measures rather than as a more direct feedback on student learning or teaching methods needs to be considered. Exhibit 1 illustrates a model of strategic consequences that arises from the use of such an approach. In Exhibit 1, the causal conditions that lead to the development of SET as well as the constraints, managing strategies, and the long-term consequences from coping with these course evaluations are shown.

The causal conditions for the expansive use of student course evaluations arose out of external public pressures for expansion in university governance that can be traced to satisfying the student unrest of the 1960s (Foote, Mayer, Fishlow and Freedman 1968; Epstein 1974). At the time, SET were only one aspect of expanded student governance that included student input on tenure decisions. Clearly the reasons for using student evaluations extend beyond simply measuring "teaching performance." These measures are a visible image for legitimizing academia accountability to students, parents, trustees, alumni, state legislators, and others. For this reason, the strong external pressures that initially developed in the 1960s continue to sustain the use of student evaluations in accounting programs today.

Note that SETs have developed within an environment of constraints identified as intervening and context conditions in Exhibit 1. Responsible evaluation statement development takes into consideration intervening and context conditions. These conditions are not controllable by instructor actions, or they are difficult to evaluate outside of wide and meaningless ranges. For example, class size has been shown to affect course ratings, but class size, level of course, or required or elective are not influenced by instructor actions. There are also constraints that arise from the inability of students to evaluate such items as the appropriateness and currency of material taught and correct textbook selections for the course. These conditions provide limits on the development of responsible evaluative statements and their administrative use.

The intervening and context conditions place innate constraints on the development of survey statements. In the face of these constraints, managing strategies are developed to reduce these difficulties. Through a strategy of using survey statements to emphasize student satisfaction measures, evaluations are managed so that a window on student satisfaction is provided, but not on student learning, which is more complex.

One strategic consequence or response of emphasizing a generalized range of student satisfaction measures is instructors' coping behavior such as pandering to students or inertia in teaching methods. Wright, et al. (1984) concluded that the use of instructor behavioral rating scales tend to discourage the use of innovative teaching approaches in accounting education. There has been a continual publication of white papers (Perspectives on Education 1989) and seminal reports (American Accounting Association 1986) critical of the accounting curricula's resistance to change. Albrecht and Sack (2000) have been even more strident in their criticisms. Their criticisms describe accounting education as lacking real-world examples, administering a conformance curriculum, being textbook-based rather than critical thinking based, resistant to developing creative styles of learning, and using broken teaching models. Accounting faculties are described as knowing what to do, but not doing it.

A second consequence of this strategy is a disconnection from accounting program mission statement goals. The mission objectives should drive the information that is collected on SETs. If a program's mission statement calls for high levels of student satisfaction, then SETs based on measuring student satisfaction define that goal and should be used. If an accounting program's mission statement includes the development of student's critical thinking skills and learning,

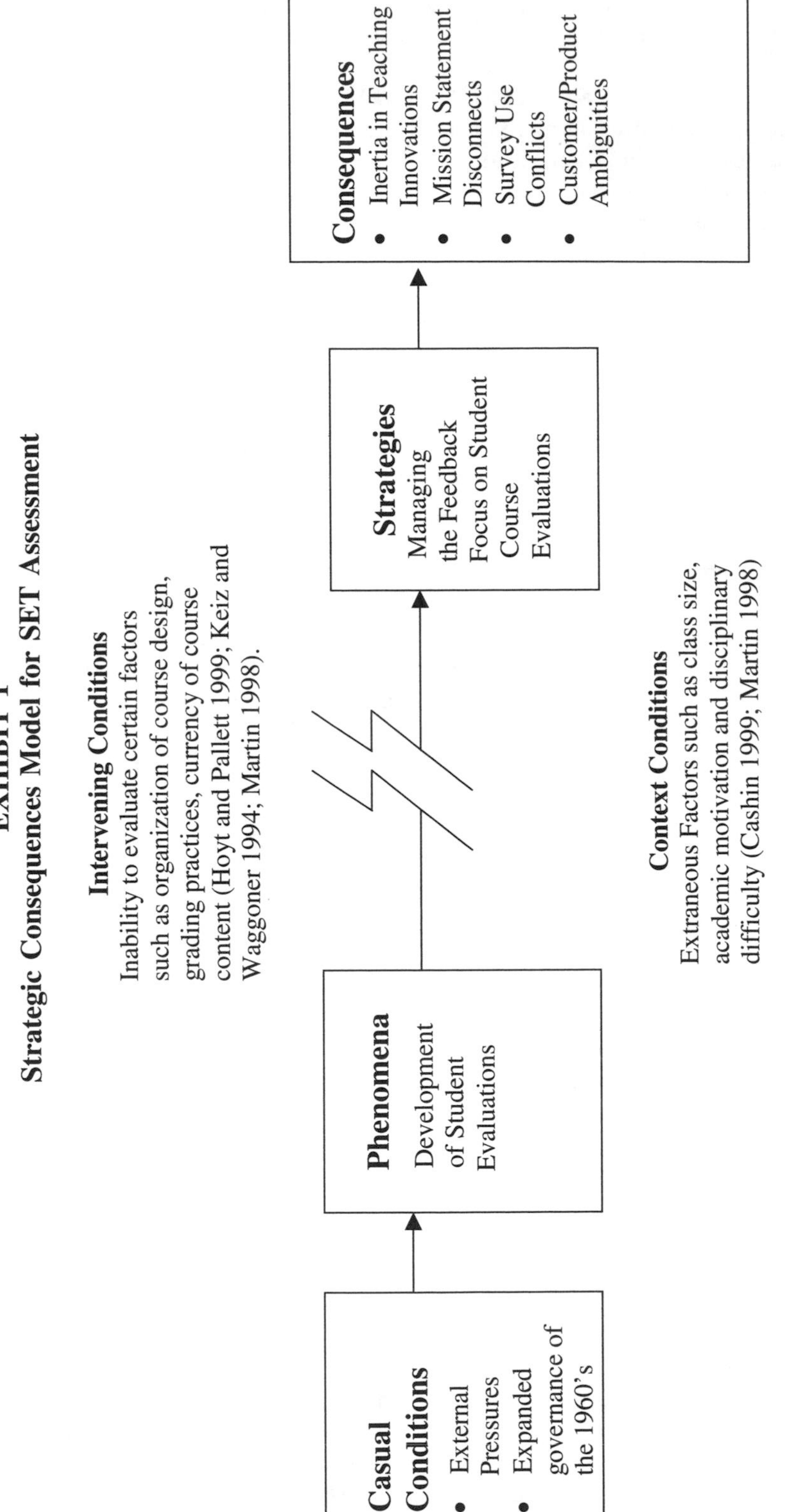
EXHIBIT 1
Strategic Consequences Model for SET Assessment
Casual Conditions
• External Pressures
• Expanded governance of the 1960's
Phenomena
Development of Student Evaluations
Intervening Conditions
Inability to evaluate certain factors such as organization of course design, grading practices, currency of course content (Hoyt and Pallett 1999; Keiz and Waggoner 1994; Martin 1998).
Strategies
Managing the Feedback Focus on Student Course Evaluations
Consequences
• Inertia in Teaching Innovations
• Mission Statement Disconnects
• Survey Use Conflicts
• Customer/Product Ambiguities
Context Conditions
Extraneous Factors such as class size, academic motivation and disciplinary difficulty (Cashin 1999; Martin 1998)

the use of student satisfaction measures based on instructor's behavior is a disconnection from the critical thinking objectives or learning identified in the mission statement. SETs should have a role in contributing toward meeting mission statement objectives, but not the primary role (Green et al. 1999).

To assume that traditional SETs are used simply to provide feedback about teaching effectiveness is to misunderstand their purpose. When the purpose of course evaluations is viewed from a perspective external to the classroom, a third consequence, survey use conflict, becomes apparent. Viewed externally, course evaluations can be seen to provide external stakeholders with views, albeit somewhat limited, into the university classroom. Academia needs to continue to show tangible data to its funding entities and patrons that it is acting responsibly, thus the dual role of these surveys becomes clearer. The surveys have been successful in making contributions to the efforts of university administrators to demonstrate that the university is stepping outside its "ivory tower" and confronting the needs of its "customers."

Unfortunately, a consequence of using course evaluations for both governance oversight functions and instructor feedback is that the two purposes conflict with each other. Administratively, a complete and detailed view of classroom teaching activities may not be truly sought, but from the instructor's perspective it is important. The classroom instructor needs to be provided with specific formative information about teaching and learning activities if the "broken education models" (Albrecht and Sack 2000) are to be changed and more innovative teaching methods introduced.

The dual purpose for using course evaluations has also contributed to ambiguity regarding customer and product identification in the university environment. This final consequence is noted in Exhibit 1.

A question that needs to be carefully considered is whether the student is a customer or a product of the university (Clayson and Haley 2005). The sampled course surveys have been largely used to rate customer satisfaction measures implicitly identifying the student's role as "customer." Customer satisfaction surveys are conducted by businesses regarding the speed of their service and their employees' consideration in providing services and products. With many commercial businesses, these factors are important, as the utility received from a service or product is short-term in nature. Usually, for a business there is a close relationship between immediate customer satisfaction and repeat business that needs to be closely traced. For an accounting program, if the "product" is identified as educating accounting students and developing critical thinking and technical skills, then the basing of course evaluations on short-term utility measures of student satisfaction may be questioned, as it was by Garner (1972) and Langbein (2008). If the student is our customer rather than our product, then shorter-term measures of satisfaction are important to ensure students are happy about their programs.

RECOMMENDATIONS

Although it is unlikely to occur, the simplest and best recommendation is to halt the widespread use of summative evaluation instruments which are used by administrators for control purposes.[8] University education would not collapse and would improve if the teaching evaluation protocols are discontinued.[9]

---

[8] Seldin (1993) also states: (1) don't let administrators develop the evaluation program and then impose it on the faculty, (2) don't fall into the trap of evaluation overkill, and (3) don't over-interpret small differences in student ratings of professors.

[9] At one time it was considered unusual to use SETs. A letter dated December 28, 1949, by the Executive Secretary of the then American Association of Collegiate Schools of Business stated that: *Of 59 schools responding, 4 reported that student rating of faculty is a regular procedure, the results being used by the deans as an aid in faculty appraisal in 3 of these 4 schools.* (American Accounting Association 1953, 232).

> The students will still learn. Education will carry on because teaching evaluation protocols have little to do with learning. Perhaps teachers will be free to teach instead of surrendering to the illusory holy grail of teaching evaluation protocols that purport to assess teaching excellence only through biased surrogates of teaching and learning. Perhaps we all might even perform at higher levels (Chonko 2006).

The dangers associated with the use of numerical measures for control purposes (e.g., tenure, promotion, and merit pay decisions) are well known (Chonko 2006; Merchant 1985; Lawler and Rhode 1976; Rideway 1956). Traditional numerical measures are unable to capture all relevant aspects of the behavior subject to control, and the controlled person tries to maximize the weaknesses in the measures rather than working toward the intended goal of improving learning (Chonko 2006; Newton 1988, 3). If SETs are used for administrative control purposes, rational self-interested instructors will alter their behavior to improve their SET scores, especially contingent faculty and those without tenure. DeBerg and Wilson (1990) gives these examples of such behavior: lobbying to teach a course where better ratings are generally achieved, making a course less rigorous for students, relaxation of grading standards, or deciding against implementation of innovative instructional techniques.

To avoid these effects, an alternative but still less-than favorable solution is to give the survey results only to the instructor for self-evaluation. Whenever the numerical measures are given to administrators, the scores are simply used (often on an uneven basis) as a means to minimize time, effort, cost, and legal liability in evaluating instructors. Yet instructor self-evaluation is unlikely to become a reality because of the alternative purpose, demonstration of administrative responsibility, for using SETs. In any case, the nature of the questions on these evaluations are often not useful for improving student learning or teaching methods, i.e., they tend to largely highlight student satisfaction.

Certainly SET results should not be made public nor should grade distribution information become public information (e.g., Texas A&M University). If administrators do not recognize the dysfunctional impact of numerical control measures, how can the general public (including students) be expected to use these measures properly? If the status quo is maintained, certainly faculty and staff should be allowed to numerically evaluate administrators and make the results available to the public in the same manner.

One way to make summative SET more reliable is to require students to identify themselves through their student number. Under the present anonymous system, students' disapproving comments only add credence to termination and negative merit pay decisions. Currently instructors have no due process for false statements made by unidentified students. If students are allowed to sue instructors, students' statements used to negatively affect an instructor's merit pay, promotion, and tenure should be identified. Instructors should be allowed to know their accusers.

Faculty members who believe the traditional SET system of evaluation is obviously flawed may seek redress from the courts.[10] If these scores are used in unfavorable tenure and promotion decisions, legal rectification is unlikely to occur, however. Courts generally will not evaluate the validity of SETs. They will only determine if the performance system was applied to everyone in a consistent and fair manner, and the burden of proof rests with the plaintiff.[11] Further, identified instructor weakness in any specific area (presentation, class organization, testing, etc.) of an overall

[10] For examples see: *Lim v. Trs. of Ind. Univ.*, 297 F.3d 575, U.S. App., Lexis 14534 (2002); *Girma v. Skidmore College*, 180 F. Supp. 2d 236 (2001); and *Hall v. Kutztown Univ. of PA, et al.*, U.S. Dist. Lexis 138 (1998). See R.E. Haskell, herein.

[11] See: *Fisher v. Vassar College*, 114 F.3d 1332 (2d Cir. 1997).

good student evaluation can be used to support the case against the faculty member.[12] Therefore, faculty coping behaviors used to raise their classroom SET scores, the practice of which have little to do with better student learning outcomes, are a required self-preservation mechanism in today's university teaching environment where traditional SETs are used.

Non-summative, formative SET instruments contain open-ended questions for comment by students. Non-summative SET may be useful for improving teaching when the questions are directed at student learning outcomes. Classroom visitation, instructor self-appraisals, evaluation of teaching materials, and non-summative SET are more appropriate means for administrative evaluation of faculty.

MEASURING FOR LEARNING

At a minimum, if traditional SETs are used they should be modified to measure student learning rather than student satisfaction.[13] The Individual Development Educational Assessment (IDEA) Survey Form developed at the Center for Faculty Evaluation and Development (Center) at Kansas State University (http://www.idea.ksu.edu) is an example of such an evaluative instrument. The IDEA form assumes that there is no one correct way to teach. Therefore, the survey is used to measure each specific instructor's learning objectives while taking into account those factors that are outside the instructor's control. The IDEA survey can be used to evaluate a course or to provide diagnostic information about the course for the instructor. The diagnostic format allows for the instructors' selection of twenty teaching methods, twelve learning objectives (from simply gaining factual knowledge to use of resources for solving problems), and five course characteristics that are beyond the control of the instructor (i.e., student motivation, student work habits, class size, student effort, and course difficulty). There is a short form of the survey that does not include choices related to teaching methods, but it does include twelve learning methods and three extraneous course characteristics (i.e., student motivation, student work habits, and class size). The short form is used for administrative decisions, not diagnostics.

Since 1975, the Center has been providing this service to universities including the processing and summarization of the results of the online or paper surveys. Numerous white papers, research and technical reports have been produced by the Center during this time (http://www.idea.ksu.edu/resources/Papers.html). Changes from a student satisfaction survey to one that measures student learning must be accompanied by new administrative and faculty understandings of the process. The Center provides consulting services and pilot programs to help with this process. In addition, the Center provides confidential surveys and feedback specifically designed to evaluate the performance of deans, other administrators, and chairpersons. The Center has databases collected from its participants that provide for effective benchmarking of survey results that go beyond internal departmental evaluations.

The IDEA approach is used by a number of universities (currently the survey has been used in 60,000 classrooms), but in those universities where course characteristics are not considered, it is still necessary to remind your department head that you teach a non-regulated course, a difficult course, a late evening course or you are older. Traditional SET scores vary between graduate versus undergraduate courses, large versus small classes, homogeneous versus non-homogeneous students, and required versus non-required courses. Of course, informing your department head of the uncontrollable factors in your class assignments may not be a successful technique. We are aware of department heads assigning specific students to specific courses. In

[12] See: *Mukhtar v. CA St. Univ., Hayward*, 219 F.3d 1073 (9th Cir. 2003).

[13] A student satisfaction survey would ask for Likert responses to a question such as "How does your instructor compare with your other instructors?" whereas a student learning survey would ask, "The instructor expected students to take their share of responsibility for learning."

one department, A and B students were assigned to a select group of professors and the remaining grade-impaired students were given to other instructors. Honor classes are multiplying, which allows an instructor to give all an A+.

A class with students of lesser ability may rate an instructor more poorly than a better class, especially when confronted with tough grading and heavy work (Stumpf and Freedman 1979). We recommend that grade distribution data and course coverage data be kept by instructors as comparative data with pandering professors' courses. In today's university environment, rigorous instructors are in a position where they must provide administrators with evidence that they are working to educate their students.[14] Such documentation is especially important when decisions about tenure, promotion, and merit pay are being made. Without administrative adjustments for these factors, the continued use of a traditional SET survey can only create more grade inflation, mission statement misalignment, and course work deflation while continuing to reduce student learning.

Professors who pander to students with easy grades and easy courses are a common sight on all campuses. A result of inflated grades is that employers must keep raising the grade point average of the students that they are willing to interview. Such actions degrade the quality of the degrees granted in a program and the respect for higher education. There are universities that have tried to administratively deal with this issue. For example, to help avoid this situation, cumulative class grade points shown on a summary sheet for each course taught in the previous semester can be used to start each new semester's faculty meeting. This policy was followed at the University of New England in Armidale, Australia, and faculty members whose grades were above departmental norms were quickly identified by other faculty. The purpose of the exercise was to ensure that grade pandering to the students was not being done by one faculty member to the detriment of the program and other faculty's student evaluations. At one time, a similar grading procedure was followed at some U.S. universities where accounting departments limited the maximum number of A's to 10% of the students in a class. In today's university culture in the United States, such procedures may not be possible.

Provost Cahn (1986, 31) has stated that "the time is long overdue for professors to return to the proper use of the grading system, and to award students the grades they deserve. In so doing faculty members will be fulfilling one of their most important responsibilities: to provide accurate evaluations." New instructors should occasionally view the 1973 movie "The Paper Chase," starring law professor Charles W. Kingsfield (played by John Houseman). On the first day of class the bald-headed professor with a bowtie and black bifocal glasses forces a student to stand up and speak loudly. "Fill this room with your intelligence!" Later when explaining the Socratic Method, Professor Kingsfield states "we do brain surgery here. I train your mind."[15]

FUTURE RESEARCH NEEDED

Major research is needed to isolate the effect of pander pollution factors on student learning. How large is it? What is the difference between acceptable SET management and abusive SET management? In 2005, Charlie Dains, an executive at a large company, related two "food for thought" ethical questions during discussion in a forensic course.

---

[14] There has been administrative recognition of these issues. Cornell's Dean of Academic Affairs, Tom Dyckman, places a value of only one-quarter to one-third to the SET rating (AACSB 1993, 15). Another example of a weighted approach to faculty evaluations can be found at Blinn College (http://www.blinn.edu/facultywork/criteria.htm). At Blinn College, the SET evaluations are given a weight of 60% with the remaining 40% divided between administrative (30%) and self evaluation (10%). But 60% is still a large percentage.

[15] Professor Kingsfield stresses one student so badly that the student throws-up his breakfast after class. Today, professors cannot teach like this under our current SET-driven reward system. Balance and fairness is needed from all those who enter the classroom.

Question One: If you are a corporate controller and your boss says "cook the books" or lose your job, what would you do? Why?

Question Two: If you are an educator and are told to give all A's or B's in order to improve your SET scores or lose your job, what would you do? Why?

The idea being expressed is that ramifications should be imposed upon instructors (i.e., pandering professors) who engage in these dysfunctional practices just as ramifications are imposed upon those controllers who "cook the books."

There is a need for a new direction for research in this area. The focus of research should be reversed to identify how to improve student learning instead of how to improve scores or traditional SET evaluative instruments. According to sociologist Sid Gilbert at the University of Guelph, we "need to know what produces learning, and what practices and procedures would measure them" (Ford 1994, 6). Does a rigorous instructor like Professor Kingsfield, in the movie *The Paper Chase,* teach more effectively than a students-are-customers instructor? Does a nice instructor impart more knowledge than a less agreeable or harsh instructor? The goal in higher education is educating students—not rewarding pandering professors. According to Brown (1976), the use of SET by university administrators can lead to rewards going to the most lenient instructors instead of our best instructors.

Research on the following topics would make a contribution to determining the effect of SET on university accounting programs:

- Analyzing if pander pollution is less in regulated courses.
- Evaluating the effect of pander pollution in required, unregulated courses.
- Identifying whether pander pollution is higher in non-required, unregulated courses.
- Studying the relationship between grade inflation and SET in more detail.
- Determining whether administrators use SET scores unevenly among faculty members.
- Analyzing the effect between the student's anticipation of high grades and SET scores.
- Determining the effects SET may have on coursework deflation.
- Analyzing SET's influence on learning levels.
- Identifying if there are differences between peer review ratings and SET ratings.
- Determining whether students intentionally and purposefully slant their responses on SET questionnaires.
- Identifying SET strategic effects in creating a dysfunctional control system.

Surely if mankind can send people to the moon, we can develop a system to measure learning and evaluate the best teachers.

CHAPTER 5

Bias, the Brain, and Student Evaluations of Teaching[1]

Deborah J. Merritt, The Ohio State University*

Professors of color have published poignant accounts of harshly negative student evaluations.[2] As the few empirical studies examining instructor race and student ratings have confirmed, minority faculty receive significantly lower evaluations than their white colleagues.[3] Students' contradictory and often hostile comments on evaluations of minority faculty, as well as their occasional direct references to gender or race, raise troubling questions about the role of bias in these

* John Deaver Drinko/Baker & Hostetler Chair in Law, Moritz College of Law, The Ohio State University. Years of conversations with colleagues have helped shape the ideas reflected in this Article. For more immediate assistance, I am indebted to Ruth Colker, Andrew Merritt, Daniel Merritt, and Elaine Shoben. Kristin Harlow provided invaluable research assistance.

1 This article is reprinted from Saint John's Law Review, 2008, Vol. 82 (1): 235–288.

2 For descriptions in the legal literature, see, for example, Okianer Christian Dark, *Just My 'Magination,* 10 HARV. BLACKLETTER L.J. 21, 21–28 (1993); Richard Delgado & Derrick Bell, *Minority Law Professors' Lives: The Bell-Delgado Survey,* 24 HARV. C.R.-C.L. L. REV. 349, 349–54, 359–61 (1989), which reports results of a survey mailed to all minority law faculty; Trina Grillo, *Tenure and Minority Women Law Professors: Separating the Strands,* 31 U.S.F. L. REV. 747, 752–54 (1997); Joyce Hughes, *Different Strokes: The Challenges Facing Black Women Law Professors in Selecting Teaching Methods,* 16 NAT'L BLACK L.J. 27, 29 (1998); Reginald Leamon Robinson, *Teaching from the Margins: Race as a Pedagogicial Sub-Text,* 19 W. NEW ENG. L. REV. 151, 151–52, 168–72 (1997); Pamela J. Smith, *Teaching the Retrenchment Generation: When Sapphire Meets Socrates at the Intersection of Race, Gender, and Authority,* 6 Wm. & Mary J. Women & L. 53, 167–69, 175–91 (1999); Donna E. Young, *Two Steps Removed: The Paradox of Diversity Discourse for Women of Color in Law Teaching,* 11 BERKELEY WOMEN'S L.J. 270, 279–80 (1996); and Vincene Verdun, *The Ugly Truth: Was the Outburst Anything but Racism?,* 3 BUS. L. TODAY, May/June 1994, at 18, 18. *See also* Emma Coleman Jordan, *Images of Black Women in the Legal Academy: An Introduction,* 6 BERKELEY WOMEN'S L.J. 1, 4–5 (1990–91) (describing the controversy over Harvard Law School's lack of a single tenured minority female professor in the spring of 1990, and noting that students made "off-the-cuff" remarks to reporters regarding their visiting tort professor, Regina Austin, a woman of color); *cf.* Mari J. Matsuda, *Voices of America: Accent, Antidiscrimination Law, and a Jurisprudence for the Last Reconstruction,* 100 YALE L.J. 1329, 1332, 1352–54 (1991) (noting the tension that exists when discrimination claims are based on negative employment decisions related to foreign-born employees' accents and describing students' negative evaluation comments regarding their Asian American professors' accents).

3 Until recently, no empirical work probed the relationship between race and student evaluations, a scholarly gap that is itself troubling. Published data on this subject from law schools remain unavailable. A recent analysis of almost 17,000 evaluations completed by undergraduate and graduate students at the University of Texas, however, reveals that minority faculty obtain significantly lower ratings than white professors, even after controlling for tenure status and course type. *See* Daniel S. Hamermesh & Amy Parker, *Beauty in the Classroom: Instructors' Pulchritude and Putative Pedagogical Productivity,* 24 ECON. EDUC. REV. 369, 373 (2005). Studies have not yet attempted to isolate the reasons for this difference.

assessments.[4] White faculty members have also noted the possibility of bias in their student evaluations, particularly based on gender, appearance, or political ideology.[5] Throughout the academy, faculty question whether student evaluations of teaching accurately reflect a professor's success in helping students learn. Many charge that evaluations actually undermine learning by encouraging lenient grading and superficial classroom presentations.[6] In an increasingly diverse and competitive workplace, can we rely upon conventional teaching evaluations to tell us what we want to know about a professor's classroom success? Or do these evaluations reflect—and perhaps reinforce—biases based on race, sex, and other unwelcome characteristics?

Despite the persistence of these questions, law schools and other academic departments continue to use traditional student evaluations of teaching. Indeed, many professors report growing reliance on these measures—particularly on isolated numerical averages—in tenure, promotion, salary, and other decisions.[7] The academy has been particularly silent in response to questions about racial bias in conventional teaching evaluations: Few articles engage the eloquent critiques that individual minority professors have raised,[8] and schools do not seem to have examined their practices in response to these concerns.[9]

It is time to take seriously the criticisms that scholars have voiced about student evaluations of teaching. Extensive research by psychologists and educators convincingly demonstrates that these evaluations *are* biased. The biases, however, are not simplistic ones based directly on race,

---

[4] *See, e.g.,* Delgado & Bell, *supra* note 17, at 361 (stating that minority faculty reported student evaluations that "are sometimes both positive and negative for a single course"); Smith, *supra* note 2, at 167 ("The intensity of their anger and hatred was frightening. Many of them attached notes to their evaluations, espousing crazy racial and/or sexist stereotypes."); Kathryn Pourmand Nordick, Essay, *A Critical Look at Student Resistance to Non-Traditional Law School Professors,* 27 W. NEW ENG. L. REV. 173, 188, 191 (2005) (observing that law school classmates' criticisms of black professors "were often harsh and condescending, while the criticisms of traditional professors were almost backward compliments" and that a recent review of randomly selected student evaluations yielded "statements that clearly indicated bias").

[5] *See, e.g.,* Richard L. Abel, *Evaluating Evaluations: How Should Law Schools Judge Teaching?,* 40 J. LEGAL EDUC. 407, 437–45 (1990); Kathleen S. Bean, *The Gender Gap in the Law School Classroom—Beyond Survival,* 14 VT. L. REV. 23, 29 (1989); Martha Chamallas, *The Shadow of Professor Kingsfield: Contemporary Dilemmas Facing Women Law Professors,* 11 WM. & MARY J. WOMEN & L. 195, 195–208 (2005); Christine Haight Farley, *Confronting Expectations: Women in the Legal Academy,* 8 YALE J.L. & FEMINISM 333, 336–40 (1996); April Kelly-Woessner & Matthew C. Woessner, *My Professor Is a Partisan Hack: How Perceptions of a Professor's Political Views Affect Student Course Evaluations,* 39 PS: POL. SCI. & POL. 495, 495–500 (2006); Deborah Maranville, *Classroom Incivilities, Gender, Authenticity and Orthodoxy, and the Limits of Hard Work: Four Lenses for Interpreting a "Failed" Teaching Experience,* 12 WM. & MARY J. WOMEN & L. 699, 716–23 (2006).

[6] *See, e.g.,* VALEN E. JOHNSON, GRADE INFLATION: A CRISIS IN COLLEGE EDUCATION 235–37 (2003); Dennis E. Clayson & Mary Jane Sheffet, *Personality and the Student Evaluation of Teaching,* 28 J. MARKETING EDUC. 149, 149, 157–58 (2006); Charles R. Emery et al., *Return to Academic Standards: A Critique of Student Evaluations of Teaching Effectiveness,* 11 QUALITY ASSURANCE EDUC. 37, 37–45 (2003); Wendy M. Williams & Stephen J. Ceci, *"How'm I doing?,"* 29 CHANGE 13, 13–14 (1997).

[7] *See, e.g.,* Judith D. Fischer, *The Use and Effects of Student Ratings in Legal Writing Courses: A Plea for Holistic Evaluation of Teaching,* 10 J. LEGAL WRITING INST. 111, 111–12 (2004); Hugh Hinton, *Reliability and Validity of Student Evaluations: Testing Models Versus Survey Research Models,* 26 PS: POL. SCI. & POL. 562, 562–63 (1993); Richard S. Markovits, *The Professional Assessment of Legal Academics: On the Shift from Evaluator Judgment to Market Evaluations,* 48 J. LEGAL EDUC. 417, 417 (1998).

[8] *But see* Nordick, *supra* note 19, at 179–87 (reviewing minority law professors' narratives regarding their experiences with students' hostile criticism).

[9] *See, e.g.,* Therese A. Huston, *Race and Gender Bias in Higher Education: Could Faculty Course Evaluations Impede Further Progress Toward Parity?,* 4 SEATTLE J. SOC. JUST. 591, 591–92, 597–601 (2006) (discussing research showing that student evaluations reveal biases against women and minority faculty and contending that "most faculty and administrators are unaware of the bias in students' course evaluations of teaching"); Smith, *supra* note 2, at 93–96 (stating that although "racism is alive and well as we enter the twenty-first century, . . . [w]hite people and institutions deny the continued existence of racism and its effects of the ability of African-Americans to survive and excel in academia"); Kathryn L. Vaughns, *Women of Color in Law Teaching: Shared Identities, Different Experiences,* 53 J. LEGAL EDUC. 496, 500 (2003) ("One aspect of the law school environment that has especially bothered me is a reluctance to acknowledge that my experiences in the classroom, and those of other people of color, may well be different—sometimes vastly so—from those of my white peers.").

gender, or other social categories. Professors do not suffer automatic, consistent penalties premised on race, gender, political ideology, or other commonly recognized categories. Indeed, some "non-traditional" professors obtain very positive teaching evaluations, accurately reflecting their teaching excellence, while some politically moderate, conventional white males receive ratings that seem unduly low.

Bias in student evaluations derives primarily from a relationship that most faculty overlook: the powerful link between student ratings and a small set of nonverbal behaviors.[10] Conventional student evaluations are strongly influenced by a professor's smiles, gestures, and other mannerisms, rather than the professor's knowledge, clarity, organization, or other qualities more clearly associated with good teaching. The way in which a professor walks into the room or smiles at the class can affect student ratings much more substantially than what the professor says or writes on the blackboard.[11] In fact, students' ratings of professors show little, if any, correlation with objective measures of what students learn.[12] Evaluations collected from students after no more than five minutes exposure to a professor accurately predict assessments gathered at semester's end, leaving little doubt of the superficiality of student evaluations.[13]

The nonverbal mannerisms that drive teaching evaluations bear little relation to learning. Many of the nonverbal behaviors that influence teaching evaluations are related to race, gender, and other immutable characteristics; they stem from physiology, culture, and habit.[14] Social stereotypes filter perceptions of these behaviors so that even when faculty engage in identical classroom behaviors, students may perceive those behaviors differently depending on the professor's race, gender, and other characteristics.[15] Women and minority faculty, therefore, may experience bias on at least two levels. At the same time, white men can also suffer unfairly negative evaluations if their facial expressions or mannerisms trigger negative reactions.

These biases do not arise because students are incapable of evaluating teaching. Under the right circumstances, the most experienced decision makers will manifest the same biases.[16] The inaccuracies in our current system occur because of the *manner* in which we gather student feedback. Psychology research demonstrates that the human mind functions along two very different tracks, one that generates automatic, instinctive reactions and another that produces more reflective, deliberative decisions.[17] The way that we currently obtain teaching assessments from students taps their instinctive rather than reflective judgments. Law schools can mitigate the biases

---

[10] Although this Article focuses on the substantial biases stemming from unconscious reactions to nonverbal behavior, other considerations can also distort law school evaluations. Some studies, for example, suggest that students award lower ratings to faculty if they receive grades before completing evaluations. *See, e.g.,* Dennis E. Clayson et al., *Grades and the Student Evaluation of Instruction: A Test of the Reciprocity Effect,* 5 ACAD. MGMT. LEARNING & EDUC. 52, 55–61 (2006). This dynamic can affect evaluations in courses like legal writing, in which students receive grades throughout the semester. *See, e.g.,* Judith D. Fischer, *How to Improve Student Ratings in Legal Writing Courses: Views from the Trenches,* 34 U. BALT. L. REV. 199, 199–202 (2004); Melissa Marlow-Shafer, *Student Evaluation of Teacher Performance and the "Legal Writing Pathology": Diagnosis Confirmed,* 5 N.Y. CITY L. REV. 115, 115–16 (2002) ("Many legal writing teachers claim that their evaluations contain degrading comments and are lower than doctrinal law professors."). Although they deserve serious attention, further discussion of these problems is beyond the scope of this Article.

[11] *See infra* Part I.

[12] *See infra* Part II.C.

[13] *See* Clayson & Sheffet, *supra* note 21, at 154; *infra* notes 84–90 and accompanying text (discussing in detail the psychological research finding a strong correlation between end-of-semester student evaluations and students' evaluations formulated after brief observations of the same professors).

[14] *See infra* Part II.A.

[15] *See infra* Part II.B.

[16] *See, e.g.,* Irene V. Blair et al., *The Influence of Afrocentric Facial Features in Criminal Sentencing,* 15 PSYCHOL. SCI. 674, 677–78 (2004) (discussing influences on sentencing by trial judges); *see also infra* notes 113–115 and accompanying text (discussing this research).

[17] Steven A. Sloman, *Two Systems of Reasoning, in* HEURISTICS AND BIASES: THE PSYCHOLOGY OF INTUITIVE JUDGMENT 379, 379 (Thomas Gilovich et al. eds., 2002); *see also infra* Part III.

in student evaluations by designing evaluation systems that allow students to offer more thoughtful assessments of teaching. The most effective processes would give students additional information about a professor's pedagogic strategies and then engage them in facilitated small-group discussions of teaching.

The first part of this Article reviews the psychology research demonstrating the strong link between student evaluations and a professor's nonverbal behavior. The second part examines why this connection is so damaging: It allows race, gender, and other immutable characteristics to bias our assessment of good teaching, while doing little to identify faculty who genuinely enhance student learning. A third section probes the cognitive processes that produce student evaluations, explaining why the evaluation process we use—rather than the students who participate—generates these unreliable results. The final section proposes a system of gathering student feedback, one that makes greater use of facilitated small group discussions, to overcome many of the cognitive biases built into the current system.

Fairness to both students and faculty demands that we look critically at the student evaluation system we currently employ. Understanding the flaws in our teaching evaluation process, moreover, illuminates deeper truths about how the brain works. The legal system depends upon judgments that people make of others, from hiring decisions and due diligence reviews to negotiating strategies and jury deliberations. Appreciating the cognitive channels that distort those assessments will help lawyers improve decision making in all aspects of their practice. This Article begins that process by exploring cognitive paths in judgments that are familiar to all students, faculty, and practicing lawyers: student evaluations of teaching.

NONVERBAL BEHAVIOR AND STUDENT EVALUATIONS

Nonverbal behaviors include a wide range of appearances and actions that influence communication apart from verbal content.[18] Smiles, frowns, raised eyebrows, and other facial expressions are nonverbal behaviors. So are shrugs, waves, and other gestures. The ways in which we move, position our bodies, and hold our arms further enrich the nonverbal repertoire. Dress, hairstyle, and other aspects of physical demeanor also contribute to nonverbal communication. So do many non-substantive aspects of speech, such as voice tone, accent, and cadence.

Humans respond instinctively and rapidly to these nonverbal cues.[19] Nonverbal behavior shapes employment interviews, coaching sessions, and other interactions in the workplace.[20] Expressions, gestures, appearances, and vocal tones influence every aspect of a judicial trial, from jury selection to sentencing.[21] Even a simple smile can communicate a wide variety of meanings, from genuine pleasure to discomfort or deception.[22] We rely constantly on nonverbal signals to detect the emotions, attitudes, and intentions of people around us.

Despite its cerebral connections, the law school classroom hums with nonverbal behavior. A quick scan of the room will tell the professor which students are paying attention and which ones are surfing the web or sending instant messages behind their laptop screens. Even in a large

[18] *See generally* JOSEPH A. DEVITO, THE INTERPERSONAL COMMUNICATION BOOK 162–92 (11th ed. 2007).

[19] *See* Y. Susan Choi et al., *The Glimpsed World: Unintended Communication and Unintended Perception, in* THE NEW UNCONSCIOUS 309, 309–10 (Ran R. Hassin et al. eds., 2005); Bella M. DePaulo, *Nonverbal Behavior and Self-Presentation,* 111 PSYCHOL. BULL. 203, 207 (1992).

[20] *See, e.g., Business Applications of Nonverbal Communication, in* APPLICATIONS OF NONVERBAL COMMUNICATION 119, 119 (Ronald E. Riggio & Robert S. Feldman eds., 2003) (providing a summary of recent research).

[21] *See, e.g.,* Michael Searcy et al., *Communication in the Courtroom and the "Appearance" of Justice, in* APPLICATIONS OF NONVERBAL COMMUNICATION, *supra* note 35, at 41, 41.

[22] *See* Paul Ekman et al., *Smiles When Lying,* 54 J. PERSONALITY & SOC. PSYCHOL. 414, 418–20 (1988); Christine R. Harris & Nancy Alvarado, *Facial Expressions, Smile Types, and Self-Report During Humour, Tickle, and Pain,* 19 COGNITION & EMOTION 655, 665 (2005); Julie A. Woodzicka & Marianne LaFrance, *Working on a Smile: Responding to Sexual Provocation in the Workplace, in* APPLICATIONS OF NONVERBAL COMMUNICATION, *supra* note 35, at 139, 139.

classroom, professors can often sense which students are engaged with the material and which ones are bored, hostile, or confused. Just as much nonverbal communication flows in the opposite direction. From the moment a faculty member walks into the room, students perceive, process, and react to the professor's nonverbal signals.

Researchers have extensively documented the effect of these signals on student evaluations, often contrasting the dominance of classroom "style" over content. One early and well-known investigation into these classroom dynamics used a charismatic, distinguished-looking, and mellifluous actor to play the role of a scholar named "Dr. Fox."[23] The experimenters created a meaningless lecture on "Mathematical Game Theory as Applied to Physician Education," and coached Fox to deliver it "with an excessive use of double talk, neologisms, non sequiturs, and contradictory statements."[24] At the same time, the researchers encouraged Fox to adopt a lively demeanor, convey warmth toward his audience, and intersperse his nonsensical comments with humor. "In short," as one of the investigators summarized, Dr. Fox "gave a very enjoyable lecture in which he offered little or nothing of substance."[25]

Fox fooled not just one, but three separate audiences of professional and graduate students.[26] Despite the emptiness of his lecture, fifty-five psychiatrists, psychologists, educators, graduate students, and other professionals produced evaluations of Dr. Fox that were overwhelmingly positive.[27] In addition to awarding him strong numerical scores, audience members praised him for an "[e]xcellent presentation," "warm manner," "[g]ood flow," "[l]ively examples," "relaxed manner," and "[g]ood analysis of subject."[28]

Fox's use of warm, enthusiastic, and lively nonverbal behaviors would have been admirable if it had complemented a substantive presentation. Most faculty use stylistic elements to engage student interest and motivate learning. The disturbing feature of the Dr. Fox study, as the experimenters noted, is that Fox's nonverbal behaviors so completely masked a meaningless, jargon-filled, and confused presentation. If style can trump substance so easily, even in the minds of a trained, professional audience, then what role do nonverbal behaviors play in more routine student evaluations?

Several researchers followed up on this question by using the Dr. Fox paradigm to conduct controlled classroom experiments.[29] These studies used videos that systematically varied a lecturer's content and nonverbal behaviors to examine their relative effect on student teaching evaluations.[30] A meta-analysis of this cluster of investigations concluded that nonverbal behaviors

---

[23] *See generally* Donald H. Naftulin et al., *The Doctor Fox Lecture: A Paradigm of Educational Seduction,* 48 J. MED. EDUC. 630 (1973).

[24] *Id.* at 631.

[25] John E. Ware, Jr. & Reed G. Williams, *The Dr. Fox Effect: A Study of Lecturer Effectiveness and Ratings of Instruction,* 50 J. MED. EDUC. 149, 150 (1975).

[26] *See* Naftulin et al., *supra* note 38, at 631–33. The first group heard Fox's presentation live, while the other two saw a videotape. *Id.* at 632–33.

[27] *See id.*

[28] *Id.*

[29] *See, e.g.,* Herbert W. Marsh & John E. Ware, Jr., *Effects of Expressiveness, Content Coverage, and Incentive on Multidimensional Student Rating Scales: New Interpretations of the Dr. Fox Effect,* 74 J. EDUC. PSYCHOL. 126, 126–27 (1982) (reviewing earlier studies finding that students could be fooled into giving favorable evaluations of teachers when lectures are delivered in an enthusiastic and expressive manner); Ware, Jr. and Williams, *supra* note 40, at 151; Reed G. Williams & John E. Ware, Jr., *An Extended Visit with Dr. Fox: Validity of Student Satisfaction with Instruction Ratings After Repeated Exposures to a Lecturer,* 14 AM. EDUC. RES. J. 449, 449–50 (1977).

[30] *See, e.g.,* Marsh & Ware, Jr., *supra* note 44, at 126. One set of studies, for example, used the same actor who had portrayed Dr. Fox to create six video lectures on the biochemistry of memory. Ware, Jr. and Williams, *supra* note 40, at 151. Two of the lectures were designedly "low content" and contained only four substantive points, two were "medium content" and included fourteen points, and two "high content" lectures conveyed twenty-six points. *Id.* Within each pair, one lecture employed a highly charismatic style while the other avoided engaging mannerisms. *Id.* at 151–52. The researchers then randomly assigned undergraduates to view the videos, gathering teaching evaluations of the lecturer afterwards. *Id.* at 151.

dramatically affected evaluations. For example, an entertaining style increased an instructor's ratings by about 1.2 points on a five point scale.[31] Lecturers who provided more content on the other hand received "inconsistent and generally much smaller" boosts in their evaluations.[32]

Other studies have isolated some of the specific nonverbal behaviors that generate positive student ratings. Based on a detailed analysis of university classes and student evaluations, Harry Murray determined that a professor's speech patterns, facial expressions, and humor had the greatest impact on student evaluations.[33] More learning-focused behaviors, such as giving "concrete examples of concepts," "point[ing] out practical applications," "repeat[ing] difficult ideas," or "providing sample exam questions" correlated less with student ratings.[34] While the Fox studies suggested that faculty could reap greater evaluation rewards by focusing on style rather than substance, Murray's investigation sounded a further disturbing note: Even when concentrating on the stylistic elements of their teaching, faculty can more effectively raise student evaluations by using certain facial expressions than by offering concrete examples or repeating difficult concepts.

A recent case study, centered on the eminent psychologist Stephen Ceci,[35] further illustrates the substantial connection between a professor's nonverbal behaviors and student evaluations of teaching. After participating in a short "teaching skills" workshop conducted by a media consultant, Ceci raised his evaluations in an introductory psychology course from an overall score of 3.08 out of five to 3.92.[36] Because he wanted to test the impact of the media training, Ceci carefully used the same syllabus, lecture content, audiovisual materials, assignments, and exams in sections of the course taught immediately before and after the training.[37] He altered only his vocal "pitch variability" and the extent of his hand gestures between the two versions of the course.[38] Notably, these small stylistic changes dramatically improved Ceci's score on *every* aspect of the college's evaluation form, including items like instructor knowledge, organization, accessibility, textbook quality, fairness in grading, and other qualities unrelated to vocal pitch or gestures.[39]

Even a mere description of a professor's manner can affect students' evaluations. In one controlled experiment, a guest lecturer appeared before a large undergraduate class on a day when

---

[31] *See* Philip C. Abrami et al., *Educational Seduction,* 52 REV. EDUC. RES. 446, 455 (1982).

[32] *Id.* at 452.

[33] *See* Harry G. Murray, *Classroom Teaching Behaviors Related to College Teaching Effectiveness, in* USING RESEARCH TO IMPROVE TEACHING 21, 26 (Janet G. Donald & Arthur M. Sullivan eds., 1985) [hereinafter Murray, *Classroom Teaching*]; *see also* Harry G. Murray, *Effective Teaching Behaviors in the College Classroom, in* 7 HIGHER EDUCATION: HANDBOOK OF THEORY AND RESEARCH 135, 148–50 (John C. Smart ed., 1991) [hereinafter Murray, *Effective Teaching*].

[34] *See* Murray, *Classroom Teaching, supra* note 48, at 25.

[35] Ceci is the Helen L. Carr Professor of Developmental Psychology at Cornell University. He has published extensively on the accuracy of children's courtroom testimony, as well as other subjects, and recently won the American Psychological Society's James McKeen Cattell Award for lifetime contributions to an area of critical social importance. *See* Association for Psychological Science: 2004 James McKeen Cattell Fellow Award, http://www.psychologicalscience.org/awards/cattell/citations/ceci.cfm (last visited Oct. 19, 2007); Cornell University, College of Human Ecology: Bio Page for Stephen Ceci, http://www.human.cornell.edu/che/bio.cfm?netid=sjc9 (last visited Oct. 19, 2007).

[36] *See* Williams & Ceci, *supra* note 21, at 16, 20.

[37] *See id.* at 16–17. Ceci and his co-author took elaborate measures to assure similarities between the semesters. Independent raters, for example, viewed videotaped lectures from both semesters and confirmed that their content was identical. *Id.* at 18. Ceci's experience with the course, which he had taught for almost twenty years, made the controls feasible. *Id.* at 16–17.

[38] *Id.* at 15.

[39] *See id.* at 19–20. Ceci's average rating in the category regarding instructor knowledge improved from 3.61 to 4.05: from 3.18 to 4.09 in regards to students' perceptions of his level of organization; from 2.99 to 4.06 for his accessibility; from 2.06 to 2.98 for textbook quality; and from 3.03 to 3.72 for fairness. *Id.* at 20. All of these shifts, as well as others on the evaluation form, were statistically significant at $p < .0001$. *Id.* at 20–21.

the regular professor was absent.[40] Students received written notes from their regular professor describing the guest as an experienced professor from another university who others considered "industrious, critical, practical, and determined."[41] Half of the notes further described the visitor as "a rather warm person," while the other half identified him as "a rather cold person."[42] Nonverbal behaviors often signal a speaker's apparent warmth or coldness to an audience. Here, the written descriptions primed the students to view the lecturer's manner through one of two contrasting lenses.[43]

After a forty minute informative lecture related to their course material, students evaluated the guest lecturer.[44] Those who had been told that he was "rather warm" rated him as significantly "more intelligent, more interesting, more considerate of the class, and more knowledgeable of his material" than did students who had read that he was "rather cold."[45] Changing just one word in the lecturer's written biography was enough to shift student perceptions of his personality, knowledge, and teaching effectiveness.[46]

The most remarkable evidence of the link between a professor's nonverbal behavior and student evaluations of teaching, however, comes from recent research into "thin slice" judgments. Harvard psychologists Nalini Ambady and Robert Rosenthal coined the phrase "thin slices" in 1992 to describe brief observations of an individual that generate judgments about that individual's

---

[40] *See* W. Neil Widmeyer & John W. Loy, *When You're Hot, You're Hot! Warm-Cold Effects in First Impressions of Persons and Teaching Effectiveness,* 80 J. Educ. Psychol. 118, 119 (1988).

[41] *Id.*

[42] *Id.*

[43] *Id.* at 118–19.

[44] *Id.* at 119.

[45] *Id.* Several other measures of personality and teaching effectiveness, including modesty, self assurance, and organization, did not differ significantly between the warm and cold conditions. *See id.* at 120. Widmeyer and Loy suggest that this confirms that the students perceived a relationship between warmth and teaching abilities, rather than a general "halo effect"—a frame of reference influencing others' total perception of an individual. *Id.*

[46] A large number of studies further explore the relationship among instructor personality, nonverbal behaviors, and teaching evaluations. These investigations confirm that an instructor's personality exerts a substantial influence on evaluations, largely through his or her nonverbal behaviors. One pair of researchers, for example, recently concluded that the impact of personality is so large that evaluations "could most accurately be called a 'likeability' scale." Dennis E. Clayson & Debra A. Haley, *Student Evaluations in Marketing: What Is Actually Being Measured?,* 12 J. Marketing Educ. 9, 12–13 (1990); *see also* Stephen Erdle et al., *Personality, Classroom Behavior, and Student Ratings of College Teaching Effectiveness: A Path Analysis,* 77 J. Educ. Psychol. 394, 404–05 (1985) (finding in part that college instructors received higher ratings when they exhibited charismatic classroom behaviors such as the use of humor or encouraging student participation); Kenneth A. Feldman, *The Perceived Instructional Effectiveness of College Teachers as Related to Their Personality and Attitudinal Characteristics: A Review and Synthesis,* 24 Res. Higher Educ. 139, 144 (1986) (finding statistically significant average correlations between students' and colleagues' perceptions of an instructor's personality traits and that instructor's ratings on student evaluations); James C. McCroskey et al., *Toward a General Model of Instructional Communication,* 52 Comm. Q. 197, 206–08 (2004) (finding that "teacher temperament is manifested in teacher communication behaviors which are observable by students" and that these behaviors were "associated with students' perceptions of their teachers' source credibility"); Harry Murray et al., *Teacher Personality Traits and Student Instructional Ratings in Six Types of University Courses,* 82 J. Educ. Psychol. 250, 259 (1990) ("[F]or any given type of course or for all types combined, student instructional ratings were strongly related to peer ratings of instructor personality traits."); Sally A. Radmacher & David J. Martin, *Identifying Significant Predictors of Student Evaluations of Faculty Through Hierarchical Regression Analysis,* 135 J. Psychol. 259, 265–66 (2001) ("This robust relationship between instructor extraversion and students' perceptions of teaching effectiveness could be interpreted to support the fear of some faculty that student evaluations are just personality contests and may not be valid measures of teaching effectiveness."); Barbara R. Sherman & Robert T. Blackburn, *Personal Characteristics and Teaching Effectiveness of College Faculty,* 67 J. Educ. Psychol. 124, 130 (1975) ("[T]he evidence leans toward the importance of the personal characteristics as the cause of the perceived instructional effectiveness."); Marie Waters et al., *High and Low Faculty Evaluations: Descriptions by Students,* 15 Teaching Psychol. 203, 203–04 (1988) (discussing how students asked to describe teachers whom they had given high ratings on evaluations remembered those teachers for their positive personality traits "such as enthusiasm, personality, sense of humor, and enjoyment of teaching").

personality, intentions, and other characteristics.[47] Through a meta-analysis of forty-four studies[48] in which subjects observed no more than five minutes of a target's behavior, Ambady and Rosenthal concluded that these very quick observations "provide a great deal of information" and can trigger detailed predictions about another person's behavior.[49] Humans, in other words, make social judgments based on very short observations of other people.

Ambady and Rosenthal applied this insight to a detailed exploration of the assessments students offer on teaching evaluations.[50] They obtained videotapes of thirteen different instructors teaching undergraduate courses at Harvard University.[51] The courses spanned the humanities, social sciences, and natural sciences, and the instructors' ratings on end-of-semester evaluations were similarly diverse.[52] For each instructor, Ambady and Rosenthal abstracted thirty seconds of videotape from a single class session: ten seconds from the first ten minutes of class, ten seconds from the middle of the class, and ten seconds from the last ten minutes. They played these tapes, without sound, to groups of undergraduates who had never met the featured teacher.[53]

These students rated the instructors on fifteen different qualities, including competence, confidence, professionalism, enthusiasm, optimism, and warmth.[54] An initial group of raters viewed the entire thirty seconds of silent video for each instructor. Subsequent groups viewed redacted versions of just fifteen or six seconds of tape for each instructor.[55] Despite their very brief exposure to the instructors, these students produced highly consistent ratings of the instructors' qualities. After viewing no more than thirty seconds of an instructor's nonverbal behavior, the students substantially agreed with one another about which instructors were more competent, professional, and possessed other positive classroom qualities.[56]

Even more startling, these ratings showed highly significant correlations with end-of-semester evaluations the instructors had received from students enrolled in their courses. For students who viewed thirty seconds of silent videotape, their global rating (a sum of their ratings on the fifteen variables) of the instructor's personality produced a correlation coefficient of 0.76 ($p < .01$) with

[47] *See* Nalini Ambady et al., *Toward a Histology of Social Behavior: Judgmental Accuracy from Thin Slices of the Behavioral Stream, in* 32 ADVANCES IN EXPERIMENTAL SOCIAL PSYCHOLOGY 201, 203–04 (2000) (defining "thin slices" as "a brief excerpt of expressive behavior sampled from the behavioral stream," where a brief excerpt is "any excerpt with dynamic information less than 5 min [sic] long"); Nalini Ambady & Robert Rosenthal, *Thin Slices of Expressive Behavior as Predictors of Interpersonal Consequences: A Meta-Analysis,* 111 PSYCHOL. BULL. 256, 256–57 (1992).

[48] *See* Ambady & Rosenthal, *supra* note 62, at 260 (describing their many studies regarding judgments based on observations of "thin-slices" of others' behavior in various contexts).

[49] *Id.* at 267.

[50] *See* Nalini Ambady & Robert Rosenthal, *Half a Minute: Predicting Teacher Evaluations from Thin Slices of Nonverbal Behavior and Physical Attractiveness,* 64 J. PERSONALITY & SOC. PSYCHOL. 431, 432 (1993).

[51] *Id.* at 431, 433.

[52] *Id.* at 433. The teachers in Ambady and Rosenthal's study were all graduate teaching assistants. *Id.* at 433. However, their work has been replicated with full-time faculty. *See infra* notes 78–68 and accompanying text.

[53] Ambady & Rosenthal, *supra* note 65, at 433. All clips focused on the teacher alone, without showing students. *Id.*

[54] *Id.* The full list of qualities was the following: "accepting, active, [not] anxious ... , attentive, competent, confident, dominant, empathetic, enthusiastic, honest, likable, optimistic, professional, supportive, and warm." *Id.* at 433–34.

[55] The fifteen-second tapes used five seconds from each of the three portions of class time, while the six-second tapes used just two seconds from each of those portions. *See id.* at 437. Nine undergraduates rated the thirty-second segments, eight rated the fifteen-second clips, and eight judged the six-second versions. *See id.* at 433, 437. The researchers chose to use female undergraduate students for the study, attributing the basis for this decision to previous research suggesting that women are better than men at decoding nonverbal behaviors. *See id.* at 433.

[56] For the first group of students that viewed thirty-second video clips, reliability of the ratings ranged from a low of .60 (accepting, attentive, and honest) to a high of .89 (active and enthusiastic) with a mean of .72. *See id.* at 433. Reliability was comparable among students who viewed fifteen-second videos, and just slightly lower for those who saw only six seconds of video. *See id.* at 437–38.

end-of-semester evaluations, explaining almost fifty-eight percent of the variance in those evaluations.[57] For students who viewed only *six* seconds of the same taped behavior, the correlation with end-of-semester evaluations was almost as high—a correlation coefficient of 0.71 ($p < .01$).[58] These correlations are strikingly high for social phenomena.[59]

Ambady and Rosenthal concluded that their findings were "quite remarkable: On the basis of observations of video clips just half a minute in length, complete strangers were able to predict quite accurately the ratings of teachers by students who had interacted with them over the course of a whole semester!"[60] Even participants who watched as little as six seconds of an instructor's silent classroom behavior "predicted with surprising accuracy" students' end-of-semester evaluations.[61] These findings confirmed "the considerable influence of very subtle affective nonverbal behaviors on the teaching process."[62]

Elisha Babad and Dinah Avni-Babad later collaborated with Rosenthal to build on the initial Ambady-Rosenthal study.[63] This second study used video clips of forty-seven different professors teaching sixty-seven different courses.[64] The instructors in this study were experienced faculty, and their teaching spanned an even greater range of course types than in the Ambady and Rosenthal study.[65] Babad and colleagues also incorporated nonverbal aspects of speech in their study by using raters unfamiliar with the language spoken by the professors. Thirty-nine American

[57] *See id.* at 434. A correlation coefficient expresses the strength and direction of a linear relationship between two variables. These coefficients range from −1.00, which signals a perfect negative relationship between the two variables, to 1.00, indicating a perfect positive association between the two. Most social scientists consider correlations between .1 and .3 (or −.1 and −.3) to be small; those between .3 and .5 to be moderate; and those over 5 to be large. *See* JACOB COHEN, STATISTICAL POWER ANALYSIS FOR THE BEHAVIORAL SCIENCES 79–81 (Lawrence Erlbaum Assocs. 2d ed. 1988) (1969); Will G. Hopkins, *A New View of Statistics: A Scale of Magnitudes for Effect Statistics,* SPORTSCIENCE (2002), http://www.sportsci.org/resource/stats/effectmag.html.

Although correlation coefficients are widely used, their relative sizes can mislead non-statisticians. For example, a correlation coefficient of .4 is not twice as large as one of .2; rather, it is four times as strong. To correct for this and offer a commonsense way of thinking about correlations, social scientists often refer to the "amount of variance" that one variable explains in another. This amount is the square of the correlation coefficient. A correlation coefficient of .2, for example, means that knowledge of one variable allows us to explain about four percent of the variation in the other variable. A coefficient of .4 means that one variable explains about sixteen percent of the variance in the other. *See generally* JACK LEVIN & JAMES ALAN FOX, ELEMENTARY STATISTICS IN SOCIAL RESEARCH 369 (10th ed. 2006).

The designation "$p < .01$" indicates the statistical significance of a correlation or other statistical relationship. The "p" level expresses the likelihood that a given relationship would have occurred purely by chance. When $p < .01$, the reported relationship would happen randomly—rather than because of an actual relationship—less than one time out of 100. By convention, social scientists accept p levels of less than .05 as "statistically significant." *See, e.g., id.* at 230.

[58] *See* Ambady & Rosenthal, *supra* note 65, at 438. The students who rated the fifteen second clips achieved a smaller, statistically nonsignificant correlation with end-of-semester evaluations ($r = .44$, $p < .05$). *See id.*

[59] *See, e.g.,* COHEN, *supra* note 72, at 81 (stating that in social psychology, correlations of .50 are "about as high as they come"); Hopkins, *supra* note 72 (showing that correlation coefficients over .7 are "very large, very high, huge").

[60] Ambady & Rosenthal, *supra* note 65, at 435.

[61] *Id.* at 438.

[62] *Id.* at 440. The correlation between thin slices of behavior and teaching evaluations is so large, in fact, that these correlations are the highest researchers have obtained in thin-slice research. *See* Ambady et al., *supra* note 62, at 217–20. An earlier study, moreover, reached very similar results. In this study, conducted by Spallings and Spencer, ten participants viewed four-minute clips of teaching behavior by each of nine university accounting instructors. The participants agreed on how these nine instructors should rank on an overall measure of effectiveness. Their rankings, moreover, correlated significantly—a correlation coefficient of .70—with the instructors' rankings on end-of-semester evaluations. *See id.* at 209 (discussing the Stallings and Spencer study).

[63] *See* Elisha Babad, Dinah Avni-Babad & Robert Rosenthal, *Prediction of Students' Evaluations from Brief Instances of Professors' Nonverbal Behavior in Defined Instructional Situations,* 7 SOC. PSYCHOL. EDUC. 3, 3 (2004).

[64] *Id.* at 9.

[65] *See id.* at 7.

undergraduates, graduate students, professors, or other professionals rated videotapes of professors teaching in Hebrew at the Hebrew University of Jerusalem.[66]

Each of these raters viewed nine seconds of tape drawn from each of the sixty-seven classes and evaluated each professor on three scales: "Likable, Warm, Friendly," "Competent, Effective, Professional," and "Boring, Passive" versus "Interesting, Active."[67] The researchers then correlated these ratings with end-of-semester evaluations offered by students enrolled in each course. Ratings of the professors' competence and ability to interest an audience, as manifested in the nine-second video clips, correlated strongly with the enrolled students' ratings of the professor's humor, enthusiasm, clarity, and overall classroom performance.[68]

Most recently, Dennis Clayson and Mary Jane Sheffet reproduced Ambady and Rosenthal's findings with more than 700 college students enrolled in business courses.[69] Clayson and Sheffet visited fourteen different sections of these courses just after the first class had convened and the primary instructor had introduced him- or herself to the students. The instructor had not yet distributed a syllabus or other materials to the class, and had spoken with the students for less than five minutes.[70] The instructor left the room after this brief exposure, while Clayson and Sheffet asked the students to complete questionnaires about the instructor's personality, rating the faculty member's agreeableness, creativity, conscientiousness, stability, and extroversion.[71] Consistent with Ambady and Rosenthal's research, the students' initial ratings of professors' personalities, based on less than five minutes of classroom contact, correlated significantly with conventional end-of-semester evaluations of the instructor's teaching.[72] Ratings of "agreeableness," "creativity,"

---

[66] *See id.* at 8–10. In this follow-up study, participants were exposed to professors' nonverbal aspects of speech such as pitch, pauses, speed, and other factors that do not depend on the content of speech.

[67] *Id.* at 10, 11. The judges showed a high degree of consistency in their ratings. *See id.* at 13.

[68] Babad and colleagues combined scores on these evaluation questions into an "instructional" composite score. *Id.* at 15. This score, in turn, correlated highly with ratings for competence and interest drawn from lecture video clips. *See id.* at 17. In this study, the ratings based on brief video clips did not correlate significantly with some end-of-semester ratings, such as those related to course workload and difficulty, instructor accessibility, readings, and course content overall. *See id.* at 15. The failure of these correlations to reach significance is understandable, given their more attenuated relation to characteristics discernible from brief video clips. The difference among ratings in this study, however, does not mean that educators can rely upon some portions of student evaluations to escape the "thin slice" effect. Multiple studies have shown that item-scores on teaching evaluations are heavily inter-correlated. No matter what specific questions a form asks, evaluations appear to tap a student's global evaluation of instruction. *See, e.g.,* Sylvia d'Apollonia & Philip C. Abrami, *Navigating Student Ratings of Instruction,* 52 AM. PSYCHOLOGIST 1198, 1199–1201 (1997).

[69] *See* Clayson & Sheffet, *supra* note 21, at 151–52.

[70] *Id.* at 151. The fourteen sections included six in Organizational Management and eight in Principles of Marketing. *Id.*

[71] These five characteristics, as Clayson and Sheffet point out, are the "Big Five" personality dimensions. *Id.* Most psychologists agree that these five dimensions define a major portion of each individual's personality, are relatively fixed within each person, depend substantially on genetics, and have little cultural component. *See id.* Individuals high in agreeableness "tend to be friendly, trusting, and cooperative," while those who are conscientious are "methodical, well organized, and respectful of their duties." *Id.* Stability denotes people who are "relaxed, less emotional, and less prone to distress," and creativity characterizes those who are "open minded, creative, and interested in culture." *Id.* Extroverted individuals, finally, "will seek out the company of others and be energized by such interactions." *Id.*

[72] Students assessed the five personality factors by rating their instructor on five 7-point Likert scales. *Id.* at 152. For example, students indicated whether they found their instructor "disagreeable" or "agreeable," with one indicating most disagreeable and seven denoting most agreeable. *Id.* In addition to examining each of the five personality dimensions individually, Clayson and Sheffet averaged the five scores to obtain a "global" measure of personality. *See id.*

The end-of-semester evaluations included six fairly standard rating scales: (1) "[T]he instructor created an atmosphere conducive of learning;" (2) "[T]he instructor explains material appropriately;" (3) "[T]he instructor shows interest in student learning;" (4) "[T]he instructor sets high but reasonable standards;" (5) "[R]ate your satisfaction with your learning in this class;" and (6) "What grade would you give your instructor?" *Id.* Students answered each of these items with a letter grade (A–F). Clayson and Sheffet averaged the responses to obtain an overall assessment. *See id.*

"conscientiousness," and "stability" each showed significant correlations with end-of-semester ratings, as did a global measure of personality combining all five dimensions.[73]

Students, in other words, rapidly form an impression of a professor's personality. An image based almost entirely on nonverbal behavior gels within the first few minutes of the semester. The students may refine their impressions as the semester progresses, but the initial image remains telling. The significant correlation between assessments completed after just five minutes of class and those offered at semester's end is daunting. Based on this correlation, Clayson and Sheffet concluded that traditional teaching evaluations "follow a seriously flawed paradigm."[74] They recommended the initiation of "research and discussions ... to replace the current ... system with some other form of evaluation."[75]

It is tempting to believe that law students are too sophisticated or well educated to react as strongly as other students to a professor's nonverbal behaviors. There is no evidence, however, to exempt any group of adults from this phenomenon. The subjects who applauded the meaningless lecture delivered in the initial Dr. Fox experiment were all graduate students or professionals, many with M.D.s and other advanced degrees.[76] Similarly, the students whose five-minute ratings of their professors accurately predicted end-of-semester evaluations were advanced business students with professional ambitions.[77] Even experienced trial judges react unconsciously to nonverbal behavior when sentencing defendants.[78] Responding to nonverbal conduct is not a sign of immaturity, low educational attainment, or carelessness; rather, these reactions are an essential element of how the brain functions.

The Shadow Side of Nonverbal Behavior

A connection between nonverbal behaviors and teaching evaluations is not itself surprising. Teaching requires effective communication, and communication entails more than simply uttering words. An enthusiastic, expressive style maintains audience attention, emphasizes main points, and kindles deeper interest in the subject. Stylistic techniques can also enhance clarity and understanding. The fact that a professor's smiles, emphatic gestures, eye contact, changes in vocal pitch, and relaxed but confident movements correlate with more positive student evaluations of teaching is neither surprising nor threatening. Nonverbal behaviors surely play some role in good teaching, and many faculty members work to polish their classroom style, as well as their substantive knowledge.[79]

Yet, the research on student evaluations is troubling. It confirms not *some* connection between a professor's style and student evaluations, but an *overwhelming* link between those two factors. Nonverbal behaviors appear to matter much more than anything else in student ratings. Enthusiastic gestures and vocal tones can mask gobbledygook,[80] smiles count more than sample exam

---

[73] *See id.* at 154. Several other studies have reached similar results, showing very high correlations between evaluations gathered early in the semester and those collected at semester's end. *See* Richard G. Kohlan, *A Comparison of Faculty Evaluations Early and Late in the Course,* 44 J. Higher Educ. 587, 589–91 (1973) (noting that evaluations collected after the first two hours of class correlated highly with those gathered during the last week of the semester); Matthew H. Sauber & R. Rodman Ludlow, *Student Evaluations Stability in Marketing,* 88 J. Midwest Marketing 41, 43–46 (1988) (demonstrating a high correlation between evaluations collected during the second week of the semester and those gathered at semester's end).

[74] *See* Clayson & Sheffet, *supra* note 21, at 159.

[75] *Id.*

[76] *See supra* notes 38–43 and accompanying text. The authors of that study commented specifically on the "educational sophistication" of the audiences they had deceived. Naftulin et al., *supra* note 38, at 633.

[77] *See* Clayson & Sheffet, *supra* note 21, at 151–52; *supra* notes 84–88 and accompanying text.

[78] *See infra* notes 113–115 and accompanying text.

[79] *Cf.* Nira Hativa, *Teaching Large Law Classes Well: An Outsider's View,* 50 J. Legal Educ. 95, 104, 107–08 (2000) (offering advice to legal educators on ways to improve teaching, including tips on nonverbal behavior).

[80] *See supra* notes 38–28 and accompanying text.

questions,[81] and impressions formed in thirty seconds accurately foretell end-of-semester evaluations.[82] The strong connection between mere nonverbal behaviors and student evaluations creates a very narrow definition of good teaching. By relying on the current student evaluation system, law schools implicitly endorse an inflexible, largely stylistic, and homogeneous description of good teaching. Rather than encouraging faculty to use nonverbal behaviors to complement excellent classroom content, organization, and explanations, the present evaluation system largely eliminates the "dog" of substance, leaving only the "tail" of style to designate good teaching.[83] Neither law students nor faculty benefit from such a narrow definition of good teaching.

The psychology literature, moreover, identifies three further difficulties with the disproportionate role that nonverbal behaviors play in student evaluations. First, the behaviors that most influence these evaluations are rooted in physiology, culture, personality, and habit. Those behaviors are difficult for any faculty member to alter and they often reflect characteristics like race, gender, nationality, or socioeconomic class.[84] Second, the current evaluation process allows social stereotypes to filter students' perceptions of instructor behaviors. Students see the nonverbal behaviors of some faculty differently than they view identical behaviors in other professors, potentially placing women and minority faculty at a greater disadvantage.[85] Finally, the ratings that students award through the present evaluation system bear little relationship to objective measures of learning.[86] The current system of student evaluations, in other words, rewards and penalizes faculty according to relatively trivial indicia, rather than what they accomplish in the classroom.[87]

NONVERBAL BEHAVIORS AND MUTABILITY

Instructors are able to modify some of the nonverbal behaviors that affect student ratings: They can learn to move around the classroom with more ease, speak directly to students rather than lecture from notes, and gesture more emphatically. With training and practice, some faculty members can improve their evaluations—and their students' learning—by mastering these kinds of actions.[88]

Many of the behaviors that substantially shape student evaluations, however, are gestures, expressions, tones of voice, and other characteristics that stem from an instructor's physiology, culture, habit, and personality. These aspects of classroom behavior are "unintended" and "unconscious,"[89] and largely immutable. Professors who manifest these behaviors or appearances will

---

[81] *See supra* notes 48–34 and accompanying text.

[82] *See supra* notes 65–62 and accompanying text.

[83] *Cf.* Clayson & Sheffet, *supra* note 21, at 158 (describing a finance professor who caused students' scores on a national exam to rise from the thirteenth to the ninety-seventh percentile, but whose scores on student evaluations "consistently placed in the lowest third of all faculty" and stating that "if good teaching is ... what a student evaluation says it is, then this professor probably should be replaced"). "Should instructors be clones when it comes to behavioral manifestations? ... If [these questions are] ignored, a hallmark of higher educational institutions, that is, diversity in its broadest sense, could become the victim." Audhesh K. Paswan & Joyce A. Young, *Student Evaluation of Instructor: A Nomological Investigation Using Structural Equation Modeling,* 24 J. MARKETING EDUC. 193, 200 (2002).

[84] *See infra* Part II.A.

[85] *See infra* Part II.B.

[86] *See infra* Part II.C.

[87] These flaws in the evaluation system, of course, do not mean that faculty members who receive high evaluations are bad teachers. A better assessment process, more focused on student learning, might identify many of the same teachers as effective. Eliminating arbitrariness and bias in the system, however, is essential for those who are unfairly penalized.

[88] The psychologist Stephen Ceci, for example, improved his teaching evaluations dramatically through media training, and recounted his experience in the case study discussed above. *See supra* notes 50–39 and accompanying text.

[89] Ambady & Rosenthal, *supra* note 62, at 256.

never raise their evaluations beyond a settled ceiling, no matter how diligently they work at effective and engaging classroom presentations.[90]

Individuals with asymmetric facial features, for example, appear less agreeable, less conscientious, and more neurotic than individuals with symmetric features.[91] Professors with subtle facial asymmetries will seem more worried, nervous, careless, and disorganized to their students, as well as less helpful or sympathetic than their colleagues with more pleasing visages.[92] Overcoming these negative impressions is difficult, given the rapidity and lasting nature of "thin slice" judgments. Indeed, some research confirms that professors with attractive faces receive more positive student evaluations than those with less desirable features.[93] Notably, the effect may be stronger for men than women, although it affects both genders.[94]

Similarly, some faces appear more competent than others and some facial structures look immature or unintelligent.[95] Although researchers have not tested this effect directly in the classroom, they have identified significant effects in several other contexts. Between 2000 and 2004, for example, the candidate with the more "competent" face won more than two-thirds of contested congressional elections.[96] Students are likely to incorporate the same biases, attributing more knowledge to faculty with "competent" faces and more warmth to those with babyish ones.[97]

Research likewise demonstrates that individuals with Afrocentric features appear more aggressive than people without those features.[98] Trial judges respond to that perception by imposing longer sentences on criminal defendants with Afrocentric features than on those without those

---

[90] *See* Ambady et al., *supra* note 62, at 205; Clayson & Sheffet, *supra* note 21, at 158 ("[I]f ... student perceptions are even marginally related to relatively long-lasting traits [in instructors], it may be true that some teachers never will receive consistently high evaluations in certain environments, irrespective of anything they do or possibly could do."); Murray, *Effective Teaching, supra* note 48, at 162.

[91] *See* Fahim Noor & David C. Evans, *The Effect of Facial Symmetry on Perceptions of Personality and Attractiveness,* 37 J. Res. Personality 339, 346 (2003); Todd K. Shackelford & Randy J. Larsen, *Facial Asymmetry as an Indicator of Psychological, Emotional, and Physiological Distress,* 72 J. Personality & Soc. Psychol. 456, 464 (1997).

[92] *See* Noor & Evans, *supra* note 106, at 346.

[93] *See, e.g.,* Hamermesh & Parker, *supra* note 18, at 369–71, 375 (detailing a regression analysis of 16,957 student evaluations completed at the University of Texas, which showed that attractive professors, as rated by undergraduates unfamiliar with the faculty member, received significantly higher evaluations than unattractive ones, with the rating difference between most and least attractive faculty constituting a full point on a five-point teaching evaluation scale); Todd C. Riniolo et al., *Hot or Not: Do Professors Perceived as Physically Attractive Receive Higher Student Evaluations?,* 133 J. Gen. Psychol. 19, 30 (2006) (detailing results of naturalistic study based on www.ratemyprofessors.com, which confirms higher ratings for professors perceived as attractive).

[94] *See* Hamermesh & Parker, *supra* note 18, at 373.

[95] *See, e.g.,* Alexander Todorov et al., *Inferences of Competence from Faces Predict Election Outcomes,* 308 Sci. 1623, 1623 (2005); Leslie A. Zebrowitz et al., *Trait Impressions as Overgeneralized Responses to Adaptively Significant Facial Qualities: Evidence from Connectionist Modeling,* 7 Personality & Soc. Psychol. Rev. 194, 194 (2003) (noting individuals with child-like features are perceived as weak and naïve more often than those with more mature faces).

[96] *See* Todorov et al., *supra* note 110, at 1624. Competent appearance was judged by individuals from other states who did not recognize the candidates or realize that they were competing for an electoral position. *Id.* After briefly viewing a single black-and-white photo of each candidate, they indicated which individual they believed was more competent. *Id.* Competence ratings correlated with election results between 66.0% and 73.3% of the time. *Id.*

[97] The overall assessment of faculty with competent or babyish faces may depend on other attributes as well as the particular classroom context. Under some circumstances students may value highly a professor's intelligence, while under other circumstances, they may be more moved by a professor's warmth and support. *Cf. id.* at 1624 (noting that, although competent-appearing political candidates win elections significantly more often than those with less mature faces, the latter may secure an advantage in races in which integrity is a primary issue). The interplay of appearance and nonverbal behaviors is complex.

[98] *See* Irene V. Blair et al., *The Use of Afrocentric Features as Cues for Judgment in the Presence of Diagnostic Information,* 35 Eur. J. Soc. Psychol. 59, 65 (2005); *cf.* Joni Hersch, *Profiling the New Immigrant Worker: The Effects of Skin Color and Height* 1–7, 14–15 (Vanderbilt Law and Econ., Working Paper No. 07-02, 2007), *available at* http://ssrn.com/abstract=927038 (finding lighter skin color correlated with higher wages among recent legal immigrants to the United States).

characteristics: A recent large-scale analysis identified a significant relationship between Afrocentric features and sentence length, even after carefully controlling for severity of the primary offense, concurrent offenses, and prior offenses.[99] The disparity, which affected both white and black defendants, was substantial: Individuals with heavily Afrocentric features received sentences seven to eight months longer than those with identical criminal histories but few Afrocentric features.[100] The same facial features that influence experienced trial judges very likely affect law students as well, prompting them to view professors with Afrocentric features as more hostile than their other professors.

Voice quality also affects interpersonal judgments. Individuals with attractive voices seem more competent, powerful, and warm than those with less desirable vocal qualities.[101] People who speak in babyish tones sound warmer than other people, but less expert or commanding.[102] Loud voices register as more authoritative and knowledgeable than soft ones.[103] A professor's natural vocal tones, therefore, influence student perceptions of the professor's competence, warmth, knowledge, power, and other qualities.

In addition to these physiological features, a faculty member's learned mannerisms significantly affect student perceptions. By adulthood, these characteristics are as much part of us as our physical features. Speech patterns, for example, differ by culture and region. Americans tend to associate rapid speech with competence,[104] even though some Americans use more leisurely speech patterns. Students in U.S. law schools are therefore likely to prefer fast speaking faculty members, rating them as more intelligent and knowledgeable than slower speaking professors, even if the two groups of faculty deliver comparable content.

Similarly, white Americans engage in frequent eye contact, believing that it demonstrates honesty, integrity, and attention.[105] African Americans value eye contact less, and employ it less frequently while speaking.[106] When mulling the answer to a question, individuals in some cultures

---

[99] *See* Blair et al., *supra* note 31, at 676–77.

[100] *Id.* at 677–78. More precisely, a hypothetical white or black defendant with Afrocentric features one standard deviation above the mean for their race group, and with mean scores for each criminal history variable, would have received a sentence seven to eight months longer than a defendant with the same mean criminal history scores but Afrocentric features scoring one standard deviation below the mean for their group. *Id.*; *see also* William T. Pizzi et al., *Discrimination in Sentencing on the Basis of Afrocentric Features,* 10 MICH. J. RACE & L. 327, 333–36 (2005) (summarizing the work of Blair and her colleagues in this area).

[101] *See, e.g.,* Diane S. Berry, *Vocal Types and Stereotypes: Joint Effects of Vocal Attractiveness and Vocal Maturity on Person Perception,* 16 J. NONVERBAL BEHAV. 41, 51 (1992) [hereinafter Berry, *Vocal Types*]. "Attractive" voices differ by sex, but people show a high degree of consensus on which male and female voices are most attractive. *See* Diane S. Berry, *Vocal Attractiveness and Vocal Babyishness: Effects on Stranger, Self, and Friend Impressions,* 14 J. NONVERBAL BEHAV. 141, 141, 146–49 (1990).

[102] Berry, *Vocal Types, supra* note 116, at 51. Attractiveness and babyishness are separate dimensions of vocal quality, so these characteristics can interact to form a variety of distinct impressions. *See id.* at 43. Attractive and mature voices, for example, appear competent and powerful, but less warm than attractive, babyish voices. *Id.* at 51. Audiences perceive the latter as especially warm, but less powerful and competent. *Id.*

[103] *See, e.g.,* Ying Peng et al., *The Impact of Cultural Background and Cross-Cultural Experience on Impressions of American and Korean Male Speakers,* 24 J. CROSS-CULTURAL PSYCHOL. 203, 214 (1993).

[104] *Id.* at 214–15; George B. Ray, *Vocally Cued Personality Prototypes: An Implicit Personality Theory Approach,* 53 COMM. MONOGRAPHS 266, 273 (1986). Speakers from other cultures, such as Korea, either disregard vocal speed in judging competence or rate slower speakers as more competent. *See* Peng et al., *supra* note 118, at 215–16 (finding that native Koreans did not associate vocal rate with competence and distinguishing an earlier study by Lee and Bolster finding that Koreans perceived slower speakers as more competent).

[105] *See, e.g.,* Elisha Babad, *Nonverbal Behavior in Education, in* THE NEW HANDBOOK OF METHODS IN NONVERBAL BEHAVIOR RESEARCH 283, 290 (Jinna A. Harrigan et al. eds., 2005).

[106] *See* Uwe Gielen et al., *Naturalistic Observation of Sex and Race Differences in Visual Interactions,* 9 INT'L J. GROUP TENSIONS 211, 213, 220 (1979); Marianne LaFrance & Clara Mayo, *Racial Differences in Gaze Behavior During Conversations: Two Systematic Observational Studies,* 33 J. PERSONALITY & SOC. PSYCHOL. 547, 549 (1976); Kyung Soon Lee & Angela Carrasquillo, *Korean College Students in United States: Perceptions of Professors and Students,* 40 C. STUDENT J. 442, 453 (2006) (discussing that white professors perceived that Korean students avoided eye contact during conversations).

look up while members of other cultures look down.[107] Cultural differences like these can prompt a classroom of predominantly white American students to believe that faculty of color or foreign-born professors are less attentive, less candid, or otherwise less engaged with the material than white faculty members who more closely track white American cultural norms.[108]

Hand gestures and body movement also differ significantly by race and culture. African Americans, on average, use more intense body language than white Americans do.[109] Conversely, Chinese Americans, Japanese Americans, and Korean Americans use less expressive body language than whites, and display their emotions less visibly.[110] Japanese Americans are also less assertive than white Americans during verbal interactions.[111] Disparities like these can prompt white students, still the majority in most law school classrooms, to view African American professors as more hostile than white ones, while they view Asian American professors as cold, uncaring, or diffident.

Recent research, finally, suggests that sexual orientation also shapes nonverbal behavior. Using the "thin slice" method described above,[112] Nalini Ambady and two colleagues found that undergraduates correctly identified another person's sexual orientation about seventy percent of the time after viewing just ten seconds of silent videotape.[113] Students may make similar inferences about a faculty member's sexual orientation based on nonverbal cues. Those inferences can affect evaluations in a variety of ways. If heterosexual students are uncomfortable with gays and lesbians, and they perceive a professor's homosexual orientation through his or her nonverbal behavior, that professor may receive more negative evaluations. Alternatively, since judgments of sexual orientation are imperfect, some students may erroneously attribute a particular orientation to a professor and respond negatively to the gestures signifying that orientation. Research on the intersection of sexual orientation, nonverbal behaviors, and social judgments is just beginning, but may uncover significant concerns about teaching evaluations.

These traits constitute only some of the many nonverbal behaviors that influence judgments that students make about faculty.[114] The pervasive influence of these behaviors, combined with their immutability, explains the difficulty that many dedicated professors have encountered in trying to raise their scores on student evaluations. Although training has improved ratings for

---

[107] *See* Anjanie McCarthy et al., *Cultural Display Rules Drive Eye Gaze During Thinking,* 37 J. CROSS-CULTURAL PSYCHOL. 717, 721 (2006).

[108] Conversely, as the percentage of non-white and international students grows among law students, white faculty may find themselves rated negatively by students offended by their eye contact. *Cf.* Babad, *supra* note 105, at 290 ("[I]n some cultures, looking someone straight in the eye is not considered positive at all, but rather aggressive, daring, and impolite."); Judith A. Sanders & Richard L. Wiseman, *The Effects of Verbal and Nonverbal Teacher Immediacy on Perceived Cognitive, Affective, and Behavioral Learning in the Multicultural Classroom,* 39 COMM. EDUC. 342, 351 (1990) (explaining that for African American students, instructor eye contact was not related to perceived cognitive learning, but that eye contact was significant for Asian, white, and Hispanic students).

[109] *See* Sanders & Wiseman, *supra* note 123, at 351 (explaining that an instructor's tense body position correlated with white students' perceived learning, but not with that of black, Asian, or Hispanic students); Stella Ting-Toomey, *Conflict Communication Styles in Black and White Subjective Cultures, in* INTERETHNIC COMMUNICATION: CURRENT RESEARCH 75, 77 (Young Yun Kim ed., 1986) (explaining that blacks showed more confrontational conflict styles than whites did). *See generally* Thomas Kochman, *Force Fields in Black and White Communication, in* CULTURAL COMMUNICATION AND INTERCULTURAL CONTACT 193 (Donal A. Carbaugh ed., 1990).

[110] *See* Min-Sun Kim, *A Comparative Analysis of Nonverbal Expressions as Portrayed by Korean and American Print-Media Advertising, in* READINGS IN CULTURAL CONTEXTS 206, 213–14 (Judith N. Martin et al. eds., 1998).

[111] *See* William B. Gudykunst et al., *Uncertainty Reduction in Japanese-American/Caucasian Relationships in Hawaii,* 51 W.J. SPEECH COMM. 256, 269 (1987).

[112] *See supra* notes 62–62 and accompanying text.

[113] *See* Nalini Ambady et al., *Accuracy of Judgments of Sexual Orientation from Thin Slices of Behavior,* 77 J. PERSONALITY & SOC. PSYCHOL. 538, 541 (1999).

[114] *See generally* Hillary Anger Elfenbein & Nalini Ambady, *On the Universality and Cultural Specificity of Emotion Recognition: A Meta-Analysis,* 128 PSYCHOL. BULL. 203, 203–04 (2002) (reviewing studies of cross-cultural emotion recognition); Donald L. Rubin, *Help! My Professor (or Doctor or Boss) Doesn't Talk English!, in* READINGS IN CULTURAL CONTEXTS, *supra* note 110, at 149, 149–50.

some faculty,[115] most professors realize modest gains at best. Even twenty weeks of professional instruction attended by one group of highly motivated faculty generated just a small increase in student evaluation scores.[116] Anecdotal reports express similar frustrations. Professors, for example, are puzzled to discover that expanding office hours and giving students detailed contact information does not improve their ratings on "accessibility outside of class."[117] As two reviewers concluded, "accessibility" as measured on student evaluations "has more to do with personality than office hours."[118] And personality, especially as reflected through unconscious mannerisms, is notoriously hard to change.

PERCEPTUAL FILTERS: STEREOTYPING

A faculty member's gestures, voice tones, facial expressions, and other nonverbal behaviors profoundly shape what students believe about that professor's teaching effectiveness. The professor's actual behaviors, however, tell only half the story. Law students, like all humans, perceive other people's behavior through filters that are socially conditioned. None of us see the world through neutral, objective lenses. Instead, our minds classify individuals according to race, gender, age, and other socially salient categories with dizzying speed.[119] We then use those classifications to interpret a speaker's behavior so that the same gestures, expressions, and other components of nonverbal behavior look different depending on the speaker's race, gender, and other characteristics.

A long line of research, for example, demonstrates that Americans perceive smiles and friendliness more readily on white faces than on African American ones. Conversely, Americans more readily perceive anger and hostility in black individuals. Birt Duncan conducted one of the earliest studies in this area, showing a series of college students one of four videotapes in which a male student shoved another student after a heated disagreement.[120] The tapes systematically varied the races of the disputing students, producing dramatically different responses among viewers. When a black student shoved a white peer, seventy-five percent of the viewers described the incident as "violent."[121] When a white student shoved a black, only seventeen percent of the viewers regis-

[115] *See, e.g.,* Williams & Ceci, *supra* note 21, at 23.

[116] *See* Harry Murray & Cheryl Lawrence, *Speech and Drama Training for Lecturers as a Means of Improving University Teaching,* 13 Res. Higher Educ. 73, 86–87 (1980). *But see* Murray, *Classroom Teaching, supra* note 48, at 31. A professional actress taught the faculty members breathing and voice exercises, directed them in enacting short dramatic scenes, and gave them corrective feedback on their lectures. The group met for two hours each week. The faculty members who participated in the training averaged a 0.2 gain in student ratings, on a five-point scale, while a control group of faculty who were not participants in the training sessions realized no gains. An earlier study by one of Murray's graduate students identified even less pay-off from more modest attempts to provide feedback to professors on their classroom behaviors, although the lowest rated instructors realized some gains from that method. *Id.* at 29–32.

[117] *See* Clayson & Haley, *supra* note 61, at 13.

[118] *Id.*

[119] *See* Ambady et al., *supra* note 62, at 231 (citing various studies); *see also* Tiffany A. Ito et al., *The Social Neuroscience of Stereotyping and Prejudice: Related Brain Potentials to Study Social Perception, in* Social Neuroscience: People Thinking About People 189, 203 (John T. Cacioppo et al. eds., 2006). Kathleen Bean describes the power of these classifications in the context of a law professor: "[T]he gender gap ... is born the moment I walk into the classroom. It has a life of its own before I open my mouth, before my body language speaks, and before my eyes make contact with anyone. My sex, and my sex alone, ... opens the gender gap." Bean, *supra* note 20, at 29.

[120] *See* Birt L. Duncan, *Differential Social Perception and Attribution of Intergroup Violence: Testing the Lower Limits of Stereotyping Blacks,* 34 J. Personality & Soc. Psychol. 590, 592–98 (1976) (discussing the phenomenon of differential social perception of intergroup violence). The subjects believed they were viewing a live encounter between two students in a nearby room, using a closed circuit television. To standardize interactions, however, the interactions were taped. *See id.* at 592.

[121] *Id.* at 595.

tered the same reaction. Instead, the students characterized this behavior as "playing around," "dramatizing," or "aggressive."[122] The race of the perpetrator, race of the victim, and interaction between the two significantly affected the viewers' perceptions.[123]

More recently, a research team led by Joshua Correll used a laboratory computer game to demonstrate dramatically different reactions when white and black actors displayed identical behaviors.[124] Correll and his colleagues constructed a game in which the researchers systematically varied the race of a series of men that appeared on the computer screen, the poses they adopted, and the objects they held. Game players were instructed to "shoot" men holding guns and "not shoot" those holding innocent objects like wallets.[125] The players proved significantly more likely to shoot blacks holding innocent objects than whites brandishing the same items.[126] They also showed a greater tendency to overlook whites holding guns than blacks.[127] Even when subjects accurately distinguished among targets, they took significantly longer to recognize whites wielding guns and blacks with innocent objects.[128]

These stereotypes affect the judgments of both black and white individuals. Correll and several other researchers have shown that both whites and blacks perceive black men as more dangerous than white men when they are engaged in identical actions.[129] Americans of both races unconsciously filter their perceptions of nonverbal behavior to see more aggression among blacks than among whites engaged in similar conduct.

Several scholars, moreover, have shown that these differences arise even in very subtle contexts. In a striking series of experiments, Kurt Hugenberg demonstrated that white students identify happy expressions on white faces significantly more quickly than they see sad or angry expressions

---

[122] *Id.*

[123] The white viewers characterized a black student shoving another black as the most violent, a black shoving a white as next most violent, white shoving a black next, and a white shoving a white as most benign. *Id.* at 595. Race also affected the attributions that viewers attached to the students' behavior. Viewers attributed shoving by the black student to the student's personal attributes—for example, his violent nature—while they attributed shoving by a white to circumstantial factors such as that a stimulus caused the student to act. *Id.* at 597.

Sagar and Schofield obtained similar results in a study of sixth grade boys. *See* H. Andrew Sagar & Janet Ward Schofield, *Racial and Behavioral Cues in Black and White Children's Perceptions of Ambiguously Aggressive Acts,* 39 J. PERSONALITY & SOC. PSYCHOL. 590, 594 (1980) (exploring the way in which the interpretation of ambiguous social behavior can be influenced by racial stereotypes and cultural differences). When asked to judge ambiguous behavior in a hypothetical story, the boys rated the actions of black children as significantly more "mean and threatening" than identical actions by white children. *Id.*

[124] *See* Joshua Correll et al., *The Police Officer's Dilemma: Using Ethnicity to Disambiguate Potentially Threatening Individuals,* 83 J. PERSONALITY & SOC. PSYCHOL. 1314, 1314 (2002) (examining the effect of ethnicity on participants' decisions to shoot or not to shoot while playing a simple video game).

[125] One computer key corresponded to "shoot," while another indicated "don't shoot," so subjects had to register a reaction one way or another. *Id.* at 1316.

[126] *Id.* at 1318–19, 1322.

[127] *Id.* at 1319 (reporting results from the second study, finding that study participants were more likely to "not shoot" at video-game images of whites brandishing weapons than blacks). These results did not reach significance in the first and third studies, although they showed the same direction.

[128] *Id.* at 1317, 1322 (reporting results from the first and third studies finding that study participants were slower to respond when a video-game image of a white man holding a gun appeared on the screen than a black man, and were also slower to determine that objects held by images of black men were harmless objects than for similarly adorned white men). The window for response times in Study Two was so small that differences in response latencies were not detected. *See* Joshua Correll et al., *Event-Related Potentials and the Decision to Shoot: The Role of Threat Perception and Cognitive Control,* 42 J. EXPERIMENTAL SOC. PSYCHOL. 120, 120–28 (2006) (replicating the same results with yet another group of students); Justin D. Levinson, Forgotten Racial Equality: Implicit Bias, Decision-Making, and Misremembering 42 (Aug. 25, 2006) (unpublished manuscript), http://papers.ssrn.com/sol3/papers.cfm?abstract_id=927547) (stating that subjects were more likely to remember aggressive acts attributed to African American actors than to white ones).

[129] *See* Correll et al., *supra* note *139,* at 1325; Sagar & Schofield, *supra* note 138, at 594–95.

on those faces.[130] The opposite pattern emerges when white students view black faces. They identify sad or angry faces on blacks significantly more rapidly than they see happy expressions on those faces.[131]

Even neutral expressions elicit different responses depending on the race of the target. Pierre Philippot and Yanélia Yabar studied this phenomenon by showing white students a series of photographs that had been carefully selected for their neutral expressions.[132] The students were significantly more likely to associate neutral black faces, rather than neutral white faces, with emotions like "show[s] aggressiveness to others," "insult[s] others," and "boil[s] inwardly."[133]

These studies confirm that "how individuals perceive and categorize facial expressions can depend quite critically on who it is that is displaying the expression."[134] In the classroom, therefore, students are likely to detect warm, happy faces more quickly on white professors, while they perceive sad, angry, or hostile expressions more readily on blacks. A neutral expression on the face of a white professor may convey warmth to students, while the same expression on a black professor's face may connote hostility.[135] These differences can markedly affect student evaluations of faculty accessibility, caring, and other qualities.[136]

Perceptual filters also bias the ways in which people perceive identical behaviors of men and women. When a male employee establishes direct eye contact with another worker, he raises his

---

[130] *See* Kurt Hugenberg, *Social Categorization and the Perception of Facial Affect: Target Race Moderates the Response Latency Advantage for Happy Faces,* 5 EMOTION 267, 271–73 (2005). Students viewed the faces on computer monitors, using keystrokes to identify the expressed emotion. Hugenberg used character animation software to construct male faces that shared identical facial characteristics, varying only in skin color and expression. Pre-testing confirmed that students readily identified the expressions as happy, sad, or angry. In the main studies, each student responded to 160 trials using eight stimulus faces in random order. *Id.* at 270–71.

[131] *See id.* at 271, 273. Hugenberg and a colleague determined that the effect is even greater among white students who show higher degrees of racial prejudice on the Implicit Attitude Test. *See* Kurt Hugenberg & Galen V. Bodenhausen, *Facing Prejudice: Implicit Prejudice and the Perception of Facial Threat,* 14 PSYCHOL. SCI. 640, 640–43 (2003) [hereinafter Hugenberg & Bodenhausen, *Facing Prejudice*]. The difference, however, occurs among even less prejudiced students. *See* Kurt Hugenberg & Galen V. Bodenhausen, *Ambiguity in Social Categorization: The Role of Prejudice and Facial Affect in Race Categorization,* 15 PSYCHOL. SCI. 342, 343–44 (2004).

[132] Pierre Philippot & Yanélia Yabar, *Stereotyping and Action Tendencies Attribution as a Function of Available Emotional Information,* 35 EUR. J. SOC. PSYCHOL. 517, 517–27 (2005). Philippot and Yabar conducted their study in Belgium, which has a significant North African immigrant population that has given rise to racial tensions and stereotypes. In particular, Philippot and Yabar state that North African immigrants in Belgium are "generally perceived as a threatening and aggressive group." *Id.* at 520.

[133] *See id.* at 523–24, 527. Philippot and Yabar tested two other stereotypes of North Africans: "Show exuberance" and "Show excitement." *See id.* at 522. It is less clear that these stereotypes mark black-white relationships in the United States. Unfortunately, Philippot and Yabar did not distinguish among reactions to these five different stereotypes.

The laboratory studies examining differential perceptions of hostility on black and white faces have been limited so far to male faces and actors. Hopefully researchers will expand these investigations to explore perceptions of black and white women. Meanwhile, accounts by black women faculty suggest that they, like black men, suffer from exaggerated perceptions of hostility. *See, e.g.,* Smith, *supra* note 2, at 114 (discussing the stereotype of black women as "Sapphire," a "tough, domineering, emasculating, strident and shrill" character).

[134] Hugenberg, *supra* note 145, at 275.

[135] Anecdotal evidence from campuses yields similar conclusions. A black student on one predominantly white campus noted: "Socially, blacks are pressed into being very passive and always grinning, otherwise they are immediately typecast as being hostile and aggressive." Carole Baroody Corcoran & Aisha Renée Thompson, *"What's Race Got to Do, Got to Do with It?" Denial of Racism on Predominantly White College Campuses, in* RACISM IN AMERICA 137, 142 (Jean Lau Chin ed., 2004).

[136] Much of the research on race biases, like this example, focuses on differences between blacks and whites. Analogous differences, however, mark comparisons of other race groups, and research is starting to illuminate these complex relations. *See, e.g.,* Glascock & Ruggiero, *supra* note 18, at 200–05 (analyzing evaluations of white and Hispanic professors by students of both ethnicities); Levinson, *supra* note 143, at 24–25, 36–48 (examining recall bias as applied to African Americans, whites, and Hawaiians); Dominic W. Massaro & John W. Ellison, *Perceptual Recognition of Facial Affect: Cross-Cultural Comparisons,* 24 MEMORY & COGNITION 812, 816–22 (1996) (comparing white American and native Japanese students).

credibility.[137] A female employee using the same behavior does not enhance her credibility; instead, she increases the perception that she will act coercively against the other worker.[138] Similarly, a relaxed facial expression in male employees connotes credibility, expert knowledge, legitimate power, and the ability to confer rewards on others.[139] A relaxed expression on the face of a male manager also suggests that the manager can make subordinates feel valued, approved, and important.[140] Calm expressions on the faces of female employees confer none of these positive benefits. Instead, a relaxed expression prompts observers to decrease their estimation of the woman's power.[141]

These biases, like those based on racial categories, can powerfully affect students' evaluations of male and female professors. Students are likely to perceive male instructors who establish eye contact with students and adopt a relaxed expression—attitudes typically effective in classroom teaching—as credible, knowledgeable, and in control of the classroom. The students will believe that the professor has legitimate authority to demand work from them and will focus on his power to reward them for good answers, rather than his authority to punish them for bad ones. They will see the professor's ability to make them feel valued, approved, and important.

Female faculty who adopt the same classroom demeanors will evoke far different responses. They are less likely to gain credibility or the appearance of expert knowledge in students' eyes. Students will be less likely to acknowledge the female faculty member's authority to make

---

[137] *See* Herman Aguinis et al., *Effects of Nonverbal Behavior on Perceptions of Power Bases,* 138 J. SOC. PSYCHOL. 455, 460–63 (1998). Aguinis and his colleagues asked 170 young adults with significant workplace experience to respond to a written vignette in which two employees, "John" and "Greg," discussed declining profits at their bank. The researchers systematically varied John's eye contact with Greg, his facial expression, and his body posture in the descriptions to capture a variety of nonverbal behaviors. *Id.* at 460. When the vignette described John as looking directly at Greg, readers rated John's credibility as significantly higher than when the vignette indicated that John looked around the room, glancing occasionally at Greg. *See id.* at 463. Credibility was assessed from reactions to a series of statements such as "John is a man who keeps his word" and "John tells the truth." *See id.* at 462.

[138] *See* Herman Aguinis & Christine A. Henle, *Effects of Nonverbal Behavior on Perceptions of a Female Employee's Power Bases,* 141 J. SOC. PSYCHOL. 537, 544–45 (2001). Aguinis and Henle used the same procedure adopted in Aguinis' earlier study, *see generally* Aguinas et al., *supra* note 152, but identified the two employees as "Mary" and "John." Aguinis & Henle, *supra,* at 541. When Mary was described as looking directly at John, readers did not believe that she was more credible than when she glanced at him only occasionally. Instead, they perceived her as possessing significantly more coercive power. *Id.* at 544–45. Coercive power is a supervisor's ability to punish a subordinate. Aguinis and Henle measured ability to coerce through reactions to statements like "Mary can give John undesirable job assignments" and "Mary can make things unpleasant on the job for John." *See id.* at 543.

[139] *See* Aguinis et al., *supra* note 152, at 463. When the vignette described the facial expression of one worker, "John," as relaxed, readers rated him significantly higher on credibility, expert power, legitimate power, and reward power—all positive attributes in the workplace. *See id.* "Expert power" measures the special expertise that a superior employee can share with an inferior. Aguinis and his colleagues measured expert power through reactions to statements like "John can share with Greg his (John's) considerable experience and/or training." *Id.* at 462. Legitimate power refers to an employee's perceived authority to command others. It was measured in this study through reactions to statements like "John can make Greg recognize that he (Greg) has tasks to accomplish." *Id.* Reward power, finally, consists of the ability to confer benefits on another worker. This study established perceptions of reward power through reactions to statements like "John can increase Greg's pay level." *Id.*

[140] *See id.* at 463. In this study, a relaxed expression on a male manager's face significantly increased ratings of "referent power." That type of power includes the perceived ability to make others feel "valued," "approve[d]," "personally accepted," and "important." *See id.* at 462.

[141] *See* Aguinis & Henle, *supra* note 153, at 544–46. Aguinis and Henle identified just one nonverbal behavior that appeared to have a positive effect on perceptions of female managers. A relaxed body position, signified by leaning back in a chair with legs crossed, increased ratings of referent power. *See id.* at 544–45. Readers, in other words, were more likely to think that this female employee could confer feelings of acceptance, value, and importance on another worker. Aguinis and Henle termed this finding "surprising" and "did not consider this a finding of strong theoretical significance" because of its incongruity with prior theoretical work. *Id.* at 545. The finding, however, may hold a clue to how female professors *do* achieve positive ratings from students. When they appear relaxed in the classroom, that appearance may connote high status, consistent with a general correspondence between those variables, which for women translates into an ability to confer "soft" benefits like feelings of value, acceptance, and importance.

assignments or demand work in the same way they will perceive that power in a male professor. They will also be less likely to focus on the female professor's ability to reward them for good work or to enhance their feelings of value and importance. Instead, students are more likely to focus on the female instructor's power to punish them for poor work.[142]

Fewer studies examine the impact of socioeconomic status on our perceptions of others, but those that exist suggest that it also shapes attitudes. One well-developed line of experiments uses vehicles—a common class marker in American life—to probe reactions to people of high and low socioeconomic class. Anthony Doob and Alan Gross performed the first of these experiments, demonstrating that drivers were significantly more likely to honk at an old, rusty car that failed to move promptly through an intersection than at an expensive, new, and well-maintained car.[143] Andrew McGarva and Michelle Steiner observed similar driver responses when testing their reactions towards being honked at by a rusty Ford pickup, the low-status vehicle, and the new Nissan Pathfinder SUV, a high-status vehicle.[144] Drivers accelerated away from the Ford pickup significantly more quickly than they drove away from the SUV after the other driver honked at them.[145]

Law students do not honk at professors who displease them, but the same attitudinal differences can affect relationships in the classroom. The "horn honking" studies expose a cultural tendency to vent frustration or hostility more readily against low-status individuals than high-status ones. Socratic classrooms, challenging material, and intense competition for grades are at least as frustrating to students as a stalled car at an intersection. Law students may express that irritation more readily on evaluations of professors with low-status mannerisms than in their assessments of faculty with more high-status appearances. Indeed, the horn-honking studies may

---

[142] This type of power is a negative one leading to "resistance . . . , lower organizational commitment, and dissatisfaction." *Id.* at 544–45. Several studies comparing student comments on teaching evaluations reveal gender differences parallel to these differences. *See, e.g.*, Farley, *supra* note 20, at 339 (stating that evaluations of female law faculty criticize them disproportionately for "being too strict or for being 'task-masters' "); Michael A. Messner, *White Guy Habitus in the Classroom*, 2 MEN & MASCULINITIES 457, 458 (2000) (describing evaluations concluding that male co-teacher was "objective," "relaxed and comfortable," "flexible," "open-minded," "good humored," and "look[ed] at all sides of an issue," while a female colleague was perceived as "biased," having "an agenda," having a "chip on her shoulder," "rigid and dogmatic," "politically correct," "grumpy and angry").

Empirical surveys suggest that female faculty do, on average, receive lower evaluations than their male colleagues. A recent, multivariate analysis of almost 17,000 student evaluations at the University of Texas revealed significantly higher evaluations for male faculty, even after controlling for course type and instructor status. *See* Hamermesh & Parker, *supra* note 18, at 370, 373. Another recent study of evaluations gathered in 741 different courses taught at twenty-one different institutions showed that women faculty received significantly lower ratings from male students than females, while male and female students did not differ in their assessment of male faculty. *See* John A. Centra & Noreen B. Gaubatz, *Is There Gender Bias in Student Evaluations of Teaching?*, 71 J. HIGHER EDUC. 17, 26 (2000). Female instructors, however, received higher ratings from female students. *Id.* Earlier studies reached mixed results, but these most recent, and most comprehensive, studies suggest that male and female faculty receive somewhat different ratings.

[143] *See* Anthony N. Doob & Alan E. Gross, *Status of Frustrator as an Inhibitor of Horn-Honking Responses*, 76 J. SOC. PSYCHOL. 213, 213–16 (1968). The drivers also honked more quickly at the low status cars and were more likely to honk repeatedly at those cars. *Id.* at 216. Andreas Diekmann and several colleagues complemented this research by finding that the status of the *blocked* car also affects responses in these situations. Drivers of higher status cars are more likely to honk their horns or flick their headlights at the waiting car than are drivers of lower status cars. Andreas Diekmann et al., *Social Status and Aggression: A Field Study Analyzed by Survival Analysis*, 136 J. SOC. PSYCHOL. 761, 761–64, 768 (1996).

[144] Andrew R. McGarva & Michelle Steiner, *Provoked Driver Aggression and Status: A Field Study*, 3 TRANSP. RES. PART F 167, 167–79 (2000).

[145] *Id.* at 173–74. The "provoking" driver also held "his mouth expressively agape" and "raised both arms impatiently." *Id.* at 172. Status influences on the road, however, may differ more among cultures than some other behaviors do. *See, e.g.*, Diekmann et al., *supra* note 158, at 768.

explain the surprising degree of overt hostility that law students express on evaluations of some minority faculty.[146] Those evaluations are a type of classroom "honking."[147]

These examples comprise just a sample of the kind of stereotypes that routinely bias perceptions based on race, gender, class, and other categories. Researchers have documented a substantial number of other biases, with still others to be uncovered.[148] The bottom line is that, especially when the mind makes judgments based on "thin slices" of nonverbal behavior—the type of judgments students seem to be expressing on teaching evaluations—these stereotypes automatically and unconsciously alter perceptions. Students, like other humans, ascribe different meaning to the same behaviors depending on the race, gender, class, and other characteristics of the actor.

Familiarity does not necessarily reduce these perceptual distortions; instead, the differences may grow through self-reinforcing cycles. If students perceive hostility in the ambiguous expression of a black professor, coerciveness in the eye contact of a woman, or obstructive behavior in a professor from an underprivileged background, they will respond to those impressions with heightened hostility of their own. The faculty member, in turn, confronts negative reactions that have no apparent source. He or she has engaged in neutral (or even positive) behaviors that appear to have provoked an angry response. Faced with this seemingly irrational hostility, the black, female, or low-status faculty member may display subtle signs of their own discomfort and anxiety. Students will perceive those behaviors, reinforcing their initial negative images. False impressions generated by stereotypes, in other words, create a cycle of mutually reinforcing behavior.[149] By the semester's end, students may feel quite justified in rating the black, female, or low-status professor as hostile and uncaring. Because humans are so sensitive to nonverbal signals of aggression, support, and other attitudes, even small differences in those perceptions have "powerful implications" for ongoing interactions.[150]

The Missing Link with Learning

The link between nonverbal behavior and teaching evaluations allows irrelevant characteristics like race and gender to distort student assessments of faculty. The same association hints that conventional evaluations bear little relationship to student learning. The professionals who lauded Dr. Fox's entertaining but meaningless discussion of mathematical theory and medical education could not have learned much: There was nothing in the lecture to learn.[151] Behaviors detectable

[146] *See supra* note 17 and accompanying text.

[147] One such comment was made in an anonymous student note given to an African American female professor:

> A black mammy like you is completely incompetent to judge anyone on anything. I do not care whether you are magna cum laude .... You do not belong in law school teaching. Black mammies should stay at home doing mammy things. Or they should stay in their place and it is not law school.

Smith, *supra* note 2, at 179.

[148] *See, e.g.*, Marc David Pell, *Evaluation of Nonverbal Emotion in Face and Voice: Some Preliminary Findings on a New Battery of Tests,* 12 TENNET 499, 502 (2002) (showing that subjects recognized neutral expressions more readily on male faces and expressions of disgust more readily on female ones); Ron Tamborini & Dolf Zillman, *College Students' Perception of Lecturers Using Humor,* 52 PERCEPTUAL & MOTOR SKILLS 427, 427–32 (1981) (demonstrating that students respond differently to male and female professors using similar humor).

[149] *See* Chamallas, *supra* note 20, at 202 (describing such a cycle when students respond critically to a female law professor); Hugenberg & Bodenhausen, *Facing Prejudice, supra* note 146, at 643; Lu-in Wang, *Race as Proxy: Situational Racism and Self-Fulfilling Stereotypes,* 53 DEPAUL L. REV. 1013, 1048–80 (2004) (discussing the phenomenon of self-fulfilling stereotypes in a variety of legal contexts); Carol O. Word et al., *The Nonverbal Mediation of Self-Fulfilling Prophecies in Interracial Interaction,* 10 J. EXPERIMENTAL SOC. PSYCHOL. 109, 119 (1974).

[150] Hugenberg & Bodenhausen, *supra* note 146, at 643.

[151] *See supra* notes 38–25 and accompanying text.

in just thirty seconds of silent videotape seem unlikely to promote solid learning, yet these elements strongly influence student evaluations.[152] Do student evaluations of faculty correlate with student learning?

The cumulative research suggests that there is little, if any, positive association between the ratings students give faculty and the amount they learn. The most recent study, in fact, suggests a negative correlation between evaluations and learning. In a particularly well-designed investigation, two business professors gathered eight full years of data on students who completed two sequential accounting courses at a Midwestern university.[153] After controlling for ACT scores, overall GPA, and grades in the first course, the researchers discovered that students who completed the first course with highly rated professors achieved significantly *lower* grades in the second course.[154] The professors with top evaluations, in other words, did not prepare students for the more advanced course as well as lower rated faculty did.

This study is particularly noteworthy because it captured multiple facets of learning. By examining performance in a subsequent course, one that built directly on material learned in the first class, the investigation tapped students' long-term retention of material, as well as their motivation for learning. Some scholars suggest that even if highly rated professors do not enhance their students' immediate achievement, they inspire an enthusiasm for learning that has longer term pay-off.[155] In the business curriculum study, however, this relationship did not hold. Students who completed the initial course with highly rated professors performed less well than students who learned the introductory material from lower rated faculty. The results of this analysis lend support to speculation that a desire for better teaching evaluations may pressure faculty to "dumb down" the material they present to students.[156]

In several other studies, teaching evaluations failed to show any correlation, positive or negative, with student achievement. An examination of students in two sequential economics courses failed to find any significant relationship between faculty evaluations in the first course and student performance in the advanced offering.[157] Professors whom students rated poorly nonetheless prepared them as effectively as more highly-rated colleagues. Another more recent study directly probed the relationship between the nonverbal behaviors that influence teaching evaluations and student performance in a course. Students enrolled in fifteen different sections of an introductory course scored their instructor's nonverbal behaviors shortly before completing a common midterm

---

[152] *See supra* notes 62–62 and accompanying text; *see also* Clayson & Sheffet, *supra* note 21, at 157–58 ("Finding an association between the final evaluation of the class at the end of the term and a personality evaluation made within 5 minutes of exposure ... makes a validity argument for the relationship between personality and evaluation difficult to defend.").

[153] Penelope J. Yunker & James A. Yunker, *Are Student Evaluations of Teaching Valid? Evidence from an Analytical Business Core Course,* 78 J. EDUC. BUS. 313, 313–14 (2003).

[154] *Id.* at 315–16. Students' overall GPA, introductory course grade, and ACT scores, which are designed to measure pre-college aptitude, on the other hand, all showed significant positive correlations with their grades in the intermediate course. *Id.* at 315. As one would expect, the students' general academic ability, as reflected by ACT score and overall GPA, their diligence, as reflected by overall GPA, and their relative performance in the initial course, all predicted achievement in the subsequent course. *See id.* The notable finding of the Yunkers' study is that, after controlling for these variables, students who learned the initial material from more highly rated professors performed less well than students who studied that material from professors with lower evaluations. *Id.* at 316.

[155] *See, e.g.,* Mike Allen et al., *The Role of Teacher Immediacy as a Motivational Factor in Student Learning: Using Meta-Analysis to Test a Causal Model,* 55 COMM. EDUC. 21, 28–29 (2006); Paul L. Witt et al., *A Meta-Analytical Review of the Relationship Between Teacher Immediacy and Student Learning,* 71 COMM. MONOGRAPHS 184, 200 (2004).

[156] *See, e.g.,* JOHNSON, *supra* note 21, at 49–50.

[157] Stephen Shmanske, *On the Measurement of Teacher Effectiveness,* 19 J. ECON. EDUC. 307, 308, 311, 313 (1988); *see also* Ganesh Mohanty et al., *Multi-Method Evaluation of Instruction in Engineering Classes,* 18 J. PERSONNEL EVALUATION EDUC. 139, 143, 146 (2005) (finding no significant relationship between student ratings of instruction and student learning as measured by comparing students' scores on tests administered both prior to and upon completion of engineering courses, although study included a small number of students).

exam.[158] Scores on the midterm showed no significant correlation with the students' ratings of their instructors.[159]

Stephen Ceci, the psychology professor who documented his success in substantially raising student evaluations by adopting minor changes in his nonverbal behavior, offers further evidence that student evaluations bear little relationship to learning. After implementing a media consultant's advice, Ceci's evaluations rose almost a full point on a five point scale.[160] The students enrolled in the post-training course, moreover, believed that they learned more from a professor who gestured emphatically and varied his voice tones. On a five point scale, these students awarded Ceci an average of 4.05 for how much they had learned, compared to just 2.93 registered by students the previous semester.[161] The media training and changes in nonverbal behavior, however, did not affect students' actual performance on quizzes and exams; those scores were virtually identical across the two semesters.[162] Ceci's changed style, in other words, improved his evaluations but did not enhance the students' learning.

A few studies do identify a positive relationship between student evaluations and learning. Harry Murray, for example, found a correlation of 0.30 between students' ratings of their instructor and final exam scores in a study of multiple sections of an introductory psychology course.[163] Differences in evaluation scores, in other words, explained about nine percent of the variance in student learning.[164] An earlier meta-analysis by Peter Cohen identified a somewhat higher correlation of 0.43 between teaching evaluations and student learning, suggesting that the former explain about 18.5% of the variance in the latter.[165] Researchers, however, have noted several flaws in Cohen's analysis: It included studies in which students rated their professors only after receiving course grades, as well as surveys based solely on students' subjective beliefs about the extent of their learning.[166] In light of these and other problems, Cohen joined two other evaluation experts in agreeing that additional research was needed.[167] Those more recent studies, as noted above, have shown no positive relationship between teaching evaluations and student learning.

---

[158] Jon A. Hess et al., *Is Teacher Immediacy Actually Related to Student Cognitive Learning?,* 52 COMM. STUD. 197, 208–09 (2001).

[159] *Id.* at 210–11; *see also* Joseph L. Chesebro, *Effects of Teacher Clarity and Nonverbal Immediacy on Student Learning, Receiver Apprehension, and Affect,* 52 COMM. EDUC. 135 (2003); Debra Q. O'Connell & Donald J. Dickinson, *Student Ratings of Instruction as a Function of Testing Conditions and Perceptions of Amount Learned,* 27 J. RES. & DEV. EDUC. 18, 19, 22 (1993) (finding that student ratings of instructor in education course failed to correlate with student learning as measured by comparing students' scores on tests administered both prior to and upon completion of the course).

[160] *See supra* notes 50–39 and accompanying text.

[161] Williams & Ceci, *supra* note 21, at 16, 20. This finding is consistent with a large number of studies finding that student evaluations of teaching correlate highly with students' perceptions of how much they have learned. *See, e.g.,* O'Connell & Dickinson, *supra* note 174, at 22; Witt et al., *supra* note 170, at 201. Students, in other words, believe that they learn more from highly-rated professors—but usually, they do not. *See* O'Connell & Dickinson, *supra* note 174, at 18–19, 22.

[162] Williams & Ceci, *supra* note 21, at 21.

[163] Murray, *Effective Teaching Behaviors, supra* note 48, at 151; *see also* Jeff Koon & Harry G. Murray, *Using Multiple Outcomes to Validate Student Ratings of Overall Teacher Effectiveness,* 66 J. HIGHER EDUC. 61, 68, 73–74 (1995) (analyzing the same data).

[164] *See supra* note 72 (explaining the concepts of correlation and variance).

[165] *See* Peter A. Cohen, *Student Ratings of Instruction and Student Achievement: A Meta-Analysis of Multisection Validity Studies,* 51 REV. EDUC. RES. 281, 295–96 (1981).

[166] *See, e.g.,* Philip C. Abrami et al., *Validity of Student Ratings of Instruction: What We Know and What We Do Not,* 82 J. EDUC. PSYCHOL. 219, 220, 222–24 (1990); Hinton, *supra* note 22, at 566. The former problem confounds attempts to correlate student achievement with faculty ratings because a high evaluation offered after receiving course grades may reflect student satisfaction with their grades rather than an independent judgment of faculty quality. *See supra* note 25 (discussing the relationship between student grades and teaching evaluations). The second flaw substantially diluted Cohen's conclusions: Most scholars consider student perceptions of learning a poor measure of their actual learning. *See, e.g.,* Witt et al., *supra* note 170, at 189.

[167] *See* Abrami et al., *supra* note 181, at 231.

In a meta-analysis of eighty-one studies published between 1979 and 2001, finally, Paul Witt and several colleagues identified a small positive relationship between "immediacy," the complex of personality and nonverbal behaviors that produce high student evaluations, and objective measures of student-achievement-like exam scores.[168] Given the relationship between immediacy and evaluations, this analysis could signal a parallel association between evaluations and learning. The correlation calculated by Witt and his colleagues, however, was just 0.122,[169] meaning that variation in the measured nonverbal behaviors explained just 1.5% of the variance in student learning. Although statistically significant, Witt and his colleagues concluded that these "low associations" were "less than meaningful" in any practical sense.[170]

The nonverbal behaviors that students reward on teaching evaluations, in other words, produce little, if any, gain in student learning. Those behaviors seem to make learning more enjoyable for students, and that is a worthwhile goal for faculty to pursue. To the extent that nonverbal behaviors are mutable, professors can attempt to learn mannerisms that will increase students' enjoyment of their classes as well as the faculty member's teaching evaluations. Dedicating substantial time to polishing these nonverbal behaviors, however, is unlikely to improve student understanding. Faculty can do more to enhance actual learning by skipping the media training sessions and devoting that time directly to their students or class materials.

The price of our current system of student evaluations, moreover, is much higher than the opportunity cost of time spent trying to change nonverbal behaviors. As the previous sections explain, student evaluations impose serious risks of bias. Some of those distortions specifically burden white women, faculty of color, and other traditionally disadvantaged groups. Others penalize any faculty member with the wrong type of face, voice, gestures, or other nonverbal behaviors. The correlation between conventional teaching evaluations and student learning would have to be very high to justify this kind of unfairness.[171] Instead, the relationship to learning outcomes is minimal at best.

THE COGNITIVE FOUNDATIONS OF JUDGMENT

The psychology literature paints a disturbingly negative picture of student evaluations: These assessments respond primarily to minor aspects of a professor's classroom style; many of those behaviors reflect characteristics like race, gender, and class; and evaluation scores bear little, if any, relationship to student learning.[172] Why are student evaluations so biased?

The problem does not lie with students. It inheres in the process we use to gather their input. Despite some claims to the contrary, students have essential feedback to offer faculty on teaching.

---

[168] *See* Witt et al., *supra* note 170, at 184–85, 196.

[169] *Id.* at 196. This figure represents the correlation of student learning with combined measures of verbal and nonverbal immediacy. *Id.* Attempts to separate verbal and nonverbal immediacy yielded even lower correlations. *Id.* "Cognitive learning" embraces all types of learning that law faculty attempt to convey. In other words, it includes thinking and analysis skills, as well as mastery of basic facts and principles.

[170] *Id.* at 200. Social science conventions agree that correlations of this magnitude are weak, with little practical significance. *See supra* note 72.

[171] Evaluations are most problematic when they are used to determine a particular faculty member's fitness for tenure, promotion, salary increase, or other reward. Even a relatively large correlation between two variables in a population tells us very little about any one population member. A hypothetical correlation of .50 between student learning and evaluations, for example, would be higher than any ever detected but still would explain only twenty-five percent of the variance in student learning. *See supra* note 72. Fully three-quarters of the variation in student learning, under these circumstances, would stem from other factors. And despite the overall correlation, some faculty with low evaluations would generate more learning in their students than professors with higher evaluations. For this reason, overall correlations provide a poor basis for judging population members individually. One observer argues that a correlation between two variables should reach .90, a very high threshold, before it is used to rate individuals. Hopkins, *supra* note 72.

[172] The extensive literature on teaching evaluations raises other questions on the validity of these measures, particularly their relationship to students' expected and actual grades. *See supra* note 25. Some of these issues are important to legal education but are beyond the scope of this Article.

They can tell professors what they learned from a course and how that compared to what they expected to learn. They can describe the educational techniques that worked for them and those that did not. They can provide suggestions for how a faculty member might teach differently. Law students can assess the quality of their educational experience in myriad ways.

Obtaining useful feedback from any evaluator, however, requires collecting information under circumstances that allow for meaningful, deliberative reflection. As the Nobel prize-winning psychologist Daniel Kahneman explains, there are two types of human thought processes: System One and System Two.[173] System One processes are "fast, automatic, effortless, associative, implicit (not available to introspection), and often emotionally charged; they are also governed by habit and are therefore difficult to control or modify."[174] System Two processes are "slower, serial, effortful, more likely to be consciously monitored and deliberately controlled; they are also relatively flexible and potentially rule governed."[175]

As rational adults, we assume that most of our judgments derive from System Two. We perceive ourselves as reasoned creatures who "think things through." In fact, however, almost all judgments begin as System One intuitions; we have gut reactions to just about everything.[176] System Two deliberations challenge and override our initial System One decisions in a surprisingly limited number of cases.[177] Instead, we are more likely to use System Two cognitive processes to justify the intuitive judgments we generate using System One's more emotional leaps.[178]

Students' evaluations of faculty begin, like most judgments, as System One processes. As such, they are heavily influenced by first impressions—even though the students have known the faculty member for at least a semester. When the brain makes a System One decision, it does not assess all of the information gathered on a subject over time as with System Two processes. Instead, the mind uses its quick-fix System One toolbox: It seizes its first impressions of the subject. In a sense, the students' minds reach back to the first impressions they formed of the instructor, using those as the basis for their evaluation. Those impressions, of course, incorporate all of the biases described above.

The dominance of System One thinking offers a possible explanation for the particularly high correlation between end-of-semester teaching evaluations and "thin slice" judgments of the same teachers. Students' assessments at a course's summation may not just correspond to those first

---

[173] Daniel Kahneman, *A Perspective on Judgment and Choice: Mapping Bounded Rationality,* 58 AM. PSYCHOLOGIST 697, 698 (2003). Kahneman credits Stanowich and West with proposing the terms "System One" and "System Two," although the framework rests on work done by Kahneman and his collaborator Amos Tversky. *Id.* Other scholars have used terms like "experiential" and "analytic," or "experiential" and "rational." *See, e.g.,* Seymour Epstein, *Integration of the Cognitive and the Psychodynamic Unconscious,* 49 AM. PSYCHOLOGIST 709, 710 (1994); Paul Slovic et al., *Rational Actors or Rational Fools: Implications of the Affect Heuristic for Behavioral Economics,* 31 J. SOCIO-ECON. 329, 330 (2002).

[174] Kahneman, *supra* note 188, at 698.

[175] *Id.*

[176] *See id.* at 716–17.

[177] *See id.* at 717. Although it is impossible to know precisely how often System Two overrides System One in daily life, Kahneman estimates that the "most common" paths of decision making are either those that involve only System One—when System Two offers no corrections at all—or those in which System Two only partially and inadequately corrects System One. *Id.* All judgments, in the common meaning of that word, do activate System Two to some extent because they require explicit choices. *Id.* at 699. As Kahneman explains, however, many judgments occur without System Two overriding the instinctive direction proposed by System One—they are "intuitive" judgments. *Id.*

[178] R.B. Zajonc, a pioneer in this area of psychology, observed:

> We sometimes delude ourselves that we proceed in a rational manner and weigh all the pros and cons of the various alternatives. But this is probably seldom the actual case ... . Most of the time, information collected about alternatives serves us less for making a decision than for justifying it afterward.

R.B. Zajonc, *Feeling and Thinking: Preferences Need No Inferences,* 35 AM. PSYCHOLOGIST 151, 155 (1980).

impressions—they may *be* those impressions. Because the process we use to collect end-of-semester evaluations does not encourage System Two—deliberative—reflection, the students' brains most likely retrieve their first impressions and report those as their current evaluation.[179]

Obtaining more meaningful evaluations from students, therefore, requires finding ways to engage System Two thinking. There are at least three reasons why the current evaluation system fails to encourage that deeper thought. First, System One works with special efficiency in deciding whether things are good or bad.[180] Research, in fact, suggests that the brain has specialized neural circuitry that renders these good/bad distinctions promptly and confidently.[181] When the brain is asked to make any good/bad judgment, it is less likely to invoke System Two's more reflective thinking because System One handles these decisions so efficiently. This does not mean that the brain invariably makes correct good/bad decisions using System One, but it does tend to rely upon that process for these decisions.

Rating a professor's teaching requires the brain to make good/bad distinctions: We ask students to indicate how "good" or "bad" various aspects of that teaching were. This is especially true of the numerical judgments that most evaluation processes demand from students. The very nature of these forms, which ask students to rate value without requiring other types of reflection, discourages the brain from moving beyond System One instinctive reactions.[182]

Second, System Two thinking requires time. Our brains excel at intuitions, first impressions, and quick judgments, but struggle to make more complex decisions. As one pair of psychologists recently observed, "human cognitive capacities are limited" so "[p]roblem solving is hard work."[183] Humans have restricted working memory, making it difficult for us to process multiple pieces of data.[184] To make thoughtful evaluations, the brain needs time to recall diverse bits of data, compare them, group pieces of information into larger chunks of partial judgments, and ultimately yield a reasoned response. Researchers have repeatedly established that time pressure induces reflexive System One thinking rather than more reflective System Two processes.[185]

For students, evaluating a professor's teaching requires more complex deliberation than most faculty members realize. As instructors, our beliefs about the teaching process are omnipresent.

---

[179] Other mechanisms may also contribute to the high correlation between evaluations of teaching based on brief observations of a professor and end-of-semester evaluations of the same professor. Different theorists have suggested that first impressions may be accurate in this context, that those impressions may be self-reinforcing, or that students may be incapable of forming deeper, more considered assessments of teaching. *See* Ambady & Rosenthal, *supra* note 65; Clayson & Sheffet, *supra* note 21. The simplest explanation, however, may be the best: The mind draws upon first impressions as part of its System One thinking.

[180] *See* Kahneman, *supra* note 188, at 701; Zajonc, *supra* note 193, at 154–56.

[181] Kahneman, *supra* note 188, at 701 (citing Joseph E. LeDoux, *Emotion Circuits in the Brain,* 23 ANN. REV. NEUROSCIENCE 155 (2000)).

[182] Many law school forms, paralleling those used in other university departments, ask students both to make numeric ratings and to offer comments. The forms, however, almost invariably seek numeric ratings before comments, channeling the brain into fairly simplistic "good/bad" thinking. The number of students who offer comments, moreover, almost always falls far short of those providing numerical scores.

[183] Klaus Oberauer & Reinhold Kliegl, *A Formal Model of Capacity Limits in Working Memory,* 55 J. MEMORY & LANGUAGE 601, 601 (2006).

[184] Some psychologists have concluded that the human brain can hold only four "chunks" of data in working memory at one time. *See, e.g.,* Nelson Cowan, *The Magical Number 4 in Short-Term Memory: A Reconsideration of Mental Storage Capacity,* 24 BEHAV. & BRAIN SCI. 87, 88 (2000). Other psychologists conceptualize the limits on working memory in other ways. *See id.* (noting seven alternative views); Oberauer & Kliegl, *supra* note 198, at 608 (proposing a particularly sophisticated model). All, however, agree that working memory is constrained.

[185] *See, e.g.,* Anton J. Dijker & Willem Koomen, *Stereotyping and Attitudinal Effects Under Time Pressure,* 26 EUR. J. SOC. PSYCHOL. 61, 72 (1996) (discussing how stereotypes exerted a greater role on decisions made under time pressure); Melissa L. Finucane et al., *The Affect Heuristic in Judgments of Risks and Benefits,* 13 J. BEHAV. DECISION MAKING 1, 1–8 (2000) (explaining that subjects perceived greater inverse relationship between risks and benefits of activities when considering them under time pressure than when assessing them without time pressure); Kahneman, *supra* note 188, at 711; David M. Sanbonmatsu & Russell H. Fazio, *The Role of Attitudes in Memory-Based Decision Making,* 59 J. PERSONALITY & SOC. PSYCHOL. 614, 614–22 (1990) (describing how impressions affect consumer decisions under time pressure).

They shape our class preparation as well as our actions in the classroom on a regular basis. Even if we do not focus consciously on how we teach, the process is salient to us. Students, however, concentrate on the product of our teaching rather than the process. They attend daily to what they are learning and what they still need to know; the underlying process is secondary. For students to evaluate a semester's worth of teaching, they must recall the assignments, lectures, explanations, and other characteristics of a professor's work, examine those memories from a new perspective, and judge their efficacy in achieving a variety of goals. Comprehensive, accurate, and reflective evaluations take more than five, ten, or even fifteen minutes.[186]

Finally, since the human brain has limited capacity, any cognitive distraction impairs System Two thinking. Laboratory research demonstrates that divided attention reduces reasoned thought and thus promotes reliance on intuitive, stereotyped, and other automatic System One processes.[187] People have trouble thinking about two issues at once or switching quickly from one mental task to another.

Students complete traditional teaching evaluations under tremendous cognitive load. They have just finished a challenging law school class. They may be filling gaps in their notes or digesting the professor's final comments.[188] With the end of the semester near, they probably are worried about their performance on final examinations. They may be thinking about an upcoming job interview, a meeting with a friend, or a reunion with family members; the mind offers a large number of distractions. Laboratory research suggests that even very small distractions, such as memorizing a nine digit number between tasks, can significantly reduce reflective thought and enhance reliance on stereotypes.[189] The cognitive demands that law students face are much more substantial than these distractions, virtually forcing them to rely on intuitive System One channels to complete teaching evaluations.

The key to more meaningful evaluations of teaching, in sum, lies in creating the circumstances that allow students to engage more reflective System Two thought processes before providing those insights. Students need time and mental space to transcend intuitive System One judgments. They need mental prompts to help them review the semester's work. Like all decision makers, they need assistance in moving beyond reflexive "good/bad" judgments. The final section of this Article explores how law schools might design such a system.

DEEPER THINKING, BETTER EVALUATION

The legal system, like all social structures, rests on judgments that individuals make about others. Lawyers decide which law graduates to hire and promote; clients choose which firms to retain. Negotiators appraise their opponents to calculate a successful offer, and deal makers judge how far they can press an advantage. Trial lawyers size up jurors while jurors assess lawyers, witnesses, and parties. Appellate advocates tailor their arguments to the bench while the judges register the advocate's sincerity. Student evaluations of teaching are just one type of interpersonal judgment occurring within a constant stream of judgments that individuals make about others.

---

[186] Although many professors allot ten to fifteen minutes of class time for students to complete evaluations, most faculty observe that students rarely use all of this time. Law students are anxious to move on to other tasks such as lunch, another class, reviewing their notes, or a meeting with a friend, and tend to complete these evaluation forms quickly.

[187] *See, e.g.,* Kahneman, *supra* note 188, at 711; C. Neil Macrae et al., *Creating Memory Illusions: Expectancy-Based Processing and the Generation of False Memories,* 10 MEMORY 63, 71–80 (2002); Sabine Sczesny & Ulrich Kühnen, *Meta-Cognition About Biological Sex and Gender-Stereotypic Physical Appearance: Consequences for the Assessment of Leadership Competence,* 30 PERSONALITY SOC. PSYCHOL. BULL. 13, 13, 17, 20 (2004).

[188] Conversely, if a professor distributes evaluations at the beginning of a class period, students may initially be focused on their previous class or the material they have come to discuss. They must put all of these thoughts aside to focus on evaluation.

[189] Sczesny & Kühnen, *supra* note 202, at 17, 20.

All of these social evaluations risk the biases described above. Humans rest their judgments of others on intuitive System One thinking. Nonverbal behaviors, filtered by social stereotypes, powerfully affect those assessments. Research that has identified aids to deliberative decision making in other contexts, therefore, can be used to design a process that promotes more reflective student evaluations of teaching. Moreover, reducing bias in student evaluations of teaching may illuminate paths to better decision making in other aspects of the legal profession.

At a minimum, thoughtful evaluation of teaching requires time and attention; otherwise, System Two thought processes fail to engage. Psychologists have identified a number of other conditions that promote more reflective, deliberative judgments. These include (1) encouraging decision makers to be as accurate as possible,[190] (2) focusing evaluators on the individuality of the person they are assessing,[191] (3) reminding decision makers to consider relevant data,[192] (4) facilitating group discussion of judgments,[193] and (5) establishing accountability to a third party.[194]

Although it is possible to identify workable processes that embrace the features that promote reflective, deliberative judgments, our current system of gathering student evaluations incorporates few, if any. Gregory Munro, for example, recommends using Small-Group Instructional Diagnosis ("SGID") to assess law school teaching.[195] In this process, a facilitator meets with small groups of students to gather their impressions of a course and instructor. The students discuss their perspectives as a group, expanding the information available to each student, checking individual biases, establishing accountability, and implicitly noting the seriousness of the process and need for accuracy.[196] These group discussions reduce cognitive overload by focusing attention and providing adequate time for thoughtful assessment.

To achieve the best results, the facilitator meets with the faculty member before these group discussions, obtaining information about the course goals, the subject matter, and the professor's pedagogic strategies.[197] The faculty member may provide a brief written statement of his or her teaching objectives, offering students further focus for their discussion. A professor may also note issues that troubled him or her during the semester, inviting student feedback on those matters.

Students who participate in these small-group discussions applaud them enthusiastically.[198] Indeed, research suggests that students do not like traditional, end-of-semester written evaluations, but prefer group discussions that promote dialogue with the professor.[199] Group discussions more

---

190 Mary E. Wheeler & Susan T. Fiske, *Controlling Racial Prejudice: Social-Cognitive Goals Affect Amygdala and Stereotype Activation,* 16 PSYCHOL. SCI. 56, 57 (2005).

191 Wheeler & Fiske, *supra* note 205, at 57.

192 Kahneman, *supra* note 188, at 711–12.

193 Richard F. Martell & Keith N. Leavitt, *Reducing the Performance-Cue Bias in Work Behavior Ratings: Can Groups Help?,* 87 J. APPLIED PSYCHOL. 1032, 1033–34 (2002).

194 Thomas E. Ford et al., *The Role of Accountability in Suppressing Managers' Preinterview Bias Against African-American Sales Job Applicants,* 24 J. PERS. SELLING & SALES MGMT. 113, 113–24 (2004); Wheeler & Fiske, *supra* note 205, at 57.

195 GREGORY S. MUNRO, OUTCOMES ASSESSMENT FOR LAW SCHOOLS 136 (2000). Professors Gerald Hess and Eric Orts have each adopted similar techniques to gather ongoing feedback from law students. *See generally* Gerald F. Hess, *Student Involvement in Improving Law Teaching and Learning,* 67 UMKC L. REV. 343 (1998) (referring to the groups as "Student Advisory Teams"); Eric W. Orts, *Quality Circles in Law Teaching,* 47 J. LEGAL EDUC. 425, 425–26 (1997) (describing his classroom use of "quality circles"). The technique derives from management tools developed by Edward Deming and implemented by Japanese industries and other businesses worldwide. *See* Hess, *supra,* at 347–48; Orts, *supra,* at 425–26.

196 *See* MUNRO, *supra* note 210, at 137.

197 *See id.* at 136.

198 *See, e.g.,* Robert D. Abbott et al., *Satisfaction with Processes of Collecting Student Opinions About Instruction: The Student Perspective,* 82 J. EDUC. PSYCHOL. 201, 203–206 (1990); Hess, *supra* note 210, at 351–52, 355–61; Orts, *supra* note 210, at 425.

199 *See, e.g.,* Abbott et al., *supra* note 213, at 201–06. That dialogue may not occur directly. When evaluating faculty for tenure or promotion, especially, it is better to use another faculty member to facilitate the student discussion. Faculty, however, can establish an ongoing discussion with their own students about their teaching, and can teach in a manner that is responsive to students' concerns.

thoughtfully involve students in assessment and underscore the school's interest in their input. Students have the opportunity to view the purposes of legal education from a perspective different from their own, often enhancing their own educational commitment and learning strategies.

Faculty members also learn more from these discussions than they do from standard teaching evaluations. Thoughtful discussion with students who possess awareness of the professor's pedagogic objectives produces more detailed and informative feedback. With modest training, law faculty can successfully facilitate these sessions for one another. As they do so, they broaden their personal knowledge of classroom techniques, student responses, and pedagogic successes or failures. The process of facilitation and evaluation may create an ongoing dialogue among faculty, underscoring their joint commitment to teaching.

Small group discussion of teaching can also inform broader curricular goals within the law school. Faculty members have few opportunities to consider the curriculum as a whole, or even the significance of their courses within a student's three-year law school career. Discussions of a particular course and instructor can include questions about why the students took the course, how it fit within their broader educational goals, how prepared they feel for advanced offerings in the area, and whether they would have preferred a different type of offering. These individual discussions can fuel broader curricular reflections within the school.

This type of faculty review, of course, takes more time than traditional student evaluations. Most institutions would find it difficult to evaluate every course every semester using small group discussions. It is unlikely, however, that schools genuinely need to assess every course and faculty member that frequently.[200] Schools might aim to evaluate each course once every three years, meaning that about one-sixth of the curriculum would undergo full evaluation each semester. Faculty eligible for tenure or promotion could be evaluated somewhat more frequently. The current evaluation system produces a large amount of data every semester, but those data have limited value. Generating smaller amounts of high-quality information would better serve institutional needs.[201]

Schools can require faculty members to continue gathering regular feedback for formative purposes in every course they teach.[202] Some faculty may do this with conventional written evaluations, although schools should explain the drawbacks of these forms. Other professors may use a modified version of the Small-Group Instructional Diagnosis, conducted by the faculty member himself or herself during the semester.[203] Other techniques for assessing one's own performance include "minute paper[s]" and informal evaluation forms designed by the professor.[204] Students particularly like these techniques when they are used mid-semester, with the faculty member responding to student suggestions.[205]

Informal evaluations of this nature would allow students to comment regularly on all courses while giving faculty members useful feedback in time to implement changes. Indeed, students

---

[200] Research suggests that even students tire of the number and repetitiveness of the evaluation forms they complete. *See, e.g.,* Abbott et al., *supra* note 213, at 201.

[201] Students currently devote about fifteen minutes per course—a total of seventy-five minutes per semester for students enrolled in five courses—to completing faculty evaluations. Thus, requiring each student instead to participate in one small group evaluation session would consume no more of the students' time while giving students a more satisfying experience and generating more productive evaluations.

[202] Evaluators distinguish between "formative" and "summative" evaluations. Formative evaluations are used to inform an ongoing process, such as a class, and help adapt the process to the participants' needs. Summative evaluations are used to evaluate an experience once it has concluded.

[203] *See* Hess, *supra* note 210, at 343 (describing a Student Advisory Team as "a group of students who meet periodically with the teacher to help the teacher improve the course"); Orts, *supra* note 210, at 425–27 (discussing the structure of "quality circles," groups that meet with the professor regularly throughout the semester and are comprised of student representatives, either voluntary or elected, of the entire class).

[204] *See* Hess, *supra* note 210, at 346.

[205] *See* Abbott et al., *supra* note 213, at 205.

would gain more from these formative evaluations—because they allow a faculty member to respond and adapt—than they do from the current overload of summative assessments that are used primarily to rate faculty after a course has finished. This combination, then, of informal evaluations administered by the professor, used to inform his or her teaching, with small group assessments in selected classes each semester, would give students the broadest opportunity to provide feedback on instruction and benefit from that process.[206]

Student-centered methods of instructional evaluation can also fit within a broader framework that includes teaching assessments offered by colleagues, alumni, education experts, and professors themselves.[207] Evaluation scholars repeatedly stress the need to complement student evaluations with other forms of assessment. Yet traditional student evaluations, so easily implemented and appearing to generate "hard" data, predictably overwhelm these other techniques. Shifting the nature of student evaluations will allow faculties to match those assessments more effectively with those offered by other evaluators.

Given the multiple benefits of replacing conventional student evaluations with more meaningful processes, law school faculties should commit any time required to work out the details of small group discussions or other new methods of evaluating teaching.[208] As scholars, we criticize others for adopting "quick fixes" rather than expending the time and resources needed for meaningful evaluations and fair processes. We should be willing to apply the same standards to ourselves. Failing to do so is particularly unjust to our minority colleagues, who appear to suffer disproportionately from current evaluation systems.[209] It is also unfair to students, who deserve both to be heard more effectively on teaching quality and to learn to thrive under instructors representing diverse races, cultures, and backgrounds.

Improving our method of evaluating teaching is not a panacea for eliminating bias and the role of intuitive judgments in that process. Stereotypes affect how we remember information, as well as how we perceive it.[210] Reasoned decisions remain anchored in first judgments, giving

---

[206] It is essential, however, that formative evaluations remain informal, confidential exercises between the professor and students enrolled in the course. Including these assessments in evaluations of faculty for promotion, salary increases, or other purposes would undercut the goals of the small group discussion process.

[207] *See* Filippa Marullo Anzalone, *It All Begins with You: Improving Law School Learning Through Professional Self-Awareness and Critical Reflection,* 24 HAMLINE L. REV. 324, 371 (2001) ("The responsibility of the legal academy is to provide the forum and incentives for faculty to become better teachers ...."); Laurie A. Babin et al., *Teaching Portfolios: Uses and Development,* 24 J. MARKETING EDUC. 35, 40 (2002) (explaining how statements from a teacher's colleagues, alumni of the institution, or clients of students in client-based classes "can provide evidence of effective teaching"); Gerald F. Hess, *Improving Teaching and Learning in Law School: Faculty Development Research, Principles, and Programs,* 12 WIDENER L. REV. 443, 458–61 (2006) (describing different ways that one's colleagues can contribute to faculty development); Melissa J. Marlow, *Blessed Are They Who Teach an Upper-Level Course, for They Shall Earn Higher Student Ratings,* 7 FLA. COASTAL L. REV. 553, 574–75 (2006) (suggesting that experts be used to evaluate teachers). *See generally* Daniel Gordon, *Does Law Teaching Have Meaning? Teaching Effectiveness, Gauging Alumni Competence, and the MacCrate Report,* 25 FORDHAM URB. L.J. 43 (1997) (comparing the usefulness of student evaluations and alumni surveys); Markovits, *supra* note 22 (discussing the use of market indicators to determine an academic's teaching skill).

[208] Law faculty and other scholars who have already devoted considerable attention to these details have cleared the way. *See, e.g.,* Hess, *supra* note 210, at 354 (describing the steps taken by one professional throughout the Student Advisory Team process); Orts, *supra* note 210, at 427.

[209] *See supra* notes 2–4 and accompanying text. Especially disheartening is the dearth, despite the extensive research and scholarly commentary on teaching evaluations, of studies focusing on the influence of race on these evaluations. Katherine Grace Hendrix, who conducted one of the few exploratory studies in this area, commented: "[R]esearchers have overlooked the classroom experiences of teachers and professors of color. In particular, the experience of being a member of a subordinate minority functioning as a professional within a predominantly White educational environment has escaped the interest of the White social scientist." Katherine Grace Hendrix, *Student Perceptions of the Influence of Race on Professor Credibility,* 28 J. BLACK STUD. 738, 739 (1998) (citation omitted); *see also* Huston, *supra* note 24, at 600–01 (commenting on the scarcity of research related to racial biases in student evaluations). Law schools have an opportunity to lead the rest of the academy in identifying and remedying these biases.

[210] *See* Levinson, *supra* note 143, at 11, 22–28.

those initial impressions lasting power.[211] Stereotypes based on race, gender, and class are persistent and resist efforts to overcome them. A professor's reputation, shaped in part by stereotypes, may influence even reasoned discussions.[212] And some influences on teaching evaluations, such as students' tendency to downgrade faculty who have graded them negatively,[213] fall outside the scope of the biases discussed in this Article. Progress in any field, however, requires taking small steps. If we do not attempt to improve the quality of our decision making, we remain trapped forever at its lowest levels.

CONCLUSION

Law and legal education assume reflective, rational decision making. Yet psychologists have shown that most of our judgments originate with intuitive preferences. The human brain reacts automatically to nonverbal behaviors and other subtle cues in the environment. Social stereotypes further shape our perceptions on an unconscious level. Creating conditions that support deliberative, reflective thinking is much harder than we believe.

As educators, we can take an important step toward understanding the interplay of intuitive and analytic thinking by examining those processes in the context of routine teaching evaluations. Those assessments draw heavily on the brain's automatic processes, allowing minor stylistic mannerisms and stereotypes to color ratings. Designing evaluation systems that prompt more reflective, rational input would accord students' enhanced respect, improve instruction, and treat faculty colleagues more fairly. Exploring such systems will also increase our own understanding of the intricate processes that drive decision making, knowledge we can apply to almost every field of law.

---

[211] *See* Kahneman, *supra* note 188, at 712.

[212] The few studies on the influence of instructor reputation on current evaluation systems find a very strong effect. *See generally* Bryan W. Griffin, *Instructor Reputation and Student Ratings of Instruction,* 26 CONTEMP. EDUC. PSYCHOL. 534 (2001) (discussing how instructor reputation correlated significantly with end-of-semester ratings, even after controlling for numerous other factors). It is possible that this effect would shape other modes of evaluation as well.

[213] *See supra* note 25.

CHAPTER 6

The Limitations of Measuring Student Learning

Patrick Moore, University of Arkansas at Little Rock
Ronald E. Flinn, Creighton University*

A key problem in higher education is measuring student learning. How do we know if graduates (e.g., especially accounting graduates) are learning what they should from a specific class? One answer is, we do not always know for sure about a specific class, but we do have some general information about how much students are learning in their college careers. This article discusses the limitations of measuring student learning in individual classes. We discuss how problems with Student Evaluations of Teaching (SET), grade inflation, course content deflation, the prestige economy of higher education, and faculty self-protection can help us understand the difficulties of measuring student learning.

Before we get to those topics, a more basic question is, why should we be concerned about measuring student learning? We all know that students learn. People in general are genetically hard-wired to adapt and learn. In addition, we also know that the typical college graduate knows more than other people. As Bok (2006, 8) has written,

> Countless studies have found that college students, overall, achieve significant gains in critical thinking, general knowledge, moral reasoning, quantitative skills, and other competencies. Most seniors agree that they have made substantial intellectual progress. The marketplace affirms these conclusions by giving large additional rewards to those who carry their education beyond high school to acquire a B.A. degree.

Given this reasonably rosy picture, why are so many people and accrediting bodies concerned today about measuring student learning and assessment in general?

One reason is national competitiveness. Mounting evidence suggests that other nations are outperforming the United States in higher education (Hebel 2006). The problem in the sciences and engineering is especially acute. In 2005, the National Bureau of Economic Research predicted that China will generate more science and engineering doctorates than the U.S. by 2010 (Hargrove 2005). The number of scientific and engineering articles published by the European Union between

* Patrick Moore is Associate Professor of English at the University of Arkansas at Little Rock, and Ronald Flinn is Associate Professor of Accounting at Creighton University.

1988 and 2003 outstripped the rate of publications of such articles by the U.S. beginning in 1998 (National Science Foundation 2006). These trends do not speak well for the international competitiveness of the U.S.

Another reason for concern about measuring student learning is complaints from business and industry about accounting graduates. Vangermeersch (2000) published an article on the decline in the quantity and quality of accounting majors. A recent panel discussion in *CPA Journal* titled, "Meeting of the Minds," discussed problems with some of the skill deficiencies of recent college graduates in accounting (Kranacher and Barragato 2008). More generally, a report from the College Board titled, *Writing: A ticket to work ... or a ticket out: A Survey of Business leaders* (2004), listed many complaints from business leaders. Quible and Griffin (2007) find that many college graduates cannot use the English language well.

Still another reason for concern about measuring student learning is the general decline in literacy, as evidenced by the National Center for Educational Statistics (NCES) (2008) data about the Adult National Literacy Survey and the Graduate Record Examination (GRE) results, and the general anxiety about the quality of U.S. higher education. Some of that general anxiety is captured in the titles of Bok's book, *Our Underachieving Colleges* (2006), Hersh and Merrow's book, *Declining by Degrees* (2005), Bacchetti and Ehrlich's book, *Reconnecting Education and Foundations* (2007), and Bauerlein's book, *The Dumbest Generation* (2008). The sweepingly general trends in these data do not give us specific information about individual classes or professors, but they suggest that all is not well.

The next five sections of this article discuss how problems with Student Evaluations of Teaching (SET), grade inflation, course content deflation, the prestige economy of higher education, and faculty self-protection help to create many of the difficulties of measuring individual student learning in specific classes.

STUDENT RATINGS OF PROFESSORS

How do we know if accounting graduates are learning anything from an accounting class? One answer to this question is to ask the students to rate their professors at the end of the term. But students have notorious problems with evaluating teaching effectiveness and classroom performance. See Crumbley and Smith, herein.

Several such problems are quickly apparent to anyone who visits the online SET site RateMyProfessors.com. RateMyProfessors.com claims "Over 6,000 schools, one million professors, 6 million opinions." The evaluations for individual professors include scores for "Easiness," "Helpfulness," "Clarity," "Rater Interest," and "Hotness." There is no rating for "knowledge obtained."

Moore spent several hours looking at ratings for accounting professors. He used two limiting criteria, but otherwise selected the professors below at random, looking for professors at large universities with nine or more evaluations. RateMyProfessors.com lists its anonymous student responses by most recent evaluation first. The order of these entries below is reversed, and errors of spelling, punctuation, and grammar have not been corrected. Here are some examples of the findings:

Accounting Department, University of Oklahoma, selected responses about Professor A (Anonymous 2008a):

> Student 1: "I thought she was terrible. Seems she suffers from burnout and disinterest therefore her students suffer. I thought her exams were very difficult and lecture very bad. I don't think she could work the problems on her own or without an answer key."

Student 2: "Very helpful and quite knowledgeable about the subject material ... but, the class is dull. You have to bust your butt to make an A, but with hard work it is possible. Do not blow this class off, [the professor] will eat you alive if you do!"

Student 3: "The lady is batty as hell. Go over old tests. The class isn't too bad but it feels like her talking never ends."

Accounting Department, University of Minnesota, selected responses about Professor B (Anonymous 2008b):

Student 1: "Accounting Nazi ... nuff said!"

Student 2: "[Professor] is an accounting machine, theres no question about that. His lectures are fast-paced but surprisingly coherent. Pay attention and come to class. His tests and assignments are ridiculously hard, but I still ended up doing ok without cracking open the book or doing any practice problems. With a little more effort, it should be easy to do well."

Student 3: "All you babies shouldn't be in the accounting field if you can't get A's on his test because they aren't that hard. The purpose of these courses are to weed people out of the field. Apparently there needs to be more weeding because there are too many babies in the accounting courses"

Accounting Department, University of Alabama, selected responses about Professor C (Anonymous 2008c):

Student 1: "I don't know what happened to her. She was my AC210 teacher and she was awesome, but now that she makes the test, the class is all but impossible. Hardest test I have ever taken. I would recommend her for AC210 but don't get her for any upper division class."

Student 2: "Well, I don't think shes that hot, good bod yes, everything else .. not so much. Anyways about her class. Its really easy. Go to lab and go to class .. it really does affect your grade .. but it's a really easy class. Everything is done online .. the tests are JUST like the homework .. same problems different numbers. Easy A."

Student 3: "If you have to take AC210 this is the teacher to have! She explains the material so everyone can understand what is going on and makes it interesting! Plus she tells you what to study for the quizzes and tests. Best teacher I've ever had! She even gives out candy sometimes :o)"

Accounting Department, University of Kansas, selected responses about Professor D (Anonymous 2008d):

Student 1: "This is a really hard class and he knows what he's talking about he just can't communicate. He is really boring and mumbles.

Student 2: "He is a huge bore. It was almost painful going to class and listening to his mumbled rants. P.U. you stink! You're better off digging ditches or working in a deli, a boring deli."

Student 3: "What are you guys talking about. [Uses professor's first name] is my favorite teacher in the whole wide world. I think he is ****. Count it."

Accounting Department, Baylor University, selected responses about Professor E (Anonymous 2008e):

Student 1: "She's a great teacher. Students that don't like her usually do not attend class very often. If you don't go to class without telling her before, she will not cut you any slack.

She is very organized and clearly explains everything you are tested on. To get an A all you have to do is go to class and do the homework. Definately [sic] recommend he[r]."

Student 2: "I have no idea exactly why [Prof. E] is still teaching. Her style is not effective. She did not appreciate students asking each other for help with what was just said, nor will repeat her statement when asked. The berating of students did not encourage respect. Pacing of her classes is not planned well. Not acceptable conduct for real world."

Accounting Department, Western Illinois University, selected responses about Professor F (Anonymous 2008f):

Student 1: "nice lady, bad teacher doesn't explain anything. if material isn't covered in enough time before a test she just flies through it."

Student 2: "she is so hot! and she is a really good teacher. however, the material covered is pretty tough. i suggest never missing a class"

Some of the student remarks in these evaluations are so irrelevant, petty, irresponsible, and gleefully insulting, and they show such a poor command of the English language, that it is hard to imagine how they could be taken seriously by anyone or be useful, even as a formative device (i.e., as a means to improve teaching). At best they are a kind of sport or entertainment. But SET are most often used in promotion and tenure decisions, sometimes as the only or the key measure of teaching effectiveness (Stone 1996).

The problems exhibited in these evaluations are well known to critics of student evaluations of teachers. As Chonko (2006, 5) states,

Research tells us that students, as evaluators

- May focus on a critical incident.
- Often don't distinguish between learning and grades.
- May evaluate teachers based on perceived similarity.
- Can be influenced by prior performance in other classes.
- May focus on style differences that relate to the match of teaching and learning styles without consideration that other learning styles may be preferred by other students in the class.
- May allow emotions to influence their ratings.
- May base evaluations on perceived friendship with teacher.
- May base evaluations on expected grade received in the course which can change any time a grade is received.

The previous small selection of quotations illustrates many of these eight points. One quotation focused on a critical incident (professor C passing out candy). One does not appear to distinguish between learning and grades (the remark about professor B: "His tests and assignments are ridiculously hard, but I still ended up doing ok without cracking open the book or doing any practice problems"). One mentioned the professor's prior performance in another class (the remark about professor C, "I don't know what happened to her. She was my AC210 teacher and she was awesome, but now ..."). Several were emotional (e.g., the remark that professor A "is batty as hell"; the remark that professor B is an "Accounting Nazi"; the remark about professor F that "she is so hot"). At least one suggested friendship by using the professor's first name (i.e., professor D). One appeared to base the evaluation on the expected grade (i.e., in another class, professor C "was awesome, but now that she makes the test, the class is all but impossible").

In addition to the problems mentioned by Chonko (2006), another issue with SET is that professors have many financial and professional incentives to manipulate them (Martin 1998; Wallace and Wallace 1998). Several experiments have demonstrated this point emphatically. Perhaps the best known is "The Doctor Fox Lecture" (Naftulin et al. 1973). One of the authors of the experiment taught an actor to teach charismatically on a subject about which he knew nothing. The topic of the bogus Doctor Fox's lecture was "Mathematical Game Theory as Applied to Physician Education" (1973, 631). Doctor Fox's lecture and question-and-answer period consisted of "an excessive use of double talk, neologisms, non sequiturs, and contradictory statements," all of which were "interspersed with parenthetical humor and meaningless references to unrelated topics" (1973, 631–32). Eleven psychiatrists, psychologists, and social worker educators heard Doctor Fox's initial presentation, which was videotaped and later presented to 44 other education and administration professionals in two showings.

After viewing the lecture, all the members of the audience were given questionnaires to evaluate the bogus doctor's presentation. The authors discovered that there were many more favorable than unfavorable responses. In addition, one audience member even claimed to have read one of the bogus doctor's non-existent publications. The authors of the Dr. Fox essay made several points, one of which was that even professional educators "can be effectively 'seduced' into an illusion of having learned if the lecturer simulates a style of authority and wit ..." (1973, 633). One of the limitations of the Doctor Fox Lecture is that it was a single lecture. Newton (1988, 9) has said that "subsequent research has substantially discredited this phenomenon in the actual classroom situation," where students can observe a speaker over a period of many weeks.

Almost a quarter of a century later, Williams and Ceci (1997) described their own experiment in seduction. Ceci had attended a faculty workshop at his university in which the leader recommended more enthusiasm in teaching to boost a professor's effectiveness in the classroom. After he finished, Ceci decided to test the validity of the workshop leader's advice. Ceci taught two sections of the same class in the exact same way, with only two stylistic differences. In one section, Ceci taught his normal way. In the second section, he "spoke with more pitch variability and used more gestures while lecturing, the 'enthusiastic style' recommended in the teaching skills workshop" (1997, 16). Williams and Ceci then gave exactly the same evaluation instruments to students in the two sections at the end of each course to see if there were differences. The differences were startling. For evaluation questions such as "How knowledgeable is the instructor," "How accessible is the instructor outside of class time," "How organized is the instructor," "How much did you learn in this course," and so on, the section in which Ceci used more vocal pitch variability and gestures received much higher evaluations. What was most amazing was that only changing his vocal pitch and adding gestures earned Ceci much higher evaluations on points such as instructor accessibility outside of class time. Ceci had not changed his accessibility outside of the class time. Ceci's minimal changes do not speak well for students' ability to correctly rate professors on how much they learn in a course.

In spite of the fact that SET are easy to manipulate, SET scores are now critically important to a professor's career. One's performance on them can make or break an instructor on annual evaluations and on promotion and tenure decisions. Early in their essay, Williams and Ceci (1997, 14) remarked parenthetically,

> Coincidentally, while writing this article, one of us heard from a friend elsewhere who was just denied tenure by a university review committee on the heels of a unanimously positive departmental vote. The reason? 'Below-average' course evaluations.

Stone (1996, 195) reported that he earned tenure in accounting even though a member of his university's tenure and promotion committee told him that "low teaching ratings almost led to your downfall." The same committee member told Stone that "the **only** measure of teaching **ever** considered by the University Promotion and Tenure Committee" (195; emphasis in text) was the one-dimensional response in the SET form to the statement, "Rate the instructor's overall teaching effectiveness" (195).

Because SET now loom so large in evaluating teaching effectiveness in academia, instructors often try to exploit their limitations. Neath (1996, 1366) explains that one instructor of his acquaintance tells his students the following when distributing end-of-term SET: "These evaluations will be used by the administration to determine whether my children, ages 4 and 6, will eat for the next 6 months." Neath unabashedly titles his essay on SET, "How to improve your teaching evaluations without improving your teaching." He lists 20 "tips" including "Be Male," "Be Organized," "Administer ratings before tests," "Entertain," "Cross-listings are bad," "Required courses are bad," "Teach only male students," "Be like your students," "Teach what they want and how they want it," and "Pick successful students," among others.

Many problems with SET will be difficult to resolve. One problem is measuring student achievement. As Johnson (2003, 152) says, "One reason that items on teacher-course evaluations are not more often tied to measures of student achievement is that there are no universally agreed-upon measures of student achievement." Neath (1996, 1364) is also aware of the problem: "In practice, there is no agreed-upon definition or criterion measure of effective teaching." After remarking that "the use of SET as the single or even most important factor in administrative evaluation of teaching effectiveness may be in conflict with good organizational control practice as taught by departments of accounting," Newton (1988, 11) adds, "Still, it is important here to note that no other single measure of teaching performance (or for that matter, other performance measures in the social sciences) has been shown to be highly valid." Given the emphasis on professorial individuality and autonomy in American higher education, the problem of accurately measuring student learning may never be solved to the satisfaction of many people.

GRADE INFLATION

Grade inflation is another important limitation on measuring student learning. If an instructor's grade at the end of a term is ***not*** an accurate measure of how much the student has learned, then how can grades be useful descriptors of a student's learning (Zimmerman 2002)?

Evidence of the existence of grade inflation in individual institutions of higher education in the U.S. is considerable. Johnson (2003) has written an entire book on the subject with considerable evidence of grade inflation. Rosovsky and Hartley (2002) have discussed some of the more elaborate studies of grade inflation. For example, one survey of 180 colleges showed that from 1960–1974 the average GPA increased 0.432 or almost one half a grade point (4). A second survey of 4,900 undergraduates showed that grades of A− or above increased from 7 to 26 percent, while C's or below decreased from 25 to 9 percent (4). Rosovsky and Hartley discussed a third survey of 52,256 college students, which showed that grades rose from 3.07 to 3.343 (4). An Internet website, gradeinflation.com, authored by Stuart Rojstaczer, has documented grade inflation at dozens of U.S. colleges and universities. The data show a clear rise in grades in several dozen colleges from 1967 to 2002. The site was last updated in March 2003. In summary, as Bok (2006, 305) says, "Colleges have allowed widespread grade inflation and shown increased tolerance of late or incomplete work."

Evidence shows that some accounting faculty inflate grades. For example, in Yunker and Yunker's (2003, 313) study on the influence of SET, they discovered that their research:

> strengthens some faculty members' concern that widespread and significant application of student teacher evaluations in faculty performance evaluation may be partially responsible for the interrelated phenomena of grade inflation and content debasement.

Addy and Herring (1996) found evidence of grade inflation when their school mandated a minimum grade point average in upper division accounting classes. Accounting faculty helped weaker students meet the minimum grade point average by inflating grades (1996, 11). A study of grade distributions at a private Midwestern U.S. university over a 15-year period by Cluskey et al. (1997) found evidence of grade inflation in the university as a whole and in the business school, and evidence of grade inflation in one of the four senior-level accounting courses.

Grade inflation creates many problems. It often creates higher evaluations for faculty on SET, at least in the short-run, but research suggests that higher student evaluations are not correlated with higher rates of learning. Instead, stringent grading is associated with higher rates of learning. For example, in their survey of accounting students, Yunker and Yunker (2003, 316) found the following:

> [C]ontrolling for ability-achievement at the individual student level, in this research we found that students in Intermediate Accounting I who have been in Introductory Accounting II courses in which the teacher has been rated more highly tend to do worse than students who have been in Introductory Accounting II courses in which the teacher has been rated less highly. ... In short, this research points toward potential invalidity of student evaluations of teaching in accounting education and suggests that they be applied cautiously in faculty performance evaluation.

Similarly, interpreting his research data from a survey of Duke University students, Johnson (2003, 161) said, "both the item that probed stringency of grading practices and the average grade in the prerequisite course suggest that stringent grading is associated with higher levels of achievement in follow-on courses." Buying higher student evaluations with inflated grades and deflated course content may help faculty careers in the short term, but the cost of such practices can be lower levels of achievement for students and a lack of respect for college and university education in general.

In addition to reducing student learning and achievement, the different levels of grade inflation in academic disciplines create destructive pressures on the distribution of resources in higher education. Johnson (2003, 237) says, "That grading practices differ systematically between disciplines is beyond dispute. Humanities faculty tend to grade most leniently; social sciences faculty, with the exception of economists, are approximately grade neutral; and economics, mathematics, and natural sciences faculty tend to grade most stringently." One result of such grading practices is to encourage students to avoid technical courses in the sciences, mathematics, and economics, and enroll in easier humanities courses. "As a consequence only of differences in grading practices between academic fields, American undergraduates take, on average, about 50% fewer elective courses in the natural sciences and mathematics than they would if grading practices across disciplines were more equitable" (Johnson 2003, 238). Discouraging American undergraduates from taking courses in sciences and mathematics reduces America's potential for technological and scientific innovation, and it affects national competitiveness in the global information economy.

One important purpose of grades is to tell future employers or graduate admissions committees if a student is hard-working and intelligent. As Pressman (2007, 97) states, "Grades differentiate the performance of students. If almost all students receive an A, this differentiation does not happen. And if one faculty member gives mainly A's but others do not, prospective employers and graduate schools cannot know whether students received good grades because they are bright and worked hard, or because they sought out faculty members who give mainly A's." For grades to serve their social function, they must be accurate. Too often they are not.

COURSE CONTENT DEFLATION

Many writers, past and present, are concerned with dumbed-down classes in American higher education. Here is a brief but representative sample of some titles:

The Dumbest Generation (Bauerlein 2008)
"Why Johnny Can't Write" (Sheils 1975)
"Students Know Less after 4 College Years" (Karni 2007)
Our Underachieving Colleges: A Candid Look at How Much Students Learn and Why They Should Be Learning More (Bok 2006)
Declining By Degree: Higher Education at Risk (Hersch and Merrow 2005)
"The dumbing down of higher education" (Simon 1996)
"Are writing deficiencies creating a lost generation of business writers?" (Quible and Griffin 2007)
"Reduced rigor and grade inflation diminish the quality and credibility of higher education" (Zimmerman 2002).

In spite of these and other works, the evidence for course content deflation is weak at best, in part because it is hard to compare what professors do in courses with what should occur in courses. Some evidence shows that students make intellectual gains from their college educations. For example, the subject matter tests of the Graduate Record Examination (GRE) (National Center for Education Statistics 2008) show that scores in Biology and Chemistry have increased from 1965 to 2006. Similarly, the Quantitative and Analytical reasoning portions of the general portion of the GRE have risen significantly over a period of several decades. On the other hand, Juhn, Kim, and Vella (2005, 303) "find some weak evidence that college graduate men from highly educated cohorts earn a relatively smaller wage premium even controlling for the relative supply effect," a result that suggests the possibility of course content deflation. Other evidence (see below) shows that the quality of student education is falling off in some areas.

One reason for the lack of clarity about course content deflation is the difficulty of obtaining concrete data. Unlike course content, grades are abstractions recorded for each student for each class taken. Grades can be easily converted into numbers, which can be added, multiplied, divided, and otherwise manipulated mathematically in the usual ways. To discover if grade inflation exists, a researcher can perform simple mathematical operations at different times to see if grades have changed at a given university over a period of years. Course content, however, is not recorded in any quantifiable way in student records. Course content varies from one section of a class to another and over time because classes are often taught by different faculty. In addition, course content can vary with the same professor, because faculty will try new things or better approaches to teaching content from term to term for the same course. As Bok (2006, 319) explains, it is "all but impossible to measure or compare" data from today with data from earlier times.

Although comparative evidence is lacking in many subject areas, there is clear evidence that the communication skills of college graduates are decreasing. The 2003 National Assessment of Adult Literacy (Kutner et al. 2007) showed that college graduates in 2003 were less literate than a cohort ten years earlier. The National Center for Education Statistics (2008) lists the Graduate Record Exam scores for the Verbal, Quantitative, and Analytical tests from 1965 to 2006. The mean Verbal test score was 530 in 1965 and 465 in 2006, a significant decline. Nie and Golde (2008, 61) analyzed data from the General Social Survey and found "that the verbal ability of graduates of all levels of education had decreased over time." The caption to Figure 5 in their article reads, "As higher percentages of men and women received 12 or more years of education, their average vocabulary scores did not rise but fell" (62).

There is also survey evidence that business leaders are unhappy with the writing skills of new hires (Quible and Griffin 2007). The College Board report, *Writing: A ticket to work ... or a ticket out: A Survey of Business leaders* (2004, 14) had many negative comments about the writing abilities of new college graduates. Here are a few:

"The skills of new college graduates are deplorable—across the board; spelling, grammar, sentence structure ... I can't believe people come out of college now not knowing what a sentence is."

"Recent graduates aren't even aware when things are wrong (singular/plural agreement, run-on sentences, and the like). I'm amazed they got through college."

"Recent graduates may be trained in academic writing, but we find that kind of writing too verbose and wandering."

Deficiencies in writing skills are a special concern for accounting professionals. In a recent panel discussion titled, "Meeting of the Minds," several participants mentioned that recent college graduates needed better writing skills (Kranacher and Barragato 2008). At least for writing skills, the opening sentence of Sheils' *Newsweek* (1975, 58) article still rings true: "If your children are attending college, the chances are that when they graduate they will be unable to write ordinary, expository English with any real degree of structure and lucidity." In our experience, students have deficient writing skills because they have little required writing to do in many classes, because faculty teaching large classes do not have the time and inclination to correct student writing carefully, because faculty are reluctant to give low grades for poor writing in content areas that are not focused on writing skills, because faculty fear retaliation on SET for low grades, and because students in many content areas such as business, science, and engineering believe that secretaries, editors, and professional writers will correct their writing for them when they get jobs in the workplace. Quible and Griffin (2007) suggest that some deficiencies in student writing are caused by English teachers who do not see themselves as "grammar police" (2007, 33) correcting sentence-level errors in student writing, and by English teachers who do not like to teach grammar.

Evidence for or against course content deflation in college accounting courses is ambiguous. The earlier reference to the Yunker and Yunker (2003) study on the influence of SET suggests that grade inflation and course content deflation are interrelated (313). Vangermeersch (2000, 52–54) also believes that accounting courses have been dumbed down. Several of the concerns in his article, "Fifty Reasons for the decline in the quantity and quality of accounting majors," point to course deflation, for example: "De-emphasized writing skills," "White paper ruled out detail-oriented persons," "Rejection of teaching the basics of accounting," "Accounting teachers bored by details," "Failure to stress mastery of the subject," "Laissez-faire attitudes on attendance and homework," and "No basic building blocks of learning in accounting." On the other hand, a longitudinal study of accounting students by Nelson et al. (2006, 1) says, "Measures of student quality continue to rise." This aforementioned article follows on the heels of an earlier essay by Nelson et al. (2002, 283), an article in which the authors took note of the accounting profession's concerns about the quality of college majors in accounting and concluded thus: "as measured by self-reported GPAs and standardized entrance examination scores, student quality appears to be rising." The 2006 essay by Nelson et al. suggests that the Federation of Schools of Accountancy (FSA) continue to conduct such a survey periodically (14).

Derek Bok (2006, 318) may have the last word on course content deflation: "no one knows whether college students are writing better or thinking more rigorously or making greater progress toward other educational goals than they were 50 years ago." But this is not a satisfactory outcome. Many people, including accounting professors and working accounting professionals, believe that course content has become deflated. But there is no certain evidence to decide the case one way or the other. The concerns over measuring the quality of course content need to be resolved, but there seem to be few ways to solve the problem. We discuss some of the reasons why "no one knows" whether students are learning more in the next two sections.

THE PRESTIGE ECONOMY

Higher education revolves around prestige. That statement is virtually a cliché. The sociologist Thorstein Veblen made a similar remark in 1918 when he said that the "felt need for prestige has a major share in shaping the work and bearing of the university. Whatever will not serve the end of prestige has no secure footing" (quoted in Rhode 2006, 6). Almost ninety years later, the English professors Pratt et al. (2005, 100) made a similar remark: "Higher education operates in a prestige economy in which reputation is the coin of the realm, and prestige will be defined in both local and national contexts." The drive for prestige is one incentive for faculty productivity.

Unfortunately, prestige in higher education is often not earned by being an effective teacher. As Rhode (2006, 33) says, "throughout the American academy, scholarship has become the principle foundation of status." Rhode's statement certainly applies to accounting departments. As Plumlee et al. (2006, 125) say in an article in *Issues in Accounting Education,* "promotion and tenure requirements at major universities require publication in top-tier journals." Ten years earlier in the same publication, Stone (1996, 188) said, "Evidence in accounting suggests that research is weighted more heavily than teaching or service in tenure decisions." When professors pursue status by elevating scholarship over teaching, they create trouble for the academy because they do not spend time teaching students. As Rhode (2006, 154) explains:

> The pursuit of status has not only compounded financial difficulties but also distorted academic priorities. Higher education faces a classic prisoner's dilemma, in which institutionally rational behavior leads to socially undesirable results. More resources are diverted into excessive salaries for academic celebrities, scholarships for economically advantaged students, glitzy amenities, and public relations campaigns. As both institutions and individuals face pressure to boost their reputations, other priorities can fall by the wayside. What loses out are activities such as teaching and advising, which are crucial to the academic mission but not readily evaluated in national rankings or in hiring, promotion, and compensation processes.

Evaluating the quality of teaching is notoriously problematic. But when faculty pursue status by emphasizing publishing over teaching, they lose credibility with parents, business leaders, and legislative funding sources, all of whom wonder why they should be paying tuition, taxes, and education allocations for people who do not want to teach or who are not effective teachers.

The conflict in the academy between the pursuit of status and the pursuit of money is partially explained in Hirsch's book, *Social Limits to Growth* (1976). As Hirsch states, "The heart of the problem lies in the complexity and partial ambiguity of the concept of economic growth once the mass of the population has satisfied its main biological needs for life-sustaining food, shelter, and clothing. The traditional economic distinction between how much is produced, on what basis, and who gets it then becomes blurred" (1). Once people satisfy their basic needs for food, shelter, and clothing, they effectively shift much of their attention from those basic needs, which are embedded in the material economy, to status needs, which are embedded in the positional economy. As Hirsch (1976, 27) states:

> The material economy is defined as output amenable to continued increase in productivity per unit of labor input.... The material economy embraces production of physical goods as well as such services as are receptive to mechanization or technological innovation without deterioration in quality as it appears to the consumer. It is assumed that a continued increase in the 'materials productivity' of output—that is, in final output obtained per unit of raw material input—will

> be sufficient to contain emerging shortages of raw materials as a result of technological progress, which is broadly what has happened up to now.

The material economy is typically a positive sum game: the rising tide that lifts all boats, in the famous analogy. In theory, everyone, or nearly everyone, can win. As Hirsch suggests, broadly speaking, that has generally happened "up to now" in Europe and America since the industrial revolution and more recently in China and India. Huge numbers of people in the developed world live in relative comfort and security with few worries about deprivations of food, clothing, shelter, and other basics of human survival.

Once their basic material needs are satisfied, however, people are free to focus more attention on attaining social status. As Hirsch (1976, 4) explains,

> So long as material privation is widespread, conquest of material scarcity is the dominant concern. As demands for purely private goods are increasingly satisfied, demands for goods and facilities with a public (social) character become increasingly active.

The pursuit of social status is a well-established human need. As Wright (2000, 26) has said, "Evolutionary psychologists—and, for that matter, non-evolutionary psychologists—have shown that human beings naturally pursue social status with a certain ferocity." Peter Singer (1999, 61) has said that "under different social and economic systems, many people will act competitively in order to enhance their own status, gain a position of power, and/or advance their interests and those of their kin."

But the pursuit of social status takes place in the positional economy, which is a zero sum game: if one person gains, another loses. Hirsch (1976, 27) says,

> The positional economy, ... relates to all aspects of goods, services, work positions, and other social relationships that are either (1) scarce in some absolute or socially imposed sense or (2) subject to congestion or crowding through more extensive use.

Higher education exists in a prestige economy, which is to say, a positional economy. This situation—that is, the very small chance of anyone winning big in the academy—is one of the factors creating problems for measuring student learning in higher education. As Rhode (2006, 13) explains: "The arms race for relative status has almost no winners and many losers. There is, in fact, no room at the top. Few academics will achieve true eminence as scholars, and even those who do typically find that there is always someone more distinguished."

The inherent problems (e.g., scarcity, congestion, crowding) in the race for status in the positional economy of academia are exposed when people try to measure student learning. If every student gets the highest score on a test, some people call foul, because most people know that some students are better than others and very high scores must be scarce if they are to have value. But if no one excels, some people also call foul, because there is crowding and congestion in the middle of rankings if everyone has the same ranking.

In addition to tests, grades and SET are supposed to measure student learning: grades present a teacher's summary of a student's performance in a given course. SET, in theory at least, present a student's summary of how effective the teacher has been in adding to the student's learning. But a definitive measure of student learning (i.e., one that sharply distinguishes the different abilities of the people being measured) creates problems for faculty and students. First, the professor who earns the highest SET score often also earns the highest social status. All the other faculty earn lower status. In the positional economy of the academy, that means disappointment for the large majority of professors, which is a lot of misery for many powerful people. Second, the student (or students) with the highest GPA earns high status, but everyone else earns lower status. For American students, that means millions of disappointed people. To spare themselves all that disappointment, many people do not want a definitive measurement of student learning, and they will fight long and hard to prevent one from coming into being.

All the conflict in the prestige economy of higher education creates a dilemma. As Rhode (2006, 154) said earlier, "Higher education faces a classic prisoner's dilemma." Here is Wright's (2000, 340) description of the prisoner's dilemma:

> In the prisoner's dilemma, two partners in crime are being interrogated separately. The state lacks the evidence to convict them of the crime they committed but does have enough evidence to convict both on a lesser charge—bringing, say, a one-year prison term for each. The prosecutor wants conviction on the more serious charge, and pressures each man individually to confess and implicate the other. She says: 'If you confess but your partner doesn't, I'll let you off free and use your testimony to lock him up for ten years. And if you *don't* confess, yet your partner does, *you* go to prison for ten years. If you confess and your partner does too, I'll put you both away, but only for three years.' The question is: Will the two prisoners cooperate with each other, both refusing to confess? Or will one or both of them 'defect' ('cheat')?

In the prestige economy (and prisoner's dilemma) of higher education, a definitive measure of student learning (e.g., accurate SET, grades, and standardized tests) will give high status (in effect, get out of jail free) to few people, but many other people will have less status (in effect, stay in jail) and may be excluded from rewards (e.g., promotion, tenure, and raises for professors; scholarships, graduation, and good jobs for students). Hence, there is a strong incentive for some people to "cooperate" in the academic version of the prisoner's dilemma: that is, to manipulate SET, to inflate grades, and to ensure course content is not standardized. Such "cooperation" in the prestige economy of the academy is an incentive for more people to gain more prestige, but at the expense of the quality of education.

The problems with incentives cited above are exacerbated by the growth of higher education. After all, Hirsch's book is titled *Social Limits to Growth*. Juhn, Kim, and Vella (2005, 303) point out that only about 5% of American men were college graduates in 1940, but by 1990, 22.6% of American men had graduated from college. By 2005, the percentage of Americans with a bachelor's degree or higher was 27.6% (Bauerlein 2008, 30–31). Juhn, Kim, and Vella (2005) found some evidence that the quality of American college graduates had declined in terms of their ability to command high wages. Similarly, Nie and Golde (2008, 63) remark, "Across 70 years and in multiple studies, vast increases in education have not caused an increase in verbal abilities." The results from Juhn, Kim, and Vella (2005) and Nie and Golde (2008) conform with what Hirsch (1976, 3) said almost 30 years earlier:

> Thus, the utility of expenditure on a given level of education as a means of access to the most sought after jobs will decline as more people attain that level of education. The value to me of my education depends not only on how much I have but also on how much the man ahead of me in the job line has.

As higher education in the United States continues to grow, there will be fewer incentives to have high educational standards, because there will be more scarcity, more congestion, and more crowding in the positional economy of higher education. More students and faculty in the prestige economy of higher education in America do not translate into better education. More and more people chase the same few rewards to the detriment of all. One casualty in many has been measuring student learning. That is, inappropriate tools like SET are used to evaluate professors, grades have become inflated, and course content has become deflated in some areas. Hirsch was right: There ***are*** social limits to the growth of higher education.

PROFESSORIAL SELF-PROTECTION

Finding and implementing an accurate measure of student learning mean changing the prestige economy of the academy. But, as Zakaria (2008, 143–44) has said, "Economic reforms produce growth, but they also produce dislocation—and those hurt by change always protest more loudly than those who benefit." Because many faculty and students profit from misleading measures of student learning, it is not likely that many faculty will voluntarily change much. Instead, they will probably protect each other. As Rhode (2006, 124) says, "The academic world is built on reciprocity." Adam Smith (1994, 821) made this same point over 230 years ago in *The Wealth of Nations* (first published in 1776):

> If the authority to which he [i.e., the teacher] is subject resides in the body corporate, the college, or university, of which he himself is a member, and in which the greater part of the other members are, like himself, persons who either are, or ought to be teachers; they are likely to make a common cause, to be all very indulgent to one another, and every man to consent that his neighbor may neglect his duty, provided he himself is allowed to neglect his own. In the University of Oxford, the greater part of the public professors have, for these many years, given up altogether even the pretence of teaching.

Many contemporary American faculties are already "very indulgent to one another." We have already discussed problems with manipulating SET, grade inflation, and course content deflation. Those are three of the most common ways that U.S. faculty protect themselves from threats of change to the status quo. All three of those problems require that professors "make a common cause" for the problems to continue. Any professor who does not make common cause will witness how tenured faculty protect themselves.

One witness to an episode of faculty self-protection was Professor William Abbott (2008) of Fairfield University. He documented grade inflation at his school, and he proposed two additions to the courses listed on student transcripts. First, he wanted a listing of "the number of students in the course section and the average grade awarded." Second, at the end of the transcript, he wanted "a cumulative average of all the grades in all of the course sections ... listed alongside the student's own cumulative average." When he proposed his changes to student transcripts to the Educational Planning Committee, its faculty members had three objections. First, some argued that in advanced classes every student might be excellent. Listing that everyone in a class earned an A might create the wrong impression to prospective employers or graduate-school admissions officers, who might think a student was merely average when the student was excellent. A second objection was "academic freedom extends to grading." A third objection was that Fairfield University students with high GPAs would be at a comparative disadvantage against graduates from other schools if prospective employers or graduate-school admissions officers noted that most students at Fairfield earned a high GPA. Students from other schools with similar GPAs but no average grade information for individual classes might look better. As Abbott said, "the desire to avoid disadvantaging any student in the job market was compelling for many of my colleagues." The Educational Planning Committee ultimately passed his proposal by a vote of 5-2-1. But then the proposal went to the Academic Council of his University where it was rejected by a vote of 10-2. Abbott said, "In the Academic Council the most vocal resistance once again came from the higher-grading schools and departments."

Abbott got off easy. He kept his job. The penalties ratchet up if professors decide to protect themselves from a talented job applicant or a talented applicant for tenure and promotion. Some faculty are remarkably thin-skinned and will not hire, tenure, or promote someone who appears competitive, independent, competent and confident. Nelson and Watt (1999, 298) have said this about some of their fellow English professors: "We have also seen insecure colleagues try to hire people who will not threaten them intellectually." The observation by Nelson and Watt is an example of Weil's Law of Academic Hiring, discussed elsewhere in this monograph: first-rate scholars and administrators tend to hire other first-rate scholars, but second-raters tend to hire third-raters, third-raters tend to hire fifth-raters, and so on, until quality diverges towards minus infinity (Halmos 1985, 123). The mediocrities (or worse) protect themselves from their betters by using an institution's system of committees and hierarchies of power and privilege to block out any person who threatens their interests.

King (2003) describes one especially offensive episode of professorial self-protection in the tenure and promotion case of Robert David (KC) Johnson. Brooklyn College of the City University of New York (CUNY) hired Johnson from Williams College as an untenured associate professor to teach U.S. political and diplomatic history. King (2003, 21–22) supplies this background:

> He had published two books, both with Harvard University Press, as well as seven peer-reviewed journal articles. Students flocked to his courses on U.S. politics, constitutional history, and international relations. He volunteered for openings in department committees, and was encouraged to do so by Chairman Philip F. Gallagher. He submitted reports promptly, revised old course offerings, and was prolific in his proposals for new ones. He was always available—in his office six or seven days a week, working away at his computer amid stacks of books and audio tapes of telephone calls recorded by former president Lyndon B. Johnson, but always eager to take off his headphones and have a conversation on the election of 2000 or the attacks of 9/11.

But Johnson ruffled feathers. As King (2003, 22) explains, an untenured assistant professor complained "to three different colleagues that Johnson set a standard of scholarly production and teaching success so high that it endangered her own chances for promotion and tenure." Johnson "was not an easy grader; he gave quizzes every week in introductory courses, and substantial reading assignments in advanced courses" (2003, 22). And Johnson, a member of the History department Appointments committee, voted "no" on a decision to offer a position teaching European history to an applicant whom he found unqualified (2003, 24).

When Johnson applied for tenure and promotion to full professor, the long knives came out. Although he was strong in the categories of research, teaching, and service, some faculty members found him lacking in "collegiality." As King (2003, 25) explains:

> The use of the collegiality standard was evident in his [KC Johnson's] interview with the divisional subcommittee on promotion on 19 March 2002. The meeting did not discuss, as was customary and expected, Johnson's scholarship and teaching. Instead, he was asked how he planned to 'heal' the department; whether he was doing enough to 'cuddle' our 'barely literate' students, and whether his website was not too demanding of them; and how he accounted for the failure of five candidates to accept the offers of employment extended as a result of the recent history department search.

On the basis of Johnson's alleged lack of collegiality, his application for tenure and promotion to full professor was not supported by his department chair and his college president.

Johnson hired an attorney and the two of them prepared a counterattack. They prepared a Memo of Law and a 114-page Statement of Facts (King 2003, 27). Johnson had collected six emails from the associate provost of his college which showed a number of procedural violations in his case. Johnson also found an unofficial file of materials assembled against him. This Shadow File, as he called it, contained letters and emails.

> They contained a number of false and defamatory statements: among them the claim that Johnson was 'corrupt' and 'immoral' because he did not favor the letter writer's preferred candidate in the European history search, and distasteful insinuations about Johnson's personal relationships with three male junior colleagues (King 2003, 27).

In the meantime, in November and December 2002, articles and editorials about the Johnson case began to appear in newspapers, magazines, and webzines. One letter and press release that was distributed had a statement by twenty-four well-known historians who decried the tenure and promotion decision against Johnson as representing a " 'culture of mediocrity' hostile to high academic standards" (King 2003, 28). Because of all the attention Johnson's case was getting, the CUNY Chancellor appointed a special faculty committee to evaluate the Johnson case and make a recommendation. After reviewing the case, the faculty committee unanimously voted to grant Johnson tenure and promotion to full professor. The CUNY Board of Trustees, on the recommendation of CUNY's Chancellor, granted Johnson tenure and promotion.

These two anecdotes demonstrate some of the strategies that faculty use to protect themselves from professors who want to measure student learning accurately, or who want to rise above the "culture of mediocrity." But many faculty protect themselves by playing along. In his essay about grade inflation, Cushman (2003, 54), a sociology professor at Wellesley College, explained how he coped with pressure to inflate grades:

> Before coming to Wellesley College, I taught at the University of Texas at Austin. There, as everywhere, grade inflation was becoming a problem and, to their credit, the dean of the college specifically cautioned new assistant professors that grade inflation would be frowned upon in the promotion process. Upon arriving at Wellesley, a very different institution, I used the entire grade scale in my first semester classes. Within a month, students (mostly the seasoned seniors who had learned to play the game) complained to the department chair, who advised me, in the interests of professional survival, that I had to adapt to local grading norms if I stood any chance of survival. This admonition was reinforced by several of my senior colleagues.

Cushman adapted and earned tenure.

Crumbley (1995, 71) has many anecdotes of professorial self-protection in an article subtitled, "Games Professors Play." Here is one:

> Another anecdotal example is shown by the opportunistic behavior of a nontenured, tough-grading instructor who was teaching at a large intercity university, and was receiving SET scores of approximately 4.5 (out of 7). When his department head reprimanded him, he improved his SET scores to 6.3 *within one semester*. ... He instituted a pizza party near the end of the semester and incorporated three pre-tests during the semester. Each pre-test had 200 exam questions which was distributed one week before each exam. The exam was composed of 50 multiple-choice/true-false questions from the pre-test. Thus, by the end of the

> semester the student knew what his or her *high* final grade would be before the distribution of the SET. There was an optional final exam, but no one took it because there was no pre-test. (Emphasis in original)

Crumbley (1995, 69) also listed 23 strategies that professors could use to maximize their SET scores, and Crumbley and Smith (herein) lists 28 Rules of the Trade of college teachers. The strategies mentioned by Crumbley (1995, 69) and others in this monograph all make measuring student learning difficult. Professors have so much power in U.S. universities that they can band together to prevent others from finding out if students are being educated effectively. Bok (2006, 39) has remarked that "recalcitrant parties in a university can block useful collaborations." That is certainly true about collaborations that focus on changes in pedagogy. Bok (2006, 49) has this to say about self-protection and the possibility for pedagogical change in U.S. universities:

> The neglect of pedagogy in faculty debates is probably rooted in an instinct for self-protection. It is relatively easy to move courses around by changing curricular requirements. It is quite another matter to decide that methods of pedagogy should be altered. Reforms of the latter kind require much more effort. Instructors have to change long-standing habits and master new skills for which many of them have little preparation. To avoid such difficulties, faculties have taken the principle of academic freedom and stretched it well beyond its original meaning to gain immunity from interference with how their courses should be taught. In most institutions (other than small liberal arts colleges), teaching methods have become a personal prerogative of the instructor rather than a subject appropriate for collective deliberation. The result is to shield from faculty review one of the most important ingredients in undergraduate education.

When Abbott (2008) proposed changing student transcripts at Fairfield University to reduce grade inflation, he discovered how his colleagues were ready to stretch the principle of academic freedom "well beyond its original meaning to gain immunity from interference" (Bok 2006, 49) in their self-serving grading policies. Thus, no one at his school or many others around the U.S. will ever know if student learning is being measured responsibly.

SOLUTIONS

Some solutions to problems with SET, grade inflation, deflated course content, the prestige economy, and professorial self-protection are often suggested by the authors of the works who discuss the problems.

Pressman (2007, 99), for example, says this about SET: "To help reduce the demand pressures for higher grades, student evaluations should be banned from college campuses." The extensive education literature on teaching effectiveness has consistently urged that multiple measures, including some form of student evaluations, should be used if the goal is to appropriately evaluate the teaching effectiveness of college professors and to access how teaching effectiveness relates to student learning (Kember and Gow 1994; Lucal et. al. 2003; O'Hanlon and Mortensen 1980). This literature documents the correlation between student learning styles and professors' teaching styles, and it recommends that this correlation or lack of correlation be taken into account in evaluating a professor's teaching effectiveness (Charkins, O'Toole, and Wetzel 1985; Grimes, Millea, and Woodruff 2004).

Chonko (2006, 2) also suggests that the quality of instructors should not be measured by SET at all, but by the number of learning opportunities an instructor provides. Besides papers, exams, projects, and presentations, he suggests evaluating the "type of faculty feedback provided, nature of the exams and assignments, instructor availability, instructor preparation quality, commitment of the faculty member to change, listening responsiveness, [and] teacher portfolios." Unfortunately, Chonko is vague about how they could be measured and evaluated. A common variation on Chonko's suggestion is to use SET, but only in concert with other kinds of evaluations, such as those Chonko suggested. Crumbley (1995, 74) also suggests that faculty can be evaluated by having administrators or colleagues visit their classes, and by self-appraisals, video recordings, and evaluations of teaching materials. Flinn and Crumbley (herein) discuss a number of alternatives to SET to measure teaching effectiveness.

Crumbley (1995, 73) has several suggestions about SET, besides abolishing summative SET outright. One of his "less favorable" solutions "is to give the results only to the instructor." Another suggestion is "to require students to sign their names (or social security number)" to the SET. Still another of Crumbley's suggestions is giving formative SET to students. Unlike summative SET, which consist only of numerical abstractions of a teacher's ability, formative SET have open-ended questions which require students to comment at some length on a professor's strengths and weaknesses. Such open-ended comments are more useful to professors and less prone to being distorted.

If formative SET indicate that some faculty are weak teachers, one way to help them is to create a faculty mentoring program. Brightman (2006) outlines such a program in his essay. He has many useful suggestions for improving teaching, and he illustrates his advice with several case studies. He emphasizes, "The mentor should only select faculty members who are excited about the mentoring. The mentor should never select a faculty member who has been pressured into the pool" (2006, 131). Unfortunately, such a policy would tend to eliminate those faculty who taught poorly but thought their teaching skills were effective.

As to solutions for grade inflation, Wilson (1999, 40–41) suggests some of the following: make schools list the average grade for the entire class with the student's individual grade on transcripts, eliminate easy courses from the curriculum, do not tolerate student complaints about low grades, give academic honors only to the top 10% of graduates, eliminate lax course dropping policies, revise SET to guard against the effects of grade inflation, and recognize that grade inflation devalues higher education. Kurtz (2006) emphasizes the value of adverse publicity. He recommends exposing the problems of grade inflation to wide audiences and shaming schools into curbing grade inflation. He also suggests listing students' class ranks on their transcripts, and he recommends quota systems in which only a certain percentage of students in a class could get A's.

Fajardo (2004) discusses many of the ideas mentioned by Wilson (1999) and Kurtz (2006) above. But the administrators at her university were so annoyed at rampant grade inflation that they sent letters to any faculty who gave all A's to their classes. The letters explained "the importance of improved academic rigor and grading standards" (2004, 72). This policy worked for some faculty, but for those who did not stop inflating grades, "the Provost and Vice-president for Academic Affairs established target GPAs of 2.75 for undergraduate courses, and 3.25 for graduate courses" (2004, 72). Her school also created a web report that listed the average GPA for every class taught. The report told faculty members how their grades measured against the target GPAs (2004, 72–73). The approach that Fajardo's school took is probably not for everyone, but it demonstrates how far some administrators will go to stop grade inflation and improve their school's reputation.

Johnson's (2002, 153) solution to the impact of grade inflation on SET is to use a different approach. He recommends "basing measures of student learning on performance in follow-on courses." If departments follow Johnson's advice, some faculty will probably complain that any low scores by students in follow-on courses are caused by the instructors in those courses. Faculty may also complain because of the inevitable discrepancies caused by students dropping out, by students waiting for several semesters or several years to take the follow-on course, and by new students transferring in with course prerequisites taken at other schools. Administrators will also complain because tracking student learning in follow-on courses will invariably be more complex and more costly. These kinds of problems will limit the chances that such follow-on measurements will be taken.

Problems with course content deflation are often addressed by requiring graduating students to pass comprehensive exit exams. Such exams are recommended by Zimmerman (2002) because they force students to avoid easy professors and get an education. But, as Bok (2006, 316) says, "fewer than one-third of all colleges nationwide conduct comprehensive evaluations to determine whether they are achieving the purposes of their general education program." The typical reaction to recommending standardized exit exams was summarized in an editorial in the *New York Times* (2006):

> [T]he chairman of the Bush administration's Commission on the Future of Higher Education recently suggested that standardized tests be used to determine how much college students are actually learning. The higher education community is up in arms about the suggestion, arguing that what colleges teach cannot be fully tested and that standardized tests would only dumb down an excellent education system.

When confronted with the specter of standardized exit exams, many faculty resist. But that still leaves the problem of deflated course content. The *New York Times* (2006) editorial suggests that "colleges and universities should join in the hunt for acceptable ways to measure student progress, rather than simply fighting the whole idea from the sidelines."

But college and university faculty will often ***not*** join in the hunt for "acceptable ways to measure student progress" because of the incentive structure of the prestige economy and professorial self-protection, two tightly interconnected subjects. Though he never mentions it directly, Hirsch (1976) is acutely aware of this clash. For professors to climb in the academic prestige economy and increase their income, privileges, and reputations, they must limit the attempts of others to control them. One method of control is the standardized test. For students to do well on standardized tests, professors need to adapt their courses to address the content of the test. But many professors see such adaptations as limitations on their freedom to pursue their interests. Thus, the professors teach whatever they want, or dumb down their classes, and resist standardized tests. But sooner or later in their striving for more money, more privileges, and higher prestige, professors find that the positive-sum game of the material economy clashes with the zero-sum game of the positional economy. Here is how Hirsch (1976, 188) explains the situation:

> Capitalism has indeed brought the silk stockings that were the privilege of queens to every factory girl; in this sphere and in this phase it has been a great leveler, as Schumpeter so evocatively showed. The achievement unfortunately does not enable it to repeat the performance with nonmaterial aspects of privilege, past or present.

In the material economy, capitalistic pursuit of individual self-interest can create the rising tide that lifts all boats. But in the positional economy of the academy, not everyone can be the top dog. As professors pursue their individual self-interests to higher and higher levels, they may earn more money and privileges in the material economy, but they create problems with other members of their social groups in the positional economy. This situation was captured neatly in a recent editorial by Mary-Jo Kranacher (2008, 80), editor-in-chief of the *CPA Journal:*

> [O]ne dean shared a story about her college's recent attempt to hire an additional faculty member—and accounting PhD—who summarily turned them down in favor of a $300,000 offer from another college. Paying that salary level to incoming accounting PhDs would break the budgets of most colleges and universities. Furthermore, such a move would probably trigger animosity and resentment among tenured faculty members who have provided loyal service to the institution for many years and earn far less.

The new accounting Ph.D.'s scarcity and self interest is going to create anger, wasted time, declining morale, and other problems in the surrounding social groups, the accounting department and the school itself.

For Hirsch (1976, 190), when an individual's pursuit of resources in the material economy clashes with the individual's pursuit of status in the positional economy, then something must give. His solution is as follows:

> This book has suggested that the prime economic problem now facing the economically advanced societies is a structural need to pull back the bounds of economic self-advancement. ... We may be near the limit of explicit social organization possible without a supporting social morality.

That is, for Hirsch, it is more important to emphasize the welfare of the group (the "supporting social morality") over the desires of individuals to advance themselves. At least since Adam Smith's *Wealth of Nations* (1994, 485), the value that Western society has placed on individual self-advancement has been predicated on the belief that one person's self-interest, joined with the self-interests of others would create the "invisible hand" of the market, which in turn would help the society as a whole. As Hirsch (1976, 187–88) stated, "The ultimate justification of the pursuit of individual economic interests and the establishment of rights in private property is that the resources available to all are thereby increased." Those increased resources are the rising tide that lifts all boats.

In society and the academy today, if people continue to believe that they should work to help the larger group, then they must focus less on themselves and more on society in general. As Hirsch (1976, 189) concludes:

> If the objective of universal participation is not abandoned, the constraints set by social limits will inexorably make society more dependent on collective provision and collective orientation. This in turn demands some adjustment in perceptions. What is involved here is not a revolutionary change in attitudes, the visionary 'change in human nature,' but an adjustment of degree.

One possible solution for the academy would be for faculty to reduce the aggressiveness of their self-advancement and self-protection and focus more on collaborating to improve teaching effectiveness and student learning. But improving teaching means that faculty must first find more accurate measures of student learning, and recognize that students bear some responsibility for learning. We recommend replacing or supplementing the now typical SET with multiple measures of teaching performance, reducing or eliminating grade inflation, and instituting standardized tests or other exacting measures of student performance to make course content more demanding.

Another solution to the problem of overaggressive faculty self-advancement is suggested by Rhode (2006, 171):

> Harvard philosopher William James once claimed that 'to give up pretensions is as blessed a relief as to get them gratified.' Whether or not the satisfactions

> are truly equivalent, letting go of certain status needs is often far preferable to the alternative. In an essay on academic success and failure, sociologist Gary Marx similarly suggests that the most dependable rewards come from practicing the craft itself, independent of external validation. ...

Perhaps reducing our pursuit of status and helping our students do well will be satisfying enough for some of us.

The problems in part with measuring student learning will not be easily solved, because those problems are a function of the prestige economy in which faculty and students work. Some conditions may encourage changes, however. As Abbott (2008) suggested, publicity about the problems with SET, grade inflation, course content deflation, the prestige economy of the academy, and professorial self-protection might turn the tide. Some universities or departments might have such enlightened leaders and faculty that they will ensure that professors collaborate to ensure that student learning is measured effectively. Or, to take a worst-case scenario, perhaps a series of scandals or some national calamity involving the incompetence of college graduates or professors could turn the tide of public opinion against the abuses of teaching, measurement, and social climbing that infect college campuses today. Whatever the outcome, the solutions we have considered in this section will require less focus on individual self-advancement and greater collaboration between faculty for the common good.

CONCLUSION

The title of this article is, in some ways, its conclusion: there are limits to measuring student learning with the current imprecise instruments. Too many powerful people do not want a precise instrument (or set of instruments) for measuring student learning and evaluating teaching because such an instrument (or instruments) would make too many people second-raters, third-raters, or worse.

Having said that, however, we should add that art, religion, history, and, yes, academia are full of examples of how people overcame conflicts and sacrificed their personal goals to work profitably together for the common good. Many university faculty already have experience working successfully with professors in different departments on committees, administrative job searches, teaching classes, and research publication. If we illuminate and publicize the reasons for the limitations on measuring student learning, then we are well along the road to transcending those limitations.

CHAPTER 7

Inputs to the Measurement of Teaching Quality: Moving Beyond Student Evaluations of Teaching

Ronald J. Huefner, State University of New York at Buffalo*

While student evaluation of teaching (SET) has been in common use for many years, recent years have seen the emergence of more direct attempts to assess student learning as a major theme by universities, accreditation bodies, and the general public. This recent emphasis on assessment reflects the duality of the teaching/learning process. Teaching reflects the input side of the process, learning the output side. Both should be considered important. While some students may manage to learn in the absence of good teaching, widespread comprehensive learning is unlikely without high quality teaching. While good inputs (teaching) do not guarantee good outputs (learning), neither are good outputs likely in the absence of good inputs. Learning outcomes do not just happen; they are the expected result of high quality teaching. Thus, appropriate assessment of learning should supplement, not replace, evaluation of the quality of teaching.

Prior to the recent emphasis on assessment, SET might have appeared to be an attempt to measure learning outputs, by seeking the opinions of the students being taught. But students are not the most objective evaluators of their own learning, in part because they lack benchmarks for their expected accomplishments. Indeed, the various learning assessment techniques generally do not include student evaluations. It is fair to conclude that SET do not have a major role to play in the assessment of learning, but instead in measuring student satisfaction.

What then, is their role? It is fair to say that SET has a role on the input side of the teaching/learning process, as *one* indicator of the evaluation of the quality of teaching. However, we have, as academics, ceded nearly the entire evaluation of teaching to student evaluations, and have done little to (a) make the case for using multiple measures of teaching quality, (b) specify what the other relevant measures are, (c) build data bases of these measures, and (d) possibly study the correlation between various measures of teaching quality and assessments of learning outcomes.

---

* Professor Huefner is SUNY Distinguished Teaching Professor in the Department of Accounting & Law, School of Management, State University of New York at Buffalo. rhuefner@buffalo.edu.

WHY ARE STUDENT EVALUATIONS SO POPULAR?

SET scores are in widespread use as a measure of teaching effectiveness and quality. On the positive side, they provide large numbers of evaluations, using a common instrument at a low cost. Perhaps no other technique can offer so many readings of whatever is being measured, and at modest cost. The large number of respondents also tends to mitigate the effect of outlier responses. While there are no doubt some irresponsible inputs and some evaluations are colored, positively or negatively, by specific interactions between a student and instructor, most responses, in the writer's opinion, provide a student's honest assessment of the classroom experience.[1]

While improvements or deteriorations of the measure over time do occur, in many cases there is a consistency that lends credence to the results. Accumulations of evaluations over time give both time-series and cross-sectional comparability, which may be examined by course or by faculty member. In any performance measurement situation, it is rare to have such an extensive database of assessments by many different evaluators, extending over a long period of time, and using a common instrument. We should cherish this wealth of information, but we should not be satisfied that it is sufficient to capture the many elements of successful teaching.

Student responses are anonymous; the good side of this means that evaluations can be provided without fear of identification or retribution. The negative side of anonymity is a lack of accountability for the assessment given. Some respondents may use the cloak of anonymity to exact revenge for perceived unfair grades, critical evaluations of their work, or other concerns. While this risk exists, the effect is likely mitigated by the responses of large number of students who do not have a personal agenda.

Perhaps the biggest concern with SET is that we do not know the respondents' criteria. Exactly what are we measuring? Are we measuring student learning or satisfaction? One study at the writer's institution found the evaluations to be most highly correlated with expected grade, implying that teaching is good if the student got at least the grade they expected. This feature readily supports the concern that use of a student evaluation system leads to grade inflation. While this proposition may have some truth, there are likely other factors leading to grade inflation as well. But it also seems true that high grades alone do not guarantee high evaluations; day-to-day class conduct is likely to play a major role as well. Further, evaluations are generally conducted before final grades are awarded, so at best it is *expected* grade that plays a role.

Grades likely play more of a role in required courses, where many students may have the limited goal of successfully getting through the course independent of learning quality. In elective courses, especially in one's major, interest in mastering the material may be greater. A personal anecdote: in a first offering of a new course (an elective for accounting majors), the writer consciously graded very softly, as I was still feeling my way with the material and the means of delivery. The result was that most students got high grades, in some cases probably above their normal performance. In the written comments that accompanied evaluations that semester, there

[1] My opinion here may be at odds with research showing that students frequently lie, in a variety of contexts. See, for example, Po Bronson, "Learning to Lie," *New York: The Magazine,* February 18, 2008 issue, online at nymag.com. Reasons cited for a high incidence of lying include avoiding disapproval or punishment; enhancing one's status, accomplishments, and power; and increasing one's sense of control. In student evaluations, however, responses are anonymous, limiting the personal benefit of lying. Expressing one's power may still be a motive, as a student can "trash" a good instructor with impunity. It perhaps should follow that the opposite lie would also occur, giving a high rating to an obviously deficient instructor. My own viewpoint is that, while a few respondents will take out their frustrations on an instructor's evaluations, most students give straightforward answers. Most instructors' evaluations tend to be highly consistent over time and over various student audiences, suggesting that random lying is not a major factor. But see Milliron 2008.

were several criticisms of my failure to be very discriminating in my grading of their work. In this situation, at least some students felt I had graded too easily.[2]

The biggest question with student evaluations remains, what is being measured? Most likely, it is *not* the amount of learning. Students are not in a good position to assess the quantity of learning (though they can—and do—assess workload).[3] Nor can they generally assess the quality of their learning, such as the extent to which material is current, comprehensive and relevant. Thus, those faculty who feel that the best teacher is the one who teaches students the most may well be frustrated by student evaluations.

Rather than disparage SET, we should first consider the kinds of desirable faculty behaviors (i.e., actions other than grade inflation) that may contribute to improved student evaluations. Second, and perhaps more importantly, we should attempt to make a positive case for at least equal consideration of various teaching characteristics into the assessment of teaching.

LIVING WITH STUDENT EVALUATIONS

While quantity and quality of learning may not come through, SET do seem to assess a number of course and class conduct features, that certainly facilitate the students' learning process.

In the writer's view, following are some characteristics whose presence tends to lead to good evaluations and whose absence tends to lead to poor evaluations:

1. **Thorough preparation.** Students expect an instructor to be well prepared for class, and can readily detect lack of preparation. Stumbling through a demonstration problem, or going down an incorrect path and then quickly amending it, are good ways to lose the students' respect. Not many of us can "wing it" through complex problems, and even those who can often succeed will inevitably have their days when things do not go right. Good preparation minimizes these problems. It also demonstrates a respect for students and for the effective use of class time.
2. **Matching material to class time.** The instructor who routinely runs out of material before the end of the period may leave the students feeling shortchanged, while the instructor who regularly has 30 minutes of material to rush through in the last ten minutes of class will surely leave the students frustrated. Class sessions should be well planned so that the material covered matches well with the class time available. While shortages and overages will occur occasionally, depending on student questions, the extent of discussion, and other variables, instructors learn by experience which topics are likely to require more time, and plan accordingly.
3. **Adherence to plan.** Students expect adherence to the syllabus. Getting several classes behind, changing exam dates or assignment due dates, and adding significant new assignments and/or readings along the way tends to upset the students who have carefully planned their work. Others may see it as another example of the instructor not being prepared up front. Occasional changes due to emerging new materials, for example, are usually tolerable. Of course, downward changes, such as dropping an assignment or extending a due date, are generally well received.
4. **Organization of the course and class session.** One of an instructor's major roles is to bring order and structure to a body of material. A well-organized course is a must, and

[2] Based on my School's grade distributions, which are summarized and distributed from time to time, my overall grading would fall about in the middle of the range of my colleagues'—not the hardest grader in the business school, but by no means the easiest either.

[3] In this regard, I tend to be evaluated as requiring a workload well above average.

each class session should have a visible organization as well. An agenda presented at the beginning of class is often useful to demonstrate a plan for the day's session.

5. **Feedback.** By whatever means—annotated returned copies, in-class discussion, web posting, handouts—students expect feedback on their exams and assignments, both generically (what is the answer) and specifically (why is my answer deficient). This work can be time-consuming, but it has learning value as well as providing some student satisfaction.
6. **Managing expectations.** Grades are important to most students, and thus it is useful to facilitate letting students know where they stand, so that surprises—especially unpleasant surprises—are minimized. If a student is in line for a D or an F, they ought to be well aware of it.[4] The writer establishes maximum grade cutoff levels; for example, if you get at least 880 out of 1,000 available points, you will be in the A or A− class. In other words, it will be specified that the cut for an A− won't be higher than 880. A student's grade is dependent only on his or her own performance, not on the performance of classmates. An experienced instructor should be able to write exams that distinguish levels of achievement, so that an appropriate grade distribution results. It is also true that each class is not equally talented, so that grade distributions will vary from class to class. Further, I will tend to make the true cut a bit below the announced cut, so that no one appears to miss the cut by just a point or two.
7. **Good exam procedures.** Consider making past exams (and solutions) available (web sites make this easy), so that everyone has access to them. Exams should reflect the material covered in the course and the desired skills to be demonstrated (such as critical thinking or creativity). In addition, exams should be time-appropriate. Anti-cheating precautions, such as alternate seating, assigned seating, multiple exam versions, no materials on the desktop, limitations on electronic devices, and vigilant proctoring, are signs that the instructor is trying to make the exam environment as fair as possible. The writer often employs "professional exam conditions;" that is, no questions are answered during the exam. The exam room is much quieter, and no one inadvertently gets any special hints.
8. **Perceived fairness and consistency.** A perception of instructor unfairness, whether in disparate treatment of different individuals, exam coverage inconsistent with emphasis in the course, grading that appears inconsistent from student to student, or inconsistency in any other course aspect, is likely to depress student evaluations. Inconsistent responses to similar requests are likewise perceived as instructor unfairness.
9. **Accommodation of special circumstances.** In a class of any size, various special student circumstances will arise (beyond the proverbial high mortality of grandmothers at exam times). An instructor with a firm "no makeups, no excuses" policy is viewed as inflexible. A careful balancing act is required to provide reasonable accommodations to such circumstances while maintaining fairness, consistency, and a strong expectation of meeting course requirements.
10. **Availability.** Students expect reasonable and dependable availability of the instructor outside of class times. Regular and reliable office hours are expected. My own approach is that, if my office door is open and I am not with someone, you are welcome. Thus real office hours far exceed announced office hours.

[4] In practice, a very late resignation date in my university (after the 10th week of the 15-week semester) leads many likely D/F students to resign the course rather than earn that grade.

11. **Instructor professionalism.** The writer strongly feels that an instructor gains respect by maintaining a professional image. Professional dress and behavior are appropriate; encouraging students to address you by your first name seems inappropriate.

In the writer's view, adhering to the above practices will lead to increased student satisfaction with one's course and should positively impact student evaluations. Moreover, most would agree that each of these is a desirable instructor behavior in its own right.

AN EXPANDED MODEL OF TEACHING EFFECTIVENESS

To reduce the dominance of student evaluations in the assessment of teaching quality, we need to develop and promote additional ways of measuring effectiveness and teaching performance.

One approach has been developed by the State University of New York (SUNY) as a guide for promotion to the rank of Distinguished Teaching Professor. The distinguished rank is a promotion above the rank of full professor. This professorship is awarded in three subcategories: *research* (simply titled as Distinguished Professor), *teaching* (Distinguished Teaching Professor), or *service to the institution* (Distinguished Service Professor). Upon a proposal by a department or school, an extensive dossier is prepared and carefully examined by a university-wide committee, and then forwarded SUNY Central for final consideration. Each campus may propose a very small number of candidates each year (generally one to three).

The criteria for selection as a Distinguished Teaching Professor serve as a model for a broader assessment of teaching performance. The criteria are stated as follows:

> *The primary criterion for appointment to the rank of Distinguished Teaching Professor is skill in teaching. Consideration shall also be given to mastery of subject matter, sound scholarship, service to the University and the broader community, and to continuing growth. The following criteria are to be used in the selection of persons to be nominated for the Distinguished Teaching Professorship:*
>
> ***TEACHING TECHNIQUES AND REPRESENTATIVE MATERIALS****—There must be positive evidence that the candidate performs superbly in the classroom. The nominee must maintain a flexible instructional policy which adapts readily to student needs, interests, and problems. Mastery of teaching techniques must be demonstrated and substantiated. Consideration should be given to the number of substantially different courses taught, the number of students per course, and the teaching techniques employed in the various courses.*
>
> *When available, student evaluations (in the form of student questionnaires administered and compiled by persons other than the nominee) presented for several different courses over a period of several years may provide the local selection committee with a clear idea of the nominee's impact on students.*
>
> ***SCHOLARSHIP AND PROFESSIONAL GROWTH****—The candidate must be a teacher or scholar who keeps abreast and makes significant contributions in his or her own field and uses the relevant contemporary data from that field and related disciplines in teaching. Examples of evidence in this category may include publications or artistic productions, grant awards, and participation in symposia in his or her discipline.*

> ***STUDENT SERVICES—****In relating to students, the candidate must be generous with personal time, easily accessible, and must demonstrate a continual concern with the intellectual growth of individual students. For this category, consideration should be given to the accessibility of the nominee to students outside of class, e.g., office hours, conferences, special meetings, the nominee's responsibility in terms of student advisement, and the nominee's teaching-related services to students.*
>
> ***ACADEMIC STANDARDS AND REQUIREMENTS, AND EVALUATION OF STUDENT PERFORMANCE—****The candidate must set high standards for students and help them attain academic excellence. Quantity and quality of work that is more than average for the subject must be required of the student. The candidate must actively work with students to help them improve their scholarly or artistic performance. The local selection committee should consider the quality, quantity, and difficulty of course-related work. Evidence of academic standards and requirements may be assessed by the accomplishments of students, including placement and achievement level.*
>
> *The candidate's evaluation of student work must be strongly supported by evidence. The candidate must be willing to give greater weight to each student's final level of competence than to the performance at the beginning of the course. Expert teachers enable students to achieve high levels of scholarship. Consequently, it is possible that the candidate's marking record may be somewhat above the average of colleagues. There must be evidence that the candidate does not hesitate to give low evaluations to students who do poorly. Grading practices should be evaluated by the local committee. In particular, grade distributions for all courses in recent academic years should be reviewed, and any seemingly unusual grading patterns examined.* (State University of New York undated, 3)

While these criteria are designed to identify the exceptional teacher, they also provide a useful model for the general evaluation of teaching performance.

COMMENTARY ON THE CRITERIA

A few comments on the above criteria for the identification of teaching excellence:

- **Teaching is not one-dimensional.** The opening paragraph above sees the distinguished teacher in a broader context than only classroom performance. One needs the whole package: subject matter expertise, scholarship, institutional and community service, and continuing growth. In this application, candidates for the Distinguished Teaching Professor appointment have already achieved full professor status in the institution, and thus have already met the requirements in many if not all of these areas.
- **Classroom performance is essential.** Student evaluations clearly play a role here. But so too does the ability to teach a variety of courses by a variety of techniques (e.g., lectures, seminars, case-based courses, independent study, etc.). The selection of approach, as well as other aspects of instructional policy, should be based on what best serves the needs and interests of the students.
- **Keeping up with one's field is essential.** In the accounting area, this likely implies the need to be current in both professional practice and academic thinking.
- **Teaching extends beyond the classroom.** The emphases on accessibility, advising, and other teaching-related services emphasize that teaching is not constrained to 50-minute class periods.
- **We should set high standards.** But note the two-part sentence. Someone who sets high standards is doing only half the job; the other half is to "help them attain academic excellence."

While some may view *low* student performance as indicative that the instructor has high standards, the message here is that high standards should yield *high* performance, both in class and beyond. We adhere to this notion in other aspects of life—that people rise to meet higher expectations.

- **Good teaching should yield good grades.** Here is the proverbial chicken-and-egg problem. Critics of student evaluations argue that the need to be seen as a good teacher (i.e., to get high evaluations) leads to grade inflation. But the message here is that, if teaching is really good, accomplishment—and hence grades—*should* be higher. This point is then balanced by the observation that poor performers should receive appropriate grades.
- **Learning is a process.** The last message above is that the final level of accomplishment is most important, not how quickly you get there. Ideally, the student who struggles early but by course's end has risen to B-level should be graded equivalently to someone who was B-level all along. This doesn't always match with our structured grading patterns.

CONCLUSION

As stated earlier, if we are to reduce the dominance of SET scores, in the assessment of teaching effectiveness, we must develop and promote the use of multiple ways of measuring teaching performance. Such measures might include:

- Assessments of the extent to which an instructor's materials are suitable to the course, are up-to-date, and reflect issues in professional practice.
- Activities by the instructor to maintain and increase his or her own knowledge of the subject matter and of teaching techniques, such as relevant research and publication efforts.
- The instructor's contributions to development of new courses, new topics within existing courses, and curricular change.

The above example of a protocol for the presentation of promotion cases to a rank of distinguished teaching professor is designed to advance our thinking about how this might be done. As a profession, we need to (a) make the case for other measures of teaching quality that include student learning, (b) specify what the other relevant measures are, (c) build data bases of these measures, and (d) possibly study the correlation between various measures of teaching quality and assessments of learning outcomes.

We also need an attitudinal change about teaching. While we subject our research to all kinds of peer review—readings by colleagues, seminar presentations, professional meetings, journal submissions—we are notoriously private about our teaching. We tend to resist peer or supervisory class visitations, and we tend to have few conversations or seminars about our teaching. This "privacy" leaves students as about the only ones who know what we are doing, so it is little wonder that their evaluations carry so much weight.

CHAPTER 8

Assessing Critical Thinking

Rebekah Heath, Pittsburg State University*

The Accounting Education Change Commission (1990, 309) has advocated "changes in the basic accounting curriculum and expansion of teaching modalities to encourage students to 'learn how to learn' and to develop their 'critical thinking skills.' " This focus is needed because formal accounting education has not kept pace with the "dynamic, complex, expanding, and constantly changing profession for which students are being educated" (AECC 1990, 307). While most instructors believe that developing critical thinking in their students is of primary importance (Albrecht and Sack 2000), few have an idea exactly what it is, how it should be taught, or how it should be assessed (Duron, Limbach, and Waugh 2006, 161). The purpose of this article is to provide answers to these questions.

WHAT IS CRITICAL THINKING?

A layman's definition of critical thinking is "thinking about your thinking while you're thinking to make your thinking better" (Paul 1995, 91). Critical thinking has been more formally defined as "purposeful, self-regulatory judgment which results in interpretation, analysis, evaluation, and inference, as well as explanation of the evidential, conceptual, methodological, criteriological, or contextual considerations upon which that judgment is based" (Facione 1990, 3). In addition, accounting practitioners have their own idea of what critical thinking entails. Their definition includes seeing the "Big Picture," transferring knowledge, recognizing when more information is needed, recognizing problem areas, and thinking ahead. Practitioners also include initiative, curiosity, confidence, and clear communication as necessary but not sufficient elements of critical thinking (Baril et al. 1998). For those readers familiar with Bloom's (1956) taxonomy, critical thinking is deemed to occur when students are required to perform in the Analysis, Synthesis, and Evaluation levels of the taxonomy.

However, critical thinking or "thinking well" is not only just a matter of higher-order thinking skills or strategic problem-solving abilities, but rather it also is a matter of attitude or disposition. Experts agree that it is not enough to teach students to perform thinking operations and tasks. They also should be taught the attitude and willingness to carry them out on their own, unasked as well as being taught the importance of having this attitude and willingness for their employment success as accountants. Ennis's (1993, 180) view of critical thinking involves broad dispositions,

* The author is Assistant Professor at Pittsburg State University, KS, and can be reached at rheath@pittstate.edu.

transferable over various domains such as being "open-minded," "drawing unwarranted assumptions cautiously," and "weighing the credibility of evidence."

The most beneficial theoretical approaches to the understanding of critical thinking entail the use of cognitive (or intellectual) development models (Kurfiss 1988). These models describe sequential developmental stages in which individuals use increasingly more complex critical thinking skills to understand, organize, and use knowledge. Several theories have developed to explain the development of critical thinking skills (e.g., Perry (1970); Reflective Judgment Model (King & Kitchener 1994); and Dynamic Skill Theory (Fischer and Bidell 1997)). Exhibit 1 provides a summary of the King and Kitchener (1994) reflective judgment model which has been used extensively in accounting research in the area of critical thinking. The common themes of these models, as outlined in Wolcott et al.'s (2002) review on critical thinking research, include:

- Critical thinking skills can be arrayed cognitively from less complex to more complex.
- Students must develop less complex skills before they can develop more complex skills.
- Most college students operate at cognitive levels that are too low for adequate critical thinking performance.
- Critical thinking skills develop slowly (if they do develop).
- Cross-curricular educational efforts and educational efforts over time are needed to give students sufficient time to practice for development of critical thinking skills (Federation of Schools of Accountancy 1999 Educational Research Committee).

There is sound empirical evidence that good knowledge and good thinking are inextricably bound together (e.g., Bereiter and Scardamalia 1993; Chi, Glaser and Farr 1988). Thus, critical thinking should be taught in the course of teaching discipline knowledge (Pithers and Soden 2000). Accordingly, all accounting instructors must become familiar with the means of teaching and assessing the critical thinking skills of their students.

HOW SHOULD WE TEACH CRITICAL THINKING?

Cunningham's 1996 article illustrates how to restructure an accounting course to help students improve their critical thinking skills while they are learning accounting. She discusses:

- means of restructuring course content by including discussions involving unresolved issues and the identification of assumptions underlying a line of reasoning;
- changing teaching methods to include less lecture and more debating, the analysis of articles, and the use of research projects;
- assessment of student learning by using fewer recall questions on quizzes and exams and more higher-level learning questions such as "Describe the similarities and differences in the ways accelerated depreciation methods and the straight-line method affect the financial statements over the life of a fixed asset," and
- development of a supportive classroom atmosphere in which students feel free to "try out" new thinking skills.

Kimmel (1995) presents a framework for integrating critical thinking into the accounting curriculum as well as strategies for developing critical thinking skills in the classroom. He argues that in the same way those rudiments of the accounting knowledge base are assigned to specific accounting courses, responsibility for specific critical thinking elements also should be assigned to specific courses. For example, Kimmel argues that a basic level case introduced in the Principles of Financial Accounting course can be used to teach the critical thinking element of "welcoming divergent views," while more complex cases that require the student to modify judgments in the light of new information would be appropriate to incorporate into the cost and audit courses. See Exhibit 2.

EXHIBIT 1
Reflective Judgment Stages

Stage	View of Knowledge	Concept of Justification
Prereflective Thinking: Stages 1, 2, and 3		
1	Knowledge is assumed to exist absolutely and concretely; it is not understood as an abstraction. It can be obtained with certainty by direct observation.	Beliefs need no justification since there is assumed to be an absolute correspondence between what is believed to be true and what is true. Alternate beliefs are not perceived.
2	Knowledge is assumed to be absolutely certain or certain but not immediately available. Knowledge can be obtained directly through the senses (as in direct observation) or via authority figures.	Beliefs are unexamined and unjustified or justified by their correspondence with the beliefs of an authority figure (such as a teacher or parent). Most issues are assumed to have a right answer, so there is little or no conflict in making decisions about disputed issues.
3	Knowledge is assumed to be absolutely certain or temporarily uncertain. In areas of temporary uncertainty, only personal beliefs can be known until absolute knowledge is obtained. In areas of absolute certainty, knowledge is obtained from authorities.	In areas in which certain answers exist, beliefs are justified by reference to authorities' views. In areas in which answers do not exist, beliefs are defended as personal opinion since the link between evidence and beliefs is unclear.
Quasi-Reflective Thinking: Stages 4 and 5		
4	Knowledge is uncertain and knowledge claims are idiosyncratic to the individual since situational variables (such as incorrect reporting of data, data lost over time, or disparities in access to information) dictate that knowing always involves an element of ambiguity.	Beliefs are justified by giving reasons and using evidence, but the arguments and choice of evidence are idiosyncratic (for example, choosing evidence that fits an established belief).
5	Knowledge is contextual and subjective since it is filtered through a person's perceptions and criteria for judgment. Only interpretations of evidence, events, or issues may be known.	Beliefs are justified within a particular context by means of the rules of inquiry for that context and by context-specific interpretations of evidence. Specific beliefs are assumed to be context specific or are balanced against other interpretations, which complicate (and sometimes delay) conclusions.
Reflective Thinking: Stages 6 and 7		
6	Knowledge is constructed into individual conclusions about ill-structured problems on the basis of information from a variety of sources. Interpretations that are based on evaluations of evidence across contexts and on the evaluated opinions of reputable others can be known.	Beliefs are justified by comparing evidence and opinion from different perspectives on an issue or across different contexts and by constructing solutions that are evaluated by criteria such as the weight of the evidence, the utility of the solution, or the pragmatic need for action.
7	Knowledge is the outcome of a process of reasonable inquiry in which solutions to ill-structured problems are constructed. The adequacy of those solutions is evaluated in terms of what is most reasonable or probable according to the current evidence, and it is reevaluated when relevant new evidence, perspectives, or tools of inquiry become available.	Beliefs are justified probabilistically on the basis of a variety of interpretive considerations, such as the weight of the evidence, the explanatory value of the interpretations, the risk of erroneous conclusions, consequences or alternative judgments, and the interrelationships of these factors. Conclusions are defended as representing the most complete, plausible, or compelling understanding of an issue on the basis of the available evidence.

Source: King and Kitchener (1994, 14–16).

EXHIBIT 2

How to Assign Critical Thinking Elements to Particular Accounting Courses in Light of Student Intellectual Stage and Course Content

Accounting Course	Student's Intellectual Stage at Time Course is Taken[a]	Critical Thinking Elements that Course Should Focus on Developing		
		Affective (Disposition)	Cognitive (Thought Processes)	Behavioral (Actions or Strategies)
Principles	I	Welcoming divergent views		Employing precise terms
Intermediate I	I/II	Tolerating ambiguity	Thinking Independently	Employing precise terms
Intermediate II and/or Advanced	II	Recognizing personal biases: Welcoming divergent views	Resisting over-generalization	Applying knowledge to new situations
Cost/Managerial	II			Modifying judgments in light of new information
Audit/Systems	II/III		Analyzing data for value and content; Synthesizing	Modifying judgments in light of new information
Tax	II/III			Gathering facts: Applying knowledge to new situations: Employing precise terms
Capstone (e.g., topics course)	III/IV		Defining problems accurately; Employing a variety of thinking processes	Encouraging critical dialogue; Distinguishing fact from opinion; Listening actively

[a] Stages of Intellectual Development (Kurfiss, 1988)
I–Assumes that knowledge is a collection of indisputable facts.
II–Recognizes ambiguity, but resolves ambiguity with unsupported opinions.
III–Collects evidence to support opinions, but feels everything is relative, that is, believes all solutions are equally valid.
IV–Can weigh alternative arguments and commit to a position.

Source: Kimmel (1995).

Several accounting researchers have put Kimmel's suggestions in practice. For example, Catanach, Croll, and Grinaker (2000, 583) use a business activity model in Intermediate Financial Accounting to teach critical thinking skills. Springer and Borthick (2004, 277) use a business simulation to shift their introductory accounting students from "knowing" to "thinking" because the simulation emphasizes communication skills, alternative viewpoints, and the effect of assumptions on business decisions. Similarly, Bamber and Bamber (2006, 267) use 10-K reports "to help students understand and start to grapple with the ambiguity and complexity inherent in real-world management accounting," while Daigle, Hayes, and Hughes II (2007, 149) assess student learning outcomes in the introductory accounting information systems course using the AICPA's Core Competency Framework and its emphasis on skills, not content. Rhoades and Rhoades (1985) have students use newspaper articles to identify and discuss different viewpoints in order to help students identify facts from opinions. For more ideas, the reader should consult Bonk and Smith (1998, 261) who discuss a myriad of critical and creative thinking techniques, activities, and examples that can be used to promote active, student-centered learning.

A technique that shows promise for developing critical thinking—at least in higher-level courses—is problem-based learning (PBL). PBL is "a method of instruction that uses problems as a context for students to acquire problem-solving skills and basic knowledge" (Banta et al. 2000, p. 1). Although several varieties of PBL exist, all recommend that instructors use case materials to teach basic technical knowledge (Johnstone and Biggs 1998, 413). Specifically, students are required to establish what the main problems are within the cases, how the problems might be resolved, how any proposed resolution might be evaluated, and what knowledge they need to acquire before they can construct a solution (Pithers and Soden 2000). The primary role of the instructor is to facilitate group processes and learning, not to provide easy answers.

The faculty at Boise State University (Bigelow 2004, 591) developed four PBL projects for use in their first management course. The first project could easily be adapted to an accounting setting. In this first project, students are given details about a hypothetical situation in which they are working in an engineering firm and are assigned to a disciplinary review committee. The committee is considering what should be done about a bridge inspector who contributed to a news article that embarrassed the firm. Students are asked to write an essay describing what they would do. After turning in an essay, students are given an opportunity to search for additional information. This information is provided in the form of an online office with clickable items but not all the materials are relevant, making it necessary for students to ascertain the relevance of various pieces of information. Students are then asked if they would change what they said in their first essay. They are asked to reflect on how they approached the problem given them and are introduced to a problem-solving model developed by the faculty. As a result of this project, students are thought to gain an appreciation for the qualities of a real-world situation (e.g., a poorly defined problem, no superior who will clarify the situation, multiple issues, and the need to do something, as opposed to simply recommending what should be done).

As evidence of PBL's value as a teaching tool, undergraduate nursing students at a university in Hong Kong showed significantly greater improvement in overall critical thinking dispositions (as measured by the California Critical Thinking Dispositions Inventory (CCTDI)) compared with lecture students (Tiwari et al. 2006). However, student satisfaction with the PBL class format is mixed. Sasse et al. (2000) cited student comments that indicate that they enjoyed the format and that it had a positive impact on their learning. However, these authors also found that many students expressed frustration because of the ill-structured nature of the format. Chye et al. (2000, 9) reported student complaints that there were too few notes, that many students preferred a passive learning style to an active one, that more studying was required, and that students were anxious about the relative ambiguity of the PBL approach, as opposed to the rigid and clear structure of the lecture approach.

HOW SHOULD WE ASSESS CRITICAL THINKING?

One of the weaknesses of prior research is that little is known about specific reasons why students' critical thinking skills improve. To provide evidence on this issue, researchers should not only explicitly identify desired educational objectives, but those objectives should be explicitly linked to educational interventions (FOSOA 1999).

Paul's (1995) intellectual standards are a useful framework for talking about educational objectives related to critical thinking. See Exhibit 3. Intellectual standards apply to thinking in every subject. Intellectual standards are more useful if they are made explicit to the students analyzing a case and to the instructors performing the assessment. Making standards explicit benefits students because "they can then see that there are standards, that the standards are not arbitrary, and that understanding the standards gives them insight into what good critical thinking is" (Paul 1995, 132). Standards benefit those doing the assessing because it fosters both uniformity in grading and a strong correlation between the grade and the skills being assessed. "Judging a response by how *clearly* and *completely* it states a position, for example, is using a critical thinking standard and dictates a certain level of assessment; judging a response by how *concisely* or how *elegantly* it states a position, on the other hand, is using a standard that is inappropriate to critical thinking assessment" (Paul 1995, 132).

A system of intellectual standards benefits instructors because such standards can readily be built into classroom instruction in the teaching of higher order thinking skills. Anecdotal evidence suggests that most accounting educators feel pressed to cover all the pertinent material related to the topic without finding time to include the teaching of critical thinking skills. However, critical thinking experts would argue that our students would be better served by being exposed to fewer facts and more good thinking, and many accounting practitioners would appear to agree. More than one-half of CPA respondents were willing to sacrifice some accounting knowledge in order to enhance thinking skills, problem-solving skills, listening skills, and writing skills (Novin and Pearson 1989).

EXHIBIT 3
Intellectual Standards
That Apply to Thinking in Every Subject

Thinking that is:		Thinking that is:
Clear	vs.	Unclear
Precise	vs.	Imprecise
Specific	vs.	Vague
Accurate	vs.	Inaccurate
Relevant	vs.	Irrelevant
Plausible	vs.	Implausible
Consistent	vs.	Inconsistent
Logical	vs.	Illogical
Deep	vs.	Superficial
Broad	vs.	Narrow
Complete	vs.	Incomplete
Significant	vs.	Trivial
Adequate (for purpose)	vs.	Inadequate
Fair	vs.	Biased or One-Sided

Source: Paul (1995, 131).

WHAT MEASURES ARE AVAILABLE TO ASSESS CRITICAL THINKING?

Two different means of assessing critical thinking exist: nationally-normed objective tests and naturalistic measures (such as rubrics to evaluate case analyses).

Nationally-Normed Objective Tests

Because empirical researchers prefer measures that are recognized as reliable, they frequently choose nationally-normed objective tests, such as the:

- Watson-Glaser Critical Thinking Appraisal (WGCTA)
- California Critical Thinking Skills Test (CCTST)
- California Critical Thinking Dispositions Inventory (CCTDI)
- Academic Profile (A. PROFILE)
- Collegiate Assessment of Academic Proficiency (CAAP)
- Collegiate Learning Assessment (CLA)
- CAAP Critical Thinking Assessment Battery (CTAB)
- Cornell Critical Thinking Test (CCTT)
- College Outcomes Measures Program—Objective Test (COMP)
- ETS Tasks in Critical Thinking (ETS TASKS)
- Measure of Intellectual Development (MID)
- Problem Solving Inventory (PSI)
- Reflective Judgment Inventory (RJI)

These commercially available critical thinking tests are limited in their ability to adequately assess changes in students' critical thinking abilities, but their careful development, standardized scoring, and general use make them good candidates for use in educational research projects (Reed 1998). The National Postsecondary Education Cooperative (NPEC 2000) performed a comprehensive review of a subset of the aforementioned tests. The NPEC separated critical thinking into seven major categories: Interpretation, Analysis, Evaluation, Inference, Presenting Arguments, Reflection, and Dispositions. No single test was found to measure every aspect of critical thinking. In fact, the NPEC concluded that even with all of the tests combined, all critical thinking skills were not assessed. A review of critical thinking measures used specifically in accounting education and assessment research can be found in the Wolcott, et al. (2002) paper.

In addition to being incomplete measures of critical thinking, these commercially available tests may lack power relative to more direct measures of student competency. In fact, some researchers have suggested that "multiple-choice tests are not valid indicators of critical thinking ability because test-takers are not free to determine their own questions or apply their own evaluative criteria" (Reed 1998). As such, several general knowledge standardized essay tests for critical thinking have been developed as alternatives to multiple-choice formats. The Ennis-Weir Critical Thinking Essay Test (Ennis and Weir 1985), the best-known and most widely-used example, requires students to read an essay on an everyday issue containing numerous reasoning errors and to construct their own response. The time and cost involved in grading open-ended assessments and the expertise required to grade them reliably has limited their use, however.

Naturalistic Measures or Rubrics

The second type of critical thinking assessment methodology consists of naturalistic, or locally-developed, measures. The main advantage of this methodology is that such measures are based on highly explicit criteria which improve measurement reliability. The American Accounting Association (AAA) offers a *Critical Thinking Skills Tool Kit* (2002) that includes information on Lynch, Wolcott, and Huber's (2001) *Steps for Better Thinking: A Developmental Problem Solving Process.* The tool kit includes detailed information on constructing rubrics to assess critical thinking skills.

A rubric is a means to embed in a course project an assessment opportunity that measures learning-goal achievements and provides students with consistent, measured feedback (Nitko 2001). Subjectivity can never be completely eliminated when educators grade students by means other than objective test questions, but a rubric at least establishes norms and ranges within which subjectivity can be controlled.

Holistic Rubrics

There are two types of rubrics: holistic and analytic. A holistic rubric requires the educator and/or researcher to score the overall process or product as a whole, without judging the component parts separately. See Exhibit 4. In contrast, with an analytic rubric, the educator scores

EXHIBIT 4
Holistic Critical Thinking Scoring Rubric

4 Consistently does all or almost all of the following:
- Accurately interprets evidence, statements, graphics, questions etc.
- Identifies the salient arguments (reasons and claims) pro and con.
- Thoughtfully analyzes and evaluates major alternative points of view.
- Draws warranted, judicious, non-fallacious conclusions.
- Justifies key results and procedures, explains assumptions and reasons.
- Fair-mindedly follows where evidence and reasons lead.

3 Does most or many of the following:
- Accurately interprets evidence, statements, graphics, questions etc.
- Identifies relevant arguments (reasons and claims) pro and con.
- Offers analyses and evaluations of obvious alternative points of view.
- Draws warranted non-fallacious conclusions.
- Justifies some results or procedures, explains reasons.
- Fair-mindedly follows where evidence and reasons lead.

2 Does most or many of the following:
- Misinterprets evidence, statements, graphics, questions, etc.
- Fails to identify strong, relevant counter-arguments.
- Ignores or superficially evaluates obvious alternative points of view.
- Draws unwarranted or fallacious conclusions.
- Justifies few results or procedures, seldom explains reasons.
- Regardless of the evidence or reasons, maintains or defends views based on self-interest or preconceptions.

1 Consistently does all or almost all of the following:
- Offers biased interpretations of evidence, statements, graphics, questions, information, or the points of view of others.
- Fails to identify or hastily dismisses strong, relevant counter-arguments.
- Ignores or superficially evaluates obvious alternative points of view.
- Argues using fallacious or irrelevant reasons, and unwarranted claims.
- Does not justify results or procedures, nor explain reasons.
- Regardless of the evidence or reasons, maintains or defends views based on self-interest or preconceptions.
- Exhibits close-mindedness or hostility to reason.

Available at http://www.insightassessment.com/pdf_files/rubric.pdf

EXHIBIT 5
Template for Analytic Rubrics

	Beginning 1	Developing 2	Accomplished 3	Exemplary 4	Score
Criteria #1	Description reflecting beginning level of performance	Description reflecting movement toward mastery level of performance	Description reflecting achievement of mastery level of performance	Description reflecting highest level of performance	
Criteria #2	Description reflecting beginning level of performance	Description reflecting movement toward mastery level of performance	Description reflecting achievement of mastery level of performance	Description reflecting highest level of performance	
Criteria #3	Description reflecting beginning level of performance	Description reflecting movement toward mastery level of performance	Description reflecting achievement of mastery level of performance	Description reflecting highest level of performance	
Criteria #4	Description reflecting beginning level of performance	Description reflecting movement toward mastery level of performance	Description reflecting achievement of mastery level of performance	Description reflecting highest level of performance	

Source: Mertler (2001).

separate, individual parts of the product or performance first, and then sums the individual scores to obtain a total score (Nitko 2001). Holistic rubrics are customarily used when errors in some part of the process can be tolerated, provided the overall quality is high (Chase 1999). Nitko (2001) further states that use of holistic rubrics is probably more appropriate when performance tasks require students to create some sort of response for which there is no definitive correct answer. The focus of a score report using a holistic rubric is on the overall quality, proficiency, or understanding of the specific content and skills. Use of holistic rubrics can result in a somewhat quicker scoring process than use of analytic rubrics as the educator is required to read through the student product only once, in order to get an overall sense of what the student was able to accomplish (Mertler 2001). However, only limited feedback is typically provided to the student as a result of scoring performance tasks in this manner.

Analytic Rubrics

Analytic rubrics are usually preferred for performance tasks in which there may be one or two acceptable responses and creativity is not an essential feature of the student's responses (Mertler 2001). Analytic rubrics result initially in several scores, followed by a summed total score. While demanding of an instructor, the analytic rubric offers a significant amount of feedback to a student. A template for analytic scoring rubrics is presented in Exhibit 5. One type of rubric is not inherently better than the other. The educator must find a format that works best for his or her course or purposes. Susan Wolcott, an expert on rubric design, uses a combination rubric most often. See Exhibit 6.

One potentially frustrating aspect of scoring student work with rubrics is the issue of converting the score to a grade. Trice (2000) suggests that in a rubric scoring system, there are typically more scores at the average and above average categories (i.e., equating to grades of "C" or better) than there are below-average categories. For instance, if a rubric consisted of nine score categories, the equivalent grade categories might look as follows:

EXHIBIT 6
Steps for Better Thinking Competency Rubric

		Performance Pattern 0 "Confused Fact Finder"	Performance Pattern 1 "Biased Jumper"	Performance Pattern 2 "Perpetual Analyzer"	Performance Pattern 3 "Pragmatic Performer"	Performance Pattern 4 "Strategic Revisioner"
Step 1 Skills	Identify relevant information Circle ALL that apply	Identifies facts, definitions, and/or experts' opinions.	Identifies information[1] that is relevant to the problem	Explores a wide range of relevant information[1]	Focuses on the most important relevant information[1]	Develops viable strategies for generating important relevant information[1] over time
	Recognize and address uncertainties[2] Circle ALL that apply	Identifies at least one reason for temporary uncertainty[2]	Identifies at least one reason for significant and permanent uncertainty[2]	Addresses significant and permanent uncertainties[2] when interpreting information	Identifies and discusses the significance of the most important uncertainties[2]	Develops viable strategies for minimizing important uncertainties[2] over time
Step 2 Skills	Integrate multiple perspectives[3] and clarify assumptions[4] Circle ALL that apply		Acknowledges more than one potential solution, approach, or viewpoint	Analyzes information from multiple perspectives,[3] including assumptions[4] and alternative objectives	Provides reasonable and substantive justification for assumptions[4] used in analysis	Argues convincingly using a complex, coherent discussion of own perspective; Articulates strengths and weaknesses of position
	Interpret and organize information Circle ALL that apply		Uses evidence logically to support a point of view; Correctly applies concepts/theories/techniques	Qualitatively interprets information and develops meaningful categories for analysis	Preserves problem complexity, but emphasizes the most important and/or most relevant and reliable information	Systematically re-interprets information as circumstances change or new information becomes available
Step 3 Skills	Use guidelines or principles to judge objectively across options Circle ALL that apply			Avoids reaching a biased conclusion	Maintains objectivity while establishing reasonable priorities for reaching a well-founded conclusion	Uses a systematic process of critical inquiry to build a solution; Articulates how problem solving approach and criteria can be refined, leading to better solutions or greater confidence over time
	Communicate and implement conclusions Circle ALL that apply				Appropriately tailors communication or implementation plans to the setting and audience	Provides appropriate information to motivate and engage others in long-term strategies
Step 4 Skills	Address solution limitations Circle ALL that apply				Focuses on most efficient ways to address limitations or to gather additional information	Articulates solution limitations as a natural part of addressing open-ended problems
	Engage in continuous improvement Circle ALL that apply					Identifies uncertainties and limitations as opportunities for continuous improvement; Engages in lifelong learning
Overall Approach to the Problem Circle ONLY ONE		Proceeds as if goal is to find the single, "correct" answer	Proceeds as if goal is to stack up evidence and information to support own conclusion	Proceeds as if goal is to establish an unbiased, balanced view of evidence and information from different points of view	Proceeds as if goal is to come to a well-founded conclusion based on objective consideration of priorities across viable alternatives	Proceeds as if goal is to strategically construct knowledge, to move toward better conclusions or greater confidence in conclusions as the problem is addressed over time

[1] Information can take many forms, including facts, descriptions, definitions, arguments, opinions, ideas, claims, theories, concepts, observations, research findings, values, perceptions, beliefs, influences, effects, and so on. Information can be obtained in many ways such as reading, seeing, hearing, touching, feeling, experiencing, interacting, thinking, etc.

[2] Uncertainties can relate to many aspects of the problem, including the problem definition, availability of solution alternatives, quality and interpretation of information, effects of alternatives, priorities and values of the decision maker and others, and so on. Temporary uncertainties relate to conditions that will become known in the future (e.g., experts will find the answer, information will become available, or effects will be knowable).

[3] Perspectives can relate to any type of grouping that is meaningful to the problem, such as categories of people, cultures, societies, roles, races, genders, hierarchies, theories, concepts, ideas, beliefs, attitudes, physical locations, time, disciplines, values, emotions, and so on.

[4] Assumptions are hypotheses, suppositions, conjectures, assertions, presumptions, beliefs, or premises that are taken for granted or that lie behind an argument. Assumptions are made because of uncertainties; the "truth" cannot be known or proven. Some assumptions are better than others. Better assumptions are more reasonable, logical, comprehensive, plausible, likely, rational, impartial, objective, justified, credible, and/or believable.

Sample Grades and Categories

Rubric Score	Grade	Category
8	A+	Excellent
7	A	Excellent
6	B+	Good
5	B	Good
4	C+	Fair
3	C	Fair
2	U	Unsatisfactory
1	U	Unsatisfactory
0	U	Unsatisfactory

Bigelow (2004) agrees that "given the long way our students have to go in learning problem-solving, it would be inappropriate to translate competency scores directly into grades (e.g., 90% is an "A", 80% is a 'B,' etc.)." Doing so would cause most students to fail the course. As such, Bigelow curves the scores and gains measures of competence (their original scores) and an acceptable grade profile (curved scores) for the course.

While most accounting researchers have focused on critical thinking assessment within individual courses, Doney et al. (1993) suggest the following assessment criteria for use in assessing critical thinking across the accounting curriculum:

1. *Students will demonstrate an increase in critical thinking in the domain-specific area of accounting.*
   Measurement: Pre-post testing using case studies both by class and by core content area
2. *Students will demonstrate development of critical thinking in general.*
   Measurement: Evaluation using a commercial test of critical thinking
3. *Students will demonstrate critical thinking by successfully passing normed tests in accounting.*
   Measurement: Examinations such as College-Level Examination Program, Subject Examination in Introductory Accounting, ACT (American College Testing Program) Examination Program: Accounting, Levels I, II and III
4. *Students will demonstrate development of critical thinking in written communication, papers, and oral presentations.*
   Measurement: Homework assignments, case studies, and group projects carefully designed to enhance the students' critical thinking abilities, rather than deterministic "answerable problem sets" and measured using instructor-developed rubrics; see Exhibit 7
5. *Employers will report satisfaction with the critical thinking skills of the accounting graduates they have hired.*
   Measurement: Focus groups, questionnaires, and interviews after hiring accounting graduates from re-focused program
6. *Graduates will report satisfaction with the level of critical thinking skills developed in the accounting curriculum.*
   Measurement: Alumni survey, focus groups, questionnaires, and qualitative research
7. *Accounting faculty will demonstrate the ability to integrate critical thinking skills with accounting knowledge.*
   Measurement: Teaching innovation/case development, simulation, internships

EXHIBIT 7
Designing Scoring Rubrics: Step-By-Step Procedures

Designing Scoring Rubrics:

Step-by-Step Procedure

Step 1: Re-examine the learning objectives to be addressed by the task.

Step 2: Identify specific observable attributes that you want to see (as well as those you don't want to see) your students demonstrate in their product, process, or performance.

Step 3: Brainstorm characteristics that describe each attribute.

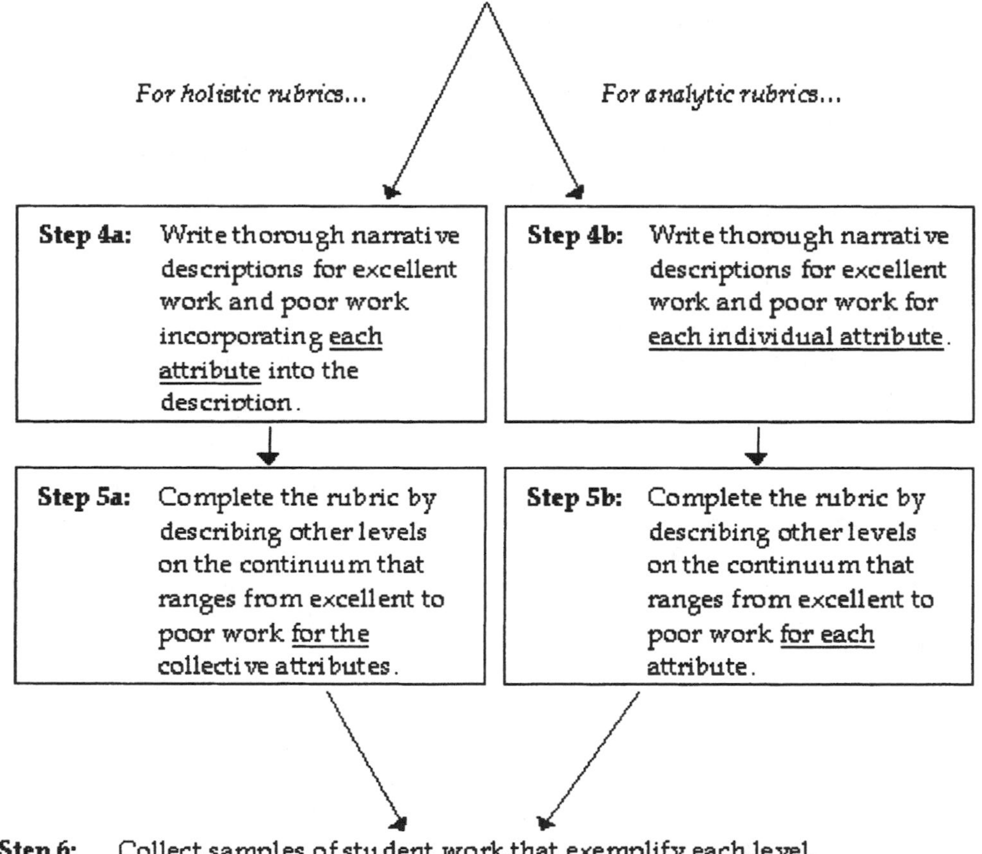

Step 6: Collect samples of student work that exemplify each level.

Step 7: Revise the rubric, as necessary.

Source: Mertler (2001).

STUDENT EVALUATIONS ROADBLOCK

The purpose of this article is to discuss different methods of instructing accounting students in sound thinking skills and to evaluate the different means of assessing students' critical thinking skills. The development of such skills should be a key desired outcome of higher education. However, a study by Smith (2004, 20) found that sampled students' course evaluations do not provide the feedback needed for developing a critical-thinking-based teaching environment. Instead the current methods of assessing instructor performance are lacking in that "the consequence of emphasizing students' satisfaction measures at the expense of students' learning measures is an unchanging accounting teaching model set in methodologies that do not support the development of critical thinking skills." The classroom instructor needs to be provided with specific information about teaching activities if the 'broken education models' (Albrecht and Sack, 2000) are to be changed.

A question for future consideration is whether the assessment of students' critical thinking skills can be used as a tool for evaluating the teaching effectiveness of individual faculty members. Currently, there is no agreement on this issue. For example, at Prince George's Community College, assessment is not linked in any way to evaluating individual faculty members (Peirce 2005). However, at Arizona State University (ASU), every academic department will have students take the Collegiate Learning Assessment, which measures critical thinking ability, beginning Fall 2007. In fact, "several of ASU's academic officials said their departments would use tests that measure how well students have learned the material to judge how professors are doing" (Gabrielson 2007).

One thing seems certain if student evaluations of critical thinking instruction are to be used in the future evaluation of faculty, the incorporation of such instruction must be done with care. Husbands (1997) finds that some course-specific characteristics hinder the educator's task of producing a satisfactory learning environment. Size of enrollment and number of other lecturers involved (e.g., in labs) were found to negatively impact student ratings, while quality of course organization positively impacted student ratings. As such, the incorporation of critical thinking exercises should be limited to those exercises that are well-written and well-organized. Cases and the associated grading rubrics are seldom perfect when first developed, but rather they need to be revised after each use (Mertler 2001). As such, the educator may decide to use a newly-developed rubric for his or her own grading purposes but not share it with students until the second or third revision.

CONCLUSION

There is no one best way to teach or measure critical thinking. Dr. Gerald Nosich (2007), a noted authority on critical thinking, suggests that the more instruments used, the better will be the overall assessment and that the more assignments assessed, the better will be the overall assessment of student learning. Only time will tell if the assessment of critical thinking skills can be used as an effective supplement to the primary means of instructor assessment, student evaluations of teachers. But at the very least, it should be used as a means of assessing the individual student's grasp of a critical component of the student's future success in our complex, expanding, and constantly changing profession.

CHAPTER 9

Multiple Teaching Performance Measurements Needed: SET Management Similar to Earnings Management

Ronald E. Flinn, Creighton University
D. Larry Crumbley, Louisiana State University*

Responsibility to students is at the core of a university's mission and of a faculty member's academic duty (Kennedy 1997, 60). The extensive education literature on teaching effectiveness, including the work of the Accounting Education Change Commission (AECC 1999), the American Accounting Association's Teaching & Curriculum Section's Committee on Promoting and Evaluating Teaching Effectiveness (the PETE report), and several articles in this monograph, have all consistently urged that multiple measures should be utilized if the goal is to appropriately evaluate the teaching effectiveness of college professors, and to determine how teaching effectiveness relates to student learning (Calderon et al. 1996; Davies et al. 2007; Green et al. 1999; Kember and Gow 1994; Lucal et al. 2003; O'Hanlon and Mortensen 1980).

As discussed in the literature and several articles herein, the current SET questionnaires, scores, and processes do not directly measure teaching effectiveness or student learning, or allow the various links (and directions) between effective teaching and student learning to be studied. At least some accounting faculty, accounting program administrators, and Deans of business schools will now admit that the extensive use of SET scores for summative evaluation of teaching effectiveness has not achieved the critical goal congruence between a professor's behavior and student learning and may in fact reduce such goal congruence.

As Marsha Huber (herein) discusses, sound education theory and all major accreditation bodies (including the AACSB), the Spellings Commission (2006), and other accrediting organizations now insist on the use of direct measures of student achievement and learning. As discussed by Ronald Huefner, and Larry Crumbley and G. Stevenson Smith (herein), SET scores do much more to measure short-run student satisfaction, which while important, is much less important than student achievement and learning. Patrick Moore (herein) argues that some faculty and administrators resist change in this area because a more direct and accurate measure of effective teaching and student learning would likely upset the *status quo*.

* Dr. Flinn is Associate Professor of Accounting at Creighton University. rflinn@creighton.edu. Dr. Crumbley is KPMG Endowed Professor at LSU. dcrumbl@lsu.edu.

While candid student feedback can be valuable to a faculty in a formative sense, the use of SET scores as the only or primary measure, for summative evaluation of teaching effectiveness has not worked and arguably has reduced student learning by causing grade inflation, course work deflation, and professors pandering to students as the use of SET has increased (Crumbley and Fliedner 2002). The notion that students are capable of critiquing their professor's teaching effectiveness grew out of the largely failed "students as customers" movement which, on balance, has reduced rather than increased student learning. Langbein (2008) argues that the extensive focus on SET scores causes faculty and administrators to have to play a socially destructive game in which professors compete for largely invalid SET scores (at least in terms of student achievement and learning) and, somewhat ironically, student learning suffers.

In the mid-90's, 90.6 percent of accounting administrators said that SET were used in promotion decisions, with 69.3 percent indicating use of SET scores in merit pay decisions (Crumbley and Fliedner 2002).

THE PETE REPORT

The PETE report (Green et al. 1999, 72–73), recommended the following:

1. Accounting departments should have a coherent framework for encouraging effective teaching. The framework requires a clearly defined mission, broad goals, specific objectives, and performance norms and targets. The mission, broad goals, and specific objectives of an institution should be tightly linked and performance norms and targets should flow from specific objectives.
2. Although it is vital to access outcomes, institutions should also focus on the processes used in teaching. Accounting departments should consider and apply the dimensions of effective teaching in evaluating the teaching process. Faculty play a dominant role in that process and the contribution of individual faculty should be assessed by examining whether the processes they use contribute to the outcomes (specific objectives) desired by the department.
3. A focus on the dimensions of effective teaching requires the use of a portfolio of information. While student evaluations of faculty teaching (SET) have the potential to shed light on important aspects of the teaching process, SET do not provide the comprehensive array of information necessary to assess all the dimensions of effective teaching. Therefore, institutions should not place excessive reliance on Student Evaluation of Teaching (SET) in evaluating faculty teaching performance. Comprehensive teaching portfolios should be used to access faculty teaching performance.
4. A modified version of the Accounting Education Change Commission (AECC) dimensions of effective teaching should be used as a framework for building teaching portfolios and for evaluating faculty teaching performance. [See AECC 1993]

OVERUSE OF SET

Sheehan's (1975, 697) concerns about the overuse of SET to evaluate teaching effectiveness are valid today:

> Should the administrative use of student ratings be discontinued? The answer is 'yes' if they are used and interpreted as perfectly valid measures of instructional effectiveness. Yet used and interpreted in conjunction with other measures (i.e., colleague ratings, self-ratings, videotaped segments of instruction, course materials, etc.), student ratings can reveal the attitudes of students as customers in the instructional process. Administrators should make use of this information

> without forgetting that classificatory errors result because of the imperfect validity of the ratings. Until instrumentation is improved, the strategy of administrators should be one of collecting as much information from as many sources as possible.

In commenting on course work deflation, grade inflation, and pandering to students caused in part by the extensive use of SET for summative purposes, Zimmerman (2002) states:

> Higher education is defined and judged by its graduates. Rigorous academic standards are the key to high quality college graduates. Individual faculty can set and maintain high standards in their classes. However, given the current situation of reduced rigor and inflated grades that exists on many campuses, faculty acting *individually often do so at their own risk* in terms of career advancement. Therefore, faculty, administrators, and students must work together to institute broad-based changes ... to reverse the tendencies for reduced rigor and grade inflation [emphasis added].

Murray (2008) asserts that instead of helping high school graduates grow up, universities prolong their childhood. He found that at his alma mater, Hamilton (1,700 students), now has 26 full-time people to manage students that required only three people in the 1960s. Internet site Pickaprof.com gives the grade point average of most professors' classes and even compares the percentage of As, Bs, and so on with previous instructors who have taught the course. Thus, students check the site and can pick the easiest professor. Many students enter a course already with an opinion of its difficulty and the difficulty of the instructor.

In his book about college education, *Higher Learning,* Derek Bok, former president of Harvard University, states:

> Teaching students to generalize methods of inquiry and to synthesize information are some of the most important goals of an undergraduate curriculum (Bok 1986, 44).
>
> ... college administrators and faculty members generally agree that upon completion of an undergraduate degree, graduates should possess these key attributes: the ability to think critically; the ability to communicate with clarity and style; and acquaintance with important fields of knowledge and modes of thought (Bok 1986, 63).

A major issue addressed in the accounting and business education literature and in this monograph is: does the present extensive use of SET for administrative control purposes and as a summative evaluation of teaching effectiveness (Crumbley and Fliedner 2002; Merritt 2008; Smith 2004) contribute to achieving the lofty goals expressed by Bok? Vasta and Sarmiento (1979) found that liberal grading resulted in higher SET scores but not more studying or better student performance. Sullivan and Skanes (1974) found that professors who focused on achievement rather than projecting enthusiasm received lower SET scores, but produced students who learned more and did better in future courses.

Outlawing SET

Would student learning cease if SET or a similar control device were not used to evaluate teaching effectiveness (Chonko 2006)? Almost no one doubts that students would continue to learn if SET or some similar control device was not used (Davies et al. 2007; Demski 2007; Wagenaar 2005; Yunker and Yunker 2003; Smith 2004). The current focus on assessment and directly measuring student learning in business colleges (Kimmell et al. 1998; Marshall 2007; Martell 2007; Shaftel and Shaftel 2007) does suggest that SET do not adequately measure learning, certainly not at the program level. Among others, Clayson and Haley 2005; Martin 1998; Newton 1988; Wallace and Wallace 1998; and Zimmerman 2002 argue persuasively that treating students as customers and the extensive use of SET as summative measures of teaching effectiveness have caused course work deflation (Fischer 2007; Holbrook 2005; Zimmerman 2002), grade inflation (Cluskey, Jr., et al. 1997), the commoditization of higher education (Singh 2002) and, more generally, professors pandering to students with the resulting decline in student learning. As in the case for corporate performance evaluation systems (Jensen 2001), an inappropriate reward system for accounting professors fosters neither goal congruence nor student learning. Teaching in universities today is like nuclear warfare. There are no winners, just survivors.

Other Means of Evaluating Teaching Effectiveness Needed

Even if SET are not replaced outright, the scholarship of teaching deserves a more appropriate and more balanced evaluation of teaching effectiveness than SET allow (Boyer 1992) or should play a more formative role in the evaluation process as originally intended. Even William Cashin (1989, 4) who has long supported the reliability and validity of SET agrees that summative SET *should not* be the only item used to evaluate teaching effectiveness:

> Nevertheless, student ratings are only one source of data about teaching and must be used in combination with multiple sources of data if one wishes to make a judgment about all of the components of college teaching. Further, student ratings are data that must be interpreted. We should not confuse a source of data with the evaluators who *use the data* to make a judgment [emphasis added].

General education research and specific accounting and business education and assessment research (Stout et al. 2005) all strongly support the notion that a broader portfolio approach should be used to evaluate an accounting professor's teaching effectiveness to more completely assess the various dimensions of effective teaching and thus promote student learning (Green et al. 1999; Newton 1988; Scarlett 2004). The extensive research on the use of SET in many disciplines supports the view that while SET certainly provide some valuable information for formative and summative purposes, SET "do not provide the comprehensive array of information necessary to assess all the dimensions of effective teaching" (Green et al. 1999, 74). Other accounting education research notes the limited nature of SET information and recommends use of a more formative or developmental approach (Hand and Rowe 2001, 157):

> Once the weaknesses inherent in an isolated end-of-module feedback [provided by SET] is acknowledged, it is necessary to develop a holistic and dynamic [assessment] model that addresses the needs of staff as well as those of other stakeholders. Evaluation and accountability can be seen as an imposition, demanding time and effort from staff with little benefit to them directly. This may particularly be true where feedback is seen as ritualistic and forms part of a regulatory framework. Such an approach, though superficially attractive because of its simplicity, has no clear follow-on and offers little to educators seeking to develop and improve their courses. Nor does it deal with contradictory perspectives. By concentrating on the use of Likert scales and other forms of measurement, regulatory approaches seek to quantify levels of satisfaction. Averaging out the richness and variety of student experience may make for easy judgments but risks the loss of fuller understanding.

> A developmental [formative] approach, on the other hand, recognizes the way in which feedback might form part of a continuous cycle of evidence-gathering, reflection, and change. Seeking out contradictions and diverse views, such an approach may expose complex issues and problems, but these are precisely the ones which must be grappled with as educators if the aim is to improve the student learning experience. At the same time, drawing on a wide range of sources, the feedback offers the opportunity to reach decisions in the light of a more rounded and nuanced understanding.

Accounting education research has determined that the following five factors are most important in creating a positive learning environment for accounting students: course content; classroom mechanics; teaching techniques; student involvement in class activities; and positive learning atmosphere (Stice and Stocks 2000). But much accounting education research suggests SET continue to be the most frequently used summative measure of teaching effectiveness (Bruns et al. 2004, 179; Stone 1996).

Thus, there continues to be a conflict between what is known to enhance learning by accounting students and the rather narrow manner in which the teaching effectiveness of accounting professors is defined (classroom instruction) and is evaluated (summative SETs) by administrators (Best 2008; Lucas and Mladenovic 2004). Student learning suffers as a result of this conflict in part because many faculty are afraid to do what they know is needed, such as assigning case studies, reading novels, requiring term papers, and using essay exams instead of giving multiple choice exams that often test memory skills rather than understanding (Langbein 2008).

In addition, administrators and faculty concerned with student learning should ask themselves if any professor, no matter how dedicated, gifted, hard-working, and knowledgeable, can effectively teach students who have a "deep distrust of anything claiming to be objectively true or generally valid" (Holbrook 2005, 5), and who are often much more concerned with the physical attractiveness ("hotness") of their professor and the ease of course work and examinations than learning (Felton et al. 2006). Administrators and faculty should also ask themselves if such students can objectively evaluate their professors' teaching efforts. Honest answers to such questions are needed to promote student learning, and perhaps ironically to improve teaching effectiveness.

The fallacy of the SET system can be illustrated by a statement from David Berri et al. (2006, 1) explaining fans' reactions to sports' teams. "When a team wins, we praise the players who we think made this happen. When our teams lose, we are just as quick, if not quicker, to blame the players who are responsible for making us feel so bad, especially the coach." When students make low grades, they blame the professor for their low grades and reduce their SET scores.

Merely forcing students to sign a honor pledge at the beginning of the SET form may encourage some of the students to be more truthful.

Alternative Measurements

Educational literature has long suggested that it is preferable to have more types of teaching activities evaluated than less. In addition, "teaching" should be defined much more broadly than classroom instruction. Some commentators have suggested that college teaching encompasses four dimensions, all of which can and should be evaluated: course organization and preparation; classroom performance; approachability and availability; and assessment of student learning (Buskist, Keeley, and Irons [undated]).

Thus, reflective self-assessments, some type of peer review, assessment of classroom instruction by students, peers, and administrators, course portfolios, teaching portfolios, and an assessment of a faculty member's other interactions with students, such as advising, meetings with accounting and business firms, sponsoring accounting organizations, conducting continuing professional education sessions, and interviews with former students should be utilized (Buskist, Keeley, and Irons).

In the mid-90s, accounting administrators indicated the following alternative evidence of teaching performance: instructor provided evidence (24%), student comments (16.6%), classroom visits (16%), peer review (15.1%), administrator visits (9.1%), former student comments (4.3%), and student performance (4%) (Crumbley and Fliedner 2002).

An informal survey was conducted at the Teaching and Curriculum (T&C) section meeting at the 2007 American Accounting Association (AAA) annual meeting in Chicago, Illinois, by Larry Crumbley, the incoming Chairperson of the T&C section. The survey asked attendees to indicate what mechanism their department uses to evaluate teaching (other than student evaluations). The results follow, with number of responses and percentages:

Peer review	33 (63%)
Input of former students	19 (36.5%)
Administrator observation	12 (23%)
Review of syllabus	4 (7.6%)
Self-assessment	4 (7.6%)
Review of teaching (course) portfolio	3 (5.7%)

Each of the following received one vote: focus group with former students and/or practitioners; department chair observation of teaching; review of grade distributions; and pedagogical innovations. The fact that these accounting faculty members were so willing to consider alternative forms of evaluating their teaching effectiveness in spite of the obvious political and other problems associated with using other forms of evaluation, suggests a rather high level of frustration with the extensive use of SET to evaluate teaching and that using one or more of the above in conjunction with SET should be seriously considered by academic accountants and administrators.

G. Smith (2004, 231) suggests the following alternative means to measure teaching effectiveness:

Junior year portfolio review
Comprehensive learning essays
Students' complaints or praise (anecdotal and informal)
Senior exit surveys
Alumni surveys
Focus groups with students
Exit exam
CPA exam results
Job placement statistics
Peer class visit and review of course
Department head class visit and review
Department head interview of faculty member regarding teaching methods
Department review of exams, syllabi, class projects, and other materials
Faculty members' annual report of all activities
Grade distribution in course
Students' performance in sequential courses
Programme intern assessments
Drop rates
Average grade point
Teaching awards

A Metric Teaching Performance Model

Most administrators are wise enough to avoid advertising specific numerical SET guidelines, because of potential legal problems. However, one private university (which put its primary emphasis on teaching and 65% of the faculty member's overall teaching performance is based on SET) provides specific maximum teaching guideline scores on the SET data collected from anonymous student questionnaires:

	For Q1–15	For Q–19
1. Outstanding	Below 1.75	Below 1.5
2. Very Good	Below 2.25	Below 2.0
3. Successful	Below 2.75	Below 2.5
4. Needs Improvement	Below 2.75–3.25	Between 2.5–3.0
5. Unacceptable	Above 3.25	Above 3.0

Question 19 is the typical summative question: "On the whole, the quality of the professor's teaching was ...," where 1 is best and 5 is worst.

Why do most department chairs perceive that a *Journal of Accounting Research* article is better than an *Issues in Accounting Education* article? Both are published in a peer-reviewed journal. At the same time most department heads believe that an easy professor teaching a graduate level course at 10:00 with a 3.83 SET score and GPA of 3.81 is better than a hard professor teaching an undergraduate level course at 8:00 (or 3:30) with a 3.21 SET score and a GPA of 2.97. They are willing to rank journals; yet they blindly rank SET scores from highest to lowest? Suppose an undergraduate course has 60% graduate students and the professor gives Cs and Ds to graduate students? One of the authors can not give D's to graduate students at his university. Why not if they deserve it?

Assuming a university is not totally controlled by SET scores like the private university example above, there is a crude approach to adjusting the SET score. One of the strongest variables for causing invalid traditional SET data results when student satisfaction is measured is a hard grader. Research clearly shows that a harder grader will receive lower SET scores.

Langbein (2008) found (in data of 7,686 students over three years at American University) that the impact of a unit increases in *expected* grade (e.g., B to A) would raise a professor's rating by an average of 0.6 on a 6-point scale (or 10%). She also found that with each increase in average *actual* grade on a 4-point scale, SET scores increase by 0.9 on a 6-point scale. Thus, she suggests that over time the effect of an additional 0.6 or 0.9 in the SET on an increase in merit pay ranking is considerable.

Other studies have found a positive relationship between expected grades and student ratings of teachers. Centra and Creech (1976) found that a student expecting an A grade gave a mean rating of 3.95, 3.74 if expecting a B, 3.41 if expecting a C, and 3.02 if expecting a D. The positive correlation between expected grade and teacher rating was 0.19. The correlation between the average expected grade for each class and the average rating of teacher effectiveness was .20 (N = 19, 194). The positive correlation was even higher with expected grade and value of the course: .26 for individual student responses and the mean correlation of .31. Greenwald and Gillmore (1997) found a standardized path coefficient to be as high as .50. Thus, standard-deviation change from half a standard deviation below the university mean rating to half a standard deviation above would be a change from the university's 31st percentile of professors to the 69th percentile.

Cashin (1989) reminds researchers that in the social sciences validity correlations above 0.70 are unusual, especially when studying complex phenomena (e.g., teaching, learning). Thus, correlations between 0.20 and 0.49 are practically useful.

A crude adjustment can be made to SET scores to place professors on a more level playing field as suggested by some researchers (Greenwald and Gillmore 1997; McPherson 2006; McPherson and Jewell 2007). Assume two professors with the following SET scores and GPA data:

Professor	A	B
SET score	2.90	3.80
GPA given	2.70	3.60
Adjustment	4.00 − 2.70 = 1.30	4.00 − 3.60 = .40
Comparable SET score	2.90 + 1.30 = 4.20	3.80 + .40 = 4.20

Here both professors have similar *adjusted* SET scores of 4.20. In today's climate, however, professor A may be fired. This approach does not adjust for instructors who have higher expectations and cover more material.

Where multiple professors teach the same course, especially when there is a departmental exam, another self-defense approach for a demanding professor is to give a pre-test and post-test during the semester. This testing procedure can demonstrate that learning has really occurred. If the professor is remanded for a low SET evaluation, there is clear documentation about learning levels. This documentation may help to support the instructor's position in promotion and tenure proceedings.

A hard grader, however, is not the only variable affecting a professor's SET score. Robert E. Haskell in his article (herein) outlines a number of contaminating variables. Further, Martin (1998) breaks the 133 confounding variables into four major categories:

1. Environment and Course-Related Variables (26).
2. Student Characteristics (28).
3. Teacher-Related Characteristics (34).
4. Controllable Teacher Practices Related to Course and Students (45). See Appendix A for these tables.

Martin's (1998, 1088) most important observation about SET, however, is that student opinions do not qualify as empirical evidence. Yet administrators (and courts) regularly treat SET opinions as evidence.

Many accounting departments and business schools spend a great deal of time and energy ranking the various top journals. These same departments and colleges should debate and decide which of these 133 variables (found in the tables at the end of this article) are more significant and use the most important ones to adjust the SET scores plus add other teaching effectiveness variables.

Although some of the earlier research found that bias or extraneous variables were not extreme in SET (ranging from 5–25 percent), Haladyna and Hess (1994) found that bias and extraneous factors accounted for 38 percent of the variance in criterion ratings (e.g., gender, age, personality, expected grade, etc.).

Hoyt (1997) found that four variables beyond the instructor's control ranged from 19 percent to 61 percent and averaged 55 percent. Hoyt suggests that administrators must make appropriate adjustments to account for extraneous circumstances. Hanna et al. (1983) indicate that student rating data should be adjusted for student motivation/preferences, class size, and similar unfair influences.

Norming Reports

The School of Business at Montclair State University recognizes that there are many confounding variables that bias SET scores, so they provide their faculty with a set of customized norming reports (Peterson et al. 2008) based upon Brightman's (2005) recommendations that SET must be reliable and valid and have a meaningful norming report. However, their norming reports seem to apply only to class session (day/evening), class level, class focus, and class type. Brightman (2005) believes that it is unfair to compare faculty members without using the correct norming reports.

Peterson et al. (2008) assert that faculty may use the norming reports to game the system (e.g., engage in actions designed to enhance their ratings but not to improve student learning). Such gaming techniques are to make easier examinations, give higher grades, teach higher-level courses, teach classes students elect to take, or teach only during the day. They suggest establishing more appropriate norming reports to more accurately evaluate faculty and "diminish the probability of 'gaming' the system" (Peterson et al. 2008, 397).

Teaching Performance Model

According to David Berri et al. (2006, 3), the analysis of numbers can be difficult. "For people who are not accustomed to looking at numbers systematically, the stories they might believe may not be consistent with the stories the numbers offer." In their book *Wages of Wins,* the authors (Berri et al., 2006) develops a metric based upon the National Basketball Association's (NBA) EFF performance measurement:[1]

$$\text{Points} + \text{Rebounds} + \text{Assists} + \text{Steals} + \text{Blocks} - \text{Missed Field Goals} - \text{Missed Free Throws} - \text{Turnovers/Games}$$

The thirty NBA professional basketball teams compute an efficiency score (EFF) for each of their players. For example, Dirk Nowitzki of the Dallas Mavericks had the highest EFF score (30.0) than any other player during the 2007–2008 season. The EFF score does not consider the salary paid to players. By dividing this EFF score into a player's salary a better evaluation measure is obtained: salary/EFF performance measurement.

Berri et al. (2006, 117) worry about comparing "apples with oranges," so they suggest a WIN Score:

$$\text{Points} + \text{Total Rebounds} + \text{Steals} + \tfrac{1}{2}\,\text{Blocked Shots} + \tfrac{1}{2}\,\text{Assists} - \text{Field Goal Attempts} - \tfrac{1}{2}\,\text{Free Throw Attempts} - \text{Turnovers} - \tfrac{1}{2}\,\text{Personal Fouls}$$

ESPN's John Hollings has developed a basketball player efficiency rating called PER which measures a player's per-minute performance, while adjusting for pace. The PER model takes into account both positive and negative accomplishments, and Hollinger distributes the final PERs in his book *Pro Basketball Forecast.* The electronic *Journal of Basketball Studies* site lists a number of methods to evaluate teams and players.[2] Why are there no academic articles developing methods to evaluate the teaching of professors along these lines?

Educators should develop a teaching model of productivity based possibly around SET scores. Shinkfield and Stufflebeam (1996) indicate that all evaluations should have four basic attributes: propriety, utility, feasibility, and accuracy.

---

[1] There are other basketball models of productivity. Dave Heeren's TENDEX formula is TENDEX = Points + Rebounds + Assists + Blocked Shots + Steals − Turnovers − All missed shots. This value is then weighted by minutes played and game pace. Bob Bellotti's Point Created model is Points Created = Points + Rebounds + Assists + Blocked Shots + Steals − Turnovers − All missed shots − ½ personal fouls.

[2] See Ronald Ratings, www.82games.com; NCAA and NFL have a pass efficiency formula. Baseball has Offensive Efficiency Rating (OER) and Earned Runs Average (ERA).

- Propriety—Ethical and fair to all parties.
- Utility—Informative, timely, and influential so educators will improve their performance.
- Feasibility—Easy to use, adequately funded, and politically viable.
- Accuracy—Based upon dependable information about relevant qualifications and performance.

The teaching model of productivity developed below should replace or compliment norming reports and should meet these four attributes much better than SET scores alone. Below is an example of an EFF score for measuring the teaching performance of a professor, based upon some of the variables in Martin's (1998) four tables (see Tables 1–4) and Peterson et al. (2008):

$$
\begin{aligned}
&\text{SET score} + (4.00 - \text{GPA}) + \underset{\text{Administrator's adjustment}}{(0 \text{ to } 1)} + \underset{\text{Peer reviewers' adjustment}}{(0 \text{ to } 1)} \\
&+ \underset{\text{If older than 40}}{[(.5)} \quad \text{or} \quad \underset{\text{If older than 55}}{(.75)]} + \underset{\text{\# of classes before 8:00/after 3:00}}{[0 \text{ to } 1]} \\
&+ \underset{\text{Difficulty of course}}{(0 \text{ to } 1)} + \underset{\text{Types of tests}}{(0 \text{ to } 1)} + \underset{\text{Amount of homework}}{(0 \text{ to } 1)} + \underset{\text{\# of preparations}}{(0 \text{ to } 1)} \\
&+ \underset{\text{Level of courses}}{(0 \text{ to } 1)} + \underset{\text{\# of new preparations}}{(0 \text{ to } 1)} + \underset{\text{XACT winners}}{(0 \text{ to } 1)} + \underset{\text{\# of publsihed textbooks}}{(0 \text{ to } 1)} \\
&+ \underset{\text{Teaching seminars/workshops attended}}{(0 \text{ to } 1)} + \underset{\text{Ph.D. Chairperson}}{(0 \text{ to } 1)} \\
&+ \underset{\text{Lectures given outside classroom}}{(0 \text{ to } 1)} + \text{Others} = \Sigma \text{ Some Amount}
\end{aligned}
$$

We have chosen not to include negatives in our formula. However, a department could add negatives if desired (e.g., missed classes, no final examinations, giving parties, etc.). One obvious argument against such a metric ranking system is its complexity. However, an academic unit can argue and vote on the various variables to use and the weight, just as they decide on the ranking of academic professional articles and the value of professional service. For example, a tax professor faces each year the fact that the *Accounting Review* is ranked much higher than the *Journal of Taxation* or *Tax Notes* because of discrimination against professional articles, even if professional articles are more relevant to a professor's teaching. Obviously, the majority rules, but at least an attempt should be made to deemphasize the weight of SET scores. Of course, teaching awards committees should use some type of norming reports or teaching model rather than relying on the satisfaction of students.

If an administrator really wishes to determine the "real" teaching performance of his or her faculty, divide each faculty member's salary by the above resulting metric to determine the most cost-efficient professors with respect to teaching and salary. Such an exercise may indicate that using low-cost contingent faculty is not cost-efficient. Certainly, if the NBA can develop an efficiency formula, higher education can develop a workable efficiency formula. Is education not more important than professional basketball? Are academic people not as smart as sports people?

Certainly if accounting professors would write as many articles of SET management as they have written on earnings management, we as professors could develop a workable metrics for measuring teaching. Why is a SET management article less valuable than an earnings management article?

Move Away from GPA on Transcripts

All of the blame can not be placed on administrators because faculty must share some of the blame. For example, University of Colorado President Hank Brown tried to tackle grade inflation by disclosing grade-point-average percentiles or class rank on student transcripts. Brown said that grades no longer reveal how you really do (Brown 2006). When Brown graduated from Colorado in 1961, class rankings were on transcripts, but the practice was abandoned as a result of grade inflation. Regrettably, a faculty-driven proposal to put the average class grade on transcripts died at the University of Colorado Faculty Council 13 years ago. An employer cannot tell from a transcript if a student got an A in a course where the class average was A. The University of Colorado law school discloses the rank of students in the top third of each class, but the rest of the university dropped that practice many years ago. The Regents approved a new policy that requires the disclosure to students who ask for it of their class standing. The standings will be calculated by college and within Arts and Science by major.

In 1997, the Duke Arts and Sciences Council voted to reject a version of nominal/real grading reporting (Kurtz 2006). Science and math professors generally voted in favor and humanities professors voted against it. Class ranking and grade-point-average percentiles would restore some form of comparative curve at the university level. For example, the highly successful George Shinn (the owner of the New Orleans Hornets) takes pride in telling people that he graduated in last place from A.L. Brown High School in Kannapolis, N.C. in 1963. (Crumbley graduated way ahead of George Shinn.)

As grades spiral skyward, some form of quota system should be installed by administrators or demanded by professors. Stuart Rojstaczer (2003) stated:

> A's are common as dirt in universities nowadays because it's almost impossible for a professor to grade honestly. If I sprinkle my classroom with the C's some students deserve, my class will suffer from declining enrollments in future years. In the marketplace mentality of higher education, low enrollments are taken as a sign of poor-quality instruction. I don't have any interest in being known as a failure.

Rojstaczer has not given a C since 2001. Harvard government professor Harvey Mansfield, Jr. now gives his students two grades: one for official records and another lower one that reflects what the student really deserves. He says, "I remember when B was an honor's grade—today a B minus is a slap in the face" (Bruno 2004).

In 2004, the Princeton faculty voted 156 to 84 to implement a quota system to restrict the number of A grades to undergraduates to 35%. A's had risen as high as 46%.

A real GPA could be calculated if a university would simply place the average GPA given in a class for the semester, course, and section. Merely publicizing the courses that have high average grades would put some pressure on pandering professors (Felton and Koper 2005). Posting class averages, however, can backfire because students search for the easy courses to take (Bruno, 2004).

Felton and Koper (2005, 3–4) suggest a simple adjustment that can compensate for grade inflation if the average GPA given in the course is provided. They suggest listing two grades on transcripts: the nominal GPA (instructor's grade) and the real GPA as a second item. The real GPA is calculated by adjusting the nominal GPA per class by the class GPA. They provide the following example (Felton and Koper 2005, 3–4).

Consider the student in Exhibit 1. Using a scale where an "A" is 4.00, an "A−" is 3.70, a "B+" is 3.30, a "B" is 3.00, a "B−" is 2.70, down to a "D−" that counts for 0.70 points, his GPA for the semester is 3.56.

This nominal GPA is computed in the usual manner by taking the course GPAs weighted by credit hours per course, as follows:

$$\text{Nominal GPA} = [3.70(3) + 3.30(3) + 3.00(3) + 4.00(3) + 3.00(1) + 4.00(3)]/16$$
$$= 3.56$$

EXHIBIT 1
Real and Nominal GPAs

Course	Letter Grade	Credit Hours	Class GPA	Nominal GPA	Real GPA
ENG 101	A−	3	2.15	3.70	3.44
MTH 216	B+	3	1.95	3.30	3.38
GEO 118	B	3	2.75	3.00	2.18
FRN 125	A	3	3.26	4.00	2.45
PED 180	B	1	3.17	3.00	1.89
ACC 100	A	3	2.98	4.00	2.68
Total Credit Hours, Weighted-Average GPAs		16	2.65	3.56	2.77

The student's Real GPA is calculated by adjusting the Nominal GPA per class by the class GPA, as follows:

$$\text{Real GPA} = \left\{\left[\frac{3.70(3)}{2.15} + \frac{3.30(3)}{1.95} + \frac{3.00(3)}{2.75} + \frac{4.00(3)}{3.26} + \frac{3.00(1)}{3.17} + \frac{4.00(3)}{2.98}\right]/16\right\} \times 2.00 = 2.77$$

The Real GPA adjusts the nominal GPA to a scale where 2.00, a "C," is average. A student with a Real GPA that is above 2.00 has outperformed the class on average, while a student with a Real GPA below 2.00 has underperformed the class on average.

Other more complicated formulas have been developed, but the Felton/Koper solution should be workable at most universities if they wanted to fix the real problem. Statistics Professor Valen Johnson proposed an Achievement Index (AI). His AI (Johnson 1997) determines a ratio based on a student's course grade, the student's relative position in the class, and the relative difficulty of the course as indicated by the grade distribution in the class.

In 1998, Indiana University introduced an Expanded Grade Context Record (EGCR). This EGCR has a record of the course, professor, grades, level of performance of the student relative to others in the course, and the majors and overall performances of other students in the class. The EGCR includes the class GPA (GPAs of all students in the class), and an index calculated as the number of the students in the course receiving the same or higher grades divided by the total number of grades given in the class (McConahy and Cote 1998). See also Nagle's Relative Performance Index (Nagle 1998).

Grieves (1982) suggests replacing the normal grade with a two-number grade. One number would be the grade earned in the class. A second number would be the average GPA given in the class for the semester, course, and section in question. Ho and Shalishali (2001) suggest a Z score. Law Professor Nicholas Georgakopoulos (1996) suggests replacing the traditional grade with a Relative Rank Index based upon the student's grade, the medium grade in the class, and the dispersion of grades in a class.

In studying SET scores of teachers in 607 economics classes over 17 semesters, McPherson (2006) found that in some situations, professors can "buy" better SET scores by inflating student grades. McPherson (2006, 13) and others suggest that administrators should therefore consider adjusting raw SET scores "to eliminate the influence of factors that either could be manipulated by instructors to their advantage (e.g., expected grade) or that might be beyond the instructor's control (such as the type of course)."

McPherson (2006, 13–17) describes a statistical method by which professors' teaching effectiveness can be ranked according to their estimated fixed-effects coefficients and according to their adjusted semester-by-semester SET scores in a manner that takes into account extrinsic influences (e.g., the professor acting in ways that will cause a student to expect higher course grade than he or she will likely earn).

Administrator Reviews

The most logical way to determine teaching effectiveness is for the immediate supervisor to randomly attend one or more classes of each faculty member each semester. The function of an administrator is to judge the teaching performance of his or her faculty members and recommend ways to improve (Brightman 2006). Over three or four years most administrators should be able to determine their best teachers based upon their observations. However, fulfilling their administrative duty would take time and energy and risk legal consequences, so most administrators prefer to shirk their administrative duties by spending about 30 minutes each semester reviewing SET and then going to the golf course or tennis court.

A demanding, strict professor should challenge his or her supervisor to randomly attend several classes each semester and provide a written report outlining ways to improve teaching effectiveness. More than likely the supervisor will not put in a written report for you to grade inflate or reduce your course coverage or difficulty. By following all written suggestions of the immediate supervisor, a demanding professor has some protection if SET scores do not improve.

There may be reluctance or fear from some professors to allow an administrator to review one's teaching. This attitude is foolish because a written report from an administrator that is unfavorable can be challenged within the university and in the courtroom, if needed. However, even though SET rankings are hearsay evidence (somewhat like raw FBI data), many courts allow SET results in the courtroom. See the article by Robert Haskell in this monograph.

Thus, since SET are anonymous, there is no way for a professor to question the reasons for students' opinions in the courtroom. Many judges believe that once the opinions are tabulated by the computer, the results are empirical evidence (and not hearsay evidence). The real problem is getting an administrator in the classrooms because they are well aware of their potential legal liability if they (rather than students) take a position about a teacher's effectiveness.

One of the authors (Crumbley) in the mid-seventies was in charge of a large Master of Tax Program. During two semesters he randomly sat in on the classes of each of the tax teachers. All but one of the professors were partners in local CPA firms. The one full-time Ph.D. professor was receiving the worst SET scores. The author found that he and the other full time professor were the only ones providing an academic education (e.g., lectures, examinations, quizzes).

The author waited until the last class period (a 3-hour evening course) to visit and observe one adjunct professor who had a history of the best SET scores (5 out of 5). The course subject was estate and trust taxation, and this professor started talking about complex trusts about midway during this last 3-hour class. The instructor should have begun talking about complex trusts around one-third of the way through the semester. The author learned that the adjunct professor was taking the students out after each class night buying them dinner and beer. He/she was merely teaching a course to recruit students for his/her CPA firm.

Marsha Huber in her article herein explains how her Director of the Center for Teaching and Learning comes to classes in the middle of the semester to hold focus groups with the students, and gathers input about her teaching. The Director then provides the professor with constructive formative feedback to enable him or her to address class concerns. Has anyone come to your classroom and provided constructive criticism?

Knowledge Gained in a Course

If SET are not reliable and valid indicators of student learning, why not simply operate on the assumption that the "best teacher" is the one who teaches student the most during a semester or term? Students would not rate the professor's teaching in any manner. Thus, any concerns that student ratings are based on the professor's popularity or other attributes not directly related to student learning would be eliminated. The professor would seem to have no incentive to deflate course work, to inflate grades given to students, or otherwise pander to students (Wallace and Wallace 1998).

Wallace and Wallace (1998) criticize the use of summative SET as causing course work reduction and grade inflation, both of which are inconsistent with the goals of a sound college or university education. Wallace and Wallace (1998, 446) advocate the use of appropriate competency exams:

> A measurement tool that is aligned with education is a competency exam, directed to the common body of knowledge of the respective areas of study. That competency exam should not be controlled by the professor and its should be administered by third parties, controlling for a number of relevant covariates, to calibrate the real teaching performance of the faculty. Student performance, rather than student happiness, is that dimension which higher education should strive to evaluate. That dimension has true relevance to assessing faculty's performance and is not a contradiction of the mission of universities.

Centra asserts that the notion of testing the knowledge gained by a student in a course is largely misguided and grew out of the culture of accountability and has a number of serious problems which make it unworkable:

- There must first be agreement among faculty and administrators as to precisely which course and learning objectives should be measured and precisely how they should be measured.
- Appropriate tests must be developed to accurately measure whether students have achieved the course objectives.
- If this is the only way that a professor's teaching effectiveness is measured, the professor has many incentives to teach to the tests which may conflict with other goals of a broadly educated college student (Centra 1972, at pp. 9–10).

Of course, teaching to a valid exam would be much less objectionable than grade inflation and course work devaluation. For more discussion of exit exams, see the Moore/Flinn article herein.

This discussion illustrates a key issue and criticism of excess use of student-opinion-based SET to evaluate teaching effectiveness: the differences between reliability and validity, particularly construct validity (Webster 1990, 15). Imagine an accounting department that is accredited by the Association to Advance Collegiate Schools of Business (AACSB) housed within a business school that is also accredited by this body and that both are housed in a "teaching" college or university. Assume the accounting department has only tenured associate professors or professors and no contingent faculty.

Many of the faculty members hold professional certifications and are active in the accounting profession. Assume that accounting majors typically receive As or Bs in their major courses (e.g., grade inflation has occurred), consistently rate all professors as very good or excellent instructors, and are generally pleased with their accounting education. Assume many of the accounting majors find appropriate entry-level employment positions. Assume, however, that contrary to the Accounting Department and business school explicit mission of educating students for a career as a professional accountant, few of the students eventually pass relevant professional exams (e.g., CPA, CMA, CIA).

This failure would seem to be a situation where SET may be reliable in terms of consistently rating their instructors on satisfaction items that student find important to them, such as ability to organize course content and ability to present it clearly and enthusiastically in a classroom setting. But if only a few students eventually pass professional accounting exams, which are widely accepted as appropriate and relevant summary measures of learning for accounting students, we must conclude that SET alone are not appropriately measuring student learning and more direct measures of student learning should be used to judge teaching effectiveness. One author (Crumbley) suggests students sue their university if they make As or Bs on their auditing classes and then flunk the auditing portion of the CPA exam. Such lawsuits by students may force universities to return to academic standards.

Imagine further that through time the accounting department is able to hire newly minted persons holding a Ph.D. in accounting as Assistant Professors to replace retiring professors. Assume that the accounting department and business school place a great deal of emphasis on SET scores, particularly the overall teaching effectiveness rating, for summative teaching effectiveness purposes (such as annual merit raises and promotion and tenure decisions). Assume that neither the accounting department nor the business school does much in the way of formative evaluation of teaching to help the new professors, who may have received little or no training in how to teach a class in their Ph.D. programs. The underlying theory is apparently that one does not need much instruction in how to teach students effectively and that neither the department's nor the business school's responsibility is to help the new professors become effective teachers. Assume that new professors quickly discover the disconnect between receiving good SET ratings (and the benefits of receiving such ratings) and teaching accounting major courses in an appropriately rigorous manner. What is the new professor to do?

Those who argue that this scenario cannot and does not occur in many of today's accounting programs must be living in a different world than the authors of this article. Imagine further that the accounting department and the business school is one in which research productivity is valued and rewarded much more highly than teaching effectiveness. The conclusion must be that SET alone are not sufficient to measure student learning in an accounting program and that SET should not be used for summative purposes or should be used in conjunction with other measures of teaching effectiveness.

Peer Review of Teaching

Research indicates that peer review of teaching is being used more frequently in business schools as the AASCB accreditation process has placed much greater emphasis on assessment and student learning (Bruns et al. 2004; Chism 1999; Gaffney and Krishnan 2000). Research suggests that while some form of peer review of teaching can certainly offer both professors and administrators valuable information about instructional objectives and classroom presentation, there are many concerns over the validity of peer observations in terms of increasing student learning and the professor's willingness to accept criticism and suggestion from faculty peers or administrators (Bruns et al. 2004, 188).

A study published in 2000 found that three specific peer review activities were especially useful to accounting professors: peer review of course syllabi as the basis for discussion about teaching methods and student learning among faculty peers; reciprocal classroom visits; and the systematic development of teaching portfolios (Gaffney and Krishnan 2000).

As noted, some form of peer assessment of teaching effectiveness was the most popular alternative to student-opinion based SET at the 2007 Teaching & Curriculum meeting. Cosser

(1998) notes that in many universities throughout the world the evaluation of teaching effectiveness is accomplished almost exclusively by student opinion survey or SET instruments (1998, 143). In arguing that a more holistic, collaborative, and balanced approach in which a comprehensive peer review of teaching should be used for both formative and summative purposes (and arguing that such purposes should generally not be separated), Cosser (1998, 160) notes that, like research and publication efforts in which peer review is an inseparable element, "teaching will be considered a worthy scholarly activity only when it is reviewed by peers."

Cosser (1998, 160) also argues that in context of continuing pressure for accountability of college and university education, peer review of teaching is most appropriate as peer review allows professors "themselves to determine the quality of their work, thereby mitigating against the bureaucratic imposition of measures of accountability from outside the university." Many faculty members at Cosser's employer, the University of Witwatersrand, Johannesburg, South Africa, were quite willing to replace the existing student evaluation of teaching effectiveness system with some form of peer review (Cosser 1998, 149).

Some arguments suggested in the literature (Cosser 1998, 143–144) against using some form of peer review to judge teaching effectiveness include:

- Peer review is incompatible with academic freedom [if so, SET are also];
- Peer review can be detrimental to faculty relationships [we must be professionals];
- Peer review does not result in the type of valid and reliable information needed for promotion and tenure decisions [if so, neither would SET];
- Peer review may be appropriate for formative and developmental purposes but not for summative purposes such as promotion and tenure decisions [why not?];
- It is not clear that any observations of teaching are necessary to form a valid and fair opinion of a professor's teaching effectiveness [not understandable];
- Various concerns exist about who will serve as reviewers and, importantly, will whoever serves provide negative observations if such comments are warranted;
- Reviewers will unduly disrupt class sessions [really flimsy excuse];
- It is not clear what reviewers should evaluate other than classroom instruction (e.g., course syllabus, examination, class handouts, class projects, etc.) [everything available];
- In many colleges and universities, research and publication are much more important than teaching effectiveness in making promotion and tenure decisions; thus peer review is unnecessary [yet faculty are fired for low SET scores].

Some literature suggests that the disadvantages of using peer review for judging teaching effectiveness far outweighs the advantages, and that the reliability of peer review of teaching effectiveness is much higher than the validity of such review in terms of measuring student learning (Webster 1990, 12). A general concern is that when business professors are asked to evaluate the teaching effectiveness of their colleagues for summative purposes, they may be reluctant to make critical comments even if warranted. However, professors must be professional and accept this responsibility.

Another concern is what occurs if a professor makes the changes in teaching techniques suggested by a competent peer reviewer and his SET scores or other measures of teaching effectiveness do not improve? Is the fact that the professor tried to improve sufficient? Surprisingly, one research study involving marketing professors found that faculty reviewers will often judge a peer's teaching effectiveness more harshly than students do (Webster 1990, 14–15).

In spite of these arguments against peer review of teaching, we believe peer review is a more reliable and valid means of evaluating teaching effectiveness than SET. Some form of peer review used in conjunction with student opinion SET will clearly be an improvement over the present almost total reliance on SET and can be a variable in our suggested teaching model of productivity.

Course Portfolios

After some form of peer review, the literature suggests that self-assessment (Buskist, Keeley, and Irons) and professor-prepared teaching portfolios are gaining popularity at least for formative purposes (Laverie 2002; New et al. 2008; Ouellett 2007). Laverie (2002) suggests that making a professor's teaching portfolio available for review allows professors to obtain a peer review of teaching effectiveness while minimizing some of the problems noted above such as class disruption (Laverie 2002). Again, class disruption seems to be a flimsy excuse, however, when students come in late, leave early, read newspapers, cell phones ring, etc. How is the class disrupted by another professor or administrator sitting in the class?

McKeachie and Kaplan (undated) note that professor-created course portfolios have many advantages as supplements to student-opinion based SET. But, like any one evaluation tool, portfolios can have the following problems:

- They can be costly to prepare and update in terms of time and resources;
- A physically attractive portfolio (complete with color, graphics, and even a videotape) may prove more persuasive to reviewers than a one with less polish;
- Some faculty members are likely more adept at creating teaching portfolios than others, particularly if the portfolio is Web based;
- College administrators and promotion and tenure committee members often have little experience or training in how to appropriately evaluate a teaching portfolio [Of course, what experience or training do students have to fairly evaluate a professor's teaching effectiveness?], and
- As with SET scores, the nature of effective teaching varies across disciplines; thus the nature of a teaching portfolio may naturally vary as well.

The literature suggests that, although there are many benefits to a professor preparing and making public course portfolios available for peer review, such portfolios have only recently become popular in college education as a tool for student, faculty, and institutional development (New et al. 2008, 9). Course portfolios are said to be a key item in the formative evaluation of teaching that will, more generally, enhance the scholarship of teaching by allowing some form of peer and/or administrator review. A typical course portfolio discusses and contains evidence of course design, teaching methods, student learning and outcomes, student evaluation of teaching, and the professor's reflection on each course taught (New et al. 2008, 12).

There are a number of obstacles to the more frequent use of course portfolios: business faculty are generally unaware of this method of documenting teaching efforts and effectiveness; very limited professional and institutional support for such efforts is generally provided; some faculty believe that including their work in a portfolio amounts to "giving away" their intellectual efforts and time, and some faculty, and administrators do not give course development, and attempts to improve teaching effectiveness much credit (New et al. 2008, 16–18).

Self-Assessment

Ouellett (2007) argues that teaching portfolios offer these advantages:

- Useful as a developmental tool to stimulate individual reflection and personal development.
- Used as a demonstration of accomplishment.
- Demonstrate how we express our priorities in teaching over a range of considerations and time.
- Allows an instructor to articulate and then demonstrate how key values and priorities suffuse course planning, implementation, and assessment.
- Can help define the role of teaching in relation to our other professional responsibilities (e.g., research and service).

Ouellett (2007, 426, 427) also provides the following helpful Internet sites:

- Creating a Teaching Portfolio—Online Information and Resources (https://www.tltc.ttu.edu/teach/teachingportfolio.asp; Texas Tech University, Teaching and Learning and Technology Center, 2007).
- Developing a Teaching Portfolio (http://depts.washington.edu/cidrweb/PortfolioTools.htm; University of Washington, Center for Instructional Development and Research, n.d.).
- Developing a Teaching Portfolio (http://ftad.osu.edu/portfolio/; The Ohio State University, 2005).
- Preparing a Teaching Portfolio (http://www.utexas.edu/academic/cte/teachfolio.html; University of Texas at Austin, Center for Teaching Effectiveness, n.d.).
- The Teaching Portfolio at Washington State University (http://www.wsu.edu/provost/teaching.htm; Washington State University, Office of the Provost, 1996).
- Teaching Strategies: Teaching Portfolios and Course Portfolios (http://www.crlt.umich.edu/tstrategies/tstpcp.html; University of Michigan, Center for Research on Learning and Teaching, 2004).

As expected, the major issue with a self-assessment or self-evaluation of a professor's teaching effectiveness is the lack of objectivity (Webster 1990, 13). In an older study of self-assessment of teaching effectiveness, Centra found significant differences between professor and student ratings with the professor's ratings typically much more favorable than student ratings on virtually all aspects of teaching effectiveness (Centra 1972, 8).

Fink (undated) states that self-assessment is an inherent part of college teaching and that self-monitoring is an immediate and constant way for a professor to judge his or her own teaching effectiveness and to determine the need for changes. In addition, at most colleges and universities a professor can arrange to have his or her classroom instruction recorded on audiotape or videotape, can consult professionals in a unit often titled Teaching and Assessment Center, or can participate in some type of instructional development program.

Teaching portfolios

The literature suggests there are many beneficial aspects of teaching (as opposed to course) portfolios, and the most significant one is that at least some aspects of a professor's teaching efforts can be made public in order to be subjectd to peer and/or administrator review. A professor can use a teaching portfolio to demonstrate how student ratings of his/her teaching effectiveness are related to student learning in his/her courses and his/her research and publication efforts (e.g., hard subject, demanding teacher, harsh grader). At one university, the Provost recommends that a teaching portfolio should be about five pages in length and that preparing or reading a portfolio should not consume an excessive amount of a faculty member's time. The precise format and contents depend largely on the professor's discipline. (The Teaching Portfolio at Washington State University).

One university has stated:

> A 'teaching portfolio' is a compilation of information about a faculty member's teaching, made by that faculty member, often for use in consideration for tenure or promotion. It is not, in itself, an instrument for teaching evaluation, but a vehicle for presenting information which may include results of evaluations and which may itself contribute to evaluation. It can therefore be selective, emphasizing the positive—to serve as a showcase for a faculty member's achievements in teaching, not necessarily a comprehensive or balanced picture of everything. (The Teaching Portfolio at Washington State University).

Regrettably, this university defeats the purpose of a teaching portfolio by stating that it is not "an instrument of teaching evaluation." Why not? For more detail of teaching portfolios, see Calderon (1996, Chapter 4).

Interviews with Former Students and Others

The results of interviews with a professor's former students, and past or present employers of such students, alumni groups, and similar attempts to judge the long-term impact of a professor on students, will not be as easily quantified or as timely as end-of-semester SET scores. But that does not make them less valuable; in fact, their results may be far more meaningful than short-run impressions and SET scores.

Many accounting faculty can easily name former students who now better appreciate what they learned in a course and why their tax professor make them digest difficult cases and read and summarize relevant articles from tax practitioner journals. Many accounting faculty can name former students who now appreciate what they learned in a course and why their accounting and auditing professors make them study corporate financial statements and audit opinions. Unfortunately, a SET instrument is unlikely to capture this longer-term view and will penalize a professor making such difficult, time-consuming assignments.

Today's college students are much different than they were in the past, have generally not been exposed to as rigorous pre-college educational experiences as in the past, and often have a pseudo-sophistication about some aspects of information technology. But many have been raised in an environment that stressed self-esteem instead of academic achievement, personal responsibility, and intellectual curiosity. As such, many students need to be taught as children and not as adults.

CONCLUSION

Student-opinion-based SET will likely continue to be used as the primary source of information for summative evaluations of a professor's teaching effectiveness because of their cost effectiveness and inertia. The literature and experience suggest that students in a classroom are the most authoritative judges of *some* aspects of teaching effectiveness—certainly classroom satisfaction. Thus, totally eliminating the use of SET in formative or summative evaluations of teaching effectiveness is not *necessarily* advocated here.

However, to continue to use a system for evaluating teaching effectiveness that is so narrow, does not promote goal congruence, has such a short-run orientation, and can penalize accounting faculty members for doing things that are different (but promote student learning) makes little sense if the goal is to truly educate students for the world in which they will live and work. A much more balanced approach should be used if accounting educators, including the more frequent academically qualified ones, are to discharge their various ethical and professional responsibilities.

SET has a number of serious limitations in terms of measuring teaching effectiveness in accounting programs, especially in terms of student learning (construct validity). If used, they should be used in a much limited manner for summative purposes than they are presently. Also, SET only should be used in conjunction with other measures that have been determined to be more reliable and valid measures of student achievement and learning.

Accountants often describe themselves as experts in measurement, and auditors often describe themselves as experts in determining if things have been measured correctly. Accounting professors should use these skills in assessing teaching effectiveness in both formative and summative evaluations to help maximize student learning. Accounting education has been notoriously resistant to change even after major events such as the failure of Enron and WorldCom (Arens and Elder 2006). Hopefully, accounting faculty and business college administrators understand that students are inventory (and not customers) and will be more willing to end the reliance on SET and start to reward teaching effectiveness. Students, their parents, and society are paying for effective teachers and not popular teachers.

APPENDIX A
CONFOUNDING VARIABLES

EXHIBIT 1

Confounding Factors in an Academic System: Environment and Course-Related Variables

Environment Related

1. Campus, e.g., location, convenience, attractiveness.
2. Building, e.g., location, convenience, attractiveness, presence of snack bar, etc.
3. Room lighting, glare; etc.
4. Type of seating, e.g., tables with chairs or desks, level of comfort, etc.
5. Seating arrangement, e.g., tiered levels, wide or shotgun style.
6. Acoustics.
7. Internal noise, e.g., from air conditioner.
8. External noise, e.g., from other classes, etc.
9. Overhead projector availability and quality.
10. Screen availability and quality.
11. Black or white board availability and quality.
12. Ability to adjust airflow and temperature.
13. Other equipment availability and quality, e.g., computers, software, etc.

Course Related

14. Size of class (Nichols and Soper [1972] cited in Wright et al. 1984; Mulford and Schneider 1988).
15. Size of class relative to room size.
16. Required or elective (Mulford and Schneider 1988).
17. Level, i.e., freshman through graduate (Kau and Rubin [1976] cited in Wright et al. 1984).
18. Level of difficulty within the university.
19. Level of difficulty within the college.
20. Level of difficulty within the major.
21. Stated or implied importance within major.
22. Time of class, e.g., regular semester, summer, morning, afternoon, night (Nichols and Soper [1972] cited in Wright et al. 1984).
23. Length of class time.
24. Relationship with other classes, e.g., prerequisites and other interdependence (Deberg and Wilson 1990).
25. Relationship of course to a professional exam, e.g., CPA.
26. Relationship of course to local employment opportunities.

Source: Martin, 1998, 1083.

EXHIBIT 2
Student Characteristics

1. Race.
2. Sex (Bledsoe [1971] cited in Wright et al. 1984).
3. Age.
4. Health.
5. Introvert or extrovert.
6. Cultural background, family values, ethics, etc.
7. Cultural characteristics, e.g., masculinity, individualism, etc. (Hofstede 1991).
8. Orientation toward McGregor's (1960) Theory X or Theory Y.
9. Marital status.
10. Academic background.
11. Academic major.
12. Level of preparation during course.
13. Current employment status.
14. Campus resident or nonresident.
15. Distance nonresidents live from campus.
16. Military status.
17. Learning style.
18. GPA (Kau and Rubin [1976] cited in Wright et al. 1984).
19. GPA in major.
20. Grades in prerequisite courses.
21. Expected grade (Kau and Rubin 1976; Nichols and Soper 1972; and Malpass 1966; Weaver 1960, all cited in Wright et al. 1984).
22. Amount learned in previous courses, particularly prerequisite courses.
23. Amount retained from previous courses, particularly prerequisite courses.
24. Attitude and bias toward the course obtained from other students or faculty.
25. Bias toward the instructor obtained from other students or faculty.
26. Proportion of classes attended.
27. Whether the student is present when student evaluations are given.
28. Characteristics in relation to those of the instructor.

Source: Martin, 1998, 1084.

EXHIBIT 3
Teacher-Related Characteristics

1. Race.
2. Sex (Bledsoe [1971] cited in Wright et al. 1984).
3. Age (Rayder [1968] cited in Wright et. al. 1984; Mulford and Schneider 1988).
4. Attractiveness.
5. Health.
6. Voice, e.g., deep, powerful, weak, squeaky, accented, monotone.
7. Verbal fluency (Coffman [1954] cited in Wright et al. 1984).
8. Expressiveness (Meier and Feldhusen [1979] cited in Wright et al. 1984).
9. Weight.
10. Energy level.
11. Personality, e.g., serious, humorous, jovial, laid back, outgoing, dynamic, caring, sensitive (Wright and Wotruba [1978] and Naflulin et al. [1973], both cited in Wright et al. 1984).
12. Number of years teaching.
13. Number of times teaching the course evaluated.
14. Innate intelligence and capacity for learning.
15. The number of different course preparations during a semester and over a long-term basis.
16. The number of different levels of courses taught during a semester and on a long-term basis.
17. Dress.
18. Self discipline.
19. Religious views.
20. Political views.
21. Enthusiasm for the course evaluated.
22. General knowledge, e.g., degrees, extent of continuous learning.
23. Extent of relevant practical experience.
24. Knowledge of course within subject area.
25. Current knowledge of subject area.
26. Knowledge of related areas.
27. Ability and willingness to bring knowledge of related areas into class.
28. Ability and willingness to keep the course (i.e., student knowledge) constant when the teacher's knowledge level is increasing.
29. Preparation for class (Mulford and Schneider 1988).
30. Ability and willingness to learn and use student's names.
31. Acting ability.
32. Willingness to act, e.g., play roles, etc.
33. The extent that the teacher is involved in service-related work, e.g., committees, etc.
34. Textbook authorship (McDaniel and Feldhusen [1971] cited in Wright et al. 1984).

Source: Martin, 1998, 1085.

EXHIBIT 4
Controllable Teacher Practices Related to Course and Students

1. Whether the objectives of the course are clearly stated.
2. Pedagogy used in the course, e.g., use of lecture, discussion format, Socratic method, cases, cooperative learning, team assignments, presentations, team presentations, papers, team papers, computer assignments, outside readings.
3. The extent that prerequisite course materials or topics from previous courses are reviewed during class time.
4. The extent that prerequisite course materials or topics from previous courses are reviewed outside of class, e.g., during office hours.
5. The extent to which the material used in the class is canned or developed by the teacher.
6. Whether the materials used in the course can be sold to the bookstore when the class ends.
7. The extent that related research of the teacher is brought into class.
8. Willingness to entertain, tell jokes, show cartoons, be dynamic or evangelical in class.
9. Time spent on entertainment or ratio of substance to puff and fluff.
10. Whether quizzes are used.
11. Relationship of the quizzes to the test.
12. Whether and how homework is counted.
13. Whether a class session is dedicated to reviewing material prior to each test.
14. Whether the tests are cumulative.
15. The ratio of difficult to easy questions on the tests.
16. The ratio of conceptual to quantitative or mechanical questions on the test.
17. The extent that critical thinking is tested, e.g., comparing and evaluating concepts, unstructured case situation questions without definitive answers, questions that require the student to choose a position and defend it.
18. Time spent teaching the test, i.e., teaching what appears on the test rather than general course content.
19. Willingness to omit the more difficult material from the tests.
20. Willingness to give out practice tests.
21. Relationship of practice tests to the actual tests, e.g., random sample of material or exact replicas.
22. The type of tests given, e.g., objective, short answer, essay.
23. Whether the tests are completed in class or taken home.
24. The number of tests given.
25. Whether the sequence of tests become more or less difficult, e.g., whether the first test is designed to weed-out low achievers or students with weak backgrounds.
26. The time pressure placed on students during the test.
27. Whether partial credit is given for incorrect answers.
28. Whether the test grades are scaled in some way.
29. The relationship between the level of difficulty taught and tested, e.g., teach at a higher level than tested.
30. Whether class participation is graded.
31. Whether credit is given for effort and improvement.
32. Whether students are allowed to keep their tests.
33. Whether re-tests are given.
34. The extent that old tests are available to students, e.g., placed on reserve in the library.
35. How the various assignments are graded and weighted in obtaining the student's final grade.
36. Whether extra credit projects are provided.
37. Whether the teacher's style is directed to the high achievers or the low achievers in the class.
38. Willingness and ability to critically evaluate students in various soft areas such as speaking and writing skills.
39. Tolerance, e.g., for student tardiness, absences, dishonesty, excuses, lack of background and lack of preparation.
40. Time spent with students during office hours.
41. Willingness to be friendly.
42. Willingness to socialize with students.
43. Time spent socializing with students.
44. Willingness to give students home phone number and return their calls.
45. Willingness to give "I" grades to students who fail the course and then let them retake the course (free) the following semester.

Source: Martin, 1998, 1086.

CHAPTER 10

Improving Teaching and Learning through SMART Classroom Assessment Techniques

Marsha M. Huber, Otterbein College*

John Amos Comenius, the "Father of Modern Education," asked in the 1600s if there was a way to teach children well, but quickly at the same time. Students in his day were taught using rote memorization and were not taught to *think* critically (McMahon 2008). Over 400 years later, this problem still exists. Although the accounting profession and employers want graduates to exercise higher order thinking skills (AECC 1990), the focus of teaching and learning often comes down to performance on exams that call for memorization rather than measuring understanding or critical thinking skills (Jones 1996; Beattie, Collins, and McInnes 1997). See R. Heath, herein.

In fact, the accounting profession uses examinations to license its professionals. One such test, the CPA exam, is a content based, licensing exam consisting primarily of multiple choice questions. The exam also uses small cases called simulations to test a candidate's work-related skills. Because of this exam, there is a tendency for some professors to teach content (and lots of it) so that students will pass the exam. My goal is not to criticize faculty members for trying to meet the demands of the profession, but to call to question what accounting educators are doing (often without thinking) in the classroom. Instead of employing "deep" teaching methods that encourage understanding and critical thinking, professors use "surface" teaching methods characterized by memorization and an emphasis on testing (Jones 1996; Beattie, et al. 1997). Students too become obsessed with testing, focusing their attention on "what will be on the test."

The Spellings Commission (U.S. Department of Education 2006) suggested that higher education must change, stating that there are "disturbing signs that many who do earn degrees have not actually mastered the reading, writing, and thinking skills that we expect of college graduates" (p. x). Although teaching accounting content is important, education is also about developing higher thinking and people skills (Diamond 1998; Appelbaum 1997). In fact, when surveyed in 2005, business school deans stated graduates should be competent in their disciplines, but also effective communicators, analytical thinkers, ethical decision-makers, leaders, lifelong learners, and problem solvers demonstrating professionalism (AACSB 2005).

The Spellings Commission (2006, 4) urged educators to "make a commitment to embrace new pedagogies, curricula, and technologies to improve student learning" to correct shortcomings

* Dr. Huber, CPA, is Associate Professor at Otterbein College, mhuber@otterbein.edu.

in educational quality. Thus, this article is about retooling ourselves when it comes to assessing student learning in the classroom. SMART assessment is part of the dialogue of good teaching. This article defines SMART assessment and the design process, gives practical examples of classroom assessment techniques, and provides guidance on "closing the assessment feedback loop."

MOVING AWAY FROM AN EMPHASIS ON TESTING

A qualitative examination of sixty accounting syllabi in 2008, from a *Google* search for different accounting classes (Principles, Tax, Intermediate, Cost, Systems, and Auditing) at thirty institutions, public and private, revealed that exams served as the primary assessment technique. Tests weighted between 75%–85% of the course grade. The remainder of the grade was based on a combination of homework, cases, projects, and participation. The tests were comprised of mainly true-false, multiple choice, and problems. There were a few outliers with on-line classes having grades based 100% on exams and one major university where tests only comprised 0–50% of the grade.

Testing, as a form of assessment, is the easiest to develop since most textbooks come with test banks. Testing measures certain types of learning, especially frequent testing, has been shown to build long-term memory of content (Tuckman and Sexton 1992). As mentioned earlier, education is also about developing higher learning and soft skills (Diamond, 1998; Appelbaum, 1989). Multiple choice exams, however, are not designed to evaluate those skills. Thus, additional assessment techniques are needed to (a) focus student attention to develop higher learning skills and (b) to assess whether or not the higher learning goals are being achieved in the class.

WHY ASSESSMENT

Every accrediting body now requires some form of assessment or accountability for student learning (Huba and Freed 2000, Suskie 2004, Fink 2003). In 1989, the Commission on Institutions of Higher Education introduced a requirement for every affiliated institution to adopt a plan of outcomes assessment. All three business accreditation bodies, the AACSB, the ASBSP, and the IACBE, include an assessment requirement in their standards. The Spellings Commission (2006, 21) stated higher education needs "to embrace and implement serious accountability measures."

The AACSB, the premiere business accrediting body, requires assessment at two levels—the macro level is known as program assessment and the micro level is called classroom assessment. The AACSB states that "Programs must evaluate instructional effectiveness and overall student achievement" (AACSB Standard 12). This type of assessment determines whether or not accounting majors are meeting the learning goals of the program at certain intervals such as by the end of their sophomore or senior years. Common types of program assessment include summative tools such as standardized testing (Educational Testing Services) or the passing rates on the CPA examination.

Assessment of learning at the micro levels involves classroom assessment techniques (CATs). Angelo and Cross (1993) defined assessment in their classic book, *Classroom Assessment Techniques,* (1993) as an ongoing process aimed at understanding and improving student learning. The AACSB requires assessment stating that "faculty must actively involve students in the learning process, encourage collaboration, and ensure frequent, prompt feedback on student performance" (Standard 13). The most common assessment tools in accounting are tests, homework, and student projects. Using assessment is consistent with Accounting Education Change Commission (AECC) objectives and provides timely feedback to help professors make changes and assess learning experiences (Cottell and Harwood 1998). Assessment, when used properly, encourages deep and self-directed learning (Steadman and Svinicki 1998).

Direct assessment is considered superior to indirect assessment. Direct assessment requires faculty to collect evidence of student learning directly from students through exams, projects, the use of portfolios, and essays. Indirect methods do not measure "student learning," but rather how students "feel" about their learning such as student evaluations of teaching (SETs). Class grades can not be used because they incorporate many things besides student learning such as attendance, participation, curves, and subjectivity in assigning letter grades.

Angelo and Cross (1993) state that good assessment encourages student-faculty interaction and active learning, gives prompt feedback, emphasizes time on task, communicates expectations, and respects diverse ways of learning. CATs are individualized for each class context and are teacher driven—with instructors deciding on what, when, and how to respond to each CAT.

Angelo and Cross (1993) share the following assumptions about assessment:

- The emphasis shift is from teaching to student learning.
- We need new techniques for new times with continuing evaluation to see if teaching techniques are working.
- The assessment goals of CATs must be explicit to students with professors providing prompt feedback to students.
- Students need to assess their own learning.

Certainly, one way to improve learning is to improve teaching effectiveness. To do so, faculty need to obtain feedback often in order to adjust their teaching practices as well as having students practice self-assessment. Self-assessment allows students to become self-directed learners by forcing them to become accountable for their own learning.

The remainder of this article discusses assessment—defining it, explaining why you need to understand it, and how to use it. Using assessment also serves as a type of action research where classroom problems are identified and corrected as faculty members gather evidence, reflect on it, and implement changes. If assessment is about improving teaching and learning, then CATs provide the evidence upon which changes can be based.

DEFINING ASSESSMENT TYPES

Frey & Schmitt (2007) classify assessment into four categories: performance, authentic, formative, and assessment for learning. The most common type of assessment is performance assessment. **Performance** assessment measures comprehension and problem solving skills. Tests, quizzes, and homework problems are common ways to assess skills progression. **Authentic** assessment measures higher thinking skills by evaluating the students' ability to solve real-world problems. This type of assessment would include case studies and simulations. **Formative** assessment provides for improvement during the semester. This approach might include a mid-semester intervention from an outside evaluator to gather information from students on how the faculty member can improve what he/she is doing in the classroom. Lastly, **assessment for learning** would include techniques that make students reflect upon their own learning such as reflection papers.

Frey and Schmitt (2007) divide what Angelo and Cross would define as "classroom assessment" into the two categories of "formative" and "assessment for learning." For purposes of this discussion, I combine those two categories into a new category called "**learning to learn.**" Learning to learn assessment is the joint responsibility of both professors and students, and a feedback loop between the two groups will help to maximize the learning experience (Angelo and Cross 1993).

Faculty members generally use traditional testing for performance assessment for 75 to 85% of the course evaluation, as stated in the 2008 *Google* study. Other forms of assessment, such as authentic assessment, were sometimes used as part of the remaining 15–25% of the course evaluation. Completely lacking from the syllabi was any indication of "learning to learn" assessment. This particular type of assessment, although popular in other disciplines, is underutilized in accounting classes. For example, writing a reflection paper might be common in an English or psychology class, but rare in an accounting class.

Exhibit 1 presents a scheme for the various forms of assessments, coined as PAL, standing for **P**erformance, **A**uthentic, and **L**earning to Learn. As outlined in PAL, accounting faculty should consider diversifying their assessment schemes to provide a more balanced approach to evaluating students.

A PARADIGM OF ASSESSMENT—RETOOLING OCCURS

In order to design assessment for classes, faculty members need to outline specific learning goals or objectives in their course syllabus. Testing would serve as the primary means of assessment for measuring comprehension of content. If faculty members think analytical and critical thinking skills are important, then they could add case studies to their classes or ask students to write critiques of accounting articles. Business deans, the AECC, the AACSB, and recruiters all maintain that there is more to education than what the traditional assessment tools measure. If the 2008 *Google* evaluation of the types of assessment used is representative of the population, then many accounting professors will need to retool themselves to provide a more balanced approach to assessment.

Administrators also often overlook the learning issue and use SETs as the primary means to evaluate the effectiveness of faculty teaching. It takes time, training, and re-programming of mindsets for other forms of assessment to be understood and valued by faculty, students, and administrators. In order to bring change, faculty members need to continually direct students to be responsible for their own learning. Furthermore, others need to be educated that CATs are an acceptable form of feedback for revising teaching. Administrators should look to alternative assessment means to see if students are learning rather than relying on SET scores, which do not measure learning.

The Assessment Process

Assessment should be SMART as it is administered throughout the term. Following is an acronym for SMART to summarize the basic principles behind assessment.

Systematic—ongoing throughout the term.
Measurable—assessing a particular learning goal.
Appropriate—congruent to the learning goal.
Relevan—meaningful to the instructor and student.
Timely—implemented at the right time during the term.

EXHIBIT 1
PAL—Assessment of Student Learning

Assessment Type	Purpose
Performance assessment	To measure knowledge and skills
Authentic assessment	To measure ability to solve real-world problems
Learning to Learn	To provide feedback to instructor to improve teaching and to students to improve learning

In addition, four steps are necessary to operationalize the SMART assessment process (Exhibit 2). First, the faculty member must develop specific learning goals. These are to be stated in terms of what students "will be able to do" at the completion of the course. Next, the learning goals must be matched to learning experiences. Learning experiences would include any activity that promotes learning comprised mainly of assignments, but could also include assessment techniques. Third, the appropriate assessment tool is selected and implemented. Last, the faculty member gathers student data (whether tests or CATs) to provide students with feedback and/or to make adjustments to teaching.

Step 1: Developing Learning Goals

Educational reform has developed over the last century with the most pervasive influences from John Dewey and Benjamin Bloom. Dewey, the "Father of Experiential Education," believed that learning should be based on critical thinking and problem solving, not memorization (1938). Bloom (1956) separated learning into three domains: cognition (knowledge), affective (values), and psychomotor (skills). Contemporary educator, L. Dee Fink (2003) developed a theory of learning that uses six learning dimensions, stating that "significant" learning takes place through the interaction of the six dimensions of foundational knowledge, application, integration, learning to learn, caring, and the human dimension. The common link among these educationists is that there are other forms of learning (e.g., affective and psychomotor) in addition to the traditional type of learning that relies heavily on mental processes.

Since accounting programs and professors have diverse learning objectives, the first step in developing learning goals is to determine what students "will be able to do" at the end of each course. By using a paradigm, such as Fink's paradigm of significant learning, faculty members are forced to expand their teaching techniques, assignments, and forms of assessment.

The 2008 *Google* examination of syllabi revealed that most accounting classes are designed to measure knowledge and application levels. Even if faculty members are teaching in Fink's other dimensions, missing are assessment techniques for integration, learning to learn, caring, and the human dimensions on the syllabi. Table 1 in Appendix A: *Congruency—Matching Learning Goals to CATs*—provides an example on how a professor could design a principles of accounting class around learning goals with congruent assessment techniques using L. Dee Fink's paradigm of significant learning.

Step 2: Matching Learning Experiences to Learning Goals

The key to assessment is congruency—the matching of learning experiences to learning goals. Some learning experiences are multi-dimensional, achieving several goals at the same time.

EXHIBIT 2
The Assessment Process

Step	
1	Develop and include learning goals stating what students "will" be able to do on the syllabus (i.e., students will be able to explain a set of financials to someone else)
2	Match each learning goal to learning experiences (assignments such as interviews, critiques, journals, and projects)
3	Select and implement the appropriate assessment techniques to measure if learning goals are being accomplished (congruency)
4	Use the data to improve student learning (feedback to students and changes in teaching).

Following are learning goals for a principles of financial accounting class for each of Fink's six dimensions of learning and the corresponding learning experiences and/or related assessment tool (summarized from Table 1 in Appendix A):

1. *Foundational knowledge*—students will have a grasp of the basic terminology and principles of accounting. Tests and quizzes are the primary source of assessment.
2. *Application*—students will apply their learning to solving problems. Tests and homework can assess this learning goal. A class project where students compare two companies' financial statements is a powerful authentic assessment tool to assess whether students can apply the material to practical and realistic problem solving.

Less common examples of learning experiences are (as presented in Table 1 in Appendix A):

3. *Integration*—students will understand how financial accounting fits into the whole. An interview with a business person who uses financial statements in decision-making as well as a critique of SOX help students understand how financial accounting relates to the business world.
4. *Learning to learn*—students will reflect on their learning. Reflection papers help students evaluate their own learning and address how they are feeling about their progress and the changes they need to make to improve. The "muddiest point" paper helps the instructor target topics that need further clarity in the classroom. A midterm intervention, where another person comes into the classroom to ask students about their learning, is a formative tool designed to give feedback to the instructor on changes that can be made, again to improve learning.
5. *Caring*—students will have opportunities to develop a caring attitude and understand the relevancy of what they are studying. An assignment such as an interview with a business person during the first week about the use and importance of financial statements helps to establish relevancy. After a lecture on internal controls, students are assigned to write a paper about the use of internal controls (or lack thereof) on their jobs as a form of authentic assessment. This project helps to develop "caring" as well as helps students to apply what they learned in the classroom to a real life situation.
6. *Human dimension*—students will improve their interpersonal skills by conversing with other individuals. Explaining a set of financial statements to a friend outside the class or interviewing business managers are ways to encourage the human dimension. For example, a friend completes a questionnaire that I use to assess how well students are able to explain the financials to others. Other types of human dimension exercises have to do with how financial accounting impacts individuals in society.

Step 3: Selection and Implementation of Assessment Techniques

There are many types of assessment tools, which faculty may not be familiar with. *Classroom Assessment Techniques: A Handbook for College Teachers* (Angelo and Cross, 1993) lists 50 different types of CATs that have been used at colleges. The Handbook classifies CATs according to Bloom's taxonomy of learning—knowledge, skills, and values. Once faculty members decide upon their teaching techniques, learning goals and related assignments, they can refer to the Handbook for the appropriate CATs. The handbook approach does not preclude the creation of new and unique CATs. Creating new CATs is something that can be most effective.

The focus of CATs is on the assessment of learning. They help both the professor and student to assess if the student is accomplishing the learning goals outlined for the class. The focus is not on the faculty member's teaching, but rather on student learning. This shift is sometimes difficult for professors and students to make. Current SET evaluations place the primary responsibility for learning on the faculty member rather than students. Most of the phaseology on SET forms ignores the collaborative aspects of teaching and learning. The forms focus attention on the professor rather than the student (Best 2008). CATs place the primary responsibility on students with the faculty member serving more as a mentor to ensure learning is taking place. The old mindset, however, is difficult to change.

My experience has shown that some students have difficulty comprehending this shift. When asked about "their" learning experiences, and "what they can do to improve it," a minority of students insist upon writing about me and not their learning experiences. They seem to want to place blame on me for not teaching them if their grades are not meeting their expectations.

The question I ask myself when deciding upon an assessment technique is: "How do I measure that learning goal?" If critical thinking is a goal, then "What CAT could I use to measure it?" Or if I want my students to take responsibility for their learning, "How can I use a CAT to instill student accountability?" Or if I want to know how long my students are studying during the term, "Is there a CAT to evaluate that?" In my typical accounting class, I use 15–20 different types of assignments and assessment tools and CATs to assess student learning. The number of techniques, however, is not important, but *congruency* to learning goals is.

SMART assessment should occur throughout the term, beginning at the first class. I use CATs to create a good learning environment by communicating to students the importance of learning.

Beginning of the Semester. On the first day of class, I use a *Prior Knowledge CAT* (Appendix A: CAT 1) which I designed to assess the students' prior knowledge of accounting. Typical questions include:

- Did you take accounting in high school?
- Is this your first time taking financial accounting (or are you repeating the course)?
- Have you ever worked in accounting before?

I also add questions about the basic concepts I want my students to learn in the class. I use this CAT to create a pre-test/post-test design bias. One confounding factor in experimental/quasi-experimental research is that participants learn from the pre-test (Campbell and Stanley 1963), but here, I want that to happen. I also ask students about their "feelings" about the class, which often strike the students as odd. They frequently write about their anxiety, apathy, and lack of desire to take the class. I, however, use the negative comments to build a rapport with the class. I read the class the comments and joke about what a "challenging job I have." I often ask them "how would you like to be in my shoes?" As the course continues I continue to evaluate their feelings to track changes, giving me another means to evaluate the "caring" dimension of learning. I also pass out two additional CATs on the first day. I distribute the *Group Assessment CAT* (Appendix A: CAT 2), which I use to communicate to my students the expectations for their group work.

The other CAT is the *Timekeeper CAT* (Appendix A: CAT 3). This timekeeper serves as a self-regulating technique. Students record the time they spend reading, doing homework, and studying for exams. I pick the timekeepers up twice during the term to evaluate class averages and to read student comments about their time management. In addition, this tool helps me set course expectations for future classes. I can see how pedagogical changes from adding new learning goals impact student effort. Lastly, I run correlations between time expended and grades. In some classes there are correlations, and in others, there are not. I use the correlations to set expectations, and to explain to students that time expended does not always correlate with higher grades.

During the Semester. I use many traditional assessment tools during the term such as quizzes, tests, homework, and case studies to assess student learning in the cognitive realm. I sometimes use *clickers* to give me immediate feedback of student learning. The clicker is an electronic device that a student uses to answer a multiple choice question that is projected on a PowerPoint slide.

Although student identities are anonymous, the distribution of answers is displayed on the screen. At this point, I can decide if I need to further explain a particular concept to the class. The students can also see how they are standing in relationship to other class members. They often comment that using clickers is "fun."

Another quick and easy CAT is the *Muddiest/Clearest Point CAT.* At different points during the term, the professor asks the students to write about the muddiest and clearest points in the lecture. This technique is time effective, taking about 2–3 minutes, and allows the instructor to quickly assess the students' understanding level of the material. If there are problems, then the instructor can re-lecture on the muddy concepts.

Using *Reflection papers* (Appendix A: CAT 4) help students reflect on their learning and how to improve it. I want to gauge how students are feeling throughout the term. Studies on self-efficacy reveal that students' success in unfamiliar classes is correlated with their self-efficacy (Tuckman and Sexton 1992). Thus, I need to know if my students are feeling satisfied or frustrated about their learning, gaining confidence as the course progresses, or blaming others for their lack of performance. I also want to evaluate their levels of engagement by asking them if they have discussed the class material with those outside the classroom. The questions on this CAT help me to respond to students who are struggling.

The *Mid-Semester Intervention CAT* is probably the best formative CAT, helping professors improve their teaching during the term. At my college, this intervention is conducted by the Director of the Center for Teaching and Learning (CTL) who comes to my class by the middle of the term. During a twenty-minute exercise, she holds focus groups with my students and gathers input about my teaching. The Director then provides me with constructive formative feedback that enables me to address class concerns. This information has helped me remove obstacles to my students' learning. For example, students felt I was trying to "get them" when I described an upcoming exam as "hard." They felt exams should be "achievable" and "challenging," but not hard. I know this problem seems to boil down to semantics, but the CTL Director told me that these simple words make a difference when it comes to student motivation levels (Appendix A).

End of Semester. At the end of the term, again, I use traditional forms of assessment such as testing, class projects, and presentations. I ask the students to complete a final *reflection paper,* the *pre-test/post-test CAT* again, and to fill out an *Assessment CAT* that asks them about their learning experience. I also moved my final to an in-class, on-line exam. The class completes the final in a computer lab under my supervision so that they can see the correct answers and final scores immediately. I want my students to learn from their mistakes on the final as well as having an opportunity to challenge the answer key.

Step 4: Closing the Loop

Closing the feedback loop is essential for classroom assessment to be successful. There are two aspects to closing the loop: (1) faculty members need to hear and respond to student input to improve their teaching practices, and (2) students need timely, relevant feedback to improve their learning (Exhibit 3).

The focus to improve remains on student learning—whether it includes changes in teaching technique or helping students understand their own responsibility in the learning process. CATs are designed to do just this.

Faculty Responsibility

Faculty members should use a variety of assessment techniques to improve what they do in the classroom. They need to set appropriate learning goals, determine congruent learning experiences, and then select appropriate assessment techniques. Assessment becomes a form of action

EXHIBIT 3
The CAT Feedback Loop

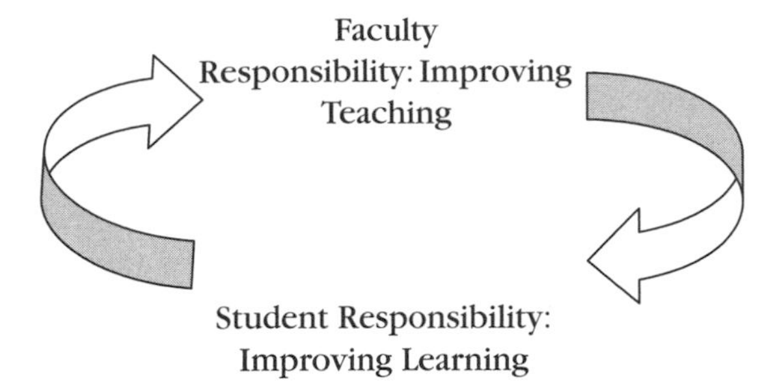

research when it is used to improve student learning. Action research is defined as an approach to improving education by encouraging teachers to be aware of their own practice, to be critical of that practice, and to be prepared to change it (McNiff 1998). Change is a deliberate process that emancipates teachers from the often unseen constraints of assumptions, habit, precedent, coercion, and ideology (Carr and Kemmis 1986).

Simply stated, when faculty members see a problem, they need to make an attempt to alleviate it. As an example, I used a simple reflection paper CAT to ask my upper level accounting students to reflect on why they performed so poorly on an Intermediate exam. Several of them wrote that they studied "what was easy" or "what they liked." I was stunned by their responses. This explanation would have never entered my imagination as a reason for poor test performance.

I began to research this topic more to see what I might do that could help my students improve their performance. Through discussions with colleagues, it became clear that the problem was not confined to my classes. My colleagues surmised many reasons for the lack of performance among my students such as "students were lazy, under prepared, did not read or want to work, could not think critically, and wanted to be coddled." These explanations sounded rational, but none provided me with a solution to help my students improve their learning. Through a literature search, I discovered a theory of self-regulation that might provide an explanation to what was occurring in my classes. Tuckman and Sexton (1992) categorized students into three groups: self-believers (those high in the belief that they can do well on any task), self-unsure (those in the middle), and self-doubters (those who doubt their abilities to perform tasks). Self-believers perform well no matter what the task or test. On the other hand, self-doubters only exert effort if they feel there is a guaranteed pay-off. Thus, self-doubters need frequent quizzes to help them retain knowledge and to give them an opportunity to score well rather than only a midterm and final where the risk of failure is higher.

Perhaps, my Intermediate class was full of self-doubters, and my testing practices were counterproductive to their learning. Might the Tuckman and Sexton's theory of self-regulation explain the problem in my Intermediate class?

I also asked colleagues and students for recommendations for change. One colleague suggested de-emphasizing exams by not giving in-class examinations, but putting them on-line. Students from the Intermediate accounting class, after participating in a mid-semester intervention with our CTL Director, suggested more frequent testing on each chapter (seemingly supportive of the self-regulation theory).

I did not change my entire Intermediate class structure, but made a few adjustments by adding on-line quizzes on the remaining chapters. As a result, the students' performance improved during the latter part of the class and on the final. Accordingly, I made changes to my tax classes the following term. I replaced the in-class midterm and final with weekly on-line, open book quizzes, and tests. The quizzes were not timed or supervised; whereas the final exam was supervised and held in a computer lab.

Thus far, I found these changes to be personally liberating—no more study sessions, review sheets, or retests to grade. It's a relief to not hear a student ask, "Is this going to be on the test?" I also like the fact that on-line quizzes and tests provide instant feedback which students can learn from.

Interestingly, the average scores on the quizzes were about 7–8 correct out of 10. The students liked this format, but could not believe how "low" their scores were on "open book" quizzes. The quizzes forced them to research each question. Some expressed satisfaction as they saw their scores improve as they improved their research skills.

Student Responsibility

CATs are intended to improve student learning, which should be the goal of education and not satisfaction. Helping students assume responsibility for their learning is the key benefit of using CATs. For example, the 2–3 minute "muddiest/clearest point CAT" causes students to review the lecture for the day, and communicate what they did or did not learn. The "Timekeeper" and "Reflection Paper" CATs force students to evaluate their use of time and studying techniques. Interestingly, my experience has been that many students will take responsibility for their lack of learning in their journals.

In a recent Tax Class, I found that my students "did not feel their grades reflected their efforts." As I thought about their statements, I realized that my students equated grades with effort, not with the quality of their work. Here I uncovered a flaw in my students' paradigm of learning. If my students focus on their effort and not the quality of their work, it is no wonder they are confused about their grades. "Quality" is not in their realm of understanding of what education is all about. Thus, this simple CAT provided me with a powerful insight into the mind of my students. I can now redirect my students to more productive thinking when I explain the issue of effort and the quality of their work.

THE LAG MODEL: CONGRUENCY IN GRADING

Grading is another compelling communicator of messages to students. Most literature on CATs state that CATs should be anonymous and not graded (Angelo and Cross 1993). I agree that formative CATs, where students could feel threatened, should be anonymous and not graded. I believe, however, that other CATs should be tied to grades. Congruency in grading is necessary to promote learning. For example, if a professor states that critical thinking is a learning goal, but 90% of the grade is tied to multiple choice exams, students will disregard the other aspects of learning. In fact, the incongruence between grading and what professors state as their values could be viewed as disingenuous.

Given that the average accounting professor is 57 years old (Previts 2007), he/she may be unfamiliar with current assessment techniques. The typical accounting professor learned under the lecture/testing model, the prevailing teaching model of the 1970s and 1980s. In fact, with the exception of the education field, few professors receive formal training in pedagogy, assessment, or teaching in their Ph.D. programs. Thus, when professors try to adopt newer measures of assessment, testing still serves as the primary determinant for grading. As a result, I propose faculty adopt the LAG Congruency Model (Exhibit 4). **L**earning Goals, **A**ssignments, and **G**rading are interrelated, and must work together to maximize student learning. If these three elements

EXHIBIT 4
LAG Congruency Model: Learning, Assignments, and Grading

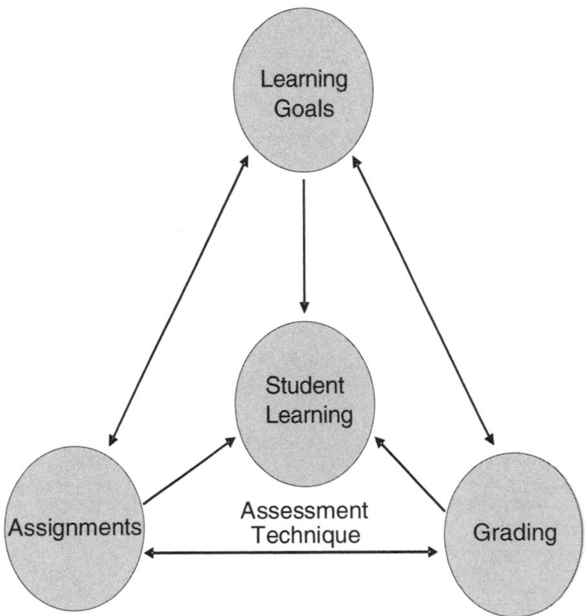

are balanced or congruent with each other, the professor's messages will be clearly communicated to today's student. If not, student learning will LAG.

The model recognizes that grading structures have a bearing on student efforts. Even if professors value other learning goals, their grading schemes could undermine their best efforts to redirect student learning. No doubt, students focus their attention where the points are (Chulkov 2006, Betts and Grogger 2003). Thus, a grading scheme must support a professor's learning goals, learning experiences, and assessment schemes. When I created the LAG model, I discovered that my grading scheme was imbalanced, leaning heavily on performance assessment, even though I believe strongly in other forms of assessment. I recently revised my grading scheme for my principles class as seen below (Exhibit 5):

Through this grading scheme, I communicate clearly to students that I value all six dimensions of learning, and I will reward them for quality work in each area.

PERFECTING OUR CRAFT

Ultimately, this article is about improving the craft of teaching effectively for professors, and the goal of learning for students. Accounting professors need to modernize what they do to reach a tech savvy generation that values relevancy. If I am good at my craft, I will use these values to my advantage.

The shift is to focus on student learning—your eyes and the students' eyes. The goal is students and their learning. I am their experienced guide, mentor, and evaluator. First, I must develop learning goals that are varied and meaningful. Second, I need to select learning experiences (assignments) that support those learning goals. Lastly, I must align assessment (grading) to communicate to students the importance of the system that I created in a substantive way.

EXHIBIT 5
Principles of Financial Accounting

Learning Goals	Assignments	Grading
Foundation Knowledge—can recite basic knowledge of accounting principles and create financial statements.	Testing, quizzes, homework, clickers.	20%
Application—can solve problems and conduct a financial analysis of two similar "real" companies and communicate the better company to an audience.	Testing, homework, and financial comparison class project.	30%
Integration—can understand how accounting fits into the business world, and understand how "cooking the books" affects society.	Interviews with business people, essay about video, SOX essay.	10%
Learning to Learn—taking responsibility for your own learning.	Muddiest point, reflection papers, timekeeper, teaching center intervention.	20%
Caring—develop interest in the topic: how accounting will affect you in the future and the business you work with.	Interviews with business people, internal control paper, retirement planning.	10%
Human Dimension—how does accounting affect others, friends, investors, and what is the influence of the public media.	Critiques of public media, essay about video, explaining financials to a friend.	10%

Developing the "craft" takes time and introspection on the part of the faculty member. The joy for me comes as I see students not only improve in their comprehension of material, but their higher learning skills as well as their professionalism. One student wrote of my transition in winter of 2006:

> This has been one of the best classes I've taken at Otterbein ... I will be able to use the knowledge in the future. I like the new way you conducted your class. It gives the students a much better understanding of the information presented to them. We do not have to get so worked up about exams and cram the night before only to forget the info the next day.

Another student in the same class wrote:

> I have more respect for the career I am pursuing. Being an accountant is an all day job. You don't really leave your work at the office ... I will have to be always ready for whatever a client brings to my office.

The challenge never ends for me. Sometimes, I find out that a particular teaching technique or technology does not work for a class. Last year, I adopted the use of clickers for my principles of financial accounting classes. I asked my students using CAT #4 to rate the clickers. My traditional students in accounting principles class ranked the use of clickers as "excellent" or "good;" whereas my non-traditional evening students ranked them as "poor." On the other hand, the evening students ranked the lectures as "excellent;" whereas the traditional students ranked them as "fair." After two terms of similar ratings, I decided not to use clickers for my evening classes. The evening students felt that the clickers detracted from a more valuable perceived use of time, which were lectures. Thus, CAT #4 helped me to differentiate the needs of my different student populations.

In conclusion, SMART assessment gives faculty members the tools to perfect the craft of teaching and learning. In fact, doing assessment well in itself is a craft. If faculty members use these principles of assessment outlined in this chapter, then the assessment process can work to the benefit of all the stakeholders involved—students, faculty, and the college.

APPENDIX A

TABLE 1
Congruency—Matching Learning Goals to CATs

Learning Objective	Description	"What Students will be Able to Do"	Assignments and Assessment Techniques
Foundation Knowledge	Terminology; content; principles of the discipline	Understand and remember key concepts, terms, and relationships related to financial accounting.	Performance: Testing, quizzes, clickers.
Application	Knowledge applied to problem solving and analytical thinking	Use the concepts learned in class to evaluate the financial statements and condition of a company and communicate their meaning to an audience.	Performance and Authentic: Testing, homework, and financial comparison class project.
Integration	Relationship with other disciplines, courses, part of the whole	Identify the interaction between accounting and business, investment, and governmental policy decisions.	Authentic: Interviews with business people, essay about video, SOX essay.
Learning to Learn	Life-long learning; self-regulating behavior	Reflect upon your learning.	Formative and Assessment for Learning: Muddiest point, reflection papers, timekeeper, teaching center intervention.
Caring	Caring about the material; seeing relevancy	Become confident about your ability to apply course material to "real world" situations.	Authentic: Interviews with business people, internal control paper, retirement planning.
Human Dimension	Impact on society as a whole and others	Engage in critical evaluation of accounting issues that you encounter in the public media. Be aware of the ethical standards that guide CPAs.	Performance/Authentic: Critiques of public media, essay about video, explaining financials to a friend.

APPENDIX A
CAT #1: Assessing Student's Prior Knowledge

1. Have you had accounting in high school?	Yes	No		
2. Have you had a college accounting level course? (Perhaps you dropped it or did not get a satisfactory grade in the past)	Yes	No		
3. Have you (or do you) work in an accounting-related field? If yes, please describe:	Yes	No		
4. Have you ever heard of financial statements before this first class?	Never heard of this	Have heard of it, but do not know what it means	Have some idea of what it means, but am not too clear	Have a clear idea of what this means and can explain it
5. Have you ever heard of the Sarbanes Oxley Act?	Never heard of this	Have heard of it, but do not know what it means	Have some idea of what it means, but am not too clear	Have a clear idea of what this means and can explain it
6. Have you ever heard of debits and credits?	Never heard of this	Have heard of it, but do not know what it means	Have some idea of what it means, but am not too clear	Have a clear idea of what this means and can explain it
7. Have you ever heard of financial ratios?	Never heard of this	Have heard of it, but do not know what it means	Have some idea of what it means, but am not too clear	Have a clear idea of what this means and can explain it
8. Have you ever heard of journal entries?	Never heard of this	Have heard of it, but do not know what it means	Have some idea of what it means, but am not too clear	Have a clear idea of what this means and can explain it
9. Have you ever heard of internal controls?	Never heard of this	Have heard of it, but do not know what it means	Have some idea of what it means, but am not too clear	Have a clear idea of what this means and can explain it
10. Have you ever heard of the auditors report?	Never heard of this	Have heard of it, but do not know what it means	Have some idea of what it means, but am not too clear	Have a clear idea of what this means and can explain it
11. What is your motivation level to take this class at this time?	I am not motivated at all and wish it was not a requirement	I have minimal interest in this class	I am moderately interested	I am very motivated and can't wait to get started

Write your **feelings** about taking this class this term:

APPENDIX A
CAT #2: Formative Group Assessment*

1. Overall, how effectively did your group work on this assignment?
   Poorly Adequately Well Extremely Well
2. Out of the ___ group members, how many participated actively most of the time?
   5 4 3 2 1
3. Out of the ___ group members, how many were fully prepared for the activity?
   5 4 3 2 1
4. Give a specific example of something you learned from the group that you wouldn't have learned working alone:

5. Give one specific example of something the group learned from you:

6. Suggest one change to the group that could improve its performance:

---

* Adopted from Angelo and Cross, Classroom Assessment Techniques (1993), p. 350.

APPENDIX A
CAT #3: Timekeeper

	Week 1							**Total**
	Sun	Mon	Tues	Wed	Thurs	Fri	Sat	
Studying/Reading								
Homework								
Studying for Tests								
	Week 2							**Total**
	Sun	Mon	Tues	Wed	Thurs	Fri	Sat	
Studying/Reading								
Homework								
Studying for Tests								
	Week 3							**Total**
	Sun	Mon	Tues	Wed	Thurs	Fri	Sat	
Studying/Reading								
Homework								
Studying for Tests								

Weeks 4–10

	Week 10							**Total**
	Sun	Mon	Tues	Wed	Thurs	Fri	Sat	
Studying/Reading								
Homework								
Studying for Tests								
	Finals							**Total**
	Sun	Mon	Tues	Wed	Thurs	Fri	Sat	
Studying/Reading								
Homework								
Studying for Tests								

Hours	
Studying/Reading	
Homework	
Studying for Tests	
Total Hours	

Midterm thoughts: How well do you think you used your time during the first half of the term? What things will you change for the second half of the term?

APPENDIX A
CAT #4: Reflection Papers

How helpful are the following to your learning?

	High	Good	Average	Low	Not at all
Working in groups in class	5	4	3	2	1
Reading the text	5	4	3	2	1
Doing "short" homework problems in the book	5	4	3	2	1
The "You Tube" video critique	5	4	3	2	1
Lectures	5	4	3	2	1
The use of clickers	5	4	3	2	1
Internal control paper	5	4	3	2	1
On-line quizzes	5	4	3	2	1
On-line midterm and final	5	4	3	2	1
Self-reflection papers	5	4	3	2	1

1. What concepts, principles, or ideas that you have learned thus far, do you think you will remember the most after you leave this class?
2. Reflect upon what you consider the most interesting thing you have learned in this class?

3. Do you see any relationship between this class and things going on in the business, investment, and/or government now?
4. How will what you have learned change your performance as a future accounting or business professional (now or in the future)?
5. What has surprised you most about this class this term?
6. How are you feeling about the class now that it is almost over?
7. Have you told anyone outside of class about information that you have learned in class? If so, list who these individuals might be.
8. Have you learned anything about yourself this term?
9. Add any comments that you would like me to read ....

Would you allow me to share your comments with a wider audience at a conference or on a paper? Yes ______ No ______

CHAPTER 11

Grades, Performance, and Reputation: Adjusting Ratings Using Expected Grades

Karen Leppel, Widener University
Hamid Zangeneh, Widener University*

Over the last half century, student evaluations of instructors have become the tool of choice for university administrators in their decision-making process for salary adjustments, tenure, and promotions. Cognizant of this fact, instructors seeking job security have bought students' approval by giving higher grades. A large amount of literature of both time series and cross sectional studies has explored the phenomenon of grade inflation and its potential adverse impact on the educational system (Langbein 2008; McPherson 2006).

In this study, we find that if a student perceives a course as easy, the student tends to give the course a high rating. Furthermore, students form views of instructors before enrolling in their courses, shopping around for better opportunities for high grades and less work. The greater the instructor reputation for being easy and the higher the students' expected grades, the higher the rating of the professor. Thus, if it is simpler to increase grades than to increase teaching quality, instructors have an incentive to do the former and ignore the latter. Students may seek the easy professors with the high grades and feel smug about their choices. However, when they are unable to perform their job with a prestigious "Big Four" accounting firm or in another employment setting, that satisfaction disappears along with respect for U.S. higher education.

BACKGROUND

Grade inflation is considered to be the consequence of using student evaluation of instructors as summative devices to evaluate teaching effectiveness (Germain and Scandura 2005). In spite of the fact that it is important and beneficial to know whether students are getting their money's worth, this customer satisfaction survey method may be a significant reason for the lower standards and higher grades awarded by faculty. If so, the educational system may be awarding raises, promotions, and tenure to those who are less deserving than the superficial evidence indicates. Instructors who are comparable in teaching quality, but do not inflate grades or deflate coursework, are given lower student evaluations, and are less likely to receive raises, promotions, and tenure

* The authors are Professors in the School of Business Administration at Widener University, One University Place, Chester, PA, 19013. Professors Zangeneh and Leppel can be reached by e-mail at hzangeneh@widener.edu and kleppel@widener.edu, or by telephone at 610-499-1140 and 610-499-1170, respectively.

than their peers who do inflate grades. As a consequence, the educational environment deteriorates in a degenerative process. The old cliché might become true; bad money chases good money out of circulation.

There is the argument that grades could be higher for reasons other than buying better evaluations. For example, better teachers may provide greater learning opportunities so that the students perform at a higher level. Alternatively, better teachers may attract better students who earn higher grades. In addition, some instructors may give higher grades because they do not see the grade system as important or their courses as relevant to their students' future. Some faculty members may not believe in themselves as experts in the area they are teaching and, therefore, they do not see themselves as the final arbiter. Also, if minority students tend to come from poorer educational backgrounds, they may perform at a lower level. Some professors may be unwilling to fail those students.

The seemingly intuitively acceptable concept of giving higher grades to secure higher ratings has resulted in a mixed, albeit lop-sided, bag of statistical evidence. On the supporting side of the ledger, a positive relationship between (expected) grades and ratings were found by Aigner and Thum (1986); Ditts (1983); Eiszler (2002); Isely and Singh (2005); Kau and Rubin (1976); Krautmann and Sander (1998); McPherson (2006); Mehdizadeh (1990); Nelson and Lynch (1984); Nichols and Soper (1972); and Zangenehzadeh (1988). On the other side of the ledger, Seiver (1983) found a positive relation using ordinary least squares and no relation using a simultaneous equations model; Decanio (1986) found no relationship using a multinomial logit model.

THE MODEL

Since, by definition, evaluation of individuals is almost never one-dimensional, a three-stage least squares method was used to account for simultaneity and avoid the biased and inconsistent results that would arise if an ordinary least squares model was used.

Three equations were estimated for three endogenous variables: professor quality, course quality, and expected grade.

In the professor quality equation, we expected that a student would rate a professor higher overall if that student rated the professor higher on performance characteristics found on a typical course evaluation form, specifically: ability of instructor to make a clear presentation; successfulness of instructor in encouraging students to think and reason about the subject matter; and accessibility of instructor outside of class. We also hypothesized that students would "punish" instructors of unpopular and challenging quantitative courses, by giving the professors lower ratings. Furthermore, as discussed above, we anticipated that students with higher expected grades would rate professors higher.

If a professor's teaching style is consistent with a student's learning style, the student is more likely to find the course appealing. Thus, a student who rates a professor higher is also likely to rate the course higher. In addition, students are generally unenthusiastic about quantitative courses and would be expected to rate them lower. Also, if students consider easy courses to be better courses, easy courses will be rated higher.

In the expected grade equation, stronger students, whose grade point averages are higher, would expect higher grades. The expected grade also would be higher when the professor is reputed to be an easy instructor. Since students tend to struggle with quantitative courses, their expected grades would tend to be lower in those courses. A course that students consider to be of higher quality may be one that is of greater interest or relevance to them; students may then expect to do better in that course. Expected grades are likely to be lower among students who feel that their grades do not reflect their effort. There are two reasons for this relationship. Sometimes students put what they believe to be a great deal of time into studying for a course. However, they may be employing ineffective study methods, may be lacking in mental aptitude for the subject, or may be underestimating the appropriate amount of time needed for the course. Consequently, their performances are poor, and the students are discontented. In addition, students who believe that their grades do not reflect their effort may be more likely to have an external rather than internal locus of control. An extensive amount of literature indicates a positive relation between internal locus of control and academic achievement, because individuals with an internal locus of control are more motivated. (See the literature review by Findley and Cooper 1983). Thus, students who feel that their current grades reflect their effort are likely to have higher expected grades.

ESTIMATION AND RESULTS

The hypotheses were tested using data from the Widener University School of Business Administration. Widener University is a comprehensive institution whose business school offers both undergraduate and master's degrees. Students were given a 28-question form, along with the regular end of semester evaluation form.[1] Participating faculty members were primarily from economics, management, marketing, finance, and information systems. A total of 754 questionnaires for 26 instructors in 54 courses/sections were collected.

Professor quality was measured by student responses to the statement "overall, I would rate the quality of the professor ...;" the choices were excellent, good, average, fair or poor. Similarly, course quality was measured by student responses to "overall, I would rate the quality of this course," using the same choices. To capture the relative ease of a course, students were asked to complete the statement "compared to other courses you have taken in the school of business at Widener, this course was" with one of the following: very easy, easy, average, hard, or very hard. To capture a professor's reputation, students were asked to complete the statement "this instructor is known to be" with one of the following: very hard, hard, fair, easy, or very easy. A course was categorized as quantitative if it was in accounting, economics, finance, operations management, quantitative analysis, or taxation. Exhibit 1 summarizes the definitions and coding of the variables that were included in the estimated equations and provides descriptive statistics for those variables.

The three-stage least squares estimation results are reported in Exhibit 2.[2] The results from the professor quality equation are consistent with other studies that concluded overall ratings of professors are positively influenced by students' expectation of their grades. A professor can buy better ratings by handing out better grades. As expected, instructor ratings also are positively and significantly related to: ability of instructor to make a clear presentation; success of instructor in encouraging students to think and reason about the subject matter; and accessibility of instructor outside of class. Surprisingly, the coefficient of the dummy variable for a quantitative course was positive as well. The anticipated negative impact of unpopular quantitative courses was not evident.

The course quality equation indicates that students who rate an instructor highly tend to rate the course highly as well. Students also consider easier courses to be higher quality courses. In addition, they dislike quantitative courses and give them lower ratings than other courses.

The expected grade equation indicates, not surprisingly, that the grade students anticipate receiving is positively related to the student's current grade point average; better students expect higher grades. Furthermore, students expect to do better in courses that they consider to be of higher quality. Expected grades are also higher when the professor has a reputation as an easy instructor. When students believe that their current grade reflects their course effort, they anticipate higher grades. Lastly, students expect to perform worse in quantitative courses. Thus, while there

[1] Questionnaires can be requested directly from the authors.

[2] When the specification was run on undergraduate day only and on all students, the signs and significance levels were essentially the same. When it was run just on graduate students, the signs were the same, but fewer coefficients were statistically significant, probably due to the small sample (n = 55).

EXHIBIT 1
Means and Standard Deviations of Variables

Variable Name	Definition	Coding	Mean	Standard Deviation
PROFQUAL	Overall professor quality rating	1 = poor, 5 = excellent	3.745	1.158
CRSEQUAL	Overall course quality rating	1 = poor, 5 = excellent	3.597	1.105
CLEARPRES	Ability of instructor to make a clear presentation	1 = poor, 5 = excellent	3.700	1.185
THINKING	Successfulness of instructor in encouraging students to think and reason about the subject matter	1 = poor, 5 = excellent	3.719	1.131
ACCESS	Accessibility of instructor outside of class	1 = poor, 5 = excellent	3.739	1.027
REFLECT	Current grade reflects student's course effort	1 = not at all, 5 = totally	3.460	1.076
EASY	Ease of course compared to other courses in the school of business	1 = very hard, 5 = very easy	2.475	0.885
EASYREP	Professor's reputation as an easy instructor	1 = very hard, 5 = very easy	2.416	0.806
EXPGRADE	Expected final grade in course	1 = F , 5 = A or A−	4.028	0.825
CURRGPA	Student's current GPA	1 = 0 to 0.99, 4 = 3.0 to 4.0	3.606	0.502
QUANT	Quantitative course dummy	1 = quantitative course, 0 = not quantitative course	0.444	0.497

Number of Observations: 754

was no direct negative impact of quantitative courses on teachers' ratings, there was an indirect negative impact. Since students anticipate poorer performance in quantitative courses, and students rate professors lower when they expect a lower grade, quantitative courses will indirectly reduce the rating of the instructors who teach them. This indirect negative impact will at least partially offset the positive direct effect mentioned above.

RANKINGS

Since students' expected grades influence their evaluations of their instructors, it is appropriate to adjust evaluations based on expected grades. Two types of adjustments, identified as Methods A and B, were explored and rankings were produced based on those adjustments. A ranking of 1 represents the best performance and a ranking of 26 represents the worst. Rankings are shown in Exhibit 3. The first and second columns of that table show the unadjusted average instructor rating and the unadjusted rankings, respectively.

Method A is based on the adjustment factor, $\overline{G}/\overline{G}_j$, where $\overline{G}$ was the average expected grade for students of all instructors, and $\overline{G}_j$ was the average expected grade for students of faculty member j. For each instructor, the average unadjusted instructor rating was multiplied by that adjustment factor. This process reduced the instructor rating for professors whose average expected

EXHIBIT 2
Three-Stage Least Squares Estimation Results

Equation	Variable Name	Coefficient	Std. Error
Overall professor quality rating 1—PROFQUAL	Intercept	−0.5279***	0.1724
	EXPGRADE	0.1587***	0.0461
	CLEARPRES	0.3780***	0.0276
	THINKING	0.3965***	0.0279
	ACCESS	0.1776***	0.0242
	QUANT	0.2184***	0.0455
Overall course quality rating 2—CRSEQUAL	Intercept	0.2434**	0.1067
	PROFQUAL	0.7980***	0.0273
	EASY	0.1637***	0.0298
	QUANT	−0.0911*	0.0513
Expected final grade in course 3—EXPGRADE	Intercept	0.3299*	0.1993
	CURRGPA	0.1881***	0.0350
	CRSEQUAL	0.5981***	0.0472
	EASYREP	0.1391***	0.0325
	REFLECT	0.1848***	0.0261
	QUANT	−0.2504***	0.0475

Instruments: ACCESS, CLEARPRES, CURRGPA, EASY, EASYREP, PROFEFF, QUANT, REFLECT, THINKING.
* significant at the 10% level
** significant at the 5% level
*** significant at the 1% level

grade exceeded the school average, and increased it for professors whose average expected grade was less than the school average. Adjusted instructor ratings and adjusted rankings using this method are shown in the third and fourth columns of Exhibit 3.

Method B is based on the coefficient of expected grade in the professor quality equation. The coefficient, b, measures the estimated impact of expected grade on instructor rating. In this adjustment process, for each student,

$$\text{Adjusted instructor rating} = \text{unadjusted instructor rating} - (b)\,(\text{expected grade}).$$

This adjusted rating was averaged over all the instructor's students, for each instructor. Ratings of all instructors were reduced by this process, but professors with higher expected grades had their ratings reduced by more than those with lower expected grades. Adjusted instructor ratings and rankings using this method are shown in the fifth and sixth columns of Exhibit 3.

For both adjustment processes, the rankings differed from the unadjusted ranking. More substantial changes in rankings were observed under Method A than under Method B. However, for both methods, instructors near the top usually remained near the top, and instructors near the bottom usually stayed near the bottom.

CONCLUSIONS

While earlier research has examined the effect of expected grades on student evaluation of teaching, the literature has not previously addressed the impact of a professor's reputation. If an instructor continually gives higher grades than may be justified by the quality of student work, the instructor can develop a reputation as an easy professor. For a given level of student performance, this reputation increases the grade expected, which in turn increases the student's rating of the professor. Instructors who develop a reputation for giving high grades for relatively low quality

EXHIBIT 3
Unadjusted and Adjusted Professor Quality Rankings

Unadjusted Instructor Rating	Unadjusted Ranking	Instructor Rating Adjusted Using Method A[a]	Adjusted Ranking (A)	Instructor Rating Adjusted Using Method B[b]	Adjusted Ranking (B)
4.86	1	4.32	8	4.14	3
4.86	2	4.42	2	4.15	2
4.85	3	4.46	1	4.16	1
4.80	4	4.39	4	4.10	4
4.79	5	4.41	3	4.10	5
4.75	6	4.17	10	4.02	6
4.73	7	3.81	14	3.93	8
4.66	8	4.32	9	3.97	7
4.45	9	3.99	12	3.74	10
4.44	10	4.35	5	3.79	9
4.23	11	3.99	13	3.55	11
4.00	12	4.03	11	3.37	12
3.90	13	4.35	6	3.33	13
3.88	14	4.34	7	3.31	14
3.82	15	3.67	16	3.15	15
3.54	16	3.67	17	2.92	16
3.50	17	3.76	15	2.91	17
3.45	18	3.56	20	2.83	18
3.45	19	3.37	21	2.80	19
3.29	20	3.56	19	2.70	20
3.26	21	3.28	22	2.63	22
3.23	22	3.66	18	2.66	21
3.13	23	3.16	24	2.50	23
3.09	24	3.26	23	2.48	24
3.08	25	3.10	25	2.44	25
3.02	26	2.94	26	2.36	26

[a] Values were calculated by multiplying instructor rating by the expected grade ratio. The expected grade ratio was computed by dividing the school's mean expected grade by the instructor's mean expected grade.
[b] Values were calculated as adjusted rating = unadjusted rating – (0.158653) (expected grade), where 0.158653 is the estimated regression coefficient of expected grade in the instructor rating equation.

student work, may reduce the incentive for students to put forth sufficient effort to achieve a high level of competence in the subject. A promotion, tenure, and merit system that rewards this behavior can cause the pattern to proliferate and can reduce the quality of the education received by the student.

Students may initially be happy with their easy classes and their high grades. However, when a student becomes involved in a co-op experience, internship, or employment and lacks the knowledge and understanding to do the assigned work, he/she will not be so content. That student will be even less satisfied when he/she graduates and is unable to pass the CPA or some other professional exam or to meet employer expectations. In retrospect, those easy classes will no longer seem like such wise choices. However, the damage done by these students to hard, demanding professors can last forever and eventually destroy education.

CHAPTER 12

Assessment Testing in the First Intermediate Accounting Course: A Three-Year Study in Comparison to Bloom's Taxonomy

Michael J. Krause, University of Indianapolis*

On the Monday of Thanksgiving week, in the years 2004–2006, Intermediate Accounting I students took the same assessment test on the "accounting cycle." The test used all 40 multiple choice questions found in Spiceland et al.'s *Intermediate Accounting* (3rd edition, chapter 2) test bank. Students received advanced notice about the test topic, but they were told *not* to prepare for the exam. Upon completing the test, students responded to a survey designed to measure attitudes about the experience. By using a second answer sheet, kept separate from the study's measurement instrument, students received immediate performance feedback from the instructor on the test day. Selection of this specific test topic was based upon my belief that a sustained competency about the "accounting cycle" is a prerequisite for further study of advanced theories and skills related to financial accounting.

In 2006 and 2005, nearly all students participated because five points were automatically added to attendees' first exam grade. Without such an incentive, only 29 out of 43 students voluntarily took the test in 2004. While the author taught 65% of the 2004 class as sophomores, all 2006 and 2005 students had other professors for introductory accounting courses. The 2006 and 2005 students used the Norton *Intermediate Accounting* text (2nd edition, 2007; 1st edition, 2006). The 2004 class, however, used Spiceland text, the source for test material. Entry into the Intermediate II course was restricted to students who earned a grade of "C" or better in Intermediate I. Over the three years observed, students who failed to qualify for the second course were 17% in 2006, 26% in 2005, and 21% in 2004.

Since 2004, I have organized measures of student performance on this specific test by categorizing test questions as concepts, examples, or calculations. After participating in an August 2006, American Accounting Association panel discussion in Washington, D.C. (on course-embedded outcomes assessment), I first saw a connection between my work and the cognitive categories found in Bloom's *Taxonomy of Educational Objectives* (1956). Specifically, I noticed a similarity between my test question categorizations for this particular assessment vehicle to the

* Professor Krause is Associate Professor of Accounting at the University of Indianapolis and Professor Emeritus at Le Moyne College. krausem@uindy.edu.

classifications found in Bloom's first three fundamental levels of cognitive development (knowledge, comprehension, and application).

ASSESSMENT LITERATURE REVIEW IN COMPARISON TO OBSERVATIONS FROM THIS THREE-YEAR STUDY

Some business schools maintain a graduation prerequisite that candidates take a comprehensive assessment test which is given outside of any particular senior business course. The School of Business at the University of Indianapolis maintains such a policy. The alternative is to embed the assessment vehicle within a capstone course to function both as a graded assignment as well as an assessment exercise. The dual purpose of grading and assessing distinguishes an embedded assessment vehicle. Peter Ewell (2003) stresses the benefits of embedded assessments. Since embedded assessments are given within the standard curriculum, they provide an opportunity to evaluate the class "as a whole." Ewell maintains that students do not take assessment activity seriously when given outside the curriculum. Of particular relevance are these comments about selecting course-embedded methods:

> Assessment results at the course level can provide information to individual students about their learning, and can lead to changes in classroom activities, assignments, and grading methods. Thus, the course is an ideal level at which outcomes assessment can create a feedback loop on the quality of learning experiences within an accounting program ... Then assurance of learning results at the course level can also flow upward to support program-level assessment and can provide evidence regarding the contribution that an individual course makes to a related learning goal of the program (Ammons and Mills 2005, 2).

Ammons and Mills (2005) also contend that course-embedded assessments improve student motivation to do their best during the evaluation process, with the additional benefit to them of timely feedback. The test in this study qualifies as a course level assessment. Students did receive quick feedback, specifically on the day of the test. Results from this study's immediate follow-up survey confirmed my belief that the students did indeed take the assessment exam seriously. While students were told not to prepare for this particular assessment exam, the observed median test score over the three-year period ranged from 60% to 70%. These results do not differ much from my personal experience when giving multiple choice questions on an Intermediate Accounting exam that counts toward the final course grade. As a direct assessment method, Ammons and Mills (2005, 6) say that objective examinations "may be a good choice ... when the outcome of interest is the demonstration of knowledge acquisition." Therefore the use of forty multiple choice questions on this study's assessment test appears to be an appropriate method to test knowledge of the accounting cycle. Future research plans are aimed at reducing the size of the testing instrument by eliminating duplication of specific accounting topics and cognitive assessment measures.

Akers *et al.* (1997, 262) detailed the Accounting Department's assessment process at Marquette University which adopted a learning outcome that "accounting graduates should possess the technical accounting knowledge necessary to obtain an entry-level accounting position." By testing the fundamental accounting cycle, this study's assessment exam was consonant with Marquette's selected intended student learning outcome. Without a working knowledge of the accounting cycle, would a student be ready for a future entry-level job or even ready now to take advanced accounting courses? Ainsworth and Plumlee (1993) describe a similar learning objective at Kansas State University. Ainsworth and Plumlee validate my objective for this test; they also ratify the objective question assessment technique. They indicate that a "lecture method of teaching, with objective testing, is very appropriate for lower-level classes where knowledge and comprehension are the desired cognitive objectives and professional skill development is not critical" (Ainsworth and Plumlee 1993, 119). While the Intermediate I course should not be classified as a lower-level class, the accounting cycle lesson is essentially a review to summarize and establish the learning that should have taken place in sophomore courses. Therefore, a multiple choice assessment test can diagnose the existence of a fundamental knowledge base from which to progress to professional skill development.

Stivers et al. (2000) share assessment lessons learned at Kennesaw State University. Of their eighteen points, the five most important to this study are:

1. Be specific in stating learning outcomes; developing general learning outcomes, such as "accounting knowledge," makes it difficult to evaluate specific competencies.
2. Plan to use multiple measures to capture different aspects of your program over time.
3. Focus on group results rather than individual student results; a group focus allows you to capture and understand your program strengths and weaknesses without incurring the additional cost (time) to focus on individual students.
4. Nationally averaged standardized tests may not meet your needs.
5. Scheduling exams can be difficult. Students may not be willing to take time outside of class and faculty may not be willing to give up class time for assessment (Stivers *et al.* 2000, 576–578).

My experience mirrors Stivers points 1–5 above. Assessment tests focused specifically on the accounting cycle which overcomes problems with setting a too general outcome (point 1). The objective test coupled with the survey was a multiple measurement event (point 2). This study developed results by each test question, thus focusing on group results (point 3) (i.e., 2004 students performed superbly on nine questions, below standard on four others). A national standardized test was not necessary (point 4) as this assessment instrument used a text test bank. By using down time in the semester, a holiday week, this study avoided scheduling difficulties (point 5). In the related survey, students consistently agreed that the "test was a good experience" and that "Thanksgiving week is a good time to take a diagnostic test." Also, I did not reduce teaching time (point 5) since a review lesson with an assessment angle was created. Over the three years studied, the students consistently indicated through the accompanying test survey that the test itself was a positive review experience (see Exhibit 3—Question 2). This finding allays the student "willingness" concerns raised by Stivers in point 5 above.

LITERATURE REVIEW (BLOOM'S TAXONOMY APPLIED)

Many diverse studies have used Bloom's Taxonomy (1956) as a framework to organize analysis and to further discussion. Bloom's educational objectives listed in progressive cognitive order are: knowledge; comprehension; application; analysis; synthesis; and evaluation. Karns, Burton, and Martin (1983) analyzed six Principles of Economics texts. They evaluated how well exam questions coordinated with stated text learning objectives using Bloom's Taxonomy to categorize text material. Hampton and Krentler (1993) used Bloom's work to classify multiple choice questions found in four Introductory Management and four Introductory Marketing texts. Davidson and Baldwin (2005) studied the end of chapter materials in forty-one Intermediate Accounting texts from 1934 to 2004. They then related their analysis to Bloom's six educational objectives to identify trends in learning goals over seventy years. Athanassiou, McNett, and Harvey (2003) provide excellent background about Bloom's theory as they attempted to shift learning management to students as a way to promote critical thinking skills. Reeves (1990) also clearly puts

Bloom's work into context as he explains its relevance to teaching Business Ethics. Perhaps most creatively, Jui-Hung Ven and Chien-Pen Chuang (2005) developed a lexicon of action verbs related to Bloom's six levels of cognitive behavior by analyzing job descriptions for information occupations in USA, Australia, and Taiwan.

The six studies mentioned generated some common findings:

- Textbooks fail to provide evaluation materials beyond basic cognitive levels (Karns et al. 1983; Hampton and Krentler 1993; Davidson and Baldwin 2005).
- The best opportunities to evaluate at highest levels of cognitive development are provided by creative personal pedagogies (Reeves 1990; Athanassiou *et al.* 2003).
- Bloom's cognitive levels are progressive. Higher levels of cognitive development requires mastery of the basic levels (Reeves 1990; Davidson and Baldwin 2005).
- Carefully selected action verbs can best describe (frame) assessment activities at the six levels of cognitive development and can guide new assessment development (Reeves 1990; Athanassiou et al. 2003; Jui-Hung Ven and Chien-pen Chuang 2005).

OBSERVATIONS

The first two tables below compare the assessment test performance of the three Intermediate Accounting I classes observed from 2004 to 2006. In particular, Exhibit 1 organizes the individual question's error rates by the three major categories established by Bloom and experienced by me. Observations show that at lower levels of Bloom's taxonomy, error rates are at or below the existence rate of such questions within a category. Only Bloom's "application" (use) category consistently showed a higher error rate than the existence percentage of test questions in that category. Unlike Exhibit 1 in which yearly error percentages established by using a denominator totaling all test errors, Exhibit 2 lists yearly error percentages observed when the denominator amount was designated as the total responses found within a subset of those questions assigned a specific Bloom's category (one of the three used in this study, and the reason why table does not add up to 100%). For all three years observed, the mean error rate for questions within a category was found to be consistently and significantly higher as the analysis ascends Bloom's scale. Exhibit 3 reporting student survey results indicate that over the three-year period, students displayed a consistently positive attitude toward the assessment test experience.

The results of the follow-up survey seem to add credibility to test results in Exhibits 1 and 2. Survey responses indicate that students appeared to be putting forth their best efforts to answer exam questions correctly. Students only responded negatively to two survey questions dealing with other semester course projects. Students apparently did not see the connection between these

EXHIBIT 1
Test Results

Bloom's Objective	Author's Category	% of Total Test	Errors as a % of Total Test 2006	2005	2004
Knowledge (recall)	Concept	27.5%	17.3%	20.0%	17.3%
Comprehension (understanding)	Example	42.5%	42.0%	43.2%	42.2%
Application (use)	Calculation	30.0%	40.7%	36.8%	40.5%
		100.0%	100.0%	100.0	100.0%
Student Population			52	44	29
Total Incorrect Answers			715	732	348

EXHIBIT 2
Mean Error Rate (Questions in a Category)

	Errors as a % of a Question		
Category (Questions in Category)	**2006**	**2005**	**2004**
Concept (n = 11)	21.7%	30.4%	18.8%
Example (n = 17)	33.9%	42.3%	29.8%
Calculation (n = 12)	46.6%	50.9%	40.5%
Standard Deviation—Question Error Rate	**2006**	**2005**	**2004**
Concept (n = 11)	10.4%	13.5%	11.2%
Example (n = 17)	14.5%	18.8%	18.2%
Calculation (n = 12)	12.5%	12.6%	12.8%

EXHIBIT 3
Comparative Survey Results
(Strongly agree assigned "1." Strongly disagree assigned "5.")

Questions Asked:	2006 Mean/ (Std. Dev.)	2005 Mean/ (Std. Dev.)	2004 Mean/ (Std. Dev.)
1. Test was a good experience	2.04/(.80)	1.81/(.55)	1.79/(.48)
2. Test helped me understand Accounting basics that I need to know	1.78/(.70)	1.86/(.56)	1.59/(.49)
3. Test helped me measure the progress that I made this semester in comprehending Financial Accounting	1.98/(.65)	1.88/(.54)	1.86/(.63)
4. (Course required) review case gave me background that helped me take this test	2.30/(.83)	2.45/(.93)	2.45/(1.07)
5. *Wall Street Journal* project gave me background that helped me take this test	3.40/(.82)	3.10/(.81)	3.38/(.81)
6. My final grade on this course will exceed "C+"	1.82/(.82)	1.93/(.91)	1.72/(.69)
7. The Thanksgiving week class is a good time to take a diagnostic test	1.68/(.73)	1.52/(.73)	1.86/(.82)
8. I did well on this test	2.52/(.67)	2.62/(.75)	2.48/(.81)
9. I intend to pursue the Accounting major all the way to graduation	1.58/(.87)	1.50/(.76)	1.31/(.65)

two required course projects (reading *The Wall Street Journal* and doing a review case) and the Accounting Cycle lessons which were the object of the assessment test they took.

Exhibit 4 displays the range of expected performance outcomes established by the Class of 2004 (best performing) and the Class of 2005 (worst performing). Assessment questions allow for direct comparison between these two benchmark years. Exhibit 5 shows that the benchmark years also can be used to analyze other class years when their performance falls between that observed for the two established outlying classes. In comparing the benchmark years themselves, Exhibit 6 shows that the 2004 class out performed the 2005 class. (Significance is defined as a difference of 15.5%.) Exhibit 6 documents, by specific test questions, how the 2004 group performed extensively better than the 2005 class.

EXHIBIT 4
Overall Comparative Performance

	2006	2005	2004
Median Correct Test Score	66%	60%	70%

EXHIBIT 5
Average Absolute Value of Difference in Performance of 2006 Class vs. Benchmark Classes Using Observed Individual Question Error Rate

Test Category	2006 versus 2005	2006 versus 2004
Concept (n = 11)	8.7%	5.2%
Example (n = 17)	11.4%	8.4%
Calculation (n = 12)	13.2%	13.4%

EXHIBIT 6
Comparative Study of Benchmark Years (2005 vs. 2004)

2005 % Incorrect	2004 % Incorrect	Type of Question	Question Topic
68.2%	27.6%	Calculation	Bad debts expense AJE
40.9%	10.3%	Example	Deferral (Revenue) AJE
68.2%	37.9%	Calculation	Bad debts expense AJE
45.5%	17.2%	Concept	Accounting Equation
52.3%	24.1%	Concept	Deferral (Revenue) AJE
54.5%	27.6%	Example	Accrual (Asset) AJE
59.1%	34.5%	Example	Accrual (Liability) AJE
65.9%	44.8%	Calculation	Cost supplies purchased
56.8%	37.9%	Example	Accrual (Liability) AJE
34.1%	17.2%	Concept	Retained Earnings Statement
40.9%	24.1%	Example	Deferral re: Cash Inflow
61.4%	44.8%	Example	Internal event transaction
15.9%	0.0%	Example	Contra a/c—accumulated depreciation
50.0%	65.5%	Calculation	Cash Flows—operating activities

The 2005 class performed better than the 2004 class on only one question which dealt with the Statement of Cash Flows (SCF). The 2004 class covered the topic only in Intermediate II; whereas the 2005 class studied the SCF in both Intermediate I and II. Given its competitive advantage of covering the SCF topic in Intermediate I prior to the November assessment test date, the 2005 class should have performed much better than the 2004 group on the SCF question. The 15% positive difference scored by the 2005 class on the SCF question mirrors the 15% negative difference it also scored on a basic review question which identified "accumulated depreciation" as a "contra" account. Since the 2004 class did poorly on a topic that it never studied in Intermediate I by the same percentage differential as the 2005 class did poorly on a simple primary accounting lesson, this fact solidifies the position that these two classes form polar opposite benchmark years.

NEXT STEPS

Assessment test format for 2004–2006 contained all forty multiple choice questions available in the Spiceland et al.'s 3rd edition *Intermediate Accounting* text chapter 2 test bank. I wanted a measurement device free from personal bias so Spiceland's questions were used unedited. With three years of observations available, a less cumbersome assessment format can be created. The creation of a revised test format can not completely eliminate my perspective on accounting education. However, at least now by using performance results accumulated over three years, I can logically explain the construction of an assessment test encompassing the accounting cycle theme.

The new assessment format will contain twenty-four questions. Three sets of eight questions each will reflect Bloom's fundamental cognitive categories of knowledge (concepts), comprehension (examples) and application (calculations). Every third question then will contain the same classification. Thus "knowledge" will be measured in questions 1,4,7,..22; "comprehension" will be measured in questions 2,5,8,..23; and finally "application" will be measured in questions 2,6,9,..24. The sixteen questions to be eliminated from the original forty will be first sorted by those that need to go to maintain a quota of eight questions per Bloom's three categories tested. Next the actual questions to be deleted will be those outlying questions within a category where student performance was the best and the worst observed.

Once the final twenty-four questions are established, the placement into the assessment instrument will be by ascending order of observed student error rates. The objective of this strategy is to sustain a positive attitude and efficient exam time management for students by placing the most challenging questions at the end of the test. Compared to the order found in Spiceland's exam bank, all "comprehension" questions will have to be rearranged, while 75% of "knowledge" and "application" questions need to be repositioned so that most difficult questions are asked last. Survey results over three years showed that when students answered the question "I did well on this test" they judged themselves very harshly. Yet, they gave "agree" results to the questions: "Test was a good experience" and "Test helped me understand Accounting basics that I need to know" (see Appendix and Exhibit 3). So question placement should build upon this inherent student goodwill found in survey results even though the former test was cumbersome and lacked assessment strategy. An initial draft of the new assessment test contains twenty-four questions with an average 2006 observed error rate of 34.78% as compared to the old test's forty questions with an average 2006 observed error rate of 34.38%. These error rates are consistent with the fact that over the three years studied the median overall test score ranged from 60% to 70% correct answers.

In addition to culling questions, the questions will be reworded to contain action verbs consonant with Bloom's taxonomy. The menu of relevant action verbs can be found in "Table 8" of the work of Jui-Hung Ven and Chien-Pen Chuang (2005). I deliberately set out to write a new test draft that avoided using the same "Table 8" action verb more than once. As a result of this strategy the following verbs were selected as the best fit into the sentence originally published in Spiceland test bank:

1. **Knowledge**—recall, indicate, label, reproduce, repeat, recite, pronounce and provide
2. **Comprehension**—retell, give, display, define, observe, articulate, clarify and scrutinize
3. **Application**—compute, perform, retrieve, report, show, present, process and capture.

Other minor changes will be made to the original Spiceland sentences to make the wording more compatible with newly inserted verbs. The most consistent change requires eliminating a sentence's passive voice.

Master's of Business Administration students (who should be developing Bloom's highest cognitive skills) could be surveyed to help identify which action verbs may be most understandable for a typical undergraduate student. The goal ultimately would be to structure four action verbs into each eight-question block that measures a specific cognitive category. This two to one ratio of questions to verbs is a strategy to select the most effective predicates without running the risk of injecting bias into student responses by overusing a key action word.

CONCLUSIONS

The assessment test and survey were an effective use of class time. A diagnostic multiple choice test is an excellent example of a course-embedded assessment tool. This fact compounds the effectiveness of the time invested to implement this exercise. With The Association to Advance Collegiate Schools of Business, Association of Collegiate Business Schools and Programs and regional accreditation bodies explicitly or implicitly adopting outcomes assessment, an objective test represents a useful approach to a requirement that education justifies its use of individual and state resources. The data and reflections presented in this report, support statements made by Ammons and Mills (2005, 2) that "assurance of learning results at the course level can also flow upward to support program-level assessment" (like preparing students to obtain entry-level accounting positions). Collecting such evidence proves the ultimate practicality of an assessment test within a time-constrained semester.

Carefully selected multiple choice questions from textbook materials can be used to assess Bloom's three basic levels of cognitive development—knowledge, comprehension and application. My classification of multiple choice questions as concepts, examples and calculations reflects Bloom's taxonomy. This study also affirms findings from previous research that text materials do an excellent job of assessing the most basic levels of cognitive development.

This study verifies that Bloom's taxonomy is indeed a valid tool to measure orderly cognitive progression. Over the three years, a comparison of a cognitive category's *error rate* (based on all observed answers for the entire assessment test) versus the percentage of questions a category holds in total test population (the *existence rate*) showed the following trends:

- The most basic cognitive level, knowledge, showed an error rate consistently below the existence rate.
- Comprehension, the next higher cognitive level, demonstrated an error rate remarkably similar to the existence rate.
- Application, the highest of the fundamental cognitive levels, displayed an error rate consistently above the existence rate.

The calculation category (application) generated the most consistent standard deviation for observed incorrect answers. Despite the fact that the overall test performance for the three class years was clearly different, all three class years struggled uniformly with the exam's highest level of cognitive development assessed.

Additional research is needed to link multiple choice testing to other assessment vehicles designed to measure more advanced cognitive development. Such research could be designed to establish that a competency at lower levels of cognitive development is a prerequisite to obtaining skills reflective of the highest levels of cognitive development.

Surveys conducted over the three years studied indicate that students had a positive reaction to the assessment test experience. In particular, the timing of the experience was favorably rated. Negative survey results (found in Exhibit 3, Questions 4 and 5) concerning the effectiveness of course-required *The Wall Street Journal* project and course-required review case showed that students did not just give responses which they perceived would please their professor.

Using the current assessment test as a prototype, a future exam construct will reduce total questions asked and thus become more proportionately reflective of the three cognitive categories assessed. Available research on "action verbs" can guide new questions creation that would minimize or eliminate dependence upon textbook materials. Such an independent test instrument could facilitate research establishing that students have truly obtained a sustained competency over an assessed topic.

A streamlined assessment instrument should be tested. Revisions can be measured to see if previously observed positive student perceptions about assessment experience get even better. If student perceptions at least remain the same as compared to the years 2004–2006, future research needs to explore if a shorter, more structured measurement vehicle does a better job of establishing achievement at Bloom's three basic levels of cognitive development. If the answer to that question is "yes," then the ground work would be established to market the idea of college consortiums to benchmark cognitive results when an agreement is reached as to the learning objective(s) to be assessed.

This study's recommendation for a revised measurement instrument is itself an example of the long-term benefits of outcomes assessment. The feedback loop created by studying the assessment test over three years will generate a more efficient and sophisticated measurement device to document a valued outcome—a student's sustained competency with lessons dealing with the accounting cycle.

The development of an improved testing instrument happens because the author also improves. Assessment is not only a means to establish that a program has added value to a student's education, it also documents the growth and adaptation skills of the educator. This study shows how the author became more aware of the benefits and the information provided by the assessment test as it was administered over a three-year period. In the effort to demonstrate continuous improvement to accreditation bodies, assessment vehicles provide individual educators insights about the group dynamics at work over a period of years. In this study Exhibit 4 shows that the overall median assessment test score ranged from 60% to 70%. This finding established ranges for normal outcomes which will help to identify future classes as strong or weak. Exhibit 4 findings also establish that the valued outcome (like comprehension of the accounting cycle) will on average yield at best a 70% retention rate. Therefore, even in a technically intensive course like Intermediate Accounting, skills training should be given a syllabus agenda item.

Diversifying the learning outcomes (a technical topic and a related skill for example) improves the chances that the educator will indeed be able to demonstrate some value added to the student's education. While assessment may have been instigated by forces outside the classroom, the individual educator who invests time in such exercises will not fail to see the benefit. This fact is especially true for accounting educators. Assessment reflects what accountants do—set up a system to collect transactions, record transactions, and then process reports. Assessment artifacts are simply an educational version of economic transactions. Assessment and accounting appear to be related disciplines.

Therefore, accounting educators should make the most of this natural relationship (a discipline advantage) and use assessment as a means for professional improvement and as a means to document professional accomplishments. In establishing the learning outcome to measure, the individual educator makes a statement about personal educational values. As educational techniques come, adapt and then go, values remain. Once such values have been enunciated, the educator will find that within class time, no opportunity will be by-passed to reinforce those educational ideals for which there is a true personal commitment.

APPENDIX
SURVEY QUESTIONS

1 = strongly agree. 5 = strongly disagree

STATEMENT

1.	Test was a good experience	1	2	3	4	5
2.	Test helped me understand Accounting basics that I need to know	1	2	3	4	5
3.	Test helped me measure the progress that I made this semester in comprehending Financial Accounting	1	2	3	4	5
4.	(Course required) review case gave me background that helped me take this test	1	2	3	4	5
5.	*Wall Street Journal* project gave me background that helped me take this test	1	2	3	4	5
6.	My final grade for this course will exceed "C+"	1	2	3	4	5
7.	Thanksgiving week class is a good time to take a diagnostic test	1	2	3	4	5
8.	I did well on this test	1	2	3	4	5
9.	I intend to pursue the Accounting major all the way to graduation	1	2	3	4	5

CHAPTER 13

Distance Learning in Accounting Education: Current State and Future Directions

Vasant Raval, Creighton University*

The field of distance education (DE) in most academic disciplines in higher education has grown over time, and with increasing pace. From correspondence courses in early 1970s to distance teaching in the nineties, to distance learning at the dawn of the 21st century—there is progress on many fronts. A survey of chief academic officers sponsored by the Sloan Consortium found that overall online enrollments for U.S.-based institutions increased from 1.98 million in 2003 to 2.35 million in 2004 (Sloan Consortium 2005). This increase represents a growth of 19 percent compared to 20 percent from 2001 to 2002, and 23 percent from 2002 to 2003.

Online enrollments have continued to grow at rates far in excess of the total higher education student population, albeit at slower rates than for previous years.

- Almost 3.5 million students were taking at least one online course during the fall 2006 term, with a nearly 10 percent increase over the number reported the previous year.
- The 9.7 percent growth rate for online enrollments far exceeds the 1.5 percent growth of the overall higher education student population.
- Nearly 20 percent of all U.S. higher education students were enrolled in at least one online course in the fall of 2006 (Sloan Consortium 2007).

Several reasons contribute to this growth in distance education. For students, especially non-traditional students, access to education via technology is crucial, particularly in the remote geographical areas. In addition, DE provides flexible delivery systems that can accommodate varying work and family schedules, and provide some degree of freedom to pace one's progress in a course. Also, for the institutions of higher learning, DE could prove to be a strategic way to grow enrollment without having to build additional physical infrastructure (class room space, dorm rooms, etc.).

The emergence of DE was initially rooted in the existing face-to-face teaching-learning model (FF), also called the traditional or legacy model. Therefore, there exists a tendency to take a comparative view of DE in relation to its established alternative, FF.

* Professor Raval is Professor of Accounting at Creighton University.

Content, delivery, learner, teacher, and learning objectives are all often examined in the DE arena in comparison to the same attributes in FF. Our experience with the legacy model has a long history and has been investigated extensively; therefore, it is imperative to think of DE as an alternative to FF rather than an altogether different market space for teaching and learning. While the comparative approach helped in some ways, it also inhibited capacity to examine and evaluate DE as an original, independent, and potentially strategic option.

A primary purpose of this chapter is to report on the current state and future directions of distance education (DE), particularly with respect to business education and where possible, specifically as related to accounting education. The discussion is organized into six broad categories: Environment, Institutional Aspects, Assurance of Quality, Student-Teacher dimension, Content, and Delivery.

ENVIRONMENT

The environment of the higher education space has changed considerably. Declining rate of enrollment growth, increasing costs, and aging faculty are just some of the factors. Faculty tenure, academic freedom, students as customers are all subject to considerable reevaluation, also.

One of the vastly impacting variables in this "industry" is information technology (IT). Just as information technology impacts other aspects of life and business, IT also impacts teaching and learning. While early attempts to launch a distance learning course were filled with many perils, the technology and infrastructure development, and support from within and outside higher education institutions have become more sophisticated. The question of participation in the distance education is now largely outside of the information technology maturity. DE is a question of strategic engagement at this time, and in the future, DE may even become one of survival of institutions.

Early problems in DE were centered on technology. Reliability of communication lines, communication bandwidth, rate of data transfer, and availability and affordability of the Internet access to students were key issues. Also included in the list of problems were student-related technology, (e.g., the compatibility of the hardware that the student has and availability of software to the student).

As learning management systems (e.g., Blackboard, BlueLine) grew in number and sophistication, most of the technology issues have been addressed to a large degree. At this stage, DE programs have become less expensive, more reliable, and more viable at least from the technology perspective. However, it should be recognized that many other variables play a part in the decision to launch DE programs. Ultimately, the human side of the inputs might weigh much more in the decision than the technology.

The technology behind distance education developments closely resembles Christensen's definition of disruptive technology (2003). He distinguished between established technologies that allow an entity to grow in a linear mode (sustaining technologies) from those technologies that start out as simple, cheap, and even inferior, but grow over time into innovative and new uses that generate exceptional economic value. Arguably, DE technology is a disruptive technology. Today, the evidence is becoming clear: despite all its problems and challenges, distance learning is here to stay, and may even dramatically change the campus scene of the legacy systems.

One potentially effective approach to address a disruptive technology is to set up an autonomous unit freely competing with the established legacy system. Universities tend to set up separate distance learning divisions internally, and state university systems could set up a separate university. Penn State's World Campus, Arizona Regents University, California Virtual Campus, and Florida Gulf Coast University are examples of such initiatives. There are similar initiatives afoot overseas, for example, the Thailand Cyber University.

INSTITUTIONAL ASPECTS

U.S. institutions of higher education, both private and public, have been impacted by many variables, such as the cost of education and a commitment of several years on the part of students. The idea of "full-time" education in "residence" mode for a period of four years or longer is being challenged. Equally important is the fact that the generational profile of student, including the most recent one, the Net Generation, creates the need to align the institution to the characteristics of its students, even in the legacy mode of learning. While the Net Generation is not the first generational change for higher education institutions, it certainly is dramatically different from the past generations.

According to the Commission on Future of Higher Education, Department of Education, 18–22 year-old full-time undergraduate student represents only 16 percent of the higher education population. About 40% study part-time, 40% attend two-year institutions, 40% are age 25 or older and 58% are age 22 or older. To work part-time while seeking an undergraduate degree is not uncommon anymore.

While online educational space is growing, a knee-jerk reaction on the part of an institution is certainly neither warranted nor should it be expected. A clear articulation of the institution's strategy and how it aligns with its mission, goals, and objectives is important. Also, crucial to the institution's success in online programs is a systematic development and execution of its strategy related to online education.

For the professional accounting students who wish to sit for the CPA examination, most State Boards of Public Accountancy require 150 hours of academic work. Since earning an undergraduate degree requires about 120 hours, students wishing to sit for the CPA examination seek choices to complete the additional hours. They likely would look for flexibility, lower costs, and coursework that meets their needs with the 150-hour requirement of the State from where they choose to take the examination.

The demand from accounting students for flexibility in taking additional credits to meet the 150-hour requirement to sit for the CPA examination is likely to generate greater amounts of interest in offering DE courses appropriate for the requirement. This need for flexibility is caused not only by the requirement of additional courses, but also by the differences between States in terms of what constitutes 150 hours. Thus, an accounting graduate from a Nebraska institution sitting for the CPA from Kansas could meet the specific Kansas requirements through DE options.

Because there is a need to support additional academic work required of professionals, there also is a need to offer continuing education programs. While these may not come under the umbrella of accreditation, the decision whether to offer them, and in what form, should be guided by similar considerations as in accredited programs.

ASSURANCE OF QUALITY

Both the regional accrediting agencies for business education and AACSB International have been emphasizing the fact that quality of education should be identical in online tracks, if offered in an accredited program. In 2001, the eight U.S. regional accrediting commissions issued a statement to guide higher education institutions in addressing quality issues in online programs. The statement addressed quality in online education in five components:

- Institutional context and commitment to online education and allocation of necessary resources.
- Curriculum development and online instruction by academically qualified faculty.
- Faculty support, such as training, workload considerations, and compensation.
- Student support, such as administrative and technical assistance.
- Evaluation and assessment of learning.

In an analysis of AACSB International's guidance and standards, Grandzol and Grandzol (2006) identify several dimensions of the accreditation requirements that point to quality issues of online education:

- Quality comparable to that in FF learning.
- Adequate student-faculty interaction to promote learning.
- Support infrastructure and resources (student support, academic assistance, career and academic advising).
- Active learning, where the student is fully engaged in the learning process and interacts with faculty and peers.

In a study conducted by the Institute for Higher Education Policy (2000), twenty-four benchmarks of quality of online education were identified. These were grouped into the following categories:

- Course structure
- Student support
- Institutional support
- Course development
- Teaching-learning
- Faculty support
- Evaluation and assessment

The pressures to prove that learning occurs in the DE environment are probably even greater than in a FF environment. FF courses and curricula have existed for a long time, and some conviction in learning assessment approaches, as applied to FF programs, has been gained over time. DE should not be mere delivery of content, but must result in the achievement of the course's learning objectives. Operationalizing this observation is a considerable challenge.

While the debate regarding best approaches to measure learning in DE environment will continue, there are many advantages to DE in this regard. For example, subject matter may be easily and cost effectively presented in various forms: instructor notes, PowerPoint slides accompanied by narration, transcript of the narration, suggested answers to assigned problems, pretests and posttests with definite opening and closing times. Students may choose appropriate documents out of these somewhat overlapping and multimedia (e.g., voice, video, image, text, etc.) deliveries. Based on their learning styles, some students, for example, may prefer to use audio accompanied by presentation slides, while others may stick to the textbook, instructor notes, and the script of the presentation. When a choice is offered, students have the benefit of picking one they believe would help them the most. In contrast, students do not really have delivery options to consider for their learning, unless a FF class is supported by a learning management system in a hybrid approach.

Despite all efforts, quality issues in online education probably will linger until institutions, and their faculty and students, climb the learning curve. Interestingly, the two key role players—teacher and student—are at the center of the scene and will certainly be key factors in decisions that impact quality of education. DE is a vastly different learning space and, combined with the new generation of tech-savvy students, creates significant challenges of offering quality academic programs.

STUDENT-TEACHER DIMENSION

In terms of technology orientation, today's college students are familiar with the technology, while the professors are frequently not so equipped. They have lived with the Internet, iPod, laptop, and mobile phones. They are impatient with pencil and paper and longer cycle times to do anything. According to some, they suffer from attention deficit order.

In contrast, their teachers—especially those who have been around for a long time—may be unfamiliar with current technology, less willing to learn the skills. Their conviction lies mostly in the tradition, and their comfort is with the legacy systems of learning, where they control the pace, content delivery, and the schedule. In contrast, distance education instructors must plan ahead, be highly organized, and communicate with learners in new ways (Howell et al. 2003).

Future students are likely to insist on student-centered learning approaches. They are more tuned to Blogs (web logs), podcasting (iPod based broadcasts), vodcasting (video on demand broadcasts), wikis (online shared space for composition and editing), RSS (Rich Site Summary/ Really Simple Syndication), and digital gaming or simulation (X-box, for example). To them, learning is an experience, filled with experimentation and self discovery. Whereas, not all content to be learned can be fitted in the new stream of options, with proper care and selection, there is room for creating excitement and motivation for learning.

Although the Net generation of students might be anxious to learn using new technology, their teachers may not be ready for them. The demand for faculty time in learning new technologies and putting them to proper use to deliver the desired learning objectives is no small task. Understandably, some, despite all accommodations and incentives, may still not be willing to retool their courses and instructions. A statistic of interest here would be the quality and quantity of faculty involvement in online education. Are we seeing a two-class system—those who teach online and those who don't—emerging, at least in the short run?

For teachers to get comfortable with the new technology tools, one option is to experiment with new vehicles of communication and sharing in "blended" courses, where a face-to-face class is supported with a learning management system. Such hybrid delivery allows faculty to comprehend how learning occurs in the new environment, and what works and what does not work in their specific course content. For the student, this option offers a chance to work with multiple channels of learning approaches built into the online segment of the blended course.

Historically, the notion that a teacher is the provider of learning and the student is the receiver is often implicit in teacher-student relationships. But students learn from their cohorts and classmates as well, including those who are shy and reluctant to get involved in the classroom. Their creativity is unleashed in ways that teachers may not be aware.

In an Accounting Information Systems (AIS) face-to-face class that the author offered, a course management platform typically used for DE was deployed. Among many other tasks that students accomplished, they were required to participate in an asynchronous discussion forum. The topic was XBRL. This forum provided the students an opportunity for myriad discoveries particularly via web-based sources of information. One student searched YouTube and found a video presentation on XBRL, and almost everyone benefited from it.

Students now and in the future will be technology proficient, for they are expected to be surrounded by technology. However, will this proficiency easily translate into skills necessary to leverage technology tools to achieve learning objectives? An assumption that this transformation will automatically happen is a big risk. In the author's opinion, there exists a significant gap between daily use of technology for esoteric purposes and knowing how to learn by deploying them appropriately. Over the next few years, while trial-and-error approach may prevail, systematic study of this dimension is crucial to the success of DE in the long run.

CONTENT

Any initial attempts to deploy DE were mostly in the form of conversion of existing courses rather than their transformation. Information systems professionals know it too well; any time a system needs to be transported to another software platform, such as an ERP, the easiest thing to do might be to just convert it from its existing form, without evaluating the possible improvements one could make because of the strengths (and weaknesses) of the new platform.

The initial development—and even current trend in some cases—has characteristically been in the spirit of taking courses and converting them on an as-is basis into a DE form, without addressing fully how the learning objectives are compromised, or can be leveraged, because of the DE medium. A primary advantage of this approach is that it requires a minimal investment of time, albeit rendering the blueprint imperfect. Such translation may even avoid the question of approving the online course because one can argue that the course existed in the bulletin, and only its delivery has changed. But the question remains: Is all content appropriate for delivery via the DE approach?

A long-term effect of such quick translation tactics could be that the traditional, well-established universities will be left with courses that are difficult to convert, while those easy-to-convert courses have already become popular with for-profit institutions in the DE space.

One might think that universities founded with a mission to serve predominantly through DE alternatives might have started with an altogether newly developed blueprint of curricula. However, a cursory look at publicly available information does not suggest so. Comparing an Introduction to Financial Accounting course from a nearly pure DE university with a comparable course at a FF university, we find that there is minimal substantive (content-related) difference between the two courses. This similarity may be because even the former has to justify curriculum equivalency for their students to transfer from, or to, locally available institutions of higher learning. Regardless of this consideration, the fact remains that we have not yet approached the examination of content for its fit with the DE approach.

DELIVERY

In any learning environment, three interrelated components should be considered: content (the subject matter of learning), context (learner and teacher characteristics, for example), and method (delivery and communication channels) (Kozma and Bangert-Drowns 1987). Of the three, a significant producer of change in the DE arena is the method. While the legacy systems afforded the teacher every opportunity to be an independent decision maker in almost all aspects of the learning process, the new scenario suggests that the teacher will have to seek support from educational technologists and course designers. Experts who understand how new technologies work in effective delivery of various learning objectives are key to the course design. Thus, the course design and delivery becomes a team effort, although the content expertise still resides with the teacher.

There are some caveats already emerging. For example, an online course must be completely ready for launching on the first day. For this to happen, meticulous planning is necessary. Faculty may have to unlearn the short windows of planning they may be familiar with in a FF learning environment. Another caveat: Not all students are geared to effective online learning; a majority of students still want face-to-face interaction. In an accounting information systems course, it would be difficult, for example, to teach online the process of data normalization, and in an auditing course, the topic of audit judgment.

A third caveat to consider is that students expect real-time responses in an online environment and no matter how good the faculty is in keeping up with the electronic communication, not all expectations of an online student will be met. In a graduate course in managerial accounting, one faculty found that the students were active over the weekend, when the instructor had to juggle family commitments.

CONCLUDING REMARKS

Compared to non-business academic programs, business programs have shown greater increase in the volume of DE courses. This trend is going to continue and in all likelihood, accelerate. Because of the expanding horizons of DE in business education, now that its presence is proven beyond doubt, the next questions in its life cycle have more to do with issues of "real" learning and assessment methods that would permit assurance of learning.

There is little doubt that DE now offers a viable and, in some cases, only learning path. Over the short span of years, the field has shown promise, accompanied by impressive improvements in the technological and infrastructure support. As current issues of quality, assessment, and the selection of learning approaches are resolved, additional concerns will emerge. For example, issues of transfer credits, flexibility of schedules, more room for self-pacing one's progress in a course, compression of timeframe for graduation, and option to take a course (equivalent or similar to the one offered FF on the campus) online will surface in the near term. In light of such demands, institutions must quickly reevaluate their policies on students' academic work, including transfer credits, and how to effectively communicate these policies to incoming students.

References

Abbott, W. M. 2008. The politics of grade inflation: A case study. *Change* (January/February 2008) 40 (1): 32–37.

Accounting Education Change Commission (AECC). 1990. Objectives of education for accountants: Position statement number 1. *Issues in Accounting Education* 5 (2): 307–312.

———. 1993. Evaluating and rewarding effective teaching. Issues Statement No. 5. Torrance, CA: Accounting Education Change Commission.

Adams, J. V. 1997. Student evaluations: The rating game. *Inquiry* 1 (2): 10–16.

Addy, N. and Herring, C. 1996. Grade inflation effects of administrative policies. *Issues in Accounting Education* 11 (1): 1–3.

Aguayo, R. 1991. *Dr. Deming: The American Who Taught the Japanese About Quality.* New York, NY: Simon & Schuster.

Aigner, D. J., and F. D. Thum. 1986. On student evaluations of teaching ability. *Journal of Economic Education* 17 (4): 243–266.

Ainsworth, P., and R. D. Plumlee. 1993. Restructuring the accounting curriculum content sequence. *Issues in Accounting Education* 8 (1): 112–127.

Akers, M. D., D. E. Giacomino, and J. P. Trebby. 1997. Designing & implementing an accounting assessment program. *Issues in Accounting Education* 12 (2): 259–280.

Albrecht, W. S., and R. J. Sack. 2000. Accounting education: Charting the course through a perilous future. *Accounting Education Series* No. 16. Sarasota, FL: American Accounting Association.

Albritton, F., Jr. 2007. Academic department best practices: Attracting students to study economics. Seminole Community College, Working Paper (March). Available at: http://ssrn.com/abstract=967387.

American Accounting Association (AAA). 1953. *Accounting Teachers' Guide.* Cincinnati, OH: South-Western Publishing Company.

———, Committee on the Future Structure, Content, and Scope of Accounting Education (The Bedford Committee). 1986. Future accounting education: Preparing for the expanding profession. *Issues in Accounting Education* 1 (1): 168–195.

———. 1993. Evaluating and rewarding effective teaching. Issues Statement No. 5. Torrance, CA: Accounting Education Change Commission.

———. 2002. *Critical Thinking Skills Toolkit.* Sarasota, FL: American Accounting Association.

———. 2008. *Accounting Faculty in U.S. Colleges and Universities: Status and Trends, 1993–2004. A Report of the American Accounting Association February 19, 2008.* Sarasota, FL.

American Association of University Professors (AAUP) 2006a. *AAUP Contingent Faculty Index 2006.* Available at: http://www.aaup.org/NR/rdonlyres/F05FF88E-B2A8-4052-8373-AF0FDAE060AC/0/ConsequencesAnIncreasinglyContingentFaculty.pdf.

———. 2006b. *Recommended Institutional Regulations on Academic Freedom & Tenure.* Available at: http://www.aaup.org/AAUP/pubsres/policydocs/contents/RIR.htm.

———. 2008a. *Treatment of Adjunct Faulted at U. of New Haven.* Available at: http://www.insidehighered.com/news/2008/05/15/aaup.

———. 2008b. *AAUP Faculty Survey.* Available at: http://chronicle.com/stats/aaup/index.php?action=result&search=&state=&year=2008&category=I&withRanks=1&limit.

Ammons, J. L., and S. K. Mills. 2005. Course-embedded assessments for evaluating cross-functional integration and improving the teaching-learning process. *Issues in Accounting Education* 20 (1): 1–19.

Anderson, D. 2007. *Up Your Business! 7 Steps to Fix, Build, or Stretch Your Organization (2nd ed).* New York, NY: John Wiley.

Anderson, M. 1992. *Impostors in the Temple.* New York, NY: Simon & Schuster.

Angelo, T. A., and K. P. Cross. 1993. *Classroom Assessment Techniques: A Handbook for College Teachers.* San Francisco: Jossey-Bass.

Angus, S. 2008. The power of integration: Assessing a recent best-practice method for large-class instructional materials generation & presentation. Monash University, Faculty of Business and Economics, Working Paper (February). Available at: http://ssrn.com/abstract=1106362.

Annand, D. 2007. Reorganizing universities for the information age. *International Review of Research in Open and Distance Learning* 8 (3): 1–9.

Anonymous. 2008a. RateMyProfessors.com. Available at: http://www.ratemyprofessors.com/ShowRatings.jsp?tid=341175 (accessed on June 15, 2008).

———. 2008b. RateMyProfessors.com. Available at: http://www.ratemyprofessors.com/ShowRatings.jsp?tid=359225 (accessed on June 15, 2008).

———. 2008c. RateMyProfessors.com. Available at: http://www.ratemyprofessors.com/ShowRatings.jsp?tid=324794 (accessed on April 2, 2008).

———. 2008d. RateMyProfessors.com. Available at: http://www.ratemyprofessors.com/ShowRatings.jsp?tid=612560 (accessed on April 2, 2008).

———. 2008e. RateMyProfessors.com. Available at: http://www.ratemyprofessors.com/ShowRatings.jsp?tid=64414 (accessed on April 2, 2008).

———. 2008f. RateMyProfessors.com. Available at: http://www.ratemyprofessors.com/ShowRatings.jsp?tid=75100 (accessed on April 2, 2008).

Appelbaum, M. I. 1989. Assessment through the Major, C. Adelmen (3d.), *Performance and judgment: essays on principles and practice in assessment of college student learning.* U.S. Department of Education Office of Educational Research and Improvement. Washington, DC: U.S. Government Printing Office.

Appleby, S. 2002. Playing the blame game with change checks. *UALR Forum* (October 9): 2–3.

Arens, A., and R. Elder. 2006. Perspectives on auditing education after Sarbanes-Oxley. *Issues in Accounting Education* 21 (4): 345–362.

———, ———, and M. Beasley. 2005. *Auditing and Assurance Services: An Integrated Approach 10th ed.* Upper Saddle River, NJ: Pearson Prentice Hall.

Argyris, C. 1991. Teaching smart people how to learn. *Harvard Business Review* 69 (3): 99–109.

Armitage. H., and J. Boritz. 1986. Integrating Computers into the Accounting Curriculum. *Issues in Accounting Education* 1 (1): 86–100.

Asan, S., and M. Tanyas. 2007. Integrating Hoskin Kanri and the balanced scorecard for strategic management: The case of higher education. *Total Quality Management & Business Excellence* 18 (9/10): 999–1014.

Aslanian, P., and J. Duff. 1973. Why accounting teachers are so academic. *Journal of Accountancy* 136 (4): 47–53.

Association for the Advancement of Collegiate Schools of Business (AACSB) International. 2003a. *Eligibility Procedures and Accreditation Standards for Business Accreditation.* (January 1). Tampa, FL.

———. 2003b. *Sustaining Scholarship in Business Schools.* (September) Tampa, FL.

———. 2005. *Eligibility Procedures and Accreditation Standards for Business Accreditation.* (January 1). Tampa, FL.

———. 2005b. *Who Will Prepare Tomorrow's Business Leaders?* Available at: http://www.aacsb.edu/resource_centers/deansresources/default.asp.

———. 2006. *2005–2006 Executive Salary Survey Summary.* Tampa, FL. Available at: http://www.aacsb.edu/knowledgeservices/home/SSExecSummary_05-06.pdf.

———. 2008a. *The AACSB Guide to Business Education: 2008 Data Direct from the Source.* Tampa, FL.

———. 2008b. Final Report of the AACSB International: Impact of Research Task Force. (February). Joseph Alutto Chair. Available at: http://www.aacsb.edu/resourcecenters/research/default.asp.

Athanassiou, N., J. M. McNett, and C. Harvey. 2003. Critical thinking in the management classroom: Bloom's taxonomy as a learning tool. *Journal of Management Education* 27 (5): 533–555.

Atkinson, M. 2001. The scholarship of teaching and learning: reconceptualizing scholarship and transforming the academy. *Social Forces* 79 (4): 217–1229.

Bacchetti, R., and T. Ehrlich (eds.). 2007. *Reconnecting Education and Foundations: Turning Good Intentions into Educational Capital.* San Francisco, California: Jossey-Bass.

Bailey, A. 1995. The Practicing Profession's Mental Model: Are We Creating the Right Mental Models for New Professionals? *Issues in Accounting Education* 10 (1): 191–195.

Baker, G. P. 1992. Incentive contracts and performance measurement. *Journal of Political Economy* 100 (3): 598–614.

Bale, J., and D. Dudney. 2000. Teaching generation X: Do andragogical learning principles apply to undergraduate finance education? *Financial Practice & Education* 10 (1): 216–227.

Bamber, E. M., and L. S. Bamber. 2006. Using 10-K reports brings management accounting to life. *Issues in Accounting Education* 21 (3): 267–290.

Banta, T., K. Black, and K. Kline. 2000. PBL 2000 plenary address offers evidence for and against problem-based learning. *PBL Insight* 5 (3): 1–7.

Bar, T. R., V. Kadiyali, and A. Zussman. 2007. Quest for knowledge and pursuit of grades: Information, course selection, and grade inflation. (September), Johnson School Research Paper Series No. 13–07. Available at: http://ssrn.com/abstract=1019580 Accessed June 3, 2008.

Baril, C. P., B. M. Cunningham, D. R. Fordham, R. L. Gardner, and S. K. Wolcott. 1998. Critical thinking in the public accounting profession: aptitudes and attitudes. *Journal of Accounting Education* 16 (3/4): 381–406.

——— (ed.). 1995. *Change in Accounting Education: A Research Blueprint.* Center for Research in Accounting, James Madison University: Federation of Schools of Accountancy.

Barnard, J. 2008. Post-Tenure Review As If It Mattered. University of San Diego, Law School. Legal Studies Research Paper No. 08-083 (July). Available at: http://ssrn.com/abstract=1161303.

Barone, L. 2008. *The Tree of Financial Economics.* Working paper, London: Goldman Sachs International. Available at: http://ssm.com/abstract=1123484.

Barrow, R. 1981. *The Philosophy of Schooling.* Brighton, Sussex: Edward Elgar.

Basil, M. D., and D. Z. Basil. 2006. The marketing market: A study of Ph.D. supply, demand, hiring institutions, and job candidates. *Journal of Business Research* 29: 516–513.

Bastable, C. 1977. Why can't Johnny account? *Journal of Accountancy* 143 (1): 63–69.

Bauerlein, M. 2008. *The Dumbest Generation: How the Digital Age Stupefies Young Americans and Jeopardized Our Future [Or, Don't Trust Anyone Under 30].* New York, NY: Jeremy P. Tarcher/Penguin.

Beattie, V., B. Collins, and B. McInnes. 1997. Deep and surface learning: A simple or simplistic dichotomy? *Accounting Education.* March. 6 (1): 1–12.

Bedford, N., and W. Shenkir. 1987. Reorienting accounting education. *Journal of Accountancy* 164 (2): 84–91.

Benjamin, E. 2003a. Editorial page. *New Directions for Higher Education* 123: 1–13.

———. 2003b. Reappraisal and implications for policy and research. *New Directions for Higher Education* 123: 79–113.

Bennis, W., and J. O'Toole. 2005. How business schools lost their way. *Harvard Business Review* 83 (5): 96–304.

Bereiter, C., and M. Scardamalia. 1993. *Surpassing Ourselves: An Inquiry into the Nature and Implications of Expertise.* Chicago: Open Court.

Berkner, L., S. He, E. F. Cataldi. 2002. *Descriptive Summary of 1995–96 Beginning Postsecondary Students: Six Years Later.* National Center for Educational Statistics. U.S. Department of Education.

Berman, E. undated. A Short Guide to Evaluating Teaching. Assessment and Enrollment Research. University of Arizona.

Berri, D. J., M. B. Schmidt, and S. L. Brook. 2006. *Wages of Wins.* Stanford: Stanford University Press.

Best, A. 2008. Student Evaluation of Law Teaching Work Well: Strongly Agree, Agree, Neutral, Disagree, Strongly Disagree. *Southwestern University Law Review* 38 (1).

Betts, J. R., and J. Grogger. 2003. The impact of grading standards on student achievement, educational attainment, and entry-level earnings. *Economics of Education Review,* Elsevier, 22 (4): 343–352.

Bigelow, J. D. 2004. Using problem-based learning to develop skills in solving unstructured problems. *Journal of Management Education* 28 (5): 591–610.

Blauvelt, H. 1993. Chaney also tutors players about life. *USA Today* (December 15): C-1 and 2.

Blooinquist, P., and J. Yeager. 2008. Using Balanced Scorecards to Align Organizational Strategies. *Healthcare Executive* 23 (1): 24–28.

Bloom, A. 1987. *The Closing Of The American Mind.* New York, NY: Simon and Schuster.

Bloom, B, M. Engelhardt, E. Furst, W. Hill, and D. Drathwohl. 1956. *Taxonomy of educational objectives: The classification of educational goals. Handbook I: Cognitive domain.* New York, NY, Toronto: Longmans, Green.

Bloom, B. S. (ed.) 1956. *Taxonomy of Educational Objectives, Handbook I: Cognitive Domain.* New York, NY: David McKay.

Bok, D. 2006. *Our Underachieving Colleges.* Princeton University Press: Princeton and Oxford.

———. 1986. *Higher Learning.* Cambridge, Mass.: Harvard University Press.

———. 1986. *The Cost of Talent.* New York, NY: The Free Press.

Bolge, R. D. 1995. Examination of student learning as a function of instructor status (full-time versus part-time) at Mercer Community College. Available at: http://eric.ed.gov/ERICWebPortal/custom/portlets/recordDetails/detailmini.jsp?_nfpb=true&_&ERICExtSearch_SearchValue_0=ED382241&ERICExtSearch_SearchType_0=no&accno=ED382241/.

Bonk, C. J., and G. S. Smith. 1998. Alternative instructional strategies for creative and critical thinking in the accounting curriculum. *Journal of Accounting Education* 16 (2): 261–293.

Bosshardt, W., and M. Watts. 2001. Comparing student and instructor evaluations of teaching. *Journal of Economic Education* 32 (1): 3–17.

Boyer, E. 1992. *Scholarship Reconsidered: Priorities of the Professoriate.* Princeton, New Jersey: The Carnegie Foundation for the Advancement of Teaching.

Bricker, R., and G. Previts. 1990. The sociology of accounting: A study of academic and practice community schism. *Accounting Horizons* 4 (1): 1–14.

Brightman, H. J. 2005. Mentoring faculty to improve teaching and student learning. *Decision Sciences Journal of Innovative Education* 3: 191–203.

———. 2006. Mentoring faculty to improve teaching and student learning. *Issues in Accounting Education* 21 (2): 127–146.

Brookfield, S. 1990. *The Skillful Teacher.* San Francisco: Jossey-Bass.

Brown, D. L. 1976. Faculty ratings and student grades: A university-wide multiple regression analysis. *Journal of Educational Psychology* (68): 573–578.

Brown, J. 2006. *Brown Assails Grade Inflation* August 31. Available at: http://www.denverpost.com/fdcp?1100401062580.

Bruno, L. 2004. *Princeton Leads in Grade Deflation.* USA Today, November. Available at: http://usatoday.printthis.clickability.com/pt/cpt?action=cpt&title=Prin.

Bruns, S., C. Jackson, P. Janell, and T. Rupert. 2004. An Investigation of the Use and Perceived Effectiveness of Peer Teaching Observation for Untenured Accounting Faculty. In *Advances in Accounting Teaching and Curriculum Innovations* 6: 173–192. Boston, MA: Elsevier Ltd.

Bryant, S. M., J. B. Kahle, and B. A. Schafer. 2005. Distance education: A review of the contemporary literature. *Issues in Accounting Education* 20 (3): 255–272.

Buckley, J. 1970. A perspective on professional accounting education. *Journal of Accountancy* 130 (2): 41–47.

Burd, S. 2003. Republican lawmakers call for more accountability in higher education. *The Chronicle of Higher Education* (23 May): A23.

Bures, A. L., J. J. DeRidder, and H. M. Tong. 1988. An empirical study of accounting faculty evaluation systems. *The Accounting Educators' Journal* (Summer): 68–76.

Burgess, L. A., and C. Samuels. 1999. Impact of full-time versus part-time instructor status on college retention and academic performance in sequential courses. *Community College Journal of Research and Practice* 23 (5): 487–498.

Burnett, M., and C. Pettijohn. 1999. Improving student performance through student mentorships: Practices, prescriptions and policies for enhanced learning. *Marketing Education Review* 9 (1): 61–70.

Buskist, W. J. Keeley, and J. Irons. undated. Evaluating and Improving Your Teaching. *Association of Psychological Science Observer.* Available at: http://www.psychologiclascience.org/getArticle.cfm?id=1974.

Cahn, S. M. 1986. *Saints and Scamps: Ethics in Academia.* Totowa, NJ: Rowan & Littlefield.

Calderon, T. G., A. L. Gabbin, and B. P. Green. 1996. *A Framework for Encouraging Effective Teaching* (Report of The Committee Promoting and Evaluating Effective Teaching, American Accounting Association). Harrisonburg, VA., Center for Research in Accounting Education.

———, and B. P. Green. 1997. Use of multiple information types in assessing accounting faculty teaching performance. *Journal of Accounting Education* 15 (2): 221–239.

Callahan, D. 2004. *The Cheating Culture: Why More Americans Are Doing Wrong To Get Ahead.* Orlando Florida: Harcourt, Inc.

Campbell, D. T., and J. C. Stanley. 1963. *Experimental and Quasi-Experimental Designs for Research.* Dallas: Houghton-Mifflin, p. 9.

Campbell, H., S. Steiner, and K. Gerdes. 2005. Students evaluations of teaching: How you teach and who you are. *Journal of Public Affairs Education* 11 (3): 211–231.

Campbell, J., and W. Lewis. 1991. Using cases in accounting classes. *Issues in Accounting Education* 6 (2): 276–283.

Campbell, K., D. Mothersbaugh, C. Brammer, and T. Taylor. 2001. Peer versus self assessment of oral business presentation performance. *Business Communication Quarterly* 64 (3): 23–42.

Caplan, E. 1971. *Management Accounting and Behavioral Science.* Reading, Massachusetts: Addison-Wesley Publishing Company.

Caron, C. 2006. Teaching with Technology in the 21st Century Law School Classroom. University of Cincinnati, Law School. Public Law Research Paper No. 06-11. Available at: http://ssrn.com/abstract=896906.

Carr, W., and S. Kemmis. 1986. *Becoming Critical: Education, Knowledge and Action Research.* London: The Falmer Press.

Carrell, S., J. West, and F. Malmstrom. 2005. Peer effects in academic cheating. Working Paper, Dartmouth College (November). Available at: http://ssrn.com/abstract=842224.

Carroll, J. 2003. Do adjuncts have time for students? *The Chronicle of Higher Education* 49 (46): 2–4.

Cashin, W. E. 1989. Student Ratings of Teaching: A Summary of the Research. IDEA Paper No. 20, Center for Faculty Evaluation & Development.

———. 1999. Student ratings of teaching: Uses and misuses. In P. Seldin & Associates (eds.). *Changing practices in evaluating teaching: A practical guide to improved faculty performance and promotion/tenure decisions* (pp. 24–44), Bolton, MA: Anker.

Catanach, Jr., A. H., D. B. Croll, and R. L. Grinaker. 2000. Teaching intermediate financial accounting using a business activity model. *Issues in Accounting Education* 15 (4): 583–603.

Cegielski, C. 2008. Toward the development of an interdisciplinary information assurance curriculum: Knowledge domain and skill sets required of information assurance professionals. *Decision Sciences Journal of Innovative Education* 6 (1): 29–49.

Center for Effective Teaching and Learning (CETaL). undated. University of North Texas at El Paso. Available at: http://www.sunconference. utep.edu/CETal/resources/portfolios/evaluate.htm.

Centra, J. A. 1972. Evaluating College Teaching: The Rhetoric and the Research. Research Memorandum. ERIC#: ED 065509.

———, and F. R. Creech. 1976. The Relationship Between Student, Teacher, and Course Characteristics and Student Ratings of Teacher Effectiveness, SIR Report No. 4, Educational Testing Service, Princeton, N.J., 24–27.

Chaker, A. 2007. Class of 2007 long slide in SAT scores, *Wall Street Journal* (August 29): D1.

Charkins, R., D. O'Toole, and J. Wetzel. 1985. Linking teacher and student learning styles with student achievement and attitudes. *Journal of Economic Education* 16 (2): 111–120.

Chase, C. I. 1999. *Contemporary assessment for educators.* New York, NY: Longman.

Chen, Y., and L. Hoshower. 1998. Assessing student motivation to participate in teaching evaluations: An applications of expectancy theory. *Issues in Accounting Education* 13 (3): 531–545.

Chi, M., R. Glaser, and M. Farr (eds.). 1988. *The Nature of Expertise.* Hillsdale, NJ: Erlbaum.

Chism, N. 1999. *Peer Review of Teaching: A Sourcebook.* Boston, Massachusetts: Anker Publishing Company.

Chonko, L. B. 2006. An essay on wisdom in the teaching evaluation process. *Marketing Education Review* 16 (3): 1–13.

Chow, C., K. Haddad, G. Singh, and A. Wu. 2007. On using journal ranks to proxy for an article's contribution or value. *Issues in Accounting Education* 22 (3): 1411–1427.

Christensen, C. M. 2003. *The Innovator's Dilemma.* New York, NY: HarperCollins.

Chulkov, D. 2006. Student response to grading incentives: Evidence from college economics courses. *Journal of Instructional Psychology,* 33 (3): 206–211.

Chye, M., L. Neo, and G. Da Silva. 2000. Student evaluation of the subject under problem-based learning mode: The case of practice of entrepreneurship. Paper presented at the Second Asia-Pacific Conference on PBL, Singapore.

Cisneros-Cohernour, E. J. 2005. Academic freedom, tenure, and student evaluations of faculty: A response to Haskell and his critics. *Education Policy Analysis Archives* 13 (32). Available at: http://epaa.asu.edu/epaa/v13n32/v13n32.pdf.

Clark, B. A. 1990. Comparison of the Achievement of Students Taught by Full-time versus Adjunct Faculty in the Chemistry of Hazardous Materials Course: Governance and Management. Text-fiche, ERIC330261.

Clark, B. R. 1960. The "cooling-out" function in higher education. *The American Journal of Sociology* 65 (6): 569–576.

Clayson, D., and D. Haley. 2005. Marketing models in education: Students as customers, products, or partners. *Marketing Education Review* 15 (1): 1–10.

Cluskey, Jr., G. R., Nathan Griffin, and Craig Ehlen. 1997. Accounting grade inflation. *Journal of Education for Business* 72 (5): 273–282.

Coalition of Contingent Academic Labor (COCAL). 2008. Available at: http://www.cocal-ca.org/viii/agenda_cocal_viii.htm.

Cochran, L. 1992. *Publish or Perish: The Wrong Issue.* Cape Girardeau, Missouri StepUp Inc.

Cohen, A. M., and F. B. Brawer. 2003. *The American Community College.* (4th ed.) San Francisco: Jossey-Bass.

College Board, The National Commission on Writing for America's Families, Schools, and Colleges. 2004. *Writing: A ticket to work ... or a ticket out: A Survey of Business leaders.* New York, NY: College Board.

Cooper, D., J. Everett, and D. Neu. 2005. Financial scandals, accounting change and the role of accounting academics: A perspective from North America. *European Accounting Review* 14 (2): 373–382.

Cosser, M. 1998. Towards the design of a system of peer review of teaching for the advancement of the individual within the university. *Higher Education* 35 (2): 143–162.

Cottell, P. G., and E. M. Harwood. 1998. Using classroom assessment techniques to improve student learning in accounting classes. *Issues in Accounting Education* 13 (3): 551–564.

Coupland, D. 1991. *Generation X: Tales from an Accelerated Culture.* New York, NY: St. Martin's Press.

Covey, S. 1989. *The Seven Habits of Highly Effective People.* New York, NY: Simon & Schuster.

Crooks, T. 1998. The impact of classroom evaluation practices on students. *Review of Educational Research* 58 (4): 438–481.

Cross, J. G., and E. N. Goldenberg. 2003. How does university decision making shape the faculty? *New Directions for Higher Education* 123: 49–59.

Crumbley, D. L. 1995. The dysfunctional atmosphere of higher education: Games professors play. *Accounting Perspectives* 1 (1): 67–77.

———, K. Smith, and L. Murphy Smith. 1998. Educational novels and student role-playing: a teaching note. *Accounting Education* 7 (2): 183–191.

———, and E. Fliedner. 2002. Accounting administrators' perceptions of student evaluation of teaching (SET) information. *Quality Assurance in Education* 10 (4): 213–222.

———. undated. Ethical dilemma of accounting professors facing an illusory accountability control system. Texas A&M University, Working Paper.

Cunningham, B. M. 1996. How to restructure an accounting course to enhance creative and critical thinking. *Accounting Education* 1 (1): 49–66.

———. 2008. Using action learning to improve learning and the classroom learning environment. *Issues in Accounting Education* 23 (1): 1–30.

Cushman, T. 2003. Who best to tame grade inflation? *Academic Questions* 16 (4): 48–56.

Daigle, R. J., D. C. Hayes, and K. E. Hughes, II. 2007. Assessing student learning outcomes in the introductory accounting information systems course using the AICPA's core competency framework. *Journal of Information Systems* 21 (1): 149–170.

Dalton, S. 2008. *Five Standards for Effective Teaching: How To Succeed With All Learners, Grades K–8.* New York, NY: John Wiley & Sons.

Davidson, R. A., and B. A. Baldwin. 2005. Cognitive skills objectives in intermediate accounting textbooks: Evidence from end-of-chapter material. *Journal of Accounting Education* 23: 79–95.

Davies, M., J. Hirshberg, J. Lye, C. Johnson, and I. McDonald. 2007. Systematic influences on teaching evaluations: the case for caution. *Australian Economic Papers* 46 (1): 18–38.

Davis, S., and J. Botkin. 1994. The coming of knowledge-based business. *Harvard Business Review* 72 (5): 165–170.

Day, M., M. Kaidonis, and R. Perrin. 2003. Reflexivity in learning critical accounting: Implications for teaching and its research nexus. *Critical Perspectives on Accounting* 14 (5): 597–614.

DeBerg, C. L., and J. R. Wilson. 1990. An empirical investigation of the potential confounding variables in student evaluation of teaching. *Journal of Accounting Education* 8 (1): 37–62.

Decanio, S. J. 1986. Student evaluations of teaching—A multinomial logit approach. *Journal of Economic Education* 17 (3): 165–176.

Demski, J. 2007. Is accounting an academic discipline? *Accounting Horizons* 21 (2): 153–157.

Dewey, J. 1938. *Experience and Education.* New York, NY: Macmillan.

Diamond, R. M. 1998. *Designing and Assessing Curricula: A Practical Guide.* San Francisco: Jossey-Bass.

DiGabriele, J. 2008. An empirical investigation of the relevant skills of forensic accountants. *Journal of Investigation for Business* 83 (6): 331–338.

Dillon, E. 2007. Leading Lady: Sallie Mae and the Origins of Today's Student Loan Controversy. Washington, DC: Education Sector. Available at: http://www.educationsector.org/research/research_show.htm?doc_id=482682.

Dilts, D., H. Samavati, and M. Rahnama-Moghadam. 2006. Economic Motivation for Post-Tenure Review in Academic Institutions. *Journal of Collective Negotiations* 31 (4): 333–341.

Ditts, D. A. 1980. A statistical interpretation of student evaluation feedback. *Journal of Economic Education* (Spring): 10–15.

———. 1983. A statistical interpretation of student evaluation feedback. *Journal of Economic Education* 11 (2): 1–5.

Doney, L. D., N. E. Lephardt, and J. P. Trebby. 1993. Developing critical thinking skills in accounting students. *Journal of Education for Business* 68 (5): 297–300.

Dosch, R., and J. Wambsganss. 2006. The blame game: Accounting education is not alone. *Journal of Education for Business* 81 (5): 250–254.

Douglas, G. 1992. *Education Without Impact: How Our Universities Fail the Young.* New York, NY: Birch Lane Press Book.

Douglas, P., R. Dombrowski, and R. Garner. 2006. An examination of alternative sources of doctoral accounting faculty. *Journal of Education for Business* 82 (1): 44–48.

Douthat, R. 2005. The truth about Harvard. *Atlantic Monthly* (March): 95–99.

Dowell, D. A., and J. A. Neal. 1983. The validity and accuracy of student ratings of instructors: A reply to Peter A. Cohen. *Journal of Higher Education* (July/August): 459–463.

Driver, M. 2001. Fostering creativity in business education: Developing creative classroom environments to provide students with critical workplace competencies. *Journal of Education for Business* 77 (1): 28–33.

D'Sousa, D. 1992. *Illiberal Education: The Politics Of Race And Sex On Campus.* New York, NY: Vintage Books.

DuCette, J., and J. Kenney. 1982. Do grading standards affect student evaluations of teaching? New evidence on an old question. *Journal of Education Psychology* 73 (3): 308–314.

Duff, A., and S. McKinstry. 2007. Students' approach to learning. *Issues in Accounting Education* 22 (2): 183–214.

Dunbar, A. 2004. Genesis of an online course. *Issues in Accounting Education* 19 (3): 321–343.

Duron, R., B. Limbach, and W. Waugh. 2006. Critical thinking framework for any discipline. *International Journal of Teaching and Learning in Higher Education* 17 (2): 160–166.

Dyball, M., A. Reid, P. Ross, and H. Schoch. 2007. Evaluating assessed group-work in a second-year management accounting subject. *Accounting Education* 16 (2): 145–162.

Eagan, K. 2007. A national picture of part-time community college faculty: Changing trends in demographics and employment characteristics. *New Directions for Community Colleges* 140: 5–14.

Eble, K. 1972. *Professors as Teachers.* San Francisco: Jossey-Bass.

Eiszler, C. F. 2002. College students' evaluation of teaching and grade inflation. *Research in Higher Education* 43 (4): 483–501.

Elliott, H. 1966. *The Effective Student.* New York, NY: Harper & Row Publishers.

Elliott, R. 1992. The third wave breaks on the shores of accounting. *Accounting Horizons* 6 (2): 61–85.

———, and P. Jacobson. 2002. The evolution of the knowledge professional. *Accounting Horizons* 16 (1): 69–80.

Ellyson, R., A. Nelson, and J. MacNeill. 1985. Educating tomorrow's CPAs. *Journal of Accountancy* 160 (4): 95–102.

Elman, S. E. 2003. A regional accreditation perspective on contingent faculty appointments. *New Directions for Higher Education* 123: 71–78.

Ennis, R. H., and E. Weir. 1985. *The Ennis-Weir Critical Thinking Essay Test.* Pacific Grove, CA: Midwest Publications.

———. 1993. Critical thinking assessment. *Theory into Practice* 32: 179–186.

Epstein, L. D. 1974. *Governing the University: The Campus and the Public Interest.* San Francisco, CA: Jossey-Bass, Inc.

Evaluating Teaching Effectiveness—Research Summary. undated. Center for Teaching & Learning. Ferris State University. Available at: http://www.ferris.edu/fctl/Teaching_and_Learning_Tips/Research.

Everett, M. 1979. Student evaluations of teaching and the cognitive level of economics courses. *Journal of Economic Education* 9 (2): 100–103.

Ewell, P. 2003. The learning curve. *Biz/Ed* (July/August): 28–33.

Eynon, G., N. Hill, and K. Stevens. 2006. Factors that influences the moral reasoning abilities of accountants: Implications for universities and the profession. *Journal of Business Ethics* 63 (2): 1297–1309.

Facione, P. A. 1990. The Delphi report: Executive summary. Millbrae, CA: California Academic Press. Available at: http://www.insightassessment.com/pdf_files/DEXadobe.PDF.

Fagan-Wilen, R., D. W. Springer, B. Ambrosino, and B. W. White. 2006. The support of adjunct faculty: An academic imperative. *Social Work Education* 25 (1): 39–51.

Fain, P., and A. W. June. 2006. The bottom line for college presidents: Money matters. *The Chronicle of Higher Education* (November 24): B4.

Fajardo, C. L. 2004. Grade inflation: Causes and consequences. *American Association of Behavioral Social Science (AABSS) Online Journal:* 68–75. Available at: http://aabss.org/journal2004/AABSS_68-75.pdf.

Federation of Schools of Accountancy (FOSOA). 1999. *Recommendations for the Design of Empirical Studies Examining Curricular Efforts to Develop Student Critical Thinking Skills.* Educational Resource Committee.

Felchikov, N., and D. Boud. 1989. Student self-assessment in higher education: A meta-analysis. *Review of Educational Research* 59 (4): 395–430.

Fellinghman, J. 2007. Is accounting an academic discipline? *Accounting Horizons* 21 (2): 159–163.

Felton, J. and P. T. Koper. 2005. Nominal GPA and real GPA: A simple adjustment that compensates for grade inflation. *Assessment & Evaluation in Higher Education* 30 (6): 561–569.

———, ———, J. Mitchell, and M. Stinson. 2006. Attractiveness, easiness, and other issues: Student evaluations of professors on RateMyProfessors.com. University of Central Michigan, Working Paper (July 2006). Available at: http://ssrn.com/abstract=918283.

———, ———, ———, and ———. 2008. Attractiveness, easiness and other issues: student evaluations of professors on all one word, assessment & evaluations. *Higher Education* (February) 33 (1): 45–61.

Fenn, A., D. Johnson, M. Smith, and J. L. Stimpert. 2008. Doing publishable research with undergraduate students. Colorado College Working Paper No. 2008-03 (February). Available at: http://ssrn.com/abstract=1095895.

Fessler, N. 2008. A 'modern' professor in 'postmodern' land: Adventures teaching accounting. *Accounting Education* 17 (2): 201–204.

Filine, P. 2005. *The Joy of Teaching: A Practical Guide for New College Instructors.* Chapel Hill, North Carolina: University of North Carolina Press.

Findley, M. J., and H. M. Cooper. 1983. Locus of control and academic achievement. *Journal of Personality and Social Psychology* 44 (2): 419–427.

Fink, D. 2003. *Creating Significant Learning Experiences: An Integrated Approach to Designing College Courses.* San Francisco: Jossey-Bass.

Fink, L. undated. Evaluating your own teaching. University of Hawaii. Available at: http://honolulu.hawaii.edu/intranet/committees/FacDevCom/guidebk/teachtip/evaluate.htm.

Finkelstein, M. J., and J. H. Schuster. 2001. Assessing the silent revolution. *American Association for Higher Education Bulletin* 54 (2): 3–7.

Finkelstein, S. 2003. *Why Smart Executives Fail and What You Can Learn from Their Mistakes.* New York, NY: Penquin Group.

Fischer, J. 2007. Implications of Recent Research on Student Evaluations of Teaching. University of Louisville. Law School. Legal Studies Research Paper No. 2007–20. Available at http://ssrn.com/abstract=1005681.

Fischer, K. W., and T. R. Bidell. 1997. Dynamic development of psychological structures in action and thought. In R. M. Lerner and W. Damon (Eds.), *Handbook of Child Psychology. Vol. 1: Theoretical Models of Human Development* (5th Ed). New York, NY: Wiley.

Fishbein, L. 1993. Curbing, cheating and restoring academic integrity. *The Chronicle of Higher Education* (December 1): A52.

Fisher, D., D. Swanson, and J. Schmidt. 2007. Accounting education lags CPE ethics requirements: Implications for the profession and a call to action. *Accounting Education* 16 (4): 345–363.

Flaherty, R. 1998. *The Accounting Education Change Commission Grant Experience: A Summary.* Sarasota, Florida: American Accounting Association.

Flanagan, J., and K. Clarke. 2007. Beyond a code of professional ethics: A holistic model of ethical decision-making for accountants. *Abacus* 43 (4): 488–518.

Fogarty, T., and G. Markarian. 2007. An empirical assessment of the rise and fall of accounting as an academic discipline. *Issues in Accounting Education* 22 (2): 137–161.

Foote, C., H. Mayer, A. Fishlow, and D. Freedman. 1968. *The Culture of the University: Governance and Education.* San Francisco, CA: Jossey-Bass, Inc.

Ford, C. T. 1994. Universities take aim on performance measures. *University Affairs* (February): 6–9.

Francisco, B., T. Noland, and D. Sinclair. 2007. Pursuing a PhD in accounting: what to expect. *CPA Journal* 77 (3): 66–68.

Francisco, W., T. Noland, and D. Sinclair. 2008. AACSB accreditation: symbol of excellence or march toward mediocrity? *Journal of College Teaching and Learning* 5 (5): 25–29.

Frankel, C. 1968. *Education and the Barricades.* New York, NY: W.W. Norton & Co.

Freedman, E. 2007. *Work 101: Learning The Ropes Of The Workplace Without Hanging Yourself.* New York, NY: Delta Trade Paperbacks.

Freeland, R. 1998. *Adjunct Faculty in the Community College.* Educational Resources Information Center Document Reproduction Service No: ED 424 899.

Frey, B., and V. Schmitt. 2007. Coming to terms with classroom assessment. *Journal of Advanced Academics* 18 (3): 402–123.

Fulton, R. 2000. The plight of part-timers in higher education: Some ruminations and suggestions. *Change* May/June: 38–43.

Gabrielson, R. July 29, 2007. ASU to gauge teaching success: All departments will assess students' critical thinking. *Tribune* (Mesa, AZ).

Gaffney, M., and J. Krishnan. 2000. Peer collaboration for teaching improvement. *Advances in Accounting Teaching and Curriculum Innovations* 3: 107–123.

Gammie, E., and M. Matson. 2007. Group assessment at final degree level: An evaluation. *Accounting Education* 16 (2): 185–206.

Gappa, J. M., and F. B. Brawer. 1997. *Two Faculties or One? The Conundrum of Part-Timers in a Bifurcated Work Force.* Washington D.C.: American Association for Higher Education.

Gardner, H. 2006. *Five Minds for the Future.* Boston, MA.: Harvard Business School Press.

Garner, D. E. 1972. New student rights and academic freedom in the classroom. *Accounting Review* 48 (22): 393–394.

Geary, W., and C. Rooney. 1983. Designing accounting education to achieve balanced intellectual development. *Issues in Accounting Education* 8 (1): 60–70.

Gendron, Y. 2008. Constituting the academic performer: The spectre of superficiality and stagnation in academia. *European Accounting Review* 17 (1): 97–127.

Geogakopoulos, N. L. 1996. Relative rank: A remedy for subjective absolute grades. *Conn. L. Rev.* 29: 445–57.

George, D. 2007. Market overreach. *Journal of Socio-Economics* 36 (6): 965–977.

Germain, M. L., and T. A. Scandura. 2005. Grade inflation and student individual differences as systematic bias in faculty evaluations. *Journal of Instructional Psychology* 32 (1): 58–67.

Glassman, R. 1988. Course evaluations: Are half of us really "below average?"*Academe* (July–August): 44.

Glenn, D. 2008. Keep adjuncts away from intro courses, report says. *Chronicle of Higher Education* 54 (30): A1.

Golde, C. 2006. *Envisioning The Future Of Doctoral Education.* San Francisco: Jossey-Bass.

Goldwater, P., and T. Fogarty. 2007. Protecting the solution: A 'high-tech' method to guarantee individual efforts in accounting classes. *Accounting Education* 16 (2): 129–143.

Grandzol, J. R., and C. J. Grandzol. 2006. Best practices for online business education. *International Review of Research in Open and Distance Learning* 7 (1): 1–18.

Green, B. P., T. G. Calderon, and B. P. Reider. 1998. A content analysis of teaching evaluation instruments used in accounting departments. *Issues in Accounting Education* 13 (1): 15–30.

———, ———, A. L. Gabbin, and J. W. Habbegger. 1999. Perspectives onimplementing a framework for evaluating effective teaching. *Journal of Accounting Education* 17 (1): 71–98.

Green, D. W. 2007. Adjunct faculty and the continuing quest for quality. *New Directions For Community Colleges* 140: 29–39.

Greenwald, A. G., and G. M. Gillmore. 1997. Grading leniency is a removable contaminant of student ratings. *Journal of Educational Psychology* 89 (4): 1209–1216.

Grenzke, J. 1998. Part time faculty: Quality issues. *Update* 4(2) Educational Resources Information Center Document Reproduction Service No: ED 417 686.

Grieves, R. 1982. A policy proposal regarding grade inflation. *Educational Research Quarterly* 7 (2): 2–4.

Griffin, R., and S. Dawkins. 1986. Current trends in intermediate accounting course content. *Issues in Accounting Education* 1 (1): 238–249.

Grimes, P., M. Millea, and T. Woodruff. 2004. Grades—Who's to blame? Student evaluation of teaching and locus of control. *Journal of Economic Education* 35 (2): 129–147.

Gunther, J. 2007. Digital Natives & Digital Immigrants. Studienverlag GmbH.

Haeger, J. D. 1998. Part-time faculty, quality programs, and economic realities. D. W. Leslie (ed.), *The Growing Use of Part-time faculty: Understanding Causes and Effects.* San Francisco: Jossey-Bass.

Haka, S. 2008. Accounting at a tipping point: You can make a difference. Keynote, The American Accounting Association, Anaheim, CA, Aug. 6, 2008.

Haladyna, T., and R. K. Hess. 1994. The detection and correction of bias in student ratings of instruction. *Research in Higher Education* 35: 669–687.

Hale, J. 2008. *A Guide to Curriculum Mapping: Planning, Implementing, and Sustaining the Process.* Thousand Oaks, California: Corwin Press.

Halmos, P. R. 1985. *I Want to Be a Mathematician.* New York, NY: Springer-Verlag.

Hammer, M., and J. Champy. 1993. *Reengineering The Corporation: A Manifesto For Business Revolution.* New York, NY: HarperBusiness.

Hampton, D. R., and K. A. Krentler. 1993. The use of management and marketing textbook multiple choice questions: A case study. *Journal of Education for Business* 69 (1): 40–48.

Hand, L., and M. Rowe. 2001. Evaluation of student feedback. *Accounting Education* 10 (2): 147–160.

Hanna, G. S., D. P. Hoyt, and J. D. Aubrecht. 1983. Identifying and adjusting for bias in student evaluations of instruction: Implications for validity. *Educational and Psychological Measurement* 43 (4): 1175–1185.

Hanson, E., and F. Phillips. 2006. Teaching financial accounting with analogies: Improving initial comprehension and enhancing subsequent learning. *Issues in Accounting Education* 21 (1): 1–14.

Hargrove, T. 2005. U.S. scholarly supremacy slipping with fewer Ph.D.s. *Arkansas Democrat-Gazette* (August 20): 2A.

Hartley, R. 2008. *Corporate Crime: A Reference Handbook.* Santa Barbara, CA: ABC-CLIO.

Haskell, R. E. 1997. Academic freedom, tenure, and student evaluations of faculty. *Education Policy Analysis Archives* 5 (16): 1–36.

———. 1997a. Academic freedom, tenure, and student evaluations of faculty: Galloping polls in the 21st century. *Educational Policy Analysis Archives 5* (6). Available at: http://olam.ed.asu.edu/epaa/v5n6.html.

———. 1997b. Abridgement of academic freedom, promotion, reappointment and tenure rights by the administrative use of student evaluation of faculty: *(Part II)* Views from the court. *Education Policy Analysis Archives* 5 (6). Available at: http://olam.ed.asu.edu/epaa/v5n17.html.

———. 1997c. Academic freedom, promotion, reappointment, tenure and the administrative use of student evaluation of faculty: *(Part III)* Analysis and implications of views from the court in relation to accuracy and psychometric validity. *Education Policy Analysis Archives 5* (6). Available at: http://olam.ed.asu.edu/epaa/v5n18.html.

———. 1997d. Academic freedom, promotion, reappointment, tenure and the administrative use of student evaluation of faculty: *(Part IV)* Analysis and implications of views from the court in relation to academic freedom, standards, and quality instruction. *Education Policy Analysis Archives* 5 (6). Available at: http://olam.ed.asu.edu/epaa/v5n21.html.

———. 1997e. On Michael Theall's (and implied et al.) A reply to Haskell and to Stake. *Education Policy Analysis Archives* 5 (3). Available at: http://olam.ed.asu.edu/epaa/v5n8c3.html.

———. 1997f. Contributed commentary on Stake response to Haskell. *Education Policy Analysis Archives* 5 (8). Available at: http://olam.ed.asu.edu/epaa/v5n8c1.html.

———. 1998. *Reengineering Corporate Training: Intellectual Capital and the Transfer of Learning.* Quorum Books (Greenwood publishing group).

———. 2000. *Transfer of Learning, Cognition, Instruction, and Reasoning.* San Diego, CA: Academic Press.

Hebel, S. 2006. Report card on colleges finds US is slipping: Progress in America slows as it is 'Outperformed by many other countries,' *Chronicle of Higher Education,* (September 15): A1, A21–A24.

Hersch, R. H., and J. Merrow (eds.). 2005a. *Declining By Degree: Higher Education at Risk.* New York, NY: Palgrave Macmillan.

———. 2005b. *What Does College Teach?* Available at: http://www.thealantic.com/doc/print/200511/measuring-college-quality.

Hirsch, F. 1976. *Social Limits to Growth.* Lincoln, NE: ToExcel.

———. 1987. *Cultural Literacy: What Every American Needs To Know.* New York, NY: Houghton Mifflin Co.

———. 1996. *The Schools We Need: Why We Don't Have Them.* New York, NY: Doubleday.

Ho, J. C., and M. K. Shalishi. 2001. A proposed approach to measure student competencies: Adjusting for grade inflation and grade variation. *Academy of Educational Leadership Journal* 5 (2): 59–68.

Hocutt, M. O. 1987–1988. De-grading student evaluations: What's wrong with student polls of teaching? *Academic Questions* (Autumn): 55–64.

Hofstede, G. 1986. The cultural context of accounting. *Accounting and Culture. Annual Meeting Plenary Session Papers.* Sarasota, FL: American Accounting Association.

Holbrook, M. 2005. Marketing miseducation and the MBA mind: Bullshit happens. *Marketing Education Review* 15 (3): 1–5.

Holthausen, R. W. 1990. Accounting method choice: Opportunistic behavior, efficient contracting, and information perspectives. *Journal of Accounting and Economics* 12 (1–3): 207–218.

Hooper, P., and J. Page. 1986. Measuring Teaching Effectiveness by Student Evaluation. *Issues in Accounting Education* 1 (1): 56–64.

Hopwood, A. 2007. Whither accounting research? *Accounting Review* 82 (5): 1365–1374.

Horn, S. 2008. How to bore people with learning math. *Omaha World-Herald* (March 25): 7B.

Horngren, C., S. Datar, and G. Foster. 2006. *Cost Accounting: A Managerial Emphasis 12th ed.* Upper Saddle River, NJ: Pearson Education.

Hosmer, L. 2008. *The Ethics of Management 6th ed.* New York, NY: McGraw-Hill.

Howard, G. S., and S. E. Maxwell. 1982. Do grades contaminate student evaluations of instruction? *Research in Higher Education* 16 (2): 175–188.

Howe, N., and W. Strauss. 2000. *Millennials Rising: The Next Great Generation.*

Howell, S. C., P. E. Williams, and N. K. Lindsay. 2003. Thirty-two trends affecting distance education: An informed foundation for strategic planning. *Online Journal of Distance Learning Administration* 6 (3).

Hoyt, D. P., and W. H. Pallett. 1999. Appraising teaching effectiveness: Beyond student ratings. Idea Paper No. 36. Kansas State University, KS: Center for Faculty Evaluation and Development.

———. 1997. Studies of the impact of extraneous variables. Idea Paper, Kansas State University. Available at: http://www.bus.lsu.edu/accounting/faculty/lcrumbley/idea.html.

Huba, M. E., and J. E. Freed. 2000. *Learner-Centered Assessment on College Campuses: Shifting the Focus from Teaching to Learning.* Needham Heights, MA: Allyn & Bacon.

Huber, M., and P. Hutchings. 2005. *The Advancement of Learning: Building the Teaching Commons.* San Francisco: Jossey-Bass.

Humphrey, C. 2005. In the aftermath of crisis: Reflections on the principles, values and significance of academic inquire in accounting: Introduction. *European Accounting Review* 14 (2): 341–351.

Hunt, T., E. Joseph, R. Nuzzi, and J. Geiger (eds.). 2003. *Handbook on Research on Catholic Higher Education.* Greenwich, CT: Information Age Publishing.

Husbands, C. T. 1997. Variations in student evaluations of teachers' lecturing in different courses on which they lecture: A study at the London School of Economics and Political Science. *Higher Education* 33 (1): 51–70.

Hwang, N., G. Lui, and M. Tung. 2005. An empirical test of comparative learning in a passive learning environment. *Issues in Accounting Education* 20 (2): 151–165.

Inanga, E., and W. Schneider. 2005. The failure of accounting research to improve accounting practice: A problem of theory and a lack of communication. *Critical Perspectives on Accounting* 16 (3): 227–248.

Institute for Higher Education Policy. 2000. *Quality on the Line: Benchmarks for Success in Internet-Based Distance Education.* Washington, DC: The Institute for Higher Education Policy.

Isely, P. and H. Singh. 2005. Do higher grades lead to favorable student evaluations? *Journal of Economic Education* 36 (1): 29–42.

Jackling, B. 2005. Perceptions of the learning context and learning approaches: Implications for quality learning outcomes in accounting. *Accounting Education* 14 (3): 171–291.

Jackson, E. 1986. A comparative study to determine the effectiveness of adjunct faculty in the business division at Fayetteville Technical Institute. Available at: http://eric.ed.gov/ERICWebPortal/custom/portlets/recordDetails/detailmini.jsp?_nfpb=true&_&ERICExtSearch_SearchValue_0=ED294622&ERICExtSearch_SearchType_0=no&accno=ED294622/.

Jacoby, D. 2006. Effects of part-time faculty employment on community college graduation rates. *Journal of Higher Education* 77 (6): 1081–1103.

James, K. 2008. A critical theory and postmodernist approach to the teaching of accounting theory. *Critical Perspectives on Accounting* 19 (5): 643–676.

Jensen, M. 2001. Corporate budgeting is broken—let's fix it. *Harvard Business Review* 79 (10): 94–101.

Johnson, C. 2006. Degrees of deception: Are consumers and employers being duped on online universities and diploma mills? Ohio State University, School of Law. Public Law and Legal Theory Working Paper Series No. 79 (2006). Available at: http://ssrn.com/abstract=925243.

Johnson, S. 1977–1978. The need for more effective classroom images. *Collegiate News and Views* XXVI (2): 8–29.

Johnson, V. E. 1997. An alternative to traditional GPA for evaluating student performance. *Statistical Science* 12 (4): 251–278.

———. 2003. *Grade Inflation: A Crisis in College Education.* New York, NY: Springer-Verlag.

Johnstone, K. M., and S. F. Biggs. 1998. Problem-based learning: Introduction, analysis, and accounting curricula implications. *Journal of Accounting Education* 16 (3/4): 407–427.

Jones, C. 1996. Assessment and accounting education. *Accounting Education* 5 (1): 99–101.

Jones, S., and R. Davidson. 2007. Measuring the problem-solving abilities of accounting and other business students: A comparison and evaluation of three methods. *Accounting Education* 16 (1): 65–79.

Juhn, C., D. I. Kim, and F. Vella. 2005. The expansion of college education in the United States: Is there evidence of declining cohort quality? *Economic Inquiry* 43 (2): 303–315.

Kamenetz, A. 2006. Generation debt: The new economics of being young. *The Village Voice* (January 24): 2.

Kaplan, R., and D. Horton. 2007. Using the balanced scorecard as a strategic management system. *Harvard Business Review* 85 (7–8): 150–161.

Karni, A. 2007. Students know less after 4 college years. *The New York Sun* (September 19, 2007). Available at: http://www.nysun.com/new-york/students-know-less-after-4-college-years/62901/.

Karns, J. M. L., G. E. Burton, and G. D. Martin. 1983. Learning objectives and testing: An analysis of six principles of economics textbooks, using Bloom's taxonomy. *The Journal of Economic Education* 14 (3): 16–20.

Karr, S. 2005. Is accounting education relevant? *Financial Executive* 21 (5): 40–42.

Katz, H., and K. O'Neill. 2007. Strategies and Techniques of Law School Teaching: A Primer for New Teachers. Cleveland State University, Law School, Research Paper 07–144 (April). Available at: http://ssrn.com/abstract=982234.

Kau, J. B., and P. H. Rubin. 1976. Measurement techniques, grades and ratings of instructors. *The Journal of Economic Education* 8 (1): 59–62.

Keim, M. C., and P. E. Biletzky. 1999. Teaching methods used by part-time community college faculty. *Community College Journal of Research and Practice* 23: 727–737.

Keiz, L., and M. D. Waggoner. 1994. *Collaborative Peer Review: The Role of Faculty in Improving College Teaching.* ASHE-ERIC Higher Education Report No. 2. Washington, DC: The George Washington University, Graduate School of Education and Human Development.

Kember, D., and L. Gow. 1994. Orientation to teaching and their effect on the quality of student learning. *The Journal of Higher Education* 65 (1): 58–74.

Kennedy, D. 1997. *Academic Duty.* Cambridge, Mass.: Harvard University Press.

Kennedy, P. 1993. *Preparing For the Twenty-First Century.* New York, NY: Vintage Books.

Kezim, B., S. E. Pariseau, and F. Quinn. 2005. Is grade inflation related to faculty status? *Journal of Education for Business* 80 (6): 358–363.

Khalifa, R., and P. Quattrone. 2008. The governance of accounting academia: Issue for a debate. *European Accounting Review* 17 (1): 65–86.

Kimmel, P. 1995. A framework for incorporating critical thinking into accounting education. *Journal of Accounting Education* 12 (3): 299–318.

Kimmell, S., R. Marquette, and D. Olsen. 1998. Outcomes assessment programs: Historical perspective and state of the art. *Issues in Accounting Education* 13 (4): 851–868.

King, M. L. 2003. The KC Johnson case: A question of collegiality. *Academic Questions* 16 (2): 21–30.

King, P. M., and K. S. Kitchener. 1994. *Developing Reflective Judgment: Understanding and Promoting Intellectual Growth and Critical Thinking in Adolescents and Adults.* San Francisco, CA: Jossey-Bass.

Kingsbury, A. 2007. The measure of learning. *U.S. News & World Report* (March 12): 53–57.

Knapp, L. G., J. E. Kelly-Reid, and R. W. Whitmore. 2007. *Enrollment in Postsecondary Institutions, Fall 2005; Graduation Rates, 1999 and 2002 Cohorts; and Financial Statistics, Fiscal Year 2005.* U.S. Department of Education, Institute of Educational Sciences.

Kohl, H. 1976. *On Teaching.* New York, NY: Schocken Books.

Kohn, A. 1993. *Punished by Rewards.* New York, NY: Houghton Mifflin Co.

Kouzes, J., and B. Posner. 2007. *The Leadership Challenge 4th ed.* San Francisco: John Wiley.

Kozma, R. B., and R. L. Bangert-Drowns. 1987. *Design in Context: A Conceptual Framework for the Study of Computer Software.* Ann Arbor, MI: National Center for Research to Improve Postsecondary Teaching and Learning.

Kranacher, M. J., and C. A. Barragato. 2008. Meeting of the minds. *CPA Journal* 78 (4): 20–27.

———. 2008. The future of the profession. *CPA Journal* 78 (3): 80.

Krautmann, A. C., and W. Sander. 1998. Grades and student evaluations of teachers. *Economics of Education Review* 18 (1): 59–63.

Kurfiss, J. G. 1988. Critical thinking: theory, research, practice, and possibilities. ASHEERIC Higher Education Report Number 2, Association for the Study of Higher Education.

Kurtz, S. 2006. Deflating grade inflation. *National Review Online.* Available at: http://article.nationalreview.com/print/?q=NDEOZjNjNjA4N2M1N2ZkMTViZjAyZjlxNTdmNGYzODA.

Kutner, M., E. Greenberg, Y. Jin, B. Boyle, Y. Hsu, E. Dunleavy, and S. White. 2007. *Literacy in Everyday Life: Results from the 2003 National Assessment of Adult Literacy.* National Center for Educational Statistics. U.S. Department of Education.

Landrum, R., and R. Dillinger. 2004. The relationship between student performance and instructor evaluations revisited. *Journal of Classroom Instruction* 39 (2): 5–9.

Langbein, L. 2008. Management by results: Student evaluation of faculty teaching and the mis-measurement of performance. *Economics of Education Review* 27 (4): 417–428.

Lavelle, L. 2007. Does your B-school make the grade? Business Week (March 19): 68–73.

Laverie, D. 2002. Improving teaching through improving evaluation: A guide to course portfolios. *Journal of Marketing Education* 24 (2): 104–114.

Lawler, E. E., and J. G. Rhode. 1976. *Information and Control in Organizations.* Pacific Palisades: Goodyear Publishing.

Lei, S. 2007. Teaching practices of instructors in two community colleges in a western state. *Education* 128 (1): 148–160.

———. 2008. Assessment techniques of instructors in two community colleges in a state-wide system. *Education* 128 (3): 392–411.

Leisenring, J., and L. Johnson. 1984. Accounting research: On the relevance of research to practice. *Accounting Horizons* 8 (4): 74–79.

Lemons, J. 1996. *Scientific Uncertainty and Its Implications for Environmental Problem Solving.* New York, NY: Wiley-Blackwell.

Leppel, K., and H. Zangeneh. 2008. Grades, performance, and ratings: An empirical study. Widener University, School of Business Administration. Working Paper. Available at: http://ssrn.com/abstract=1102470.

Leslie, D. W., and J. M. Gappa. 2002. Part-time faculty: Competent and committed. *New Directions for Community College* 118: 59–68.

Lilly, G., and T. Tiemann. 2006. Research across the curriculum: Teaching undergraduates to complete a good senior capstone paper. Elon University, Working Paper. Available at: http://ssrn.com/abstract=925728.

Linn, D. 2007. Issue Brief: Higher Education Accountability for Student Learning. February 23, National Governors Association.

Liu, A. 2007. Sources and information: Community colleges and part-time faculty. *New Directions for Community Colleges* 140: 83–88.

Livingston, W. 1992. Looming demands on higher education. *Issues in Accounting Education* 7 (1): 80–86.

Lombardi, J. 2005. Grade Inflation and Abdication. Inside Higher Education (June 3). Available at: http://www.insidehighered.com/views/2005/09/03/lombardi.

Lucal, B., C. Albers, J. Ballantine, J. Burmeister-May, J. Chin, S. Dettmer, and S. Larson. 2003. Faculty assessment and the scholarship of teaching and learning: Knowledge available/knowledge needed. *Teaching Sociology* 41 (2): 46–161.

Lucas, C., and J. Murray, Jr. 2002. *New Faculty: A Practical Guide for Academic Beginners.* New York, NY: Palgrave.

Lucas, U., and R. Mladenovic. 2004. Approaches to learning in accounting education. *Accounting Education* 13 (4): 399–407.

———. 2008. Being "pulled up short": Creating moments of surprise and possibility in accounting education. *Critical Perspectives on Accounting* 19 (3): 383–403.

Lynch, C. L., S. K. Wolcott, and G. E. Huber. 2001. *Steps for better thinking: A guide for students.* Available at: http://www.WolcottLynch.com.

Lyons, R. 1999. Adjunct instructors: a priceless resource. *Community College Week* 11 (13): 4–6.

Maeroff, G. I. 2005. The media: Degrees of coverage. *In Declining Degrees.* New York, NY: Palgrave MacMillan.

Mahoney, D. 2008. *Ethics in the Classroom: Bridging the Gap Between Theory and Practice.* Lanham, Massachusetts: Rowman & Littlefield Education.

Mangan, K. 2003. New accreditation rules give business schools more leeway on faculty hiring. *Chronicle of Higher Education* 49 (35): A15.

Mantzke, K., G. Carnes, and W. Tolhurst. 2005. Incorporating professional ethics throughout an accounting curriculum. *CPA Journal* 75 (9): 66–69.

Markie, P. 1994. *A Professor's Duties: Ethical Issues in College Teaching.* Lanham, Maryland: Rowman & Littlefield.

Marsh, H., and J. Hattie. 2002. The relation between research productivity and teaching effectiveness: Complementary, antagonistic, or independent constructs? *The Journal of Higher Education* 73 (5): 603–641.

Marshall, L. 2007. Measuring assurance of learning at the degree programming academic major levels. *Journal of Education for Business* 83 (2): 101–109.

Marshall, P. D., R. F. Dombrowski, and R. M. Garner. 2006. An examination of alternative sources of doctoral accounting faculty. *Journal of Education in Business* 82 (1): 44–48.

Martell, K. 2007. Assessing student learning: Are business schools making the grade? *Journal of Education for Business* 82 (4): 189–195.

Martin, J. R. 1998. Evaluating faculty based on student opinions: Problems, complications, and recommendations from Deming's theory of management perspectives. *Issues in Accounting Education* 13 (4): 1079–1094.

McConahay, M., and R. Cote. 1998. The expanded grade context record at Indiana University. *CAUSE/EFFECT Journal* 21 (4): 47.

McGregor, D. 1960. *The Human Side of Enterprise.* New York, NY: McGraw-Hill.

McKeachie, W., and M. Kaplan. undated. Persistent Problems In Evaluating College Teaching. Available at: http://cedar.olemiss.edu/depts/vc_academic_affairs/problems.html.

McMahon, C. M. 2008. Available at: http://www.apuritansmind.com.

McNiff, J. 1998. *Action Research: Principles and Practice.* London: Routledge.

McPherson, M. A. 2006. Determinants of how students evaluate teachers. *Journal of Economic Education* 37 (1): 3–20.

———, and T. Jewell. 2007. Leveling the playing field: Should student evaluation scores be adjusted? *Social Science Quarterly* 88 (3): 868–881.

McVay, G., P. Murphy, and S. Yoon. 2008. Good practices in accounting education: Classroom configuration and technological tools for enhancing the learning environment. *Accounting Education* 17 (1): 41–63.

Medley, D. M. 1979. The effectiveness of teachers. P. L. Peterson and H. J. Walberg (eds.). *Research on Teaching: Concepts, Findings, and Implications.* Berkeley, CA: McCutchan Publishing Corporation.

Mehdizadeh, M. 1990. Loglinear models and student course evaluations. *Journal of Economic Education* 21 (1): 7–21.

Merchant, K. A. 1985. *Control in Business Organizations.* Boston, MA: Pittman.
———, and W. Van der Stede. 2003. *Management Control Systems: Performance Measurement, Evaluation and Incentives.* Essex, England: Pearson Education Limited.
———. Why interdisciplinary accounting research tends no the impact most North American academic accountants. 2007. *Critical Perspectives on Accounting* 19 (6): 901–908.
Merritt, D. 2008. Bias, the brain, and student evaluations of teaching. *St. John's Law Review* 82 (1): 235–287.
Mertler, C. A. 2001. Designing scoring rubrics for your classroom. *Practical Assessment, Research & Evaluation* (25). Available at: http://PAREonline.net/getvn.asp?v=7&n=25.
Metzger, L. 2007. The control environment and decision-making. *Journal of Government Financial Management* 56 (4): 38–46.
Milliron, V. 2008. Exploring millenial student values and societal trends: Accounting course selection preferences. *Issues in Accounting Education* 23 (3): 405–419.
Mintz, S. 1990. Ethics in the management accounting curriculum. *Management Accounting* LXXI (12): 51–54.
Mitchell, R. 1981. *The Graves of Academe.* Boston, MA: Little, Brown, and Company.
Moore, T. 2006. Teacher evaluations and grades: Additional evidence. *The Journal of American Academy of Business* 9 (2): 58–62.
Mulford, C. W., and A. Schneider. 1988. An empirical study of structural and controllable factors affecting faculty evaluations. *Advances in Accounting:* 205–215.
Murray, Charles. 2008. College daze: Instead of helping high school grads grow up, college prolongs childhood. *Forbes Magazine* (September 1). Available at: http://www.forbes.com/business/forbes/2008/0901/032.html.
Naflulin, D. H., J. E. Ware, and F. A. Donnelly. 1973. The Doctor Fox lecture: A paradigm of educational seduction. *Journal of Medical Education* 48: 630–635.
Nagle, B. 1998. A proposal for dealing with grade inflation: The relative performance index. *Journal of Education for Business* 74 (1): 40–43.
Nance-Nash, S. 2007. Vanishing profession. *Insight* (Illinois Society of CPAs) (January–February): 22–23.
National Center for Education Statistics. 2008. Table 319, Scores on graduate record examination (GRE) general and subject tests: 1965–2006. Available at: http://nces.ed.gov/programs/digest/d07/tables/dt07_319.asp.
National Postsecondary Education Cooperative. 2000. *The NPEC Sourcebook on Assessment, Volume 1: Definitions and Assessment Methods for Critical Thinking, Problem Solving, and Writing.* NPEC, Student Outcomes Pilot Working Group: Cognitive and Intellectual Development.
National Science Foundation, Division of Science Resources Statistics. 2006. Worldwide Trends in Article Output. *Science and Engineering Indicators 2006.* Available at: http://www.nsf.gov/statistics/seind06/c5/c5s3.htm#c5s311.
Neath, I. 1996. How to improve your teaching evaluations without improving your teaching. *Psychological Reports* 78: 1363–1372.
Nelson, A. 1983. Accounting for education's coming crises. *Journal of Accountancy* 136 (4): 47–53.
———. 1989. The Human Resource Dilemma In Accounting. Accounting *Journal of Accountancy* 168 (2): 46–52.
Nelson, C., and S. Watt. 1999. *Academic Keywords: A Devil's Dictionary for Higher Education.* New York, NY: Routledge.
Nelson, I. 1995. What's new about accounting education change: An historical perspective on the change movement. *Accounting Horizons* 9 (4): 62–75.
———, V. P. Vendrzyk, J. J. Quirin, and R. D. Allen. 2002. No, the sky is not falling: Evidence of accounting student characteristics at FSA schools, 1995–2000. *Issues in Accounting Education* 17 (3): 269–287.
———, ———, ———, and S. Kovar. 2006. Trends in accounting student characteristics: Results from a 15-year longitudinal study at FSA schools. Available at: http://www.thefsa.org/downloads/2006_fsa_Study_(Working_Paper).pdf.
Nelson, J. P., and K. A. Lynch. 1984. Grade inflation, real income, simultaneity and teaching evaluations. *Journal of Economic Education* 15 (1): 21–37.

Neu, D., and D. Green. 2006. *Truth Or Profit? The Ethics and Business of Public Accounting.* Black Point, Nova Scotia: Canada.

New, J., J. Clawson, R. Coughlan, and J. Hoyle. 2008. How course portfolios can advance: The scholarship and practice of management teaching. *Journal of Management Education* 32 (1): 8–22.

New Leadership for Student Learning and Accountability: A Statement of Principles, Commitments to Action. 2008. Association for American Colleges and Universities and Council for Higher Education Accreditation.

Newton, J. D. 1988. Using student evaluation of teaching in administrative control: the validity problem. *Journal of Accounting Education* 6 (1): 1–14.

The New York Times. 2006. Editorial: Proof of learning at college. (February 26). Available at: http://www.nytimes.com/2006/02/26/opinion/26sun3.html.

Nichols, A., and J. C. Soper. 1972. Economic man in the classroom. *Journal of Political Economy* (80): 1069–73.

Nie, N. H., and S. D. Golde. 2008. Does education really make you smarter? *Miller-McCune* (June/July 2008): 56–64.

Nightingale, J. 2008. *Think Smart—Act Smart: Avoiding the Business Mistakes that Even Intelligent People Make.* Hoboken, New Jersey: John Wiley.

Nitko, A. J. 2001 *Educational assessment of students* (3rd ed.). Upper Saddle River, NJ: Merrill.

Noddings, N. 2007. *Philosophy of Education* (2nd ed.). Boulder, CO: Westview Press.

Noel, C., and S. Trebucq. 2005. Accounting education and business ethics after Enron: The European illusion. *International Journal of Accounting, Auditing and Performance Evaluation* 2 (4): 414–425.

Norton, C. L., M. A. Diamond and D. Pagach. 2007. *Intermediate Accounting,* 2nd edition, Boston, MA: Houghton Mifflin Company.

Nosich, G. M. 2007. *Learning to Think Things Through: A Guide to Critical Thinking Across the Curriculum.* Upper Saddle River, N.J.: Pearson Education.

Novin, A. M., and M. A. Pearson. 1989. Non-accounting-knowledge qualifications for entry-level public accountants. *Ohio CPA Journal* 48 (4): 12.

Nutting, M. M. 2003. Part-time faculty: Why should we care? *New Directions for Higher Education* 123: 33–39.

Oblinger, D., and A. Verville. 1998. *What Business Wants From Higher Education.* Phoenix, Arizona: Oryx Press.

———, and J. Oblinger (eds.). 2005. Educating the Net Generation. Educause.

O'Donnell, J., and J. Moore. 2005. Are accounting programs providing fundamental IT control knowledge? *CPA Journal* 75 (5): 64–66.

O'Hanlon, J., and L. Mortensen. 1980. Making teacher evaluation work. *The Journal of Higher Education* 51 (6): 664–672.

Oldenguist, A. 1983. The decline of American education in the '60s and '70's. *American Education* 5: 12–18.

Olian, J. D., D. R. LeClair, and B. J. Milano. 2004. Supply, demand, and the making of tomorrow's business scholars. *The Presidency* 7 (2): 30–34.

Oppenheimer, M. 2008. Judgment day. *New York Times Magazine* (September 19). Available at: http://www.nytimes.com/2008/09/21/magazine/21wwln-evaluations-t.html?ref=magazine.

Orin, R. 2008. Ethical guidelines and constraint under the Sarbanes-Oxley Act of 2002. *Journal of Accounting, Auditing & Finance* 23 (1): 141–171.

Orr, T. 2007. *American's Best Colleges for B Students 2nd ed.* Belmont, California: SuperCollege LLC.

Ouellett, M. L. 2007. Your teaching portfolio: Strategies for initiating and documenting growth and development. *Journal of Management Education* 31 (3): 421–433.

Patten, R., and D. Williams. 1990. There's trouble—right here in our accounting programs: The challenge to accounting educators. *Issues in Accounting Education* 5 (2): 175–179.

Paul, R. 1995. *Critical Thinking: How to Prepare Students for a Rapidly Changing World.* Edited by Jane Willsen & A. J. A. Binker. Santa Rosa, CA: Foundation for Critical Thinking.

Peirce, W. 2005. The Year of Critical Thinking at Prince George's Community College: An Integrated Professional Development Program. In Christine McMahon (Ed.), *New Directions for Community Colleges* 130 (79–85). San Francisco: Jossey-Bass.

Pelikan, J. 1992. *The Idea of The University.* New Haven, Ct: Yale University Press.

Perry, W. G., Jr. 1970. *Forms of Intellectual and Ethical Development in the College Years.* New York, NY: Holt, Rinehart and Winston.

Perspectives on Education: Capabilities for Success in the Accounting Profession. 1989. New York, NY: Arthur Andersen & Co., Arthur Young, Coopers & Lybrand, Deloitte Haskins & Sells, Ernst & Whinney, Peat Marwick Main & Co., Price Waterhouse, and Touche Ross.

Peterson, R. L., M. L. Berenson, R. B. Misra, and D. J. Radosevich. 2008. An evaluation of factors regarding students' assessment of faculty in business school. *Decision Sciences Journal of Innovative Education* 6 (2): 375–402.

Phillips, G., D. Gouran, S. Kuehn, and J. Wood. 1994. *Survival in the Academy: A Guide for Beginning Academics.* Gresskill, NJ: Hampton Press Inc.

Pinker, Steven. 2002. *The Blank Slate: The Modern Denial of Human Nature.* New York, NY: Viking.

Pithers, R. T., and R. Soden. 2000. Critical Thinking in Education: A Review. *Educational Research* 42 (3): 237–249.

Plumlee, R. D., S. J. Kachelmeier, S. A. Madeo, J. H. Pratt, and G. Krull. 2006. Assessing the shortage of accounting faculty. *Issues in Accounting Education* 21 (2): 113–125.

Porcano, T. M. 1984. An empirical analysis of some factors affecting student performance. *Journal of Accounting Education* 2 (2): 111–126.

Porter, J. 2007. The best undergraduate B-schools. *Business Week* (March 19): 60–66.

Porter, L., and L. McKibbin. 1988. *Management Education And Development: Drift Or Thrust Into The 21st Century.* New York, NY: McGraw-Hill.

Powell, R. W. 1977. Grades, learning, and student evaluation of instruction. *Research in Higher Education* 7: 193–205.

Pratt, L. R., P. Armstrong, F. De Naples, J. L. Mitchell, W. Moffat, and J. Stevenson. 2005. Report of the ADE ad hoc committee on changes in the structure and financing of higher education. *ADE Bulletin* 137: 89–102.

Pressman, S. 2007. The economics of grade inflation. *Challenge* 50 (5): 93–102.

Previts, G. 2007. Keynote speech delivered at the American Accounting Association national meeting, Aug. 2007.

PricewaterhouseCoopers. 2003. *Educating for the Public Trust.*

Quible, Z. K., and F. Griffin. 2007. Are writing deficiencies creating a lost generation of business writers? *Journal of Education for Business* 83 (1): 32–36.

Quinn, S. S. 2005. The organization-based self-esteem, institutional belongingness, and career development opportunities of adjunct faculty at a small Northeastern College. *Dissertation Abstracts* International Section A: Humanities and Social Sciences. 66 (1–A): 252.

Rankine, G. and E. Stice. 1994. Using articles from the popular press in the introductory accounting course. *Issues in Accounting Education* 9 (1): 142–150.

Rawls, John. 1971. *A Theory of Justice.* Cambridge, MA: Harvard University Press.

———. 2001. *Justice as Fairness: A Restatement.* Edited by E. Kelly. Cambridge, MA: Harvard University Press.

Rebell, M. A. 1990. Legal Issues Concerning Teacher Evaluation. Millman, Jason & Darling-Hammond, Linda, (Eds.), The New Handbook of Teacher Evaluation. Beverly Hills, CA: SAGE.

Reed, J. H. 1998. *Effect of a Model for Critical Thinking on Student Achievement in Primary Source Document Analysis and Interpretation, Argumentative Reasoning, Critical Thinking Dispositions, and History Content in a Community College History Course.* Ph.D. Dissertation: University of South Florida.

Reeves, M. F. 1990. An application of Bloom's taxonomy to the teaching of business ethics. *Journal of Business Ethics* 9 (7): 609–616.

Regional Accrediting Commissions. 2001. Best practices for electronically offered degree and certificate programs. Available at: http://wiche.edu/attachment_library/Accrediting_BestPractices.pdf.

Renner, R. R. 1981. Comparing professors: How student ratings contribute to the decline in quality of higher education. *Phi Delta Kappa* (October): 128–131.

Rezaee, Z., K. Lambert, and W. Harmon. 2006. Electronic Commerce Education: Analysis of Existing Courses. *Accounting Education* 15 (1): 73–88.

Rhoades, L., and G. Rhoades. 1985. Using the daily newspaper to teach cognitive and affective skills. *The Clearing House* December: 162–164.

Rhode, D. L. 2006. *In Pursuit of Knowledge: Scholars, Status, and Academic Culture.* Stanford, CA: Stanford University Press.

Rideway, V. F. 1956. Dysfunctional consequences of performance measurements. *Administrative Science Quarterly* (September): 240–247.

Rifkin, T. 1998. Differences between the professional attitudes of full- and part-time Faculty. Available at: http://eric.ed.gov/ERICWebPortal/custom/portlets/recordDetails/detailmini.jsp?_nfpb=true&_&ERICExtSearch_SearchValue_0=ED417783&ERICExtSearch_SearchType_0=no&5accno=ED417783/.

Riker, W. H. 1986. *The Art of Political Manipulation.* New Haven: Yale University Press.

Robb, J. 2008. Adding up problems with math education. *Omaha World-Herald* (March 13): 1A.

Robbins, L. 1935. *An Essay on the Nature and Significance of Economic Science.* London: Macmillan & Co.

Rojstaczer, S. 2003. Where All Grades Are Above Average. January 28. Available at: http://www.washingtonpost.com/ac2/wp-dyn/A52648-2003Jan27?la.

Romano, L. 2005. Literacy of college graduates slipping, new adult study finds. *Arkansas Democrat-Gazette* (December 26): 4A.

Rosovsky, H., and M. Hartley. 2002. *Evaluation and the Academy: Are We Doing the Right Thing?* American Academy of Arts & Sciences. Available at: http://www.amacad.org/publications/monographs/Evaluation_and_the_Academy.pdf.

Roueche, J. E., S. D. Roueche, and M. D. Milliron. 1995. *Strangers in Their Own Land: Part-time Faculty in American Community Colleges.* Washington, D.C.: Community College Press.

Rubin, R. 2006. The Academic Journal Review Process As A Framework For Student Developmental Peer Feedback. *Journal of Management Education* 30 (2): 378–398.

Rushkoff, D. 1996. *Playing the Future: How Kids' Culture Can Teach Us to Thrive in an Age of Chaos.* New York, NY: HarperCollinsPublishers.

Sacks, P. 1996. *Generation X Goes to College: An Eye-Opening Account of Teaching in Postmodern America.* Peru, Il.: Open Court/Carus Publishing.

Sadker, M., and D. Sadker. 1994. *Failing At Fairness: How America's School Fail Girls.* New York, NY: Maxwell Macmillian.

Saje, N. 2005. Teaching for tips. *Liberal Education* 91 (1): 48–50.

Sasse, C., J. Davis, and C. McConnell. 2000. Using problem-based learning: A multidisciplinary investigation (A Rockhurst University Carnegie Seminar Project). Available at: http://cte.rockhurst.edu/cargegie/PBL.htm.

Sax, L. J. 2003. Our incoming students: What are they like? *About Campus* 8 (3): 15–20.

Scarlett, M. 2004. *The Great Rip-Off In American Education: Undergraduates Undeserved.* Amhest, NY: Prometheus Books.

Schell, E. 2001. Toward a New Labor Movement in Higher Education: Contingent Labor and Organizing for Change (June). Workplace: A Journal for Academic Labor 4.1. Available at: http://www.cust.educ.ubc.ca/workplace/issue7/schell.html.

Schiff, M., and A. Lewin. 1974. *Behavioral Aspects Of Accounting.* Englewood Cliffs, NJ: Prentice Hall.

Schipper, K. 1989. Earnings management. *Accounting Horizons* (December): 91–102.

Schultz, J. 1989a. The Bedford Committee report: Prospects for implementation. *Issues in Accounting Education* 4 (1): 218–221.

——— (ed). 1989b. *Reorienting Accounting Education: Reports on the Environment, Professoriate, and Curriculum of Accounting.* Sarasota, Florida: American Accounting Association.

Schuster, J. H. 2003. The faculty makeover: What does it mean for students? *New Directions for Higher Education* 123: 15–22.

Schwartz, B., S. Williams, and P. Williams. 2005. US doctoral students' familiarity with accounting journals: insights into the structure of the US academy. *Critical Perspectives on Accounting* 16 (3): 327–348.
Seiver, D. A. 1983. Evaluations and grades: A simultaneous framework. *Journal of Economic Education* 14 (3): 32–38.
Seldin, P. 1984. *Changing Practices in Faculty Evaluation: A Critical Assessment and Recommendations for Improvement.* San Francisco, CA: Jossey-Bass.
———. 1993a. *Changing Practices in Faculty Evaluation.* San Francisco, CA: Jossey-Bass.
———. 1993b. The use and abuse of student ratings of professors. *The Chronicle of Higher Education* (June 12): A40.
———. 1999. *Changing Practices In Evaluating Teaching: A Practical Guide to Improved Faculty Performance and Promotion/Tenure Decisions.* Bolton, MA: Anker Publishing Company.
Senge, P. 1990. *The Fifth Discipline: The Art & Practice of the Learning Organization.* New York, NY: Currency/Doubleday.
Shaftel, J., and T. Shaftel. 2007. Educational Assessment and the AACSB. *Issues in Accounting Education* 22 (2): 215–232.
Sharman, P. 2007. The Ph.D. shortage. *Strategic Finance* 88 (10): 8, 55.
Sheehan, D. 1975. On the invalidity of student ratings for administrative personnel decisions. *The Journal of Higher Education* 46 (6): 687–700.
Sheils, M. 1975. Why Johnny can't write. *Newsweek.* December 8: 58–65.
Sheldon, T., and W. Hoffman. 2005. Does higher education make the grade in institution-wide ethics and compliance programs? *Business & Society Review* 110 (3): 249–267.
Shinkfield, A. J., and D. L. Stufflebeam. 1996. *Teacher Evaluation: Guide to Professional Practice.* Norwell, MA: Kluwer Academic Press.
Shulman, L. 2004. *Teaching As Community Property.* San Francisco: Jossey-Bass.
Simon, W. E. 1996. The dumbing down of higher education. *The Wall Street Journal* (March 19, 1996): A18.
Singer, P. 1999. *A Darwinian Left: Politics, Evolution, and Cooperation.* Yale University Press, New Haven, Connecticut.
Singh, G. 2002. Educational consumers or educational partners: A critical theory analysis. *Critical Perspectives on Accounting* 13 (5–6): 681–701.
Sloan Consortium. 2005. *Growing by Degrees: Online education in the United States.* Available at: http://www.sloan-c.org/resources/growing_by_degrees.pdf.
———. 2007. I. E. Allen and J. Seaman. Online Nation: Five Years of Growth in Online Learning. Available at: http://www.sloan-c.org/publications/survey/pdf/online_nation.pdf.
Smith, Adam. 1994. *An Inquiry into the Nature and Causes of the Wealth of Nations.* Ed. by E. Cannan. New York, NY: The Modern Library.
Smith, G. S. 2004. Assessment strategies: What is being measured in student course evaluations? *Accounting Education* 13 (1): 3–28.
Smith, L. M. (ed). 2006. *Reflections on Accounting Education Research.* Sarasota, Florida: Teaching and Curriculum Section, American Accounting Association.
Snyder, C. R., and M. Clair. 1976. Effects of expected and obtained grades on teacher evaluation and attribution of performance. *Journal of Educational Psychology* 68 (1): 75–82.
Songster, A., G. Stoner, and P. McCarthy. 2007. Lessons for the classroom from Luca Pacioli. *Issues in Accounting Education* 22 (3): 447–457.
Sonner, B. S. 2000. A is for "Adjunct": Examining grade inflation in higher education. *Journal of Education for Business* 76 (1): 5–8.
Sowell, T. 1994. We suffer the consequences of '60s liberalism. *AFA Journal* (January): 14.
———. 2002. *A Conflict of Visions: Ideological Origins of Political Struggles.* New York: Basic Books.
Spellings, M. 2006. *A Test of Leadership—Charting the Future of U.S. Higher Education.* A Report of the Commission Appointed by Secretary of Education Margaret Spellings. Washington, DC: U.S. Department of Education.
Spiceland, J. D., J. F. Sepe, and L. A. Tomassini. 2004. *Intermediate Accounting,* 3rd edition, New York, NY: Irwin-McGraw-Hill.

Springer, C. W., and A. F. Borthick. 2004. Business simulation to stage critical thinking in introductory accounting: Rationale, design, and implementation. *Issues in Accounting Education* 19 (3): 277–303.

St. John, E. P. 2004. Policy research and political decisions. *Public Funding of Higher Education.* St. John, E. P. and M. D. Parsons, Eds. Baltimore, MD: The Johns Hopkins University Press.

Stake, J. 1997. Response to Haskell: Academic Freedom, Tenure, and Student Evaluation of Faculty. *Education Policy Analysis Archives* 5 (8). Available at: http://epaa.asu.edu/epaa/v5n8.html.

State University of New York. Undated. *Distinguished Teaching Professorships Policies and Procedures.* Albany, NY: SUNY.

Steadman, M. H., and M. Svinicki. 1998. CATs: A student's gateway to better learning. T. A. Angelo (Ed.), *New Directions for Teaching and Learning:* Classroom assessment and research: An update on uses, approaches, and research findings, No. 75, 13–20. San Francisco: Jossey-Bass Publishers.

Steiner, S., and M. Watson. 2006. The Service Learning Component in Business Education: The Values Linkage Void. *Academy of Management Learning & Education* 5 (4): 422–434.

Stice, J., and K. Stocks. 2000. Effective teaching techniques: Perceptions of accounting faculty. *Advances in Accounting Education* 2: 179–191.

Stivers, B. P., J. E. Campbell, and H. M. Hermanson. 2000. An assessment program for accounting: Design, implementation, and reflection. *Issues in Accounting Education* 15 (4): 553–581.

Stone, D. N. 1996. Getting tenure in accounting: A personal account of learning to dance with the mountain. *Issues in Accounting Education* 11 (1): 187–201.

Stout, D., J. Borden, M. German, and T. Monahan. 2005. Designing and implementing a comprehensive assessment plan for a graduate accounting programme. *Accounting Education: An International Journal* 14 (4): 395–410.

Strait, A., and I. Bull. 1992. Do academic traditions undermine teaching? *Journal of Accountancy* 174 (3): 69–73.

Stumpf, S. A., and R. D. Freedman. 1979. Expected grade co-variation with student ratings of instruction: individual vs. class effects. *Journal of Education Psychology* 71 (3): 293–302.

Sue-Chan, C., and G. Latham. 2004. The relative effectiveness of external, peer, and self-coaches. *Applied Psychology: An International Review* 53 (2): 260–278.

Sullivan, A. M., and G. R. Skanes. 1974. Validity of student evaluation of teaching and the characteristics of successful instructors. *Journal of Educational Psychology* 66 (4): 584–590.

Sundem, G. 1999. *The Accounting Education Change Commission: Its History and Impact.* Sarasota, Florida: American Accounting Association, Accounting Education Series 15. Available at: http://aaahq.org/aecc/history/cover.htm.

Suskie, L. 2004. *Assessing student learning: A common sense guide.* Bolton, MA: Anker.

Swartz, J., T. Swartz, and P. Liang. 2007. Market meltdown: Recruiting quality business faculty. *Journal of Education for Business* 82 (6): 337–342.

Sykes, C. 1988. *Profscam: Professors and the Demise of Higher Education.* New York, NY: St. Martin's Press.

———. 1995. *Dumbing Down Our Kids: Why America's Children Feel Good About Themselves but Can't Read, Write, or Add.* New York, NY: St. Martin's Press.

Tagomori, H. T. 1993. A content analysis of instruments used for student evaluation of faculty in schools of education at universities and colleges accredited by the national council for accreditation of teachers' education. Unpublished dissertation. University of San Francisco.

The Teaching Portfolio at Washington State University. Office of the Provost. Washington State University. undated. Available at: http://www.wsu.edu/provost/teaching.htm.

Texas A&M University. undated. Measurement and Research Service, Student Ratings of Faculty. Available at: http://www.tamu.edu/mars/ratings.index.htm.

Theall, M. 1997. On drawing reasonable conclusions about student ratings of instruction: a reply to Haskell and to Stake. *Education Policy Analysis Archives.* Available at: http://epaa.asu.edu/epaa/v5n8c2.html.

———, and J. Franklin. 1990. Student Ratings of Instruction: Issues for Improving Practice. *New Direction for Teaching and Learning,* No. 43. San Francisco: Jossey-Bass.

Thompson, K. 2003. Contingent faculty and student learning: Welcome to the Strativersity. *New Directions for Higher Education* 123: 41–47.

Thomson, A., M. Fernandez, S. Burnick, and A. Boston. 2008. APLG panel on academic and the accounting profession: The Big 4 respond. *Issues in Accounting Education* 23 (2): 209.

Tiwari, A., P. Lai, M. So, and K. Yuen. 2006. A comparison of the effects of problem-based learning and lecturing on the development of student's critical thinking. *Medical Education* 40 (6): 547–555.

Tomsho, R. 2007. Report Raises Questions About High-School Courses. *Wall Street Journal* (February 23): B1.

Topping, K. 1998. Peer assessment between students in colleges and universities. *Review of Educational Research* 68 (1): 249–276.

Townsend, R. B. 2003. Changing relationships, changing values in the American classroom. *New Directions for Higher Education* 123: 23–59.

Tracy, J. 2005. I see and I remember; I do and understand: Teaching fundamental structure in legal writing through the use of samples. *Touro Law Review* 21: 297–348.

Trice, A. D. 2000. *A Handbook of Classroom Assessment.* New York, NY: Longman.

Trout, Paul. 1997. How to improve your teaching evaluation scores without improving teaching. Available at: http://mtprof.msun.edu/Fall1997/HOWTORAI.html.

Tuckman, B., and T. L. Sexton. 1992. Self-believers are self-motivated; self-doubters are not. *Personality and Individual Differences,* 13: 425–428.

Umbach, P. D. 2007. How effective are they? Exploring the impact of contingent faculty on undergraduate education. *Review of Higher Education* 30 (2): 91–123.

U.S. Department of Education. 2006a. *National Study of Postsecondary Faculty (NSOPF:04): Report on Faculty and Instructional Staff in Fall 2003.* Washington DC: U.S. Department of Education.

———. 2006. A test of leadership—Charting the future of U.S. higher education. A report of the Commission appointed by Secretary of Education Margaret Spellings. Washington DC: U.S. Department of Education.

Vangermeersch, R. 2000. Fifty reasons for the decline in the quantity and quality of accounting majors. *CPA Journal* 70 (1): 52–54.

Van Wyhe, G. 2007a. A history of U.S. higher education in accounting, Part I: Situating accounting within the academy. *Issues in Accounting Education* 22 (2): 65–181.

———. 2007b. A history of U.S. higher education in accounting, Part I: Reforming accounting within the academy. *Issues in Accounting Education* 22 (3): 481–601.

Vasta, R., and R. F. Sarmiento. 1979. Liberal grading improves evaluations but not performance. *Journal of Educational Psychology* 71: 207–210.

Ven, J-H., and C-P Chuang. 2005. The comparative study of information competencies—Using Bloom's taxonomy. *The Journal of American Academy of Business, Cambridge* 7 (1): 136–143.

Venezia, C. 2005. The Ethical Reasoning Abilities of Accounting Students. Journal of *American Academy of Business* 6 (1): 200–207.

Vik, G. 2001. Doing more to teach teamwork then telling students to sink or swim. *Business Communication Quarterly* 64 (4): 112–119.

Waddock, S. 2005. Hollow men and women at the helm ... Hollow accounting ethics? *Issues in Accounting Education* 20 (2): 145–150.

Wagenaar, T. 2005. Student evaluation of teaching: Some cautions and suggestions. *Teaching Sociology* 23 (1): 64–68.

Waitzkin, J. 2007. *The Art Of Learning: A Journey In The Pursuit Of Excellence.* New York, NY: Free Press.

Wallace, J., and W. Wallace. 1998. Why the costs of student evaluations have long exceeded their value. *Issues in Accounting Education* 13 (2): 443–447.

Wallin, D. L. 2005. (ed.) *Adjunct Faculty in Community Colleges: An Academic Administrator's Guide to Recruiting, Supporting, and Retaining Great Teachers.* Bolton, MA: Anker.

———. 2007. Part-time faculty and professional development: Notes from the field. *New Directions for Community Colleges* 140: 67–73.

Ward, D., and J. Dugger. 2002. A comparison of selected categories of accreditation standards of the National Association of Industrial Technology, the Technology Accreditation Commission of the Accreditation Board for Engineering and Technology and the American Association of Collegiate School of Business. *Journal of Industrial Technology* 18 (3): 2–8.

Washburn, K., and J. Thornton (eds.). 1996. *Dumbing Down: Essays On the Strip-Mining of American Culture.* New York, NY: W. W. Norton.

Webb, D. E. 2008. Adjunct faculty: A boon or burden? Dissertation Abstracts International Section A: Humanities and Social Sciences 68 (7-A): 2759.

Webb, N. 1995. Group collaboration in assessment: Multiple objectives, processes, and outcomes. *Educational Evaluation and Policy Analysis* 17 (2): 239–261.

Webster, C. 1990. Evaluation of marketing professors: A comparison of student, peer, and self-evaluations. *Journal of Marketing Education* 12 (1): 11–17.

Weimer, M. 1990. *Improving College Teaching.* San Francisco, CA: Jossey-Bass Publishers.

White, E. M. 1993. Too many campuses want to sweep student plagiarism under the rug. *The Chronicle of Higher Education* (February): A44.

White, J., W. Levernier, and M. Miles. 2005. The unintended effects of AACSB's 2003 accreditation standards. *The Coastal Business Journal* 4 (1): 43–50.

Wiesenfeld, K. 1996. Making the grade. *Newsweek* (June 17): 16.

Williams, D. 1996. A Seminar on the Teaching of Accounting. *The Accounting Review* 41 (3): 542–549.

Williams, J. (Project Director). 1988. *A Framework for the Development of Accounting Education Research.* Sarasota, Florida: American Accounting Association.

Williams, W. M., and S. J. Ceci. 1997. How'm I doing? *Change* 29 (5): 12–23.

Wilson, B. P. 1999. The phenomenon of grade inflation in higher education. *National Forum* 79 (4): 38–41.

Wilson, S. 2005. Serving time the six-year rule. Available at: http://www.insidehighered.com/views/2005/06/22/wilson.

Winsor, J. L. 1977. A's, B's, but not C's? A comment. *Contemporary Education* (Winter): 82–84.

Wolcott, S. K. 1998. Critical thinking development in the accounting curriculum: focusing on ambiguity in introductory accounting courses. D. F. Fetyko (Ed.), *Changes in accounting education: implementation in specific accounting courses and subject areas.* St. Louis: Federation of Schools of Accountancy.

———, C. P. Baril, B. M. Cunningham, D. R. Fordham, and K. St. Pierre. 2002. Critical thought on critical thinking research. *Journal of Accounting Education* 20: 85–103.

———. 2005. Assessment of critical thinking. T. G. Calderon & K. D. Martell (Eds.). *Assessment of Student Learning in Business Schools: Best Practices Each Step of the Way,* Vol. 1, No. 1. AACSB International and Association for Institutional Research (AIR).

Wood, M., and C. Des Jarlais. 2006. When post-tenure review policy and practice diverge: Making the case for convergence. *Journal of Higher Education* 77 (4): 561–588.

Wood, P. 2007. Homicides in higher education: Some reflections on the moral mission of the university. *Academic Questions* 20: 277–294.

Worthington, A. G., and P. T. P. Wong. 1979. Effects of earned and assigned grades on student evaluations of an instructor. *Journal of Educational Psychology* 71 (6): 764–775.

Wright, P., R. Whittington, and G. E. Whittenburg. 1984. Student ratings of teaching effectiveness: What the research reveals. *Journal of Accounting Education* 2 (Fall): 5–30.

———, and T. Wotruba. 1978. Models of student evaluations. Paper presented to A.A.C.T.E., February, Chicago, IL.

Wright, R. 2000. *Nonzero: The Logic of Human Destiny.* New York, NY: Vintage Books.

Wyatt, A. 2004. Accounting professionalism—They just don't get it! *Accounting Horizons* 18 (1): 45–53.

Wyles, B. A. 1998. Adjunct faculty in community colleges: Realities and challenges. *New Directions for Higher Learning* 104: 89–94.

Yang, A. 2006. Yale median GPA is 3.6, study finds. *The Daily Princetonian* (October 11). University Wire: Lexis-Nexis.

Yining, C., A. Gupta, and L. Hoshower. 2006. Factors that motivate business faculty to conduct research: An expectancy theory analysis. *Journal of Education for Business* 81 (4): 179–189.

Young, R. 1977. *No Neutral Ground: Standing By the Values We Prize in Higher Education.* San Francisco: Jossey-Bass.

Yunker, P. J., and J. A. Yunker. 2003. Are student evaluations of teaching valid? Evidence from an analytical business core course. *Journal of Education for Business* 78 (6): 313–317.

Zakaria, F. 2008. *The Post-American World.* New York, NY: W. W. Norton.

Zangenehzadeh, H. 1988. Grade inflation: A way out. *Journal of Economic Education* 19 (3): 217–226.
Zimmerman, A. 2002. Reduced rigor and grade inflation diminish the quality and credibility of higher education. *NACTA Journal* (December). Available at: http://findarticles.com/p/articles/mi_qa4062/is200212/ai_n9151533/print.